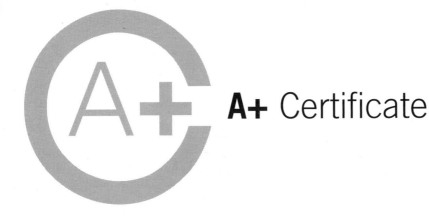

A+ Certificate

Computer Maintenance and Installation

Jenny Lawson

www.heinemann.co.uk
✓ Free online support
✓ Useful weblinks
✓ 24 hour online ordering

01865 888058

Inspiring generations

Heinemann Educational Publishers
Halley Court, Jordan Hill, Oxford OX2 8EJ
Part of Harcourt Education

Heinemann is the registered trademark of
Harcourt Education Limited

Text © Jenny Lawson, 2004

First published 2004

09 08 07 06 05 04
10 9 8 7 6 5 4 3 2 1

British Library Cataloguing in Publication Data is available
from the British Library on request.

ISBN 0 435 45638 5

All photographs by Gareth Boden

Typeset by J&L Composition, Filey, North Yorkshire

Printed in the UK by Scotprint

Acknowledgements

Every effort has been made to contact copyright holders of material reproduced in this book. Any omissions will be
rectified in subsequent printings if notice is given to the publishers.

Websites

There are links to relevant websites in this book. In order to ensure that the links work, and that the sites are not
inadvertently linked to sites that could be considered offensive, we have made the links available on the Heinemann
website at www.heinemann.co.uk/hotlinks. When you access the site, the express code is 6385P.

Contents

Acknowledgements

I send my thanks to all those who helped me to produce this A+ text:

- To Matt Jackman at Heinemann for his constant support and encouragement throughout the writing of this book.
- To Julia Sandford at Heinemann for her hard work in pushing the manuscript through the production process.
- To Barnfield College for allowing us to use their facilities during the photo shoot.
- To Jane Hance at Heinemann, and Gareth Boden and Tony Poole for their speed and efficiency in producing the many photos during the photo shoot at Barnfield College.
- To Andrew Smith for his timely advice and insights into teaching A+, his contribution of so many screen grabs, and his review of draft material.

Introduction

About this book

This book is written to help you – an A+ student – to pass your tests and to gain the A+ certificate in computer maintenance.

- The text is written in a user-friendly way, with lots of diagrams and screen grabs to explain all the things that you need to know.
- Descriptions are kept to a minimum, so you don't need to wade through pages of background information to find out what you want to know.
- Tables are used to summarise important information.
- Annotated screen shots are used to explain each process for you.
- **How To** features give you brief and clear instructions on how to install, configure and upgrade computer systems
- **CHAT** will remind you to share your knowledge with others and tell them what you have learnt
- **WATCH OUT!** will identify important health and safety issues, and tips about how to avoid disasters
- To help you to consolidate your knowledge, **Check Your Understanding** questions make sure that you have understood the material just covered. Further multiple choice revision questions are available at www.heinemann.co.uk.
- To help you to demonstrate your practical skills, **Go Out And Try** activities invite you to try things out for yourself.
- You will be applying your knowledge and skills in the workplace so **case studies** are included to show you examples of how things are done in real-life.

There are other books that cover the A+ course, or at least some of the material within it. It makes sense to refer to more than one book, especially if there is a topic that you are finding difficult. However, your best source of additional material is the internet. Follow the links to this book from www.heinemann.co.uk/hotlinks for some suggestions of useful websites.

About the A+ course and Certificate

The A+ course is an opportunity for you to launch – or enhance – your career in the IT industry as a service technician.

The A+ Certificate in Computer Maintenance and Installation recognises achievement of the essential knowledge and understanding – the things that you need to know to work within the computer maintenance and support industry. It assesses what you know about the operating systems and hardware – the things you would need to know if you were working as a break/fix microcomputer service technician.

The specification is based on the A+ Certificate. This is an internationally recognised validation of the technical knowledge and skills required of a computer service technician. The A+ certificate is sponsored by CompTIA in the USA. In the UK, OCR is working in partnership with CompTIA to offer national recognition of this qualification.

A+ is also a core unit of the OCR iPRO ICT Systems Support Certificate.

What is CompTIA?

CompTIA is a non-profit organisation. It has over 7500 member organisations, drawn chiefly from the IT sector. This includes global organisations such as IBM, Compaq, Novell, Microsoft and Hewlett-Packard. These member organisations contribute to the content review of the CompTIA certificates such as A+.

Will the A+ Certificate help you to get a job?

Yes. At least, it will help you to be shortlisted for an interview. Whether or not you get the job is up to you!

The A+ Certificate is designed to meet your needs: to achieve an internationally recognised credential as a competent computer service professional. Like all other professional certifications, having an A+ certificate gives you a passport: it's the first step towards more specialised certificates. Major computer hardware and software vendors back this qualification. Many see the A+® Certificate as an introductory award prior to gaining more product-specific accreditation (e.g. MCSE, Novell, etc). With an A+ certificate, a prospective employer will know that you have the IT skills they are looking for.

What will you learn about?

Courses leading to this qualification should provide you with basic knowledge:

◆ How to install, configure and upgrade computer systems, particularly within a Windows environment
◆ How to diagnose and resolve faults with ICT systems in a Windows environment

You will develop knowledge and understanding of the computer maintenance and installation industry, especially the environment in which microcomputer service technicians operate, and gain an awareness of health and safety issues that will affect you.

By the end of the course, you should have the skills expected of a technician with six months' on-the-job experience.

The knowledge and technical skills that you learn are vendor-neutral. So, when you have finished this course, you will be able to work on a variety of computers and understand the general principles involved in being service technician.

Full details of the A+ course specification, with complete details of the topics you will need to understand, can be found on CompTIA's and OCR's website (see www.heinemann.co.uk/hotlinks for more details).

About the A+ examination

Who decides on the exam questions?

An industry-wide job task analysis, validated through a worldwide survey of 5000 A+-certified professionals established the knowledge needed by an IT support technician. A worldwide survey was used to decide the assessment categories. It was also used to make sure that the weighting towards examination content matches what you need to know to do the job of a service technician. A committee representing the entire IT industry then oversees the A+ test. Considerable resources have been contributed to assure its accuracy, validity and reliability.

Note, however, that since Intel is one of the organisations involved in the development of the A+ examination specification, you should expect questions about Intel products, more so than other manufacturers who have not contributed to this course.

Why should I take the A+ test?

Passing the A+ test will prove that you are competent to take the post of a service technician. It is not a substitute for on-the-job experience, but the training that you will receive during your A+ course will prepare you for quicker and higher levels of service. You can then move on, up the ladder, to a job within the IT industry as a service technician.

What do I have to do to pass?

To achieve a full A+ Certificate in Computer Maintenance and Installation, you need to pass both units:

◆ Unit One: Core Hardware Service Technician Concepts
◆ Unit Two: Operating System Technologies Concepts

These are assessed at one of the licenced testing centres by external examination, set and marked by CompTIA. You will take the test at a computer, and your answers will be marked by computer.

Each test lasts for 30 minutes and you will be set 20 to 30 questions. Results are graded as pass or fail. For each test, the pass mark is 65%.

Examination technique

There are two formats for the questions in the computerised tests:

◆ For the **multiple choice questions** you need to choose one option that best answers the question or completes a statement. The option can be embedded in a graphic so you may need to point or click on something to show your choice.
◆ For the **multiple response questions**, more than one option best answers the question or completes the statement – and you have to decide on these.

To understand the questions, even before you decide which might be the correct answer, you need to understand the many terms that are used, and in particular all the abbreviations that may be included. A full list of abbreviation is given on the website.

When you take the examination, remember that you are sitting an adaptive test. This means that how you answer the first few questions will determine what questions you will be asked next, and this will affect the total score available to you. Suppose the test is marked out of 100. This table shows how getting just the first few questions correct could guarantee you a good score, even if after that you had difficulty in getting any answers correct.

First few questions	Score range available	Minimum score	Maximum score
All correct	70–100	70	100
Some wrong	35–85	35	85
All wrong	20–50	0	50

If you make a hash of the first few questions, you will limit yourself to a low mark, and although the remaining questions may be quite easy, you cannot make up for this poor start.

So take great care with all questions, but especially those at the beginning. Take care to calm down at the very start and have your wits about you. The test lasts only a short time – so you cannot afford to linger on questions, or to think about questions you have already answered, worrying about whether you were right or wrong.

◆ Once you've answered a question, forget it.
◆ Don't worry about the questions you have yet to see.
◆ Give your full concentration on the question facing you now.

For more information about the test, visit CompTIA's A+ Adaptive Test FAQ page by following the links from www.heinemann.co.uk/hotlinks.

The Heinemann website (www.heinemann.co.uk) also contains multiple choice questions for each unit in this book. These are like the questions you'll answer in the A+ examination so are a good way of revising.

How to

Unit 1
Core Hardware Service Technician Concepts

This unit focuses on the generic knowledge and understanding required of a computer service technician. There are six elements in this unit, each one contributing to the test questions:

Element	Topic	Marks in test (%)
1.1	Installation, configuration and upgrading	30
1.2	Diagnosing and troubleshooting	30
1.3	Preventive maintenance	5
1.4	Motherboard/processors/memory	15
1.5	Printers	10
1.6	Basic networking	10
Total		100

In completing this unit, you should have three aims:

◆ To demonstrate that you understand how to install, configure and upgrade computer systems.

   How to panels give you brief and clear instructions on how to install, configure and upgrade computer systems.

◆ To use IT to communicate with others, in much the same way as you will when working within a team of service technicians.

   Chat will remind you to share your knowledge with others and tell them what you have learnt.

◆ To show that you understand health and safety issues that will be important in your work as a service technician – maintaining and installing computer systems.

   Watch out warnings will identify important health and safety issues.

◆ This book will help you to keep these three aims in mind.

Chapter 1 Installation, configuration and upgrading

Before you start delving inside a PC, you do need to understand a bit about electricity and electronics. Take a look at page 358 and make sure that you understand the basic principles explained there.

Check Your Understanding 1.1

1 Explain these terms: 'current', 'circuit'.
2 Explain how these are measured: strength of a current; pressure of a current; resistance of a wire.
3 Which law links the volts, amps and ohms in a circuit?

As a service technician, you also need the tools for the job. Check that you have access to each of the tools listed on page 362, and know how to use them, especially the **multimeter**.

What does it mean?

A multimeter is a tool that will let you test and measure the electrical properties of your PC and its components.

Check Your Understanding 1.2

1 Name the most essential item in your toolkit.
2 What can be used to clean fans, grills, inside the PC case and between the keys of a keyboard?
3 Describe each of these types of screwdriver: Phillips, slotted, hex and Torx.
4 What tool can be used to check a serial or parallel port is working properly?
5 Which tool can be a combination of a voltmeter, an ammeter and an ohmmeter?
6 What range of values is used when measuring VDC?
7 How can you check for continuity?

CASE STUDY   Josie, trainee technician

Josie is working as a receptionist for PCs-4-U, a computer supplier. She has her own PC and has studied ICT courses at school. She is keen to become a computer technician but does not know what the job entails – or what qualifications she needs. You know Josie from school and she has emailed you to ask about your job and the training that you are doing.

1 Write an email to Josie explaining how you found your job as a computer maintenance technician.

2 In the body of your email, include brief details of the kinds of things you do each day at work.

3 Attach to the email an up-to-date copy of your CV, showing what qualifications you gained at school and any you have gained since then. Mention the A+ course that you are studying.

1   Functions of system modules

You should understand how each of these modules works during normal operation, and during the boot process (page 17).

- BIOS
- CMOS
- Firmware
- LCD (portable systems)
- Memory
- Modem
- Monitor
- PDA (personal digital assistant)
- Ports
- Power supply
- Processor/CPU
- Storage devices
- System board

First, though, you need to be able to identify each module. Figure 1.1 shows a PC, with some **peripherals** attached.

What does it mean?

A peripheral device is one that is outside the PC case, e.g. a printer.

- A **light** may show that the PC is turned on. Another may show that a hard disk is being accessed.
- **Cabling** connects the PC power supply to the power source at the socket.
- A **modem** links the PC to other computers via a communications link, e.g. a telephone line.
- **Portable computers** – laptops and PDAs – usually have an LCD screen; this is flatter and lighter than that used on a standalone PC.
- **Storage devices** may be housed within the PC casing, or externally.
- **Ports** provide the link between peripherals and CPU. Not all peripherals need a cable to link them to the port. **Wireless technology** means you can send emails, for example, using the infrared port on a laptop and a mobile phone.

Figure 1.1   **A PC**

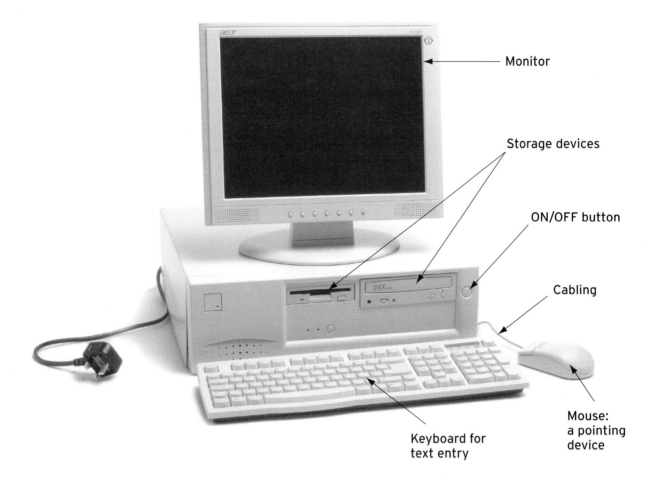

Monitor

Storage devices

ON/OFF button

Cabling

Mouse:
a pointing
device

Keyboard for
text entry

Working with a group of friends, take it in turns to describe an item of equipment that is shown in Figure 1.1. Your friends then have to identify it.

Peripherals fall into three groups:

◆ **Input devices** provide a way for the user to put data into the PC and to give commands, e.g. to decide which application to use.

◆ **I/O devices** – also known as **storage devices** or the **backing store** – provide a place, other than the PC, to store data. They also allows data to be transferred from one PC to another, e.g. on a CD-ROM. These devices may read from/write to **magnetic storage media** (such as DAT or AIT tape, or a Zip drive) or **optical storage media** (such as CD-ROM or DVD).

◆ **Output devices** present the results of any processing to the user.

What does it mean?

I/O = input/output.

CD-ROM (compact disk – read only memory) and DVD (digital versatile disk) are forms of backing store used to hold large amounts of data – an optical storage technology that uses a laser to read data from (and possibly to) its media.

Examples of input, output and I/O devices are listed in Table 1.1.

Table 1.1 *Examples of input, output and I/O devices*

Input	I/O (input/output)	Output
Keyboard	Floppy disk drive	Screen/monitor/VDU
Mouse	Hard disk drive	Printer
Trackerball	CD-ROM drive	Actuator*
Joystick	Zip drive	Loudspeaker
Scanner		
Barcode reader		
Digital camera		
Microphone		

*An actuator is a motor that powers a device, e.g. the wheels of a turtle.

CHAT *Discuss with friends the list of peripherals given in Table 1.1. Think of other peripherals that you may use with your PC.*

You should be able to recognise all the peripherals listed in Table 1.1 and shown in Figure 1.2, but will also need to know how to connect and disconnect them from the PC, how to take care of them and how to fix problems that arise with them.

◆ Physically adding and removing peripherals is covered in section 2 (page 38).

◆ The software settings that are needed to install and configure these devices are covered in section 3 (page 68) and, as printers are so important a topic, they occupy the whole of Chapter 5 (page 214).

◆ Diagnosing problems and troubleshooting is the topic of Chapter 2 (page 128), and preventive maintenance fills Chapter 3 (page 167).

Figure 1.2 shows (a) the rear view of a PC and (b) the rear and side panels on a laptop computer:

◆ **Ventilation holes** in the casing are an essential part of the cooling system.

◆ A **voltage switch** means you can use a PC in, for example, the USA, where the power supply is 110 V, as well as in Europe, where it is 200 V.

◆ The **power cord connector** for a PC expects a standard 3-pin power cord.

◆ A **laptop power supply** will be via an AC adaptor.

◆ **Ports** provide the link between peripherals and CPU.

The variously shaped ports provide a link between what is outside the case and what is inside. You will study ports and the cables used to connect peripherals to the PC via these ports in section 4 (page 87).

Go and try out 1.1

1 For a PC that you use regularly, look carefully at how each peripheral device is connected externally to the PC via the ports.
2 List the devices and, for each one, sketch both ends of the cable used as a connector, and the connectors into which these fit, both on the PC and on the device.
3 Compare your notes with others in your group. Check for differences in your sketches.

When you eventually open up the PC, you should see the **motherboard** and many more components linked to it, within the case (see Figure 1.3 on page 9).

Watch out

Don't open a PC case just yet. This section gives an overview of the inside of a PC but you need to learn about safety procedures before delving inside.

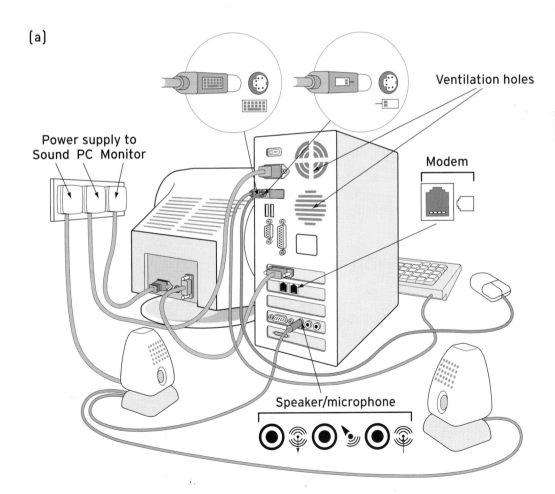

Figure 1.2

(a) The rear of a PC

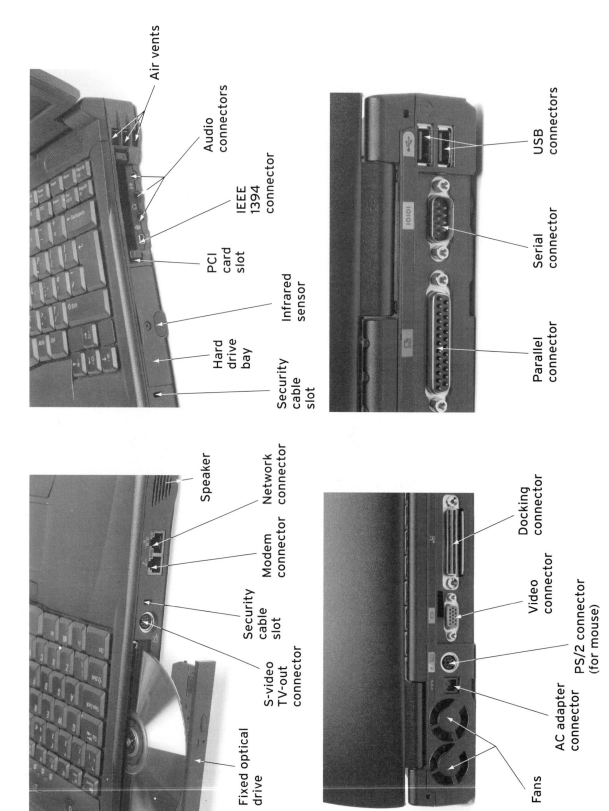

Figure 1.2   (b) The sides of a laptop

(a)

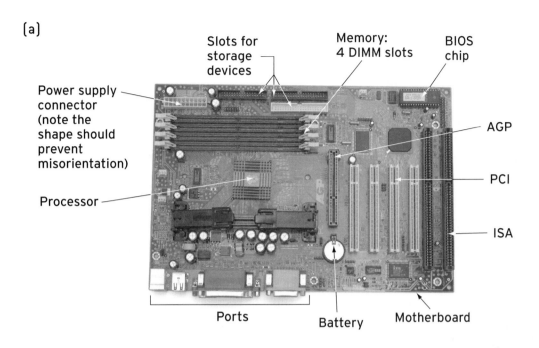

Slots for storage devices

Memory: 4 DIMM slots

BIOS chip

Power supply connector (note the shape should prevent misorientation)

Processor

AGP

PCI

ISA

Ports

Battery

Motherboard

(b)

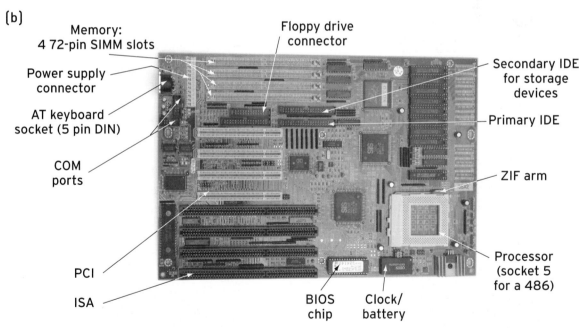

Memory: 4 72-pin SIMM slots

Floppy drive connector

Secondary IDE for storage devices

Power supply connector

Primary IDE

AT keyboard socket (5 pin DIN)

COM ports

ZIF arm

Processor (socket 5 for a 486)

PCI

BIOS chip

Clock/ battery

ISA

Figure 1.3   **The internal workings of a PC: (a) AT form factor; (b) ATX form factor**

What does it mean?

Motherboards have been known by other names in the past: system boards, logic boards and planar boards.

The motherboard is as important to a computer as the skeleton is to a human, or the chassis to a car. The components that are attached to the motherboard, collectively, are called the motherboard's **chipset**. For more information about the chipset, see Chapter 4 (page 196).

The layout of these components depends on the **form factor** of the motherboard.

What does it mean?

The form factor of a motherboard defines its shape and size: See page 191 for more details of form factors.

- The **power supply** provides electrical energy to the computer from the power source at the socket.
- The **battery** provides power for essentials like the system's date/time clock when the PC is turned off.
- **Ports** link the peripherals to the CPU, via the motherboard.
- The **system board** – or **motherboard** – holds all the circuitry for the PC.
- The **processor/CPU** is the very heart of the computer; it is situated on the motherboard and controls everything.
- The **CMOS** is an essential hardware part of the motherboard, and it holds the **BIOS**, an essential software part of the motherboard.
- **Firmware** is the name given to ROM chips; once written, unlike software, it cannot be changed.
- **Memory** comes in many forms, e.g. ROM and RAM.
- **Storage devices**, such are floppy disk drives and hard disk drives, are used to hold more information that could not be held within the PC's memory.
- **Expansion boards** provide flexibility in the configuration of peripherals for a PC. They can be used for networking two or more PCs, adding sound to a PC and/or adding video.

Notice that there is a tangle of wires, of many different colours, from the PSU (power supply unit) and that some cables look like ribbons. You will learn more about these connecting cables in section 2 (page 38).

Go and try out 1.2

Most of your time may soon be spent looking at things inside a PC case, but while it is still closed, study the outside of the casing and notice the placement of screws.

1 Which ones might be used to open up the case?
2 What type of screwdriver might you need to open up the PC?

Page 46 explains how to open a PC casing.

Some modules are introduced in the first section of this chapter so that you have at least met them and can understand some of the terminology that surrounds them:

◆ The power supply unit (below)

◆ The boot process, including an introduction to the BIOS and CMOS (page 17)

◆ The processor/CPU (page 24)

◆ Memory (page 27)

◆ Storage devices (page 30)

You then need to take a more detailed look at how to add and remove some of the internal components physically, such as IDE/EIDE devices (section 5), SCSI devices (section 6) and other peripheral devices (section 7). Finally, this chapter completes the overview of the modules by looking at methods of upgrading system performance by replacing components (section 8).

Some modules within your PC deserve much more attention and have a complete section or a chapter devoted to them later in the book:

◆ Motherboards/processors/memory are considered in great detail in Chapter 4.

◆ Printers have their own chapter: Chapter 5.

◆ Networks are the focus of Chapter 6.

First on the list for this introductory chapter is an essential part of the inner working of any PC: the power supply.

The power supply

Within a PC, the **PSU (power supply unit)** is a black or silver-coloured box, with a fan inside it and cables coming from it (Figure 1.4).

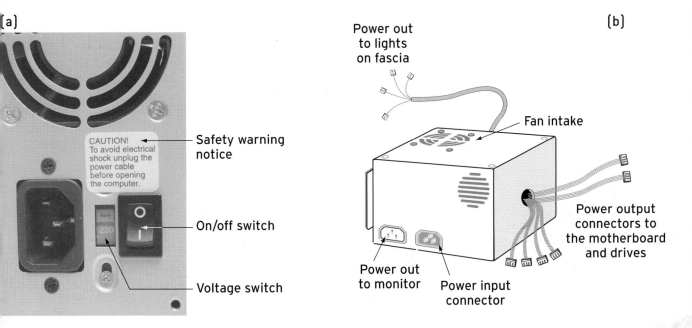

Figure 1.4   **The power supply for a PC: (a) connections on the case and (b) the PSU**

Watch out

If the fan fails to turn on when you power up your PC, do not think about sticking anything into the fan to force it to move!

The PSU has various features, depending on the age of the PC:

- On older PCs, a **passthrough connector** may be located on the back of the PSU. This would allow you to plug a monitor into the power supply and to use the PC power switch to activate the monitor.

- A **power switch** may extend through the case wall of the PSU to a back corner of the PC or more recently to the front of the PC. On more modern PCs, the on/off switch is electronic (rather than manual) and is attached directly to the motherboard, which then connects to the PSU.

- For PCs that may be used worldwide, there may be a **110/220 V selector switch**.

The main job of the PSU is to supply power to the various components of the PC. There are two types of power: internal and external.

- The **external power** via the socket provides AC (alternating current) of 110–115 V.

- The **internal power** needed by the various components within the PC is either 5 V or 12 V of DC (direct current).

What does it mean?

AC (alternating current) is a type of electricity; different from DC (direct current). With DC, the power runs from negative charge to positive charge, always in the same direction. This works fine for battery-powered devices where the power has only a short distance to travel. With AC, the direction alternates (very quickly) – and this provides an efficient way of supplying power over long distances. Since PC components work on DC and the power from the wall socket supplies AC, the PSU has to convert AC to DC.

So, the PSU converts the incoming supply of power to one that is needed.

Check Your Understanding 1.3

1 What type of current is used for most household appliances?
2 What type of current is used within a PC by the components?
3 What is the primary function of the PSU?

Go and try out 1.3

1 Where is the power supply unit on a laptop?
2 How is it connected to the power supply at the wall socket?
3 How is it connected to the motherboard of the laptop PC?

The other task of the PSU is to cool the PC, and it houses a fan that controls airflow through the PC case. Components such as the motherboard generate heat, and this heat needs to be extracted. Otherwise, components overheat and may fail. The cooler the air is that enters the fan the better. So, it is helpful to run the computer in a cool and moderately humid environment. It is also essential that the airflow is not interrupted.

There are two main methods of cooling, dependent on the **form factor** of the motherboard:

What does it mean?

The form factor is the size and shape of a device – used to describe its physical dimensions. See page 191 for more details on form factors.

- The Baby AT cools the PC by pulling air into the case and blowing it out through the fan. This does suck dust into the case!
- The ATX PSU pushes air out of the case, creating a negative pressurisation and helping to keep the inside of the PC case clear of dust. The PSU is placed close to the processor and RAM, providing them with much needed cooling, but most modern PCs also have cooling features or **heat sinks** to maintain the optimum temperature of components.

What does it mean?

ATX is one of several motherboard form factors: one that allows easy installation of full-length expansion cards and cables. It is also easier to cool.

RAM (random access memory) is volatile memory (i.e. it retains its data while the power is switched on) that offers the same access time for all locations within it.

Figure 1.5 shows how the power switch for the PSU extends the casing of a PC.

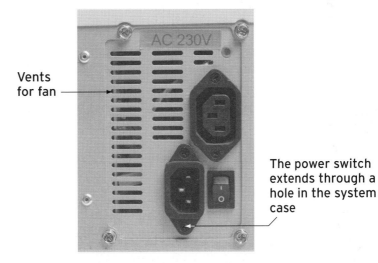

Vents for fan

The power switch extends through a hole in the system case

**Figure 1.5
The PSU within the PC case**

As with most air-conditioning units, the PSU fan works best when the PC case is closed. Expansion slot filler slides should also be in place to provide the best cooling conditions within the case.

Check Your Understanding 1.4

1 What are the two main functions of the power supply unit?
2 What is the difference between the current of internal power and that of external power?
3 How does the ATX form factor improve on the cooling performance of the PSU?

The PSU is a **switching power supply**, in that it takes the incoming 110 V and changes it to 3.3 V, 5 V or 12 V (as required by various components – see Table 1.2) by switching the power supply off and on. More simply, imagine that the 230 V supply is switched on for only a tenth of second, every second; the resultant power is then about one tenth of 230 V i.e. 23 V.

Table 1.2	*Standard voltages*
Voltage	**Device notes**
3.3 V	Motherboards with processors above 100 MHz (Pentium, Pentium Pro)*
+5 V	Motherboards with processors below 100 MHz and many peripheral boards
+12 V	Disk drive motors and other similar devices Modern motherboards passing this voltage on to ISA bus expansion slots

*Upgraded motherboards have to convert the incoming 5 V signal into the 3.3 V required.

What does it mean?

ISA (industry standard architecture) bus is one of several standard designs used by various types of IBM-compatible microcomputers.

Older PCs used −5 V and −12 V, and a PSU may include it just for compatibility, but these voltages are rarely used on modern PCs.

CHAT

Discuss the cooling arrangements for a laptop. Note that the PSU for a laptop is a separate unit housed outside the laptop. This generates heat but is far enough away from the processor not to cause problems. In addition to this, on the most powerful laptop models, there is a fan.

A PSU has a maximum power demand that it can meet, and this is measured in watts. It uses whatever amount of this power as it needs, according to the demand of the devices that are attached to the PC. So, unlike a light bulb that may be 40 W or 60 W or 100 W and burns brightly using electricity according to this wattage, the PSU takes the wattage but may not used it. You might think, then, that the PSU power should be kept down to what is required. However, if you decide to upgrade a PC and this involves adding extra devices, you will be putting a greater load on the PSU and may have to upgrade the PSU as well. A balance needs to be drawn between having enough power to be able to upgrade, but not so much that a lot is wasted on high electricity bills.

Processors use two levels of power (Table 1.3):

1   The **external voltage** – or **I/O voltage** – is the power used for devices mounted on the motherboard.

2   The **internal voltage** is a measure of how much heat the processor generates: the smaller the better.

Table 1.3 *Pentium processor voltage levels**		
Processor	**External voltage**	**Internal voltage**
Pentium 60–66	5	5
Pentium 75–200	3.3/3.5	3.3/3.5
Pentium MMX	3.3	2.8
Pentium Pro 150	3.1	3.1
Pentium Pro 166+	3.3	3.3
Pentium II	3.3	2.8
Pentium II Celeron/Xeon	3.3	2.0
Pentium III	3.3	2.0
Pentium III Xeon	3.3	1.65

*You do not need to try to remember all these different voltages. Just notice that newer models aim to minimise the internal voltage and hence reduce the amount of heat being generated by the processor.

Watch out

When testing a PSU at least one component must be connected so that power is in demand.

Check Your Understanding 1.5

1   What are the five voltages generated by the PSU?
2   What unit is used to measure the maximum power output of the PSU?

The external power is not a smooth non-fluctuating source of power. It is the task of the PSU to smooth out any irregularities in the incoming power supply, but there can be spikes and other problems with the supply which the PSU cannot handle and which may harm components within the PC:

◆ **Line noise** is caused by small variations in the voltage of the power line. With a shared power source, your PC may be competing with other electrical equipment.

◆ A **power surge** – or **power spike** – can be caused by an anomaly in the electrical supply grid, e.g. a **lightning strike**. This results in a very large voltage for a very short period of time.

◆ The opposite phenomenon of the power spike is called a **brownout**. This under-voltage may be caused by excessive demand on the electrical supply grid.

◆ A **blackout** is a complete loss of power. Some activities are more serious if interrupted, e.g. if you are midway defragmenting your disk. More of a problem may be the power surge that can happen when the power returns.

What does it mean?

Defragmentation is a process which tidies up the disk, reusing the disk space more efficiently after some files have been deleted.

The effect on your PC can be **catastrophic** (destruction of the entire PC in a single event) or there may be **degradation**, in which a device may be damaged but you will not notice the effect, apart from an intermittent fault, and then it eventually begins to fail. To learn about how to protect your PC against these problems, see Chapter 3 (page 167).

Check Your Understanding 1.6

1 Distinguish between a brownout and blackout power problem.
2 Explain what is meant by a power surge.

Go and try out 1.4

1 Find out what is meant by clamping voltage and clamping speed.
2 Find out which POST error codes indicate a problem with the PSU.

What does it mean?

POST (power-on self-test) is a hardware diagnostic routine that is run during the start-up boot sequence which checks configuration settings held in CMOS. Your power supply can also be protected using a UPS (uninterruptible power supply); see page 173.

Assuming the PSU is working correctly, what should happen when you turn on the power?

CHAT

Discuss with your friends the sequence of events that happens when you turn on a PC. Agree a list of events between you. You can check how right you are the next time you turn on your PC.

When you turn on, what happens next depends on what else is within the PC case and how everything has been installed and configured. There are several very important components:

◆ The CPU/processor (pages 24–26).

What does it mean?

CPU (central processing unit) is the main part of a computer. It comprises registers (accumulator, etc.), the ALU (arithmetic logic unit) and the control unit. It may also include the main memory IAS (immediate access store).

◆ The memory (pages 27–30).
◆ Storage devices (pages 30–38).

These and other component parts of a PC are produced by a variety of different manufacturers, each one trying to create the best solution in their particular field: memory, disk drives and so on. As a result, all these components tend to work at different speeds:

◆ Some are very slow (printers).
◆ Some are fast (disk drives).
◆ Some are very fast (memory).

However, there are not just these three categories of speed, and part of the challenge in designing a PC is to cope with synchronising the signals moving between the many component parts. These signals move along buses (see page 197) under the control of the BIU (see page 24).

First, though, the next section looks at the **boot process**, an automated process that happens every time you power up, and – hopefully – is successful so that you can start to use the PC.

Discuss how the speed of various devices is measured. What units are used? See page 362 for details of units of speed for a PC.

The boot process: booting the computer

The process of starting a computer is called booting the computer. There are two ways of starting up a PC:

◆ A **cold boot** involves turning the PC on by turning on the power. This is usually a button to be pressed on the processor casing. Cold booting involves a series of steps as shown in Figure 1.6.
◆ A **warm boot** involves restarted or resetting the computer – with the power remaining on. This may be done by pressing Ctrl/Alt/Delete. The warm boot process does not include the POST process – it is assumed that if everything was okay when the computer was first turned on, it will still be okay.

Power is not supplied straightaway to all devices. Instead, the power supply system checks what power supplies are needed for the rest of the PC. This process is called **initialising the power supply**. If the proper voltages can be supplied, it sends a POWER GOOD message to the chipset. The chipset then sends on a SYSTEM RESET signal to the processor, and the processor moves on to the next stage of the boot process: identifying the jump address and **loading the BIOS** into RAM.

BIOS (basic input–output system) is the part of the operating system that handles the input and output of the computer, allowing the operating system to use particular features of hardware within the configuration.

RAM (random access memory) is volatile memory (i.e. it retains its data while the power is switched on) that offers the same access time for all locations within it.

Figure 1.6

The steps involved in the boot process

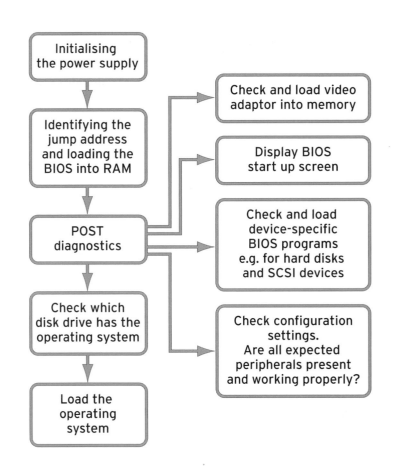

The boot process: loading the BIOS

The **BIOS** is a collection of software utilities that forms part of the operating system. The PC BIOS is fairly standardised, so it is quite possible to update the operating system (e.g. Windows 3.X to Windows 9X) without having to update the BIOS. The BIOS is usually on a ROM chip that comes with the computer, called the **ROM BIOS**. Being on RAM, the BIOS is not affected by disk failure and makes it possible for the computer to boot itself.

So, what does the BIOS do?

◆ The BIOS boots up the PC, i.e. it starts up a PC every time it is turned on.

◆ The BIOS checks the actual hardware configuration against the configuration data. It ensures the **integrity** of the computer system and can therefore prove to be the most important diagnostic tool available to you.

◆ The BIOS handles the input and output of the computer, allowing the operating system to use particular features of hardware within the configuration.

When the computer is turned on, its memory is empty, apart from one set of hardwired instructions that are located at an address called the **jump address**. These important few instructions, when executed, will load the BIOS into memory. So the computer 'jumps' to the jump address, starts executing instructions and this results in the BIOS being loaded. Figure 1.7 shows the standard memory allocation for DOS.

Figure 1.7
Standard DOS memory
allocation

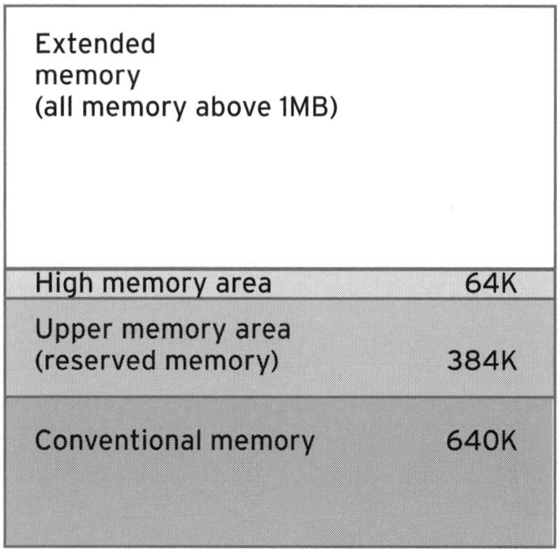

Extended memory (all memory above 1MB)	
High memory area	64K
Upper memory area (reserved memory)	384K
Conventional memory	640K

The BIOS program is placed in a location called the **high memory area** (the first 64 K of second megabyte of RAM, in memory addresses F000h to FFFFh).

Go and try out 1.5

In older computers, to speed up the boot process, a technique called **ROM shadowing** was used. In groups, research the Internet to discover more about this process.

The processor then starts executing the BIOS program – and the next stage of the boot process begins: **POST diagnostics**.

What does it mean?

POST (power-on self-test) is a hardware diagnostic routine that is run during the start-up boot sequence to check the configuration of settings held in CMOS.

CASE STUDY   Nigel the novice PC user

Nigel is nine years old and has just been given a new PC as a birthday present. He has been reading the manual that came with the PC and some of the terminology is alien to him. He does not need a detailed understanding, and does not need to know very much at all to use his PC, but he has asked you to explain things simply to him.

1 Explain the difference between a cold boot and a warm boot.

2 Explain the difference between ROM and RAM.

3 Define the BIOS.

Discuss with your friends how your answer to a nine-year-old might differ from that given to a grown-up.

The boot process: POST diagnostics

During the boot process, the hardware is checked to make sure everything is functioning as it should. If there are problems at this early stage, the system will sound an error beep. The use of sound – available directly from a speaker on the motherboard – is necessary until the monitor is running properly.

It is possible to buy a special debugging card which fits into an ISA slot. This takes error codes output from the BIOS and helps you to see where the problem lies.

1   Research the Internet to find out more about this debugging aid.
2   Compare your notes with your friends.

The BIOS loads the device BIOS of the video adaptor into memory. From then on, communication can be on-screen – and instead of beeps, error codes can be displayed. Details of the error codes and their meanings are shown in Table 9.2 on page 322.

The process then continues, loading any other device-specific BIOS programs (e.g. for hard disks or SCSI devices). For example, the IDE/ATA hard disk BIOS is loaded from high memory and executed.

SCSI (small computer systems interface) is one of five hard drive technologies. It is not an interface; instead it acts as a system bus structure and allows several SCSI devices to connect to a microcomputer (e.g. disk drives and scanners which need a high data transfer rate) by sharing a common interface.

The boot process then displays the **BIOS start-up screen**.

The boot process: the BIOS start-up screen

Figure 1.8 shows the details that are usually seen during the boot process – although some may pass too quickly for you to see them:

- **Version:** the manufacturer, program version number and date uniquely identify the BIOS version.
- **Start-up program keys:** if you need to interrupt the boot process, you must press a combination of keys as specified on the start-up screen. It may be a function key (e.g. F1) or the delete key (Delete) or a combination of keys (e.g. Ctrl + Esc).
- **Logo:** the logo of each manufacturer – of the BIOS, your PC and the motherboard manufacturer.
- **Energy Star:** the Energy Star signifies that your BIOS supports the Energy Star standard (or Green standard).

Manufacturer ——————

Manufacturer logo ——————

Version ——————

Energy star

Pressing DEL will interrupt the bootup and allow you to look at and change the CMOS settings

Serial number ——————

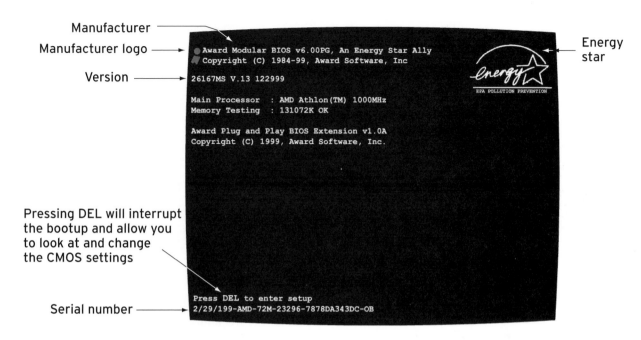

```
Award Modular BIOS v6.00PG, An Energy Star Ally
Copyright (C) 1984-99, Award Software, Inc

26167MS V.13 122999

Main Processor  : AMD Athlon(TM) 1000MHz
Memory Testing  : 131072K OK

Award Plug and Play BIOS Extension v1.0A
Copyright (C) 1999, Award Software, Inc.




Press DEL to enter setup
2/29/199-AMD-72M-23296-7878DA343DC-OB
```

Figure 1.8   On-screen display during boot up

◆ **Serial number:** the BIOS serial number identifies the combination of motherboard, chipset and BIOS program version. It may appear at the end of the display or at the bottom of the screen.

What does it mean?

Energy Star: the US EPA (Environmental Protection Agency) energy efficiency guidelines aim to reduce the amount of electricity consumed. The Green Star programme recognises devices with a standby program that activates a sleep mode when the device has been idle for a given period. In sleep mode, the device reduces 99% of its normal power consumption and no more than 30 watts of power.

CHAT

Without powering up your PC, discuss with friends how closely the start-up screens on your own PCs match that given in Figure 1.8. You can check next time you power up both how much you notice what is on the screen and exactly how close the match is.

During the POST process, the configuration settings (held on CMOS) are checked by the **system BIOS**. Peripherals as specified in the configuration settings are confirmed as present and working properly, and all devices are tested for device speed and access mode.

What does it mean?

Details of the PC configuration – the ones that are checked by the POST process – are held in CMOS. For more details of CMOS, see page 204.

Figure 1.9 shows the details that are displayed while the BIOS checks the configuration settings:

Figure 1.9

On-screen display during boot up

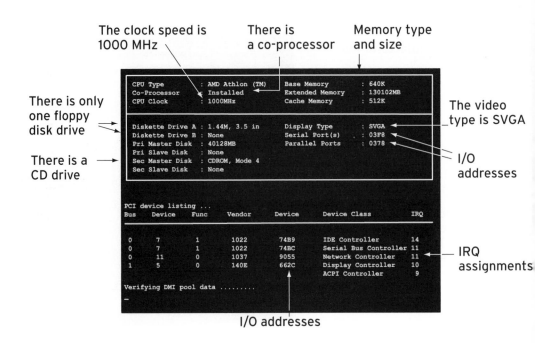

The clock speed is 1000 MHz

There is a co-processor

Memory type and size

There is only one floppy disk drive

There is a CD drive

The video type is SVGA

I/O addresses

IRQ assignments

I/O addresses

```
CPU Type        : AMD Athlon (TM)    Base Memory      : 640K
Co-Processor    : Installed          Extended Memory  : 130102MB
CPU Clock       : 1000MHz            Cache Memory     : 512K

Diskette Drive A : 1.44M, 3.5 in     Display Type     : SVGA
Diskette Drive B : None              Serial Port(s)  .: 03F8
Pri Master Disk  : 40128MB           Parallel Ports   : 0378
Pri Slave Disk   : None
Sec Master Disk  : CDROM, Mode 4
Sec Slave Disk   : None


PCI device listing ...
Bus   Device   Func    Vendor    Device    Device Class          IRQ

 0      7        1       1022      74B9      IDE Controller        14
 0      7        1       1022      74BC      Serial Bus Controller 11
 0      11       0       1037      9055      Network Controller    11
 1      5        0       140E      662C      Display Controller    10
                                             ACPI Controller        9

Verifying DMI pool data .........
-
```

- **Processor type:** this is usually the general 'family' of processor. Newer BIOS recognise Intel-compatibles.

- **Coprocessor:** a maths coprocessor or FPU may be identified as installed (i.e. as a separate unit) and/or integrated (part of the processor).

- **Clock speed:** the processor clock speed is measured in megahertz.

- **Floppy disk drives:** identifies the number of drives, their size and the capacity of the disks.

- **IDE/ATA hard disk drives**; **CD-ROM** and **DVD drives:** lists manufacturer, capacity and access mode for each drive. May also indicate primary master and slave drives and an secondary masters and slaves.

- **Memory size:** a count is made of memory detected on the PC: **base memory** (always 640 Kb), extended memory (less that set aside for the BIOS) and cache memory.

What does it mean?

Base memory is the same as conventional memory.

- **Memory type:** shows the number, type and configuration of memory banks or module and the technology.

- **Video/display type:** shows that the video adaptor is detected.

- **Serial ports:** serial ports are assigned their identities (e.g. COM1, COM2) during the boot up, and the system resource address is displayed.

- **Parallel ports:** serial and parallel ports are assigned their identities (e.g. LPT1, LPT2) during the boot up, and the system resource address is displayed.

- **Plug and Play devices:** lists PnP adaptor cards that are detected.

Check Your Understanding 1.7

Figure 1.9 includes lots of terms that you need to understand before you take your test at the end of the course.

1 Identify any terms that you do not yet understand and make a list of them.
2 Compare your list with a friend. Help each other by explaining things that are on one list but not on the other.
3 For terms that neither of you understand, refer to the index to find out where you can find a definition in this book. Make a note of these page numbers on your list.
4 Share the workload of looking up these terms, and then spend time explaining to each other what you found out.
5 Confirm that you now understand all the terms used on Figure 1.9.

Finally, the configuration is confirmed, and so this POST process ensures that the PC – with all its peripherals – is ready for use. However, it will also tell you if there is something that may need attention. See page 321 for more details about POST process and the error codes and signals.

Last, but not least, the BIOS checks the CMOS data to identify from which disk drive the operating system is to be loaded, e.g. drive A: (floppy drive) or drive C: (hard drive). It looks for the operating system's master boot record at cylinder 0, head 0, sector 0. See page 32 for details of cylinders, heads and sectors.

If it finds it, the operating system is loaded and the code in the boot sector takes over from the BIOS. If the boot record is not where it was expected to be, the BIOS looks elsewhere, exhausting all disk drives before displaying the message 'No boot device available'.

Discuss this situation with others: you turn on the computer and it displays the message 'Non-system disk error'. Why does this happen? What can you do to avoid this problem? What can you do to recover from this problem?

Check Your Understanding 1.8

1 What name is given to the type of software that does hardware checks, system tune-ups and reports on system status?
2 Name one effective tool that runs every time you power up your PC.
3 Explain the requirements for a device to be awarded the Energy Star.
4 What does BIOS stand for?
5 What is a warm boot?
6 Where are the configuration settings stored?
7 What type of ROM can be reprogrammed using flashing?
8 Where in memory is the BIOS loaded?
9 How do you know that the boot sequence has been completed successfully?

Now that you have met the boot process, we can take a closer look at the important components that you will find within the PC casing:

◆ The processor/CPU (see below).
◆ The memory (pages 27–30).
◆ Storage devices (pages 30–8).

Processor/CPU

The **processor** – or **CPU** (**central processing unit**) – is the most important component on the motherboard. Motherboards deserve their own chapter: see Chapter 4 (page 181).

What does it mean?

386, 486, Pentium and P2/3 are all examples of processors.

Figure 1.10 shows the most important parts of a PC's microprocessor:

◆ The most important part is the **control unit** (**CU**), which controls the processor in that it instructs other parts of the processor, telling them what to do, what data to work on, where to find it and where to put the results.
◆ The second most important part is the **bus interface unit** (**BIU**) which looks after all transfers of data over the internal and external bus systems.

To carry out instructions, several units contribute:

◆ The **pre-fetch unit** (**PFU**) preloads instructions whenever the BUI is not busy. This keeps data moving and keeps the CPU with a steady supply of instructions to carry out.
◆ The **decode unit** interprets the command part of a program instruction and identifies the individual steps that need to be carried out for this single instruction to be executed.

To do arithmetic, the CPU has two components:

◆ The **ALU** (**arithmetic and logic unit**) does all the simple calculations: addition, subtraction, division, and so on, of whole numbers. It also uses comparative logic to give a true or false decision for a given criterion, e.g. to test whether a data item is greater than zero.
◆ The **floating point unit** (**FPU**) – or **maths coprocessor** – does more complicated calculations, i.e. those involving numbers with decimal places that have to be stored as floating point numbers. The FPU can handle more complex functions such as trigonometric functions (sine, cosine and tangent, etc.) and logarithms.

The **memory management unit** (**MMU**) keeps track of where data is stored, in RAM and cache memory. It copes with the segmentation of memory, paging allocations, and it works out physical addresses of data from logical addresses. This allows addresses that are used by the CPU to be stored at a different physical location, e.g. in a multi-user or multi-tasking environment. See also 'Memory addressing' on page 69.

Figure 1.10
The most important parts of a PC's microprocessor

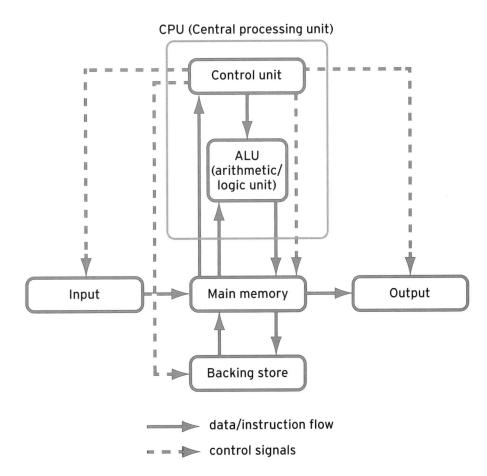

CPU (Central processing unit)

Control unit

ALU (arithmetic/ logic unit)

Input

Main memory

Output

Backing store

→ data/instruction flow

⇢ control signals

Registers are special memory locations used by the CPU temporarily to hold important data such as the IRQ flags and the current instruction being executed.

What does it mean?

IRQ (interrupt request): a primary system resource used to allow peripherals to interrupt processing and gain attention from the CPU.

One component, the **protection test unit (PTU)**, will generate an error message if anything goes wrong; it acts with the CPU to make sure everything happens according to plan. All CPUs do the same thing – control the PC – but, physically, they differ in their **packaging** (Figure 1.11). Packaging is made from ceramic or plastic material to protect the core – or **die** – of the microchip together with an arrangement of pins through which (electronic) connection can be made:

◆ The earliest chips were the **DIPP (dual in-line pin package)** with pins down two long sides of the chip. Pressure was needed to push these into place, and pins could easily be damaged.

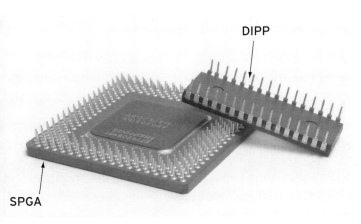

DIPP

SPGA

Figure 1.11   **Different types of CPU packaging**

◆ Square chips with pins on all four sides were then developed. To avoid the pin damage problem, these were soldered on to the motherboard, but then they could not be removed at all.

◆ With a **PGA** (**pin grid array**), the pins are arranged in concentric squares on the underside of the chip. CPGA (ceramic) and PPGA (plastic) versions were developed. Then, early Pentiums adopted the SPGA which fitted more pins in by staggering the arrangement of pins (Figure 1.12). Pin damage became less common but could still happen, but then the ZIF sockets solved this problem. Another alternative to PGA is the PBGA (plastic ball grid array) which does not have the mounting pins underneath the chip.

(a)   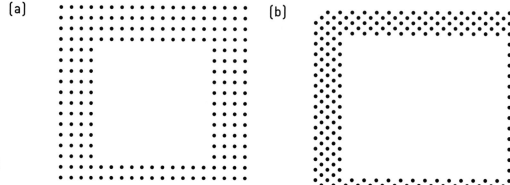   (b)

Figure 1.12

Pin patterns:
(a) concentric square pattern of CPGA; and
(b) staggered pin arrangement of SPGA

What does it mean?

The ZIF (zero insertion force) sockets have a lever that grips and releases the chip. See Figure 4.14 on page 203.

◆ The **SEC** (**single-edge connector**) has a continuous edge of connections and is mounted vertically on the motherboard (as with expansion cards and memory modules). See Figure 4.11 on page 201. Apart from the lack of pins – that could not be bent or damaged – having the board vertical allowed cooling of the processor chip, there being a greater surface area exposed to the air.

CASE STUDY   Nigel the novice PC user

Nigel wants to understand a bit more about how a processor works. Remember that he is only nine years old.

1 Draw up a table to list the components within the processor.

2 Write brief notes on what each component does.

3 Sketch the three types of packaging that might be used: DIPP, PGA and SEC.

Memory

The memory of a computer system is used for two main purposes:

◆ To store programs that are being run

◆ To store the data that the program works on

Programs are actually treated like data; the computer executes a program, instruction by instruction, and these instructions are the 'data' of the fundamental program cycle:

◆ fetch instruction

◆ decode instruction

◆ execute instruction.

The address of the next instruction to be fetched is also just data. So everything in a computer's memory is data!

There are then two main types of memory within the PC, and lots of variations of these:

◆ **ROM (read-only memory)**: PROM, EPROM, EEPROM.

◆ **RAM (random access memory)**: DRAM, EDO RAM, RIMM, SRAM, VRAM and WRAM.

What is the difference between ROM and RAM?

◆ RAM is **volatile memory**. You can write to it and read from it, but it loses its data when the power is turned off – e.g. when your computer crashes and you have to turn it off to restart it.

◆ ROM is **non-volatile memory**. It does not lose its data when the power supply is off, so it can be used to store data that is needed when you next turn on, e.g. for the BIOS chip. ROM means 'read only' memory but, depending on the type of ROM, you may or may not be able to write to it. (See Table 1.4.)

Table 1.4	*Different types of ROM*
Type of ROM	**Notes**
PROM (programmable ROM)	A PROM is a blank ROM chip – all bits are set to 1 initially. A PROM burner can be used to change the binary 1s into binary 0s, so as to store data and/or instructions on the PROM. This process cannot be reversed; once 'burnt', the 0s cannot be turned back into 1s. WYBIWYG = what you burn is what you get.
EPROM (erasable PROM)	An EPROM (pronounced 'e-prom') is the same as a PROM but with a quartz crystal window. This allows the circuitry to be accessed with UV (ultraviolet) light to turn the 0s back into 1s. The EPROM has to be removed from the PC for reprogramming.
EEPROM (electronically erasable PROM)	An EEPROM (pronounced 'e-e-prom') is the same as an EPROM except you do not need to remove it to reprogram it. This makes it very easy to upgrade. The reprogramming – using a software utility available from the chip manufacturer – is called **flashing** and the chip is called **flash ROM**.

Programs that are written and stored in RAM are called **software**; the instructions can be overwritten. The instructions written to a simple ROM chip – which cannot be rewritten – are called **firmware**. Of the two types of memory, RAM is the quicker for the CPU to access. So, to improve performance during the boot process, the BIOS instructions (held on ROM) may be copied on to RAM; this process is called **shadowing**.

Discuss with friends the similarities between the evolution of ROM and the progress from CD to CDR to CDRW. Think in particular about the changes in equipment needed to read and write these CDs.

There are also different types of RAM – SRAM and DRAM – and different ways of packaging these:

◆ **DIP** (**dual inline packaging**) is a through-hole component that fits through holes in the motherboard. These are arranged in rows called **banks**.

◆ **SIMM** (**single inline memory module**) is a small circuit board – a mini expansion board – that holds a group of eight or nine memory chips.

◆ DIMMs and RIMMs and SODIMMs are similar to SIMMs but hold more memory.

For more details on the different types of RAM, and how these are packaged, see page 185.

Check Your Understanding 1.9

1 Explain the meanning of the term 'volatile'.
2 What is flash ROM, and how is it made?
3 How is RAM packaged?

CASE STUDY

Nigel the novice PC user

Nigel has been reading his manual again – and other books about computers – and needs your help in explaining some more terminology:

1 What is the memory of a PC used for?

2 Explain the terms ROM and RAM, and the difference between them.

3 Explain the difference between PROMs, EPROMs and EEPROMs.

Cache memory

What does it mean?

Cache memory is a form of fast memory that is used as a data buffer between the CPU and RAM.

Cache memory may be internal or external:

◆ **Internal cache** is located inside the CPU chip; also called **primary cache** or 'on the die'.

◆ **External cache** is still on the motherboard but not within the CPU chip; also called **secondary cache**.

Cache memory can also be categorised according to it closeness (proximity) to the CPU:

◆ **Level 1 (L1) cache** is closest to the CPU and, like internal cache, is housed within the CPU chip.

◆ **Level 2 (L2) cache** is not so close. It may still be on the CPU chip (just behind the L1 cache) or it may be external cache.

Note: L1 cache cannot be upgraded without changing the CPU. L2 cache can be upgraded; on some motherboards the modules plug into special mounts or expansion sockets on the motherboard.

Why is cache memory needed? Central to the operation of a PC is the communication between the CPU and RAM. These two components (like many others within a computer) work at differing speeds:

◆ The CPU works in megahertz (millionths of seconds).

◆ The RAM works in nanoseconds (billionths of seconds).

 CHAT *Discuss with friends the different measure of time used in PCs. (Page 362 explains how time is measured on a PC.)*

Even though the RAM is so much quicker, it takes time to find the data that is needed and to bring it via the data bus to the CPU for processing. To aid the process, the CPU interacts with the RAM by having a series of **wait states**; it actually pauses for a while to allow the data it wants to be transferred from RAM into the registers within the CPU. Data may be coming far afar, e.g. from a hard disk, and so it has to be transferred from the disk to RAM and then from RAM to the CPU. So extra wait states may be necessary.

What does it mean? *A wait state is a time of inactivity for the CPU to allow other devices to catch up with it.*

Even when the data is within RAM, there is a delay in transferring data within the PC called **latency**. Anyway, wherever the data is, the CPU has to wait – and an idle CPU is not acceptable!

What does it mean? *Latency is a time delay.*

The cache memory is there to help to solve this problem. It acts as a buffer between RAM and CPU, and holds data that the CPU will need (e.g. things that are used a lot). Like a printer buffer, the cache memory is there to make up for the mismatch between the speed of the two devices: CPU and RAM. There may also be a **disk cache** – either in RAM or on the disk controller – to compensate for the speed difference between the hard disk and RAM.

Caching involves some guesswork by the system – what will the CPU need next?

◆ A good guess for the disk cache is that it will be whatever comes next on the disk.

◆ For the internal cache, a good guess would be whatever lies in the next section of RAM.

This guesswork uses the principle of **locality of reference**. Most of the time, it is a good guess – and so the net effect is a more effective use of CPU time. Cache memory is often a small SRAM (see page 186 for more details).

What does it mean?

SRAM (static RAM) is a special type of RAM. The transistors in SRAM, unlike the capacitors which make up DRAM, do not need to be frequently refreshed. SRAM is very fast but relatively expensive (many times more than DRAM) and takes up valuable space, so it is used for cache memory rather than primary memory.

SRAM offers access speeds of 2 ns or faster. While adding more cache memory (at L1 or L2) can increase the speed, the time it takes the CPU to keep the cache filled can decrease the performance overall. So, a balance is needed: enough to keep the CPU supplied, but not so big that the CPU spends all its time guessing what it will need next. For example, adding 256 K of L2 might increase the speed; the next 256 K added to L2 may adversely affect performance.

Check Your Understanding 1.10

1 What type of memory is most commonly used for L2 cache?
2 List all the terms used as measures of time, with an explanation for each.
3 Explain the meaning of the terms 'wait state' and 'latency'.

CASE STUDY   Nigel the novice PC user

Nigel has more questions. Answer these, using simple terminology that he can understand:

1 What is cache memory?

2 Why does the PC need cache memory?

3 How long is a nanosecond?

Go and try out 1.7

1 Pentiums may offer a cache memory for 64 MB of RAM. What was on offer on earlier machines?
2 Research the Internet to find out how much cache memory is used in a number of different spec PCs.

Storage devices

Memory can be temporary or permanent:

◆ The PC's memory is a form of **temporary storage**. When the computer is turned off, the data is lost.

◆ The **permanent storage** devices are used to hold data that would not otherwise fit within the memory of the PC and/or that needs to be portable, i.e. allowing you to take it to another PC.

Memory outside the PC – e.g. on a storage device like a floppy disk or a hard disk – is therefore more properly called storage, or **backing storage**.

What does it mean?

The peripheral that reads or writes the data is called a storage device.

The basic storage element is the **bit** (*bi*nary digit). These are grouped into bytes and/or words; then into blocks or packets, into files, and so, on according to the storage medium and what you plan to do with the data.

What does it mean?

The material on which the data is written in called the storage medium.

Storage media can be magnetic or optical:

◆ **Magnetic media** include tape and disks (floppy and hard).
◆ **Optical media** include CD-ROMs and DVDs.

The data can be read/written on to the storage medium in one of two ways:

◆ serially, one record after another
◆ directly, accessing data in a random order, just as it is needed.

Magnetic tape is a serial device, and so the data cannot be accessed other than in the order it has been written. Direct-access devices include floppy disks, hard disks and optical disks. *Note:* direct-access devices can be accessed serially if required.

Backing storage is a non-volatile form of memory so that large amounts of data – too much to retain within a PC – can be taken from one computer to another, or just kept safe in case of a PC failure. The process of **backing up** is the copying of data and/or instructions from memory within a PC on to a backing storage device.

Storage devices can be **fixed** (as in the hard disk on your PC) or **removable** (as with a magnetic tape, floppy disk, CD-ROM or DVD). On a floppy disk, the data is organised into **tracks** and **sectors** (Figure 1.13):

◆ Floppy disks have 8–36 sectors per track; hard disks have perhaps 700 sectors per track.
◆ Each sector is uniquely addressable so data can be found when needed.

Hard disks have two or more **platters**. As well as tracks and sectors, a **cylinder** is formed from one track on each platter (Figure 1.14). The most efficient use of the read/write heads of a hard drive is to access one cylinder at a time; these are numbered from 0 at the outer edge of the disk pack.

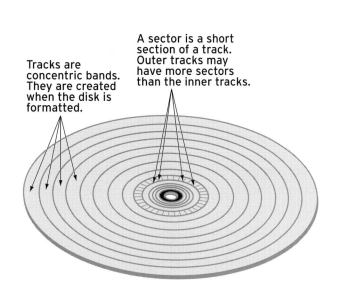

Tracks are concentric bands. They are created when the disk is formatted.

A sector is a short section of a track. Outer tracks may have more sectors than the inner tracks.

Figure 1.13   Storage on a floppy disk

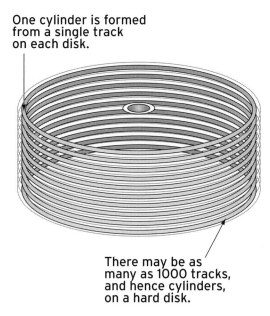

One cylinder is formed from a single track on each disk.

There may be as many as 1000 tracks, and hence cylinders, on a hard disk.

Figure 1.14   Organisation of a hard disk into cylinders

The **geometry of a disk** determines its organisational structure and is important information for the BIOS:

◆ CHS (**cylinder**, **head**, **sector**) specifies where to position the read/write heads (by the cylinder), which platter surface to access (by the head) and whereabouts on the track to find the data (by the sector).

◆ ECHS (**extended cylinder/head/sector**) addressing also identifies data on a disk by the cylinder, head and sector. Also known as **large mode** by some BIOS systems, this translation mode helped to break the 504 MB barrier for some IDE drives.

Check Your Understanding 1.11

1 Explain these terms: 'temporary storage', 'permanent storage' and 'backing storage'.
2 Name two different types of media and give one example of each.
3 Distinguish between these terms: 'backing storage' and 'backing up'.
4 Give one example of a fixed storage device and one example of a removable storage device.

CASE STUDY   Nigel the novice PC user

Nigel wants to know how data is written on to a hard disk:

1 Draw a diagram to explain to Nigel what is meant by the geometry of a hard disk.

2 Label your diagram and write brief notes to explain these terms: 'sector', 'track', 'platter'.

Partitioning a hard disk

A hard disk can then be subdivided into partitions, each of which can be formatted separately. The first partition 'cuts' the hard disk into two:

◆ A **primary partition** that cannot be split further

◆ An **extended partition** that can be further subdivided if necessary

The physical drive is not actually split up, but **logical drives** are created, each with its own drive letter (Figure 1.15).

Figure 1.15
Partitioning a disk

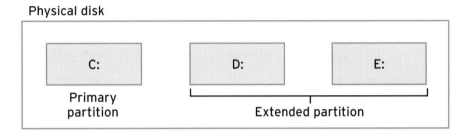

The two partitions – primary and extended – can be designated as system and boot partitions as well:

◆ The **system partition** holds all the files needed to boot an operating system. This is usually the **'active' partition.**

◆ The **boot partition** holds all the .EXE files for the operating system plus the support files.

What does it mean?

EXE is the file extension for an executable file. See Table 7.10 (page 280) for a list of file extensions and their meanings.

So, the primary partition is bootable, i.e. when you power up, the boot process will access the primary partition to start running. In certain circumstances, however, it is possible to boot from a second operating system in another partition; see **dual-booting** on page 300.

Why would you want to partition a hard disk?

◆ Partitioning divides the disk into logical sub-drives and you can address these as if they were separate hard drives.

◆ The separate areas of the disk allow you to install more than one operating system on the same PC.

◆ If you choose to keep programs in one partition and data in a separate partition, this can make selecting files for backing up a simpler process.

◆ Partitioning can improve disk efficiency. **Cluster** sizes are generally linked to the disk size so a partition of the entire disk will have a smaller cluster size than for the entire disk.

What does it mean?

A cluster – also known as a file allocation unit – is the smallest number of sectors used to hold a file or a part of a file.

- ◆ Some of the earlier operating systems could only access the hard disk up to a certain storage capacity. So, if you had a very high-capacity hard drive, it was necessary to partition it. Otherwise, you could not make full use of the entire disk.

Exactly how you partition a hard disk depends on which operating system is installed:

- ◆ MS-DOS/Windows 9X: use the FDISK utility.
- ◆ Windows 2000 and XP: go through Windows Setup, or the Disk Management utility.

How to partition a hard disk is explained on page 289.

Check Your Understanding 1.12

1 Explain the differences between a primary partition and an extended partition.
2 Explain why you might want to partition a disk.

Formatting a disk

Before a disk can be used to store data files, it has to be formatted. There are two levels of formatting:

- ◆ **Physical (low-level) formatting** creates the cylinders, tracks and sectors on a hard disk. For a floppy disk, there are only tracks and sectors to create. For both types of disk, this involves scanning the surface for imperfections and setting aside those sectors that cannot be used.
- ◆ **Logical (high-level) formatting** prepares the disk for files by creating the operating system's file system and management tables and files.

Formatting procedures for the PC user depend on the type of disk:

- ◆ The two levels of formatting of a floppy disk are done using a single FORMAT command available with your PC's operating system. If you decide to reformat a floppy disk, you can opt for a **quick format** which just redoes the high-level formatting.
- ◆ Low-level formatting of a hard disk is done at the factory, so only the logical formatting is done using a utility on your PC. However, the hard disk has to be partitioned (if at all) prior to high-level formatting.
- ◆ With a CD-R disk, the formatting is done automatically when you write to the disk, so you don't have to worry about it beforehand.

MS-DOS and Windows operating systems format disks to have 512 data bytes per sector. Each sector also has some **header information** so that it can be identified, and **trailer information** so that the operating system knows where the data for that sector ends. The raw capacity of a disk (e.g. 2 MB on a floppy disk) is therefore reduced during formatting (e.g. to 1.44 MB) due to this overhead of data in each sector.

The high-level formatting process writes material to allow the operating system to interact with the disk: the boot sector; the root directory table; and the FAT (file allocation table) table.

The **boot sector** is a sector near the centre of the disk, set aside to hold data about how data is organised on the disk:

- The number of sectors
- The number of hidden sectors
- The number of sectors per cluster: this is usually 1 or 2 on floppy disks
- The number of sectors per track: this can be 9, 15, 18 or 36 for a floppy disk
- The number of bytes per sector
- The number of FATs
- The size of the root directory
- The program needed to load the operating system

This last item is the program that searches and loads files needed to boot the disk. If the necessary files are not on the disk, then the disk is not bootable. For details of the files that are needed for a boot, see page 252.

The **root directory table** has an entry for each file on the disk:

- The name of the file
- The file extension (see page 279)
- The file attribute (see page 278)
- The date and time that the file was created or last updated.
- The position where the start of this file is to be found on the disk (cluster number).
- The length of the file.

Since the clusters are too short to store whole files of data, a file will be stored in a number of clusters and these need not be consecutive on the disk. The file is then called **fragmented**. Keeping track of the many fragments of a file falls to the FAT. It records which clusters are used for which files.

What does it mean?

Defragmentation is a process which tidies up the disk, reusing the disk space more efficiently after some files have been deleted. For more details, see page 263.

Because the FAT is so important, two copies of it are kept and they are synchronised with each other. If your PC crashes, it may happen midway through saving a file, and there may be a discrepancy between the two FAT files. Utilities such as ScanDisk check for this. See Table 2.1 on page 131 for more details of ScanDisk and other utility programs that you can use to check your disk.

There are different versions of FAT – FAT16, FAT32 and NTFS – according to the operating system in use. You will learn more about these in Unit 2 (pages 281 and 289). Exactly what is written on the hard disk during formatting depends on the operating system. For more details of the formatting process, see page 295.

Optical disks have their own filing systems, and Windows 98 and 2000 support both of these:

◆ **CDFS (compact disk file system)** is used for optical disk files.

◆ **UDF (universal disk format)** is one of several Windows files systems and is replacing CDFS.

Hard drive technologies are listed in Table 1.5. Note that the ST506 and ESDI technologies are now outdated and most modern-day PCs use IDE/EIDE or an SCSI drive.

Table 1.5 *Hard drive technologies*

Technology	Development	Connection
ST506 ESDI (enhanced small device interface)	Outdated technology of AT PC; big and slow; complex to install and replace. Required low-level formatting and high-level formatting before the operating system could be installed	Controller board mounted on an expansion slot on the motherboard
SCSI (small computer systems interface)	SCSI is not an interface; instead it acts as a system bus structure and allows several SCSI devices to connect to a microcomputer, e.g. disk drives and scanners which need a high data transfer rate, by sharing a common interface. Useful for file servers	Connection is via an expansion board
IDE (integrated drive electronics)	Developed as inexpensive alternative to SCSI; now most popular for tape drives, hard drives, CD-ROMs and DVDs. IDE is the ATA (AT attachment) interface. Standard for IDE interface for tape drives, CD-ROMs and DVDs is the ATAPI (ATA packet interface). Originally supported two 504 MB drives; now supports greater capacity drives. Low-level formatting done at factory. High-level formatting done with FORMAT command. Costs of adding hard disks are reduced by building the IDE interface into the hard disk.	Controller board integrated into the drive assembly; hence its name. A 40-pin connector to the pass-through board or to the motherboard via a 40-wire ribbon on cable. Maximum of 18-inch ribbon protects the integrity of data passing through it. Card may be multifunctional and support serial drives, floppy drives and game ports. Motherboard may have one or two IDE/EIDE controllers.
EIDE/ATA-2 (enhanced IDE)	Post-1995 PCs enhancement of IDE; BIOS systems handling of bigger disk drives (over 504 MB, up to 8.4 GB). ATA-2 is an ANSI (American National Standards Institute) standard that is backward compatible with ATA IDE drives	ATA-2 supports **LBA (logical block addressing)**, a facility for **block transfer** of data, grouping many read/writes into a single interrupt

The **ATA IDE interface standard** determines features and translation modes used between the disk drive and the PC:

◆ **PIO (programmed input/output)** modes are the standard protocol controlling how data passes between the disk drive and the CPU. Five rates exist, each with a different maximum data transfer rate (Table 1.6).

◆ **IDE DMA (direct-memory access)** modes – also known as **bus mastering** – allows the hard drive to control the transfer of data to and from the PC's memory without going through the CPU. It requires a PCI bus and works independently of any other DMA functions of the PC. Table 1.7 shows the different modes available.

Table 1.6   *PIO rates**

Mode	Transfer rate (Mbps)	Supported by?
0	3.3	ATA IDE
1	5.2	ATA IDE
2	8.3	ATA IDE
3	11.1	ATA-2
4	16.6	ATA-2

Table 1.7   *IDE DMA rates**

Mode	Maximum data transfer rate (Mbps)	Supported by?
Single word 0	2.1	ATA IDE
Multiword 0	4.2	ATA IDE
Multiword 1	13.3	ATA-2
Multiword 3/DMA-33	33.3	ATA-2

* The rates in Tables 1.6 and 1.7 will be out of date; progress is continuous. So check current rates.

What does it mean?

IDE DMA is not the same as the DMA used with the ISA bus structure that may be included in the system chipset.

PCI (peripheral component interconnect) is a standard design for local buses used in IBM-compatible microcomputers.

A drive would normally use PIO or IDE DMA, rarely both. As a technician, you do not need to know the fine detail of these rates of transfer for the various standards. However, you should be aware that if you have more than one IDE hard drive sharing the same IDE cable, each drive having different standards, then both will perform according to the slower of the two standards. So, adding a drive may increase capacity, but if is not as high a specification as the current drive, it will reduce performance of the existing drive.

The ATA standard continues to be developed, each one incorporating some new feature. They are numbered ATA-1, ATA-2, ATA-3 and so on, with ATA-6 being the version for 2000. With ATA-4 came UltraDMA, a technology which doubled the width of the ribbon so as to reduce the risk of electromagnetic interference between the wires, so while it still carried only 40 streams of data, it could do so at a much faster rate.

Go and try out 1.8

Working with a friend, research the Internet for information on the ATA standards. Make notes.

Check Your Understanding 1.13

1 Explain the difference between low-level formatting and high-level formatting.
2 Distinguish between the purpose of the root directory table and the FAT file.
3 Apart from the various speeds of transfer, explain the main difference between PIO and IDE DMA.

CASE STUDY   Nigel the novice PC user

Nigel wants to store some images on a disk and give them to a friend to load on their PC. Nigel has some floppy disks that have been used before and also some brand-new blank CD-Rs. He has these questions for you:

1 When I tried to format the floppy disk, the PC asked if I wanted a Quick format. What does this mean?

2 Which of the two types of disks would be best to store the images that I want to give to my friend? (Give your reasons.)

3 How do I format the CD-R disks?

2   Adding and removing field-replaceable modules (FRMs)

You need to be able to add and remove a number of system modules, including some for portable systems. The background details about each FRM are given in the text and then the 'How to' panels give you brief instructions that you can follow. After reading through the notes, check that you are confident in adding and removing each module listed by doing it yourself, and then complete the checklist on page 68, adding your own notes as necessary.

How FRMs are connected – and why – depends on the characteristics of each module:

◆ Some can be replaced without opening the PC casing. You may just need to disconnect one module (like the keyboard) and plug a new one in its place. These external devices tend to be attached by a cable to a port on the rear of the PC (and/or at the side of a laptop case).

◆ For the internal devices, you will need to open up the PC case and know what you are doing.

Having physically replaced an FRM, you may need to change some software settings. This is covered in Unit 2. Here, first of all, let's concentrate on external devices; they are the easiest to add and remove.

External input devices

Some devices are wireless. They rely on infrared communication between the PC and the peripheral. Connecting them does not involve any physical connection, but you do have to set up the software to recognise that the peripheral is to be used; see page 86.

For input devices that do have a cable, at the PC end there is a connector which needs to be fitted into one of the ports on the PC casing. The full range of connectors is covered in section 4 (page 87), but details of the ones you might expect to find are given here. So, for input devices, like the keyboard or mouse, which have a cable already attached, you need to identify the port on the outside of the PC casing that matches the connector on the cable (Figure 1.16).

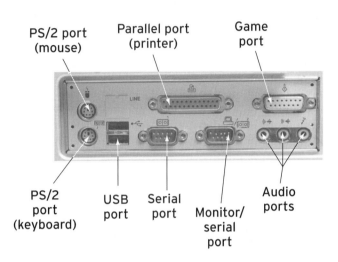

Figure 1.16
The rear view of a PC

 CHAT *Discuss with a friend the ports shown in Figure 1.16. Can you recognise each of them with confidence?*

Adding/removing a keyboard

Regardless of the layout of the keyboard, unless it is of the wireless variety, a cable runs from within the keyboard and is terminated with a connector which can be one of three types (Figure 1.17):

◆ A DIN-type 5-pin connector.
◆ A mini-DIN 6-pin – also known as a **PS/2 connector**.
◆ A USB connector.

What does it mean? *DIN is an acronym for a German phrase meaning 'German industry standard'.*

What does it mean? *USB (universal serial bus) is a higher-speed serial connection standard that supports low-speed devices (mice, keyboards, scanners) and higher-speed devices (digital cameras). For more information on connectors, see section 4.*

Figure 1.17

Connector options for a keyboard

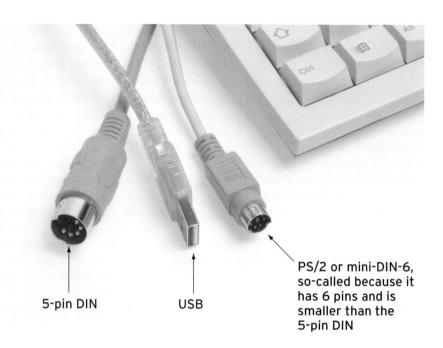

5-pin DIN   USB   PS/2 or mini-DIN-6, so-called because it has 6 pins and is smaller than the 5-pin DIN

The connector on the keyboard cable should fit into one port on the PC casing. Sometimes, both the connector and port are colour coded, and/or the port may have an icon to represent the peripheral that is expected.

If you cannot find a matching port, you may need a **keyboard adaptor**. This will interface between a DIN connection and a PS/2 connection.

On the connector at the end of the cable, there may also be an etching to show where 'top' is. Be sure to insert it the correct way up, with firm pressure, but being careful not to bend any of the pins.

If you want to install a wireless keyboard, you need to install a device driver using a 'normal' keyboard. Then you can disconnect the normal keyboard and use the wireless one instead. See page 307 for more information about installing device drivers.

How to add/remove a keyboard

Watch out

Think about whether your PC should be turned on or off when you are connecting or disconnecting peripherals. If in doubt, turn it off.

To add a keyboard, follow these steps:

1 Check the end of the keyboard cable and identify its type.

2 Locate the matching port on the PC case.

3 Making sure the connector has the correct orientation way, press it firmly into place.

Removing a keyboard simply involves running your hand along the cable from the keyboard to the port on the PC casing, and pulling the connector from the port.

Adding/removing a mouse

Connecting a mouse is similar to attaching a keyboard: identify the connector type, find the correct port and then plug in – the right way up. There are three basic types of mouse (Figure 1.18):

◆ The **mechanical mouse** has a rubber or metal ball on its underside that can roll in all directions. Mechanical sensors (rollers) within the mouse detect the direction the ball is rolling in and move the screen pointer accordingly.

◆ The **optomechnical mouse** uses optical sensors, rather than rollers, to detect the motion of the ball.

◆ An **optical mouse** uses a laser to detect the mouse's movement. Because there are no moving parts, they respond more quickly and more precisely, but are more expensive than the other two forms of mouse.

For each of these three types, the mouse can be connected in one of three ways to the PC:

◆ For a serial mouse, the RS232C serial port or PS/2 port offers the simplest connection.

◆ PS/2 mice need to be connected to a PS/2 port.

◆ Cordless mice are not connected. Instead, communication is via infrared or radio waves.

 CHAT

Discuss situations where a cordless mouse would be more useful, not just cleaner, than any other type of mouse.

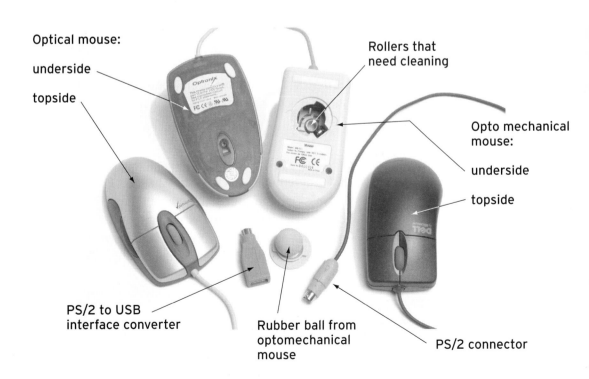

Optical mouse:

underside

topside

Rollers that need cleaning

Opto mechanical mouse:

underside

topside

PS/2 to USB interface converter

Rubber ball from optomechanical mouse

PS/2 connector

Figure 1.18
Types of mouse

How to add/remove a mouse

1 Check the end of the mouse cable and identify its type.

2 Locate the matching port on the PC case.

3 Making sure the connector has the correct orientation, press it firmly into place.

Removing a mouse simply involves running your hand along the cable from the mouse to the port on the PC casing, and gently pulling the connector from the port.

Go and try out 1.9

1 Using a PC that has a mouse and a keyboard attached, examine the connectors on both.

2 Notice which type of connector and which port has been used.

3 Look at any other input devices attached, and check which port they use, and the type of connector. Make notes.

Section 4 (page 92) explains what the pins in the connectors do.

Watch out

Think about whether you should turn a PC off before detaching or attaching peripherals. If in doubt, turn it off.

External output devices

There are a variety of output devices that you could connect to a PC. Two are considered here: a monitor and a printer.

Other output devices, like a scanner, are connected in very much the same way but, in any case, you should follow the manufacturer's instructions.

Monitors

Apart from the monitor, your PC should have a video card inside the case – and, together, these two FRMs determine what your display looks like, and form the **video system**. Video card installation is covered later in this section (page 60). Here, we simply consider how to add or remove the monitor. The port for the video is a female D-subconnector and the monitor should have a male D-subconnector, as shown in Figure 1.19. Notice the shape of this connector – of the longer two edges, one is longer than the other. This makes it easy to spot which way round to make the connection.

What does it mean?

A male connector has pins.
A female connector has holes into which the pins fit.

How to add a monitor

1 Position the monitor so that, once in place and connected, you do not have to move it.

2 Locate the D-subconnector on the PC casing.

3 Push the video cable into place, making sure you have the correct orientation.

4 Tighten the fixing screws so that they are hand tight.

To remove the monitor, run your hand along the cable from the monitor to the port on the PC casing, undo the fixing screws until they no longer hold the connector in place and then gently pull the connector from the port.

Figure 1.19
Connecting a monitor

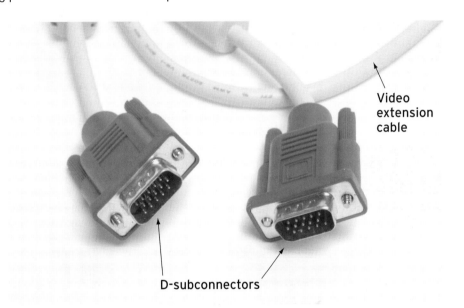

Video extension cable

D-subconnectors

Discuss the variety of pin arrangements in the cabling you have used for the keyboard, mouse and monitor. Why do you think these different arrangements were developed?

Printers

It is possible to connect a printer using an IrDa (Infrared Data Association) interface (see page 94). This is a wireless connection, so there is no cabling. However, you have to set up the software so that your PC recognises the peripheral and can communicate with it. Otherwise, you need to connect a printer cable and, unlike other peripherals looked at so far, the printer cabling has to be attached at both ends: to the printer and to the PC (Figure 1.20).

You then have two choices:

◆ Using a **serial connection** to the serial port or via the USB

◆ Using a **parallel connection**, via the parallel port

Figure 1.20
Printer-connecting cables

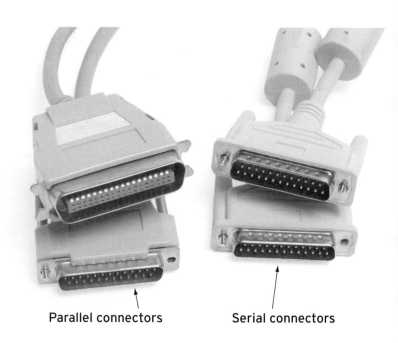

Parallel connectors   Serial connectors

The types of cabling used are very different: serial cabling is circular in cross-section; parallel cabling is a ribbon.

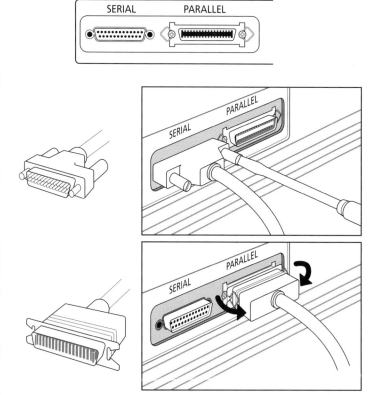

The ports on the PC are also very different, and so are the connectors that fit into them (Figure 1.21):

◆ The **serial port** conforms to the RS232c standard. This was a standard that required a 25-pin male port, but PCs only use nine of these pins so it can be and often is replaced by a 9-pin male port.

◆ The **parallel port** on the PC offers a female 25-pin DB (databus) connector. A male 25-pin DB connector on one end of the printer ribbon cable will clip or screw into place. At the other end of the cable, at the printer end, is the 36-pin Centronics connector.

The connection points on the printer are simple (Figure 1.22). Most modern printers have the option for parallel connection and USB connection. Using the USB port can free up the parallel port for another peripheral, e.g. a scanner or Zip drive. If the printer does not have a USB connection, you can use an adaptor cable. This has the standard Centronics connector (to attach to the printer) and a USB connector (to attach to the PC).

Figure 1.21   The ports on a PC

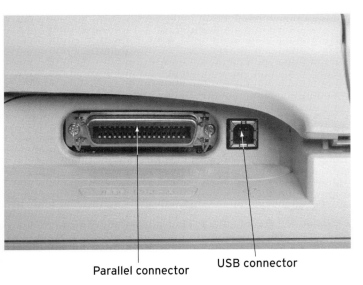

Parallel connector   USB connector

Figure 1.22   The ports on a printer

So, having decided whether the transmission is to be serial or parallel, you need to have the correct cabling to support this connection. If a parallel cable is used, to protect data integrity during transfer the maximum length of cable should be 15 feet, although 9–12 feet is even better. Newer IEEE-1284 cables could be 30 feet in length, and 50-foot high-end cables are also available. However, if you need to be more than 10 feet from a printer, you should have a networked configuration.

How to add/remove a printer

1 Decide which type of connection you need: parallel or serial. Obtain the correct type of cabling.

2 Connect the printer end of the cable to the printer.

3 Connect the other end of the cable to the PC, using the appropriate port.

When removing the printer, disconnect from the PC. Leaving the printer cable attached to the printer will make it ready to be attached to the next PC.

Go and try out 1.10

1 For each PC in your school or college, look at the type of cabling used to connect the printer to the PC. Make notes.
2 Look also at what other peripherals are connected to each PC and check that you recognise all ports and connectors.

Internal modules

To access the internal modules, you will need to open up the case.

Watch out

Follow the safety rules whenever working on a PC:

1 Be prepared: have the right tools to hand.
2 Obey the dress code: nothing dangling that will trap you.
3 Wear your ESD wrist band …!
4 Before starting, turn off the PC and disconnect the AC power cord.
5 Read the manual – don't do things from memory.
6 Ground yourself by touching the chassis to discharge any static electricity that has accumulated on your clothing or body.
7 Handle all parts gently, holding components by their edges, not by the connector.
8 Remember that some components may be too hot to touch safely.
9 Have a 'buddy' – someone nearby who can call an ambulance if things go horribly wrong!
10 Take your time and think carefully before acting.

CHAT *Discuss with your friends: under what circumstance should you not open the case of a PC?*

How to open up a PC case

Tip: You may need a Phillips screwdriver to open the case. Make sure you have all your tools to hand before you start this procedure.

1 Disconnect any peripherals so that there are no cables connected to the ports on the PC case. *Tip:* If you are uncertain that reconnecting will be straightforward, e.g. if you are not sure which cable belongs to which connector, label them as you disconnect each one.

2 Having separated the PC case from all the peripherals, move them out of the way, and take this opportunity to clean the outside of the case. This will prevent excessive amounts of dust getting into the case when you open it.

3 Check to see if the case has any protective edges or appearance bezels. These were common on older PCs but can be removed quite easily.

Screw holes

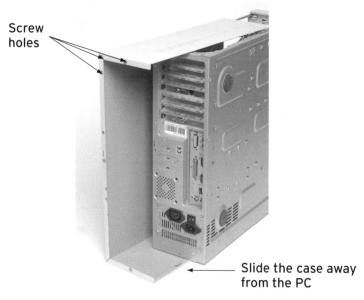

Slide the case away from the PC

Figure 1.23   **Opening a PC case**

4 Removing the case cover will depend on the type of case: tower case or standard desktop case. The older-style standard desktop cases usually have two pieces that fit together, so the front panel is attached to the case top and the back panel is attached to the case bottom. Tower cases come in a variety of designs. They may have no screws at all, and you just slide a panel away. Or there may be a base section and a U-shaped cover that you need to remove. Look for two or four Phillips or thumbscrews on the back edge of the case.

5 Before removing any screws, though, make sure they are the fixing crews for the case and not for a component within the case such as the power supply unit. *Tip:* When you do start to remove screws, set them aside in a safe place so that they can easily be found when the time comes to put everything back together.

6 Removing the cover may be a case of lifting it off, or sliding it. Consult the PC documentation to be absolutely sure. Screwless cases have a release mechanism which you will have to find. Pressing the right spot will allow a panel to be removed easily. Again, consult the PC documentation to check exactly how to open the casing.

Within the PC casing, the internal devices all need power and this may involve a connection to the PSU. All devices need also to be connected to the motherboard. In this section you will learn how to add or remove most of these components. Your first task, having opened the PC casing, and before you touch any component, is to identify what is inside.

Go and try out 1.11

Your teacher will present you with a PC so that you can identify component parts within it:

1 Referring to the How to panel on page 46, open the PC casing.
2 Do not touch anything! Draw a plan view sketch of the inside of the PC, roughly to scale.
3 Locate these components: PSU, CPU, BIOS, CMOS. As you identify each component, sketch it on your diagram.

Refer to Figure 1.3 (page 9) for a photo that should help you to identify each component in your PC.

CHAT *It would be rare for all the PCs that your group is looking at to have exactly the same arrangement inside, so compare notes with each other. Explain to each other the location of the essential components within your casing.*

Storage devices

Any one of several storage devices may need to be replaced, or you may want to install an extra floppy disk drive, hard disk drive, or CD drive.

The floppy and hard drives are installed in the 3.5″ bays; the CD drive goes in the 5.25″ bay (Figure 1.24).

CHAT *Discuss what the 5.25″ bay might have been used for before CDs were invented.*

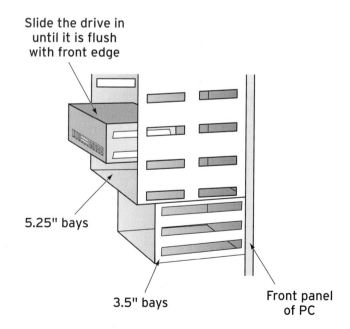

Slide the drive in until it is flush with front edge

5.25″ bays

3.5″ bays

Front panel of PC

Figure 1.24
Storage devices and their bays

A **floppy disk drive** is attached to the motherboard by a data cable, and to the PSU by a power cord (Figure 1.25):

◆ The **data cable** could be attached to an adaptor card or be connected directly to the motherboard. It is a 34-pin two-connector flat ribbon cable with a coloured stripe down one edge. This is to help you to connect the cable the right way around. There is also a

Figure 1.25

Floppy disk drive and its connectors and cabling

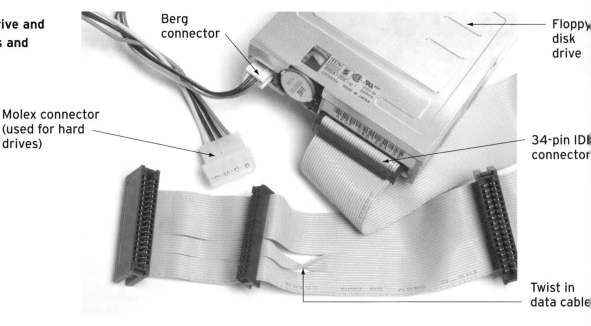

Berg connector

Molex connector (used for hard drives)

Floppy disk drive

34-pin IDE connector

Twist in data cable

twist in the ribbon. The drive attached behind the twist is recognised as logical drive A, and is therefore the default drive when you boot up your PC.

◆ The **power cord** is a four-pronged cable that is inserted into the back of the drive.

You may need to replace a floppy drive, or just install a new one. Installing an extra one should be straightforward: you just need a spare slot, a power cable and a data cable, and the fixing screws. If you don't have a spare power cable, you can use a Y-splitter so that both floppy drives work from the same power cable.

Before removing a floppy drive – even one that does not appear to be working – you need to make sure that you can boot the computer from another floppy drive, or from the hard disk. Otherwise, if things don't work after the replacement, you will be faced with a dilemma:

◆ Was it not working before you started working on it?

◆ Did you do something to stop it working?

So, check that you know the condition of the PC before attempting to replace a floppy disk drive.

How to add/remove a floppy disk drive

Think about your own safety, and that of the components, before starting to work on a PC.

To remove a floppy disk drive, follow these steps:

1 Turn off the computer and open the case.

2 Before you disconnect the data cable, notice its orientation: the coloured edge shows pin 1 and this is matched with pin 1 on the circuit board. Notice also the position of the twist in the data cable: this determines which drive is (logical) drive A and which is (logical) drive B. Disconnect the data cable from the motherboard.

3 Disconnect the power cable from the PSU.

Be care not to apply too much pressure when disconnecting the power cable; you might damage the board.

4 Undo the fixing screws that hold the floppy drive in its bay. Be sure not to remove any other screws, and keep the ones that you do remove safe.

5 Check whether you need to slide the drive out of its bay, or whether you have to lift a catch to release it.

To add a replacement floppy drive, or to install a new one, follow these steps:

1 You may need to remove a cover by reaching inside the PC and pushing the cover out.

2 Slide the floppy disk drive into the bay, until the front of it lines up with the front of the computer case.

3 The screw holes on the side rails of the case should also line up with those on the drive. Use the fixing screws to hold the drive in place.

4 Connect the drive to the motherboard using the data cable. Be careful with the orientation; match pin 1 on the board with the coloured edge of the ribbon. Check also the position of the twist; this determines the setting for drive A/drive B.

5 Connect the drive to the PSU using the power cord.

6 Turn on the PC and test the drive. If it works, turn off the PC and replace the casing.

If the PC does not work, turn the PC off before checking all the connections.

The installation and configuration of the other two storage devices – hard drive and CD-ROM – require more detailed treatment. Hard drives are IDE devices and these are covered in section 5 (page 95). CD-ROMs can be installed using an IDE interface but they may also use a SCSI interface, or be controlled by an expansion card. The CD-ROM drive might even be a portable drive that you plug into an external port on your PC, either the USB port or a SCSI port. CD-ROMs are considered in section 6 (page 100).

Check Your Understanding 1.14

1 In small groups, brainstorm the different types of floppy disks available.

2 In what way do they differ? In what way are they similar? Draw up a table to list all the types with their characteristics.

Memory

In adding (or removing) memory, your objective may be to increase (decrease) the capacity of your PC. You need to decide which type of memory to add/remove: SRAM and/or DRAM (see page 186).

The transistors in SRAM (static RAM), unlike the capacitors which make up DRAM (dynamic RAM), do not need to be frequently refreshed. SRAM is very fast (access speeds of 2 ns or less) but relatively expensive (many times more than DRAM) and takes up valuable space, so it is used for cache memory rather than primary memory.

You also need to take into account the **memory access time**, i.e. the time it takes for data to be made available. You may want the fastest possible time, but this will be limited by your PC's capability of adding faster memory. You do need to avoid mixing memory access speeds within a single PC:

◆ Fill each memory bank with the same type, speed and technology of memory.

◆ If you must mix speeds, put the slowest memory in the first bank. Then, if auto-detection is being used to determine the access speed, the slowest speed (in the first bank) will be applied to all banks. (If you put the faster speed in the first banks, other memories may be accessed at too fast a rate, with disastrous results.)

To find out how much memory is installed already, turning the PC off and then on will put it through its POST diagnostic routine and this displays the amount of RAM installed. With the case open, you should be able to identify the RAM chips. Each RAM chip should display a manufacturer's name, its type, capacity and speed. Adding up the capacity of each will give you the total RAM for your PC.

There is (at least) one other way of finding out how much RAM is installed on your PC without opening the case. Discuss with friends where this information might be stored.

Hint: Try right clicking on My Computer and looking at the Properties.

There will be a maximum amount of RAM that can be supported by the motherboard; this information will be in the manual for the motherboard, or you could find it by using the Internet.

Go and try out 1.12

1 Find out how much memory is on a given PC by various methods.
2 Check that you can reconcile the information you discover.

There are three main types of packaging: DIP, SIMM and DIMM (see page 189 for more details of these memories and RIMMs):

◆ The pins on either side of the **DIP chip** need to be inserted into holes on the motherboard, arranged in banks. The width of the bus determines the number of DIP chips that are needed to make a bank. You must fill a bank before you start the next one. The pass-through mounting allows the connection to the circuitry beneath the DIP socket.

◆ The Pentium processor uses a 64-bit path to memory and **SIMM**s are 32-bit, so you need to install them in pairs. You must fill each SIMM bank before moving on to the next.

SIMM (single in-line memory module) package is a mini-expansion board, with either surface-mounted SOF or TSOP DRAM soldered on to one or both sides of a circuit card. The edge connector has either 30 or 72 pins, and its capacity ranges from 1 Mb to 16 Mb.

◆ A **DIMM** can be installed into any available memory slot.

How to add/remove memory

Installing DIPs: Avoid touching any components unless you have to. Grease from your fingers can provide a surface for dust to collect. If you have to touch a component do so by its edges, and gently!

1 Align the pins of the DIP chip with the holes in the socket along one side (Figure 1.26).

Align the pins with the holes

BIOS chip

Socket for BIOS

Notice the jumpers here

Figure 1.26   Aligning the pins on a DIP chip

2 Gently align the pins on the other side until the chip is parallel to the board.

3 Press gently into place.

Installing SIMMs:

1 Align the SIMM at about 45° to the socket (Figure 1.27).

2 Raise the SIMM into the vertical position and seat it into the socket.

3 The clamping clips will grab the SIMM and hold it in place.

To remove a SIMM, release the clamping grips, rock the module gently so that it is at 45° to the socket and then lift it out.

Installing a SIMM

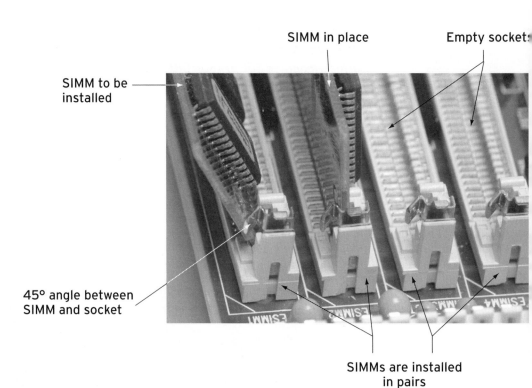

SIMM to be installed

SIMM in place

Empty socket

45° angle between SIMM and socket

SIMMs are installed in pairs

Installing DIMMs:

1 Align the DIMM to the memory socket.

2 Press firmly into place until it is well seated; it will lock into place with a snap (Figure 1.28).

Installing a DIMM

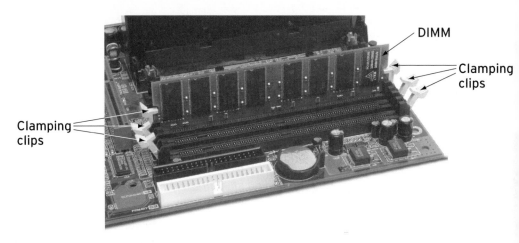

DIMM

Clamping clips

Clamping clips

To remove a DIMM, use the ejector tab; this will release the DIMM and it will pop out of the socket so that you can carefully remove it.

Installing a RIMM is similar to installing a DIMM (using locking clips), but they go into RIMM connectors and these come in pairs (Figure 1.29). You will need to refer to the motherboard documentation to help you to identify these sockets.

What does it mean?

RIMM (rambus inline memory module) is a special type of RAM; it is the trademarked name for the Direct Rambus memory module.

The RIMMs are installed in pairs; or you may install a single RIMM together with a C-RIMM (continuity RIMM) which does not contain any memory – it simply serves as a pass-through module to complete the memory channel.

Figure 1.29
Installing RIMMs

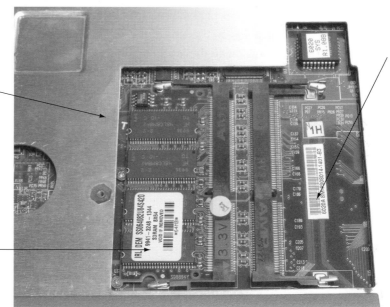

Underside of laptop computer

Empty RIMM slot

RIMM in place

Check Your Understanding 1.15

1 What is the main difference between DIP and SIMM/DIMM packaging?
2 Why must SIMMs be installed in pairs on a Pentium PC?

The motherboard

Jumper cap allows current to flow between these two jumper pins

Jumper pins

The motherboard is the main component within the PC case. Before installing a motherboard, you really must read the manual that comes with it. If you make a mistake, you may damage the motherboard and render it useless; this would be a costly mistake. So, while the instructions given here will give you a general idea of the procedure to follow, you must find out the specific details by reading the manual. Motherboards are an important topic and have a complete chapter – Chapter 4.

To prepare the motherboard for installation, you may need to set the **jumpers** or **DIP switches** (Figure 1.30). These are used, for example, to control the system bus frequency or the CPU frequency multiple. Exactly what settings you need will be explained in the manual.

Figure 1.30 **Jumpers and DIP switches**

Next, you may need to prepare the CPU. This may be a SECC and before it can be installed on the motherboard, you may need to attach a heat sink or fan (Figure 1.31). Look to see how the fan/heat sink might be attached. There may be braces which you need to align with holes on the side of the SECC. Make sure that the fit is snug; any air gap between the two will mean the fan/heat sink cannot do its job properly.

Figure 1.31

Attaching a heat sink/fan to a CPU SECC

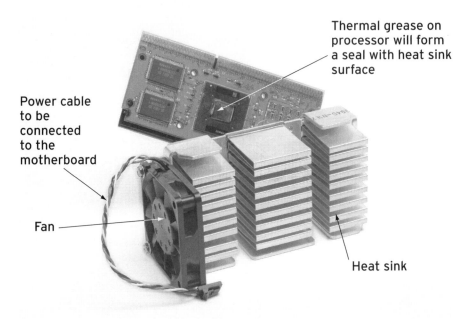

Thermal grease on processor will form a seal with heat sink surface

Power cable to be connected to the motherboard

Fan

Heat sink

The CPU, complete with its heat sink/fan, may then slip into a URM (Figure 1.32). The arm should snap into position when the SECC is properly seated.

You may then lock the SECC into position. Finally, connect the power cord for the fan into the power connection on the motherboard (Figure 1.33).

To install the motherboard within the case, you need a faceplate and some standoffs:

◆ The **faceplate** – or **I/O shield** – is a metal sheet that fits over the ports (see the foreground of Figure 1.34). You need to choose the faceplate that matches the motherboard (i.e. its ports) and the case in which you plan to install the motherboard.

◆ Position the faceplate in the rear wall of the PC case.

Figure 1.32
The SECC going into the URM

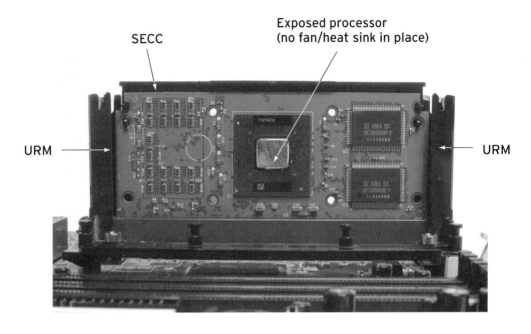

SECC

Exposed processor
(no fan/heat sink in place)

URM

URM

Figure 1.33
Connecting the power cord for the fan

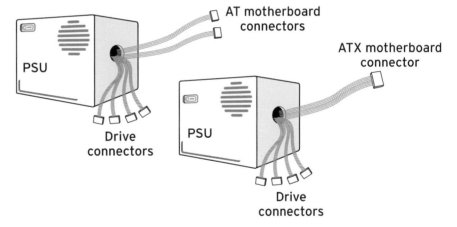

PSU

AT motherboard
connectors

ATX motherboard
connector

Drive
connectors

PSU

Drive
connectors

Figure 1.34
The faceplate in rear wall of a PC case with the motherboard screwed into place

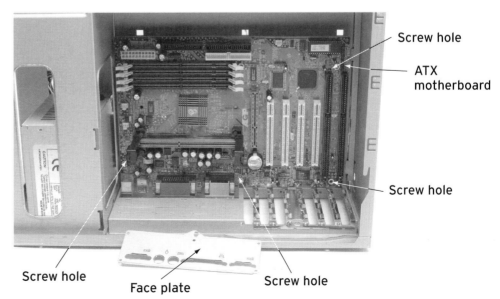

Screw hole

ATX
motherboard

Screw hole

Screw hole

Screw hole

Face plate

◆ **Standoffs** – or **spacers** – are needed to create a space barrier between the motherboard and the case so that components on the motherboard do not come into contact with the case. These round pegs are made of plastic or metal and need to be placed so that they match the screw holes on the motherboard.

 CHAT *If you had to remove a standoff/spacer, which of your tools do you think you might need to use?*

The motherboard is then attached to the case by at least four screws that fit into the standoffs. There may be more than four holes, and you should use as many as you can.

The motherboard is powered by the PSU, so you will need to connect the power cord from the PSU to the motherboard (Figure 1.35):

(a)

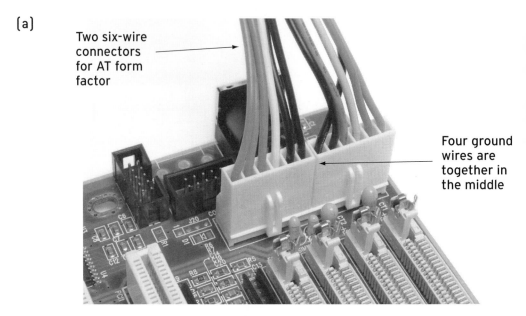

Two six-wire connectors for AT form factor

Four ground wires are together in the middle

(b)

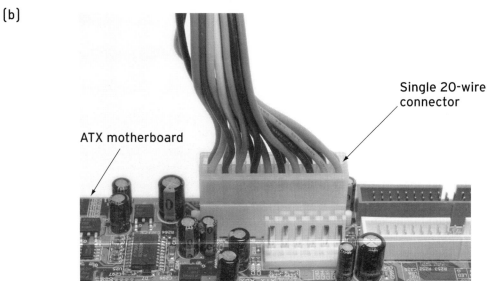

Single 20-wire connector

ATX motherboard

Figure 1.35
(a) P8 and P9 connections for the Baby AT
(b) 20-wire connector for the ATX

- For the Baby AT form factor, the two 6-wire connectors of the PSU are right next to each other. They may be labelled P8 and P9, matching those on the motherboard. The connectors are oriented correctly if all four ground wires (black) are together in the middle. Any other arrangement may damage the motherboard.
- The ATX PSU, used with the ATX motherboard, is a simple attachment of the single 20-wire keyed connector. This has a prong, lip or finger that prevents you from connecting it incorrectly. The ATX has additional voltage and power lines used to signal and control the power supply.

There will be some wire leads for the switches and wires on the front of the PC case (Figure 1.36). You will need to refer to the manual for the motherboard to make sure you match these wires correctly, although if you do muddle these you should do no harm; things just won't work as intended:

- The **power LED** controls a light that is used to indicate that the power is on.
- The **HDD LED** controls a light which indicates that an IDE device is in use.
- The **reset switch** is used to reboot the computer.
- The **remote switch** controls the power supply to the motherboard and needs to be connected for the PC to power up.
- The **speaker switch** controls the speaker!

Discuss with friends how to tell which is pin 1 on a motherboard connector.

How to install a motherboard

1 Prepare the motherboard: set jumpers and DIP switches according to the manual.

2 Prepare the CPU: attach the heat sink/fan and attach the CPU to the motherboard.

3 Fit the faceplate and standoffs, and screw the motherboard into place.

4 Connect the power by attaching the power cord from the PSU to the motherboard.

5 Connect up the wiring for the front of the PC casing.

Discuss the process of installing a motherboard to check that you are clear about the general process.

1 Explain the purpose of DIP switches and jumpers.
2 Why do some boards have heat sinks attached to them?
3 What is the purpose of a faceplate?
4 What is another name for a standoff?

Filling the expansion slots

Expansion slots allow the life of a computer to be extended, since new technology can be added as it becomes available. They allow you to add various cards to your PC, e.g. for a modem, a sound card and/or a NIC.

Speaker switch

Power LED

Hard disk drive LED

Power switch

Reset switch

Figure 1.36

Wire leads connected to instruments on the front of the PC

The expansion slots are long and thin socket connections, located on a motherboard or on a riser board, connected to buses which carry the data to and from the CPU:

◆ The grey/brown one is the **AGP slot** for a video card.

◆ The white slots are **PCI slots** – used for high-speed I/O devices.

◆ The black slots are **ISA slots** – used for older and/or slower devices.

For more information of slots and sockets, see page 203.

Each slot has two rows of metal springs which guide the expansion card connectors into place (Figure 1.37):

◆ On an ATX motherboard, the expansion slots run parallel to the short edge of the motherboard.

◆ On an AT motherboard, the expansion slots are parallel to the long edge of the motherboard.

Note: It is important that the expansion slots, when occupied, do not block access to a memory socket, the ROM BIOS, the password-clear jumper or the CMOS battery. If one does block access, this may cause you problems when trying to repair the PC.

Go and try out 1.13

1 Locate the expansion slots within a PC and list them (1 to 6), noting any expansion cards that are in the slots.
2 Repeat this activity on other PCs, noting differences between the form factors of the motherboards, and the cards that are present in the slots.

Watch out

When a PC is moved from one place to another, an expansion board may be jolted out of its seat. Before reusing the PC, check all expansion boards are properly seated and all connectors secure.

Figure 1.37
Expansion slots

(a) ATX motherboard

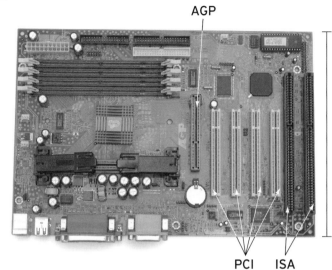

AGP

Expansion slots run parallel to the short side

PCI   ISA

(b) AT motherboard

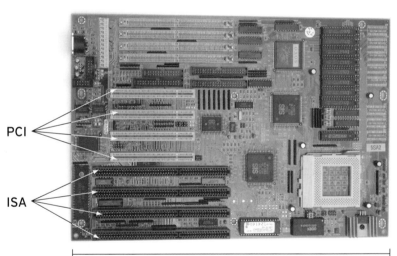

PCI

ISA

Expansion slots run parallel to the long side

There are a variety of different expansion boards – or expansion bus architectures. The 'How to' panels concentrate on just two:

◆ video board
◆ NIC.

What does it mean?

NIC (network interface card) – also called a network adaptor – provides the physical and logical link between a PC and a network.

A **video board** – or **video card** or **video adaptor** – lets your PC display images on the monitor screen. It determines the depth and resolution of the image. How good a video card you need depends on the applications you intend to use. For games, you need a better resolution and a more advanced card than if you were just doing word processing.

A video board is easy to identify – it has a port on one end of the card (Figure 1.38). Like other components, parts of the video card can get hot, so some have a heat sink or fan on the GPU (graphics processing unit). Notice that some information is written on the board (e.g. manufacturer and URL, and model number). Apart from the information written on the box that the card came in, and/or any instructions that were supplied by the manufacturer, this will help you to discover information about this particular video board's key features and system requirements.

Figure 1.38
Video card

Graphics controller chip

AGP graphics card

Graphics connector to monitor

AGP slot

How to add/remove a video board

Think about whether you should unplug the PC before working on it. For a Baby AT, leaving it plugged in provides an earth ground. Otherwise, you are better advised to unplug the PC

1 Check that you know which slot you are going to use, and that you have the correct board for your PC.

2 Be careful to handle the card by its non-connecting edges. Otherwise, you may leave traces of grease and/or dirt from your fingers.

3 Gently place the video card into the slot and press it into place.

4 To remove a board, release the locking mechanism and then slide the board gently out of its slot.

Watch out

Remember to place the component in an antistatic bag for protection.

1 For one video board, visit the manufacturer's site and find out as much as you can about the board. Compare notes with others in your group.
2 Find out about different types of video adaptor card standards: MDA, CGA, EGA, VGA and AVGA. In particular, discover what resolution they offer/support and how many colours they can display.

How to add/remove a NIC

1 Check that you know which slot you are going to use, and that you have the correct NIC board for your PC (Figure 1.39).

**Figure 1.39
A NIC with its
connectors**

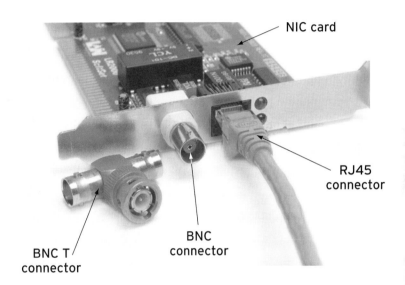

NIC card

RJ45
connector

BNC
connector

BNC T
connector

2 You may need to set a DIP switch or a jumper for the NIC card, so check the documentation.

3 Be careful to handle the card by its non-connecting edges. Otherwise, you may leave traces of grease and/or dirt from your fingers.

4 Gently place the NIC card into the slot and press it into place.

5 To remove a board, release the locking mechanism, and then slide the board gently out of its slot.

Watch
out

Remember to place the component in an antistatic bag for protection.

Having installed cards in expansion slots, you will need to complete the installation using software, so you will need to close the case and start up the PC.

Check Your Understanding 1.17

1 Explain the purpose of an expansion slot.
2 How can you distinguish between the different types of slots: AGP, PCI and ISA?
3 What does NIC stand for?

Power supply unit

Replacing a PSU should be a rare event, and it may involve temporarily moving other components to gain access. In practice, then, you would need skills on removing whichever components were blocking your access before attempting to replace a PSU. The PSU has to be attached to the motherboard and must be compatible with it, according to the form factor of the motherboard. See Figure 1.35, page 56, for a photo of the connectors. For details of form factors, see page 191.

Watch out

The ATX power supply is always on because the power is supplied through the motherboard even when the system power is off. So always disconnect the power cord from the main supply before starting to work on an ATX.

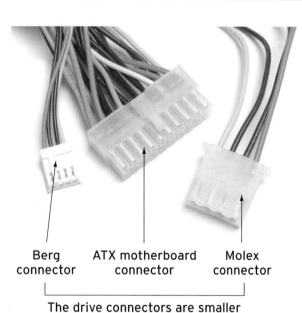

Berg connector   ATX motherboard connector   Molex connector

The drive connectors are smaller than the motherboard connector

Figure 1.40
Molex and Berg connectors

The PSU will have three or four 4-wire power connectors for internal drives. The two types and sizes of connector are easy to recognise (Figure 1.40):

◆ The larger of the two, called the **Molex connector**, is used to connect hard drives, CD-ROM and DVD drives and the larger (5.25 inch) floppy disk drives.

◆ The smaller one, the **Berg connector**, is used for the regular (3.5 inch) floppy disk drive and some tape drives.

You would only want to replace the PSU if you knew it to be faulty or had to upgrade it to allow an improved configuration to function properly. If you are not sure whether a PSU is at fault, you could disconnect the suspect PSU, and without actually removing it from the case, reconnect the peripherals to the new PSU. If the system then works, you can go ahead with the replacement. If it does not work, then maybe the PSU does not need changing.

How to add/remove a power supply

1 Turn off the power and disconnect all external power cables.

2 Remove the PC casing.

3 One by one, disconnect all power cords that are linked to devices within the PC.

4 Look carefully to see what other components you might have to remove before you can safely remove the PSU. Decide what order you will remove them.

Watch out

If you have to remove components to access the PSU, store them temporarily in antistatic bags.

5 Remove other components as necessary so that you have clear access to the PSU.

6 On the outside of the casing, locate and undo the holding screws of the PSU. Put the screws somewhere safe.

7 Examine the back or bottom of the PC casing to see how the PSU will come out. It may be in a slot and need to be slid one way.

8 Take the old PSU out and place the new PSU in position.

9 Replace the holding screws for the PSU.

10 Replace any components that you had to remove.

11 Reconnect the power cords for the devices.

12 Without replacing the cover, power up and check that the PC is working.

13 Turn off the power and replace the casing.

Check Your Understanding 1.18

1 What is the purpose of the PSU?
2 Describe the two types of connector: the Molex and the Berg.
3 When you have removed a component from a PC, what should you do to keep it safe?

Portable system components

A **PDA (personal digital assistant)** is the most portable of portable systems (Figure 1.41). This pocket-sized device – a **palm top** – is used with a pen-like stylus moving over a screen to make selections and to input text. Its software recognises handwriting so it can be used as a note-taker.

PDAs may be used as personal notebooks, but they are also used in other situations, especially for taking signatures. Brainstorm some uses for PDAs.

Laptop PCs provide more processing power while still remaining portable:

◆ A laptop can be used without access to mains power, using a battery; otherwise, it would not be considered to be portable!

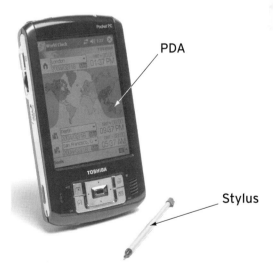

Figure 1.41 **A PDA**

◆ A laptop can be used while connected to mains power, using an AC adaptor/DC controller. The laptop still runs off the battery, but the AC adaptor recharges the battery and hence allows longer usage.

◆ A laptop may be 'docked' so that it works off a network of computers, giving access to the network for data and hardware.

A laptop can run on its battery, but only for a limited time. Exactly how long depends on the type of battery:

◆ **Alkaline batteries** are the type that you use in a calculator and may be found in palmtop computers. They are not rechargeable.

◆ **NiCad (nickel cadmium)** batteries are rechargeable, and provide a cheap but heavy source of power.

◆ **NiMH (nickel metal hydride)** batteries are an environmentally friendly option. They hold more power than NiCad batteries (for the same weight) but have a shorter life and cost more.

◆ **LiON (lithium ion)** batteries are the most expensive type but offer twice the power and half the weight with a comparable lifespan.

You could keep replacing the battery, but a better option is to have a mains power connector, which recharges the battery. In Figure 1.42, the **AC adaptor** and **DC controller** are housed within one slim box.

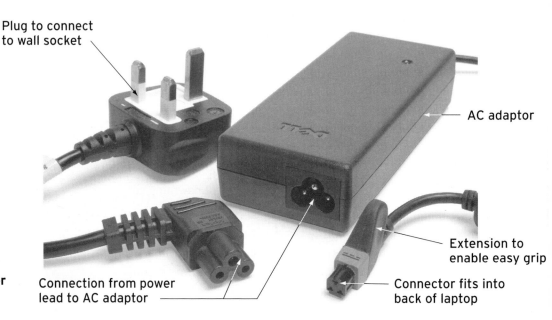

Plug to connect to wall socket

AC adaptor

Extension to enable easy grip

Figure 1.42

AC adaptor and power lead connections

Connection from power lead to AC adaptor

Connector fits into back of laptop

How to add/remove an AC adaptor

1 Connect the lead from the AC adaptor to the port on the rear of the laptop.

2 Connect the power lead to the AC adaptor, plug it in and turn on the power.

Figure 1.2b (page 8) shows views of the four sides of a laptop. Components such as the battery and the floppy drive may just click in and out of position (Figure 1.43).

Figure 1.43
Floppy drive and battery components on a laptop

Removable floppy disk drive

Battery can be removed and replaced

 CHAT *Discuss why you might want the battery on a laptop PC to be removable.*

Flash memory can be added to a notebook or palmtop computer using a PC card. This fits into a slot, usually at the side of the casing – never open the casing of a portable PC. The **hot-swapping** feature allows you to insert or remove the PC card while the portable PC is running.

Go and try out 1.15

1 Look carefully at the ports on a laptop PC. Make a sketch of each side and identify the ports and components.
2 List the peripherals that could be attached, and the type of connector that would need to be used.
3 Are there any restrictions on what could be attached to a given laptop?

An **LCD panel** is essential for any laptop PC, but may also be found on other less portable PCs, mainly because they take up so much less space than the conventional CRT design of monitor.

What does it mean? *LCD (liquid crystal display) technology relies on the ability of certain liquids to reflect or transmit light.*

LCD panels are flat (unlike CRT monitors) and about ½ inch thick. There are, then, two main types of LCD panel:

- An **active matrix display** uses **TFT (thin film transistor) technology**, with one transistor for every pixel of the display. This gives a very crisp image but is costly on power.
- A **passive matrix display** has one transistor per row of pixels and one transistor per column of pixels. Wires from these transistors form a matrix across the screen. To control one pixel, power is sent along the appropriate row and column. This system uses less power than TFT (because there are fewer transistors) but loses quality on the image (for the same reason).

Passive matrix displays then have two options for addressing each pixel:

- **DSTN (double-layer supertwist nematic)** is the older method.
- **HPA (high-performance addressing)** is the more modern method and has an advantage in that only someone looking directly at the screen sees the image displayed. This is particularly useful when the PC is being used to enter or view sensitive information.

A laptop has its LCD screen built into the top of the case so that it can be viewed when the laptop is opened. Other PCs can have an LCD screen attached using the USB port.

Discuss your preference for LCD screens versus CRT monitors with a group of friends.

A **digital camera** may also be attached to a PC via the USB port. Alternatively, you may 'fill' a PC card with images and then feed the card into a card reader so that the images can be uploaded to your PC (Figure 1.44).

Figure 1.44
A digital camera

The flash memory card fits into the rear of the digital camera

USB connector

Flash card reader

What does it mean?

PC card: a card used to add more memory and peripherals to a portable computer. Its dimensions are 85.6 mm by 54 mm with a thickness depending on its type: 3.5 mm, 5.5 mm or up to 10.5 mm, each to suit a variety of portable computers and requirements (see also page 202). All three types use a 68-pin connector.

How to add/remove a PC card

Note: You do not need to turn the laptop off when replacing a PC card.

1 Locate the PC card slot on the side of the laptop. Remove any dummy cards.
2 Slide the PC card into place.

Check Your Understanding 1.19

1 What does PDA stand for?
2 How is a laptop powered?
3 What is meant by 'flash memory'?
4 What does LCD stand for?
5 Explain the difference between active and passive matrix displays.

Go and try out 1.16

1 If you have not done so already, work through the 'How to' panels and check that you know how to add and remove all the FRMs listed in the following checklist.
2 Use the right-hand column of the checklist on page 68 to make notes for yourself.

Having attached a module, you may have some additional tasks to complete before it can be used:

◆ Some devices require DIP switches to be set (page 53).
◆ Some devices require jumpers (page 104).
◆ For most you have to set system resources (IRQs, I/O addresses, etc. – see page 68).

The PnP standard aims to save you this effort. In theory, you just plug the device in – and the system automatically recognises it, and sets up drivers, etc., to prepare for its use. PnP is not available on all systems:

◆ The bus of the expansion slot into which the device is connected must support PnP.
◆ Your motherboard and the associated chipset must support PnP.
◆ Your system BIOS has to support PnP.
◆ The operating system must support PnP.

So which systems do support PnP?

◆ Windows 95 onwards (although Windows NT only partially supports it).
◆ Architectures ISA, EISA, MCA and PCMCIA, and PCI devices and adaptors are all compatible with PnP.

CHAT *Discuss with friends: all PCI devices are PnP, but are all PnP devices PCI devices?*

Checklist	*Adding and removing field- replaceable modules*		
Module	**Page number of 'How to' panels**	**I can do this (tick here)**	**Things to remember**
External			
Keyboard		☐	
Mouse		☐	
Monitor		☐	
Printer		☐	
Internal			
Hard drive		☐	
Memory		☐	
NIC		☐	
Power supply		☐	
Processor/CPU		☐	
Storage device		☐	
System board		☐	
Video board		☐	
Portable			
AC adaptor		☐	
DC controller		☐	
Digital camera		☐	
LCD panel		☐	
PC card		☐	
Pointing devices		☐	

3 IRQs, DMAs and I/O addresses, and procedures for device installation and configuration

This section introduces the concept of logical devices before explaining IRQs, DMAs and I/O addresses. It then goes on to look at the procedures for installing these devices:

◆ modems

◆ floppy drive controllers

◆ hard drive controllers

◆ USB ports

USB = *universal serial bus.*

◆ infrared ports.

But, first, you need to understand the hexadecimal addressing system.

Addressing memory

The logic circuits within a digital computer are made from semiconductors which can store only one of two toggled values: off or on (Figure 1.45).

Figure 1.45

A semiconductor: on and off

Semiconductors	ON	ON	ON	ON	ON	ON	ON	ON
	OFF	OFF	OFF	OFF	OFF	OFF	OFF	OFF
Values	ON	ON	OFF	ON	OFF	OFF	ON	ON
Binary representation	I	I	0	I	0	0	I	I

The **binary numbering system** uses only two digits (0 and 1) and, in the digital computer, the on/off of a semiconductor is interpreted as a **bit** (**binary digit**) of data having value of either 0 or 1. A series of semiconductors, each set to on or off, can then represent a string of bits and, together, these can be used to represent larger numbers. Data and instructions are stored in the memory of the PC and travel within the computer on data buses. These data buses vary in size: 8-bit, 16-bit, 32-bit or 64-bit. The stringing together of bits – in memory or on a data bus – relies on the use of **place value** (Figure 1.46).

Figure 1.46

Column place values

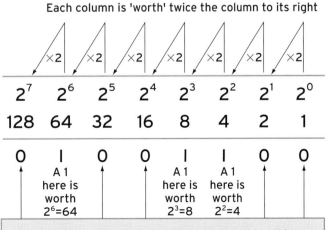

Each column is 'worth' twice the column to its right

2^7 2^6 2^5 2^4 2^3 2^2 2^1 2^0

128 64 32 16 8 4 2 1

0 I 0 0 I I 0 0

A 1 here is worth $2^6=64$

A 1 here is worth $2^3=8$

A 1 here is worth $2^2=4$

The zeros are place savers. They are 'worth' nothing.

What does it mean?

Place value: each 'column' is worth twice as much as the one to its right.

Binary can be used to represent data (as numbers or characters), but it may also be used to represent the address of an instruction where data can be found. The number of bits available for an address puts an upper limit on the amount of memory that can be accessed within the PC (Table 1.8).

Table 1.8 *Limits on addressing memory*

Number of bits	Values that can be represented	Maximum address that can be accessed	Hex addressing
8	0 to $2^8 - 1$	$2^8 = 128$	0000–00FF
16	0 to $2^{16} - 1$	$2^{16} = 65536$	0000–FFFF
32	0 to $2^{32} - 1$	$2^{32} = 4294967296$	
64	0 to $2^{64} - 1$	$2^{64} = 18446744073709600000$	

Note: The bigger the bus, the higher an address that instructions can point to and in which data can be stored.

Because so many bits are needed to represent larger numbers, the location of an address in memory is normally written in hexadecimal.

What does it mean?

Hexadecimal: 'hex' means six and 'decimal' means ten, so hexadecimal means sixteen.

The **hexadecimal numbering system** used 16 digits (0, 1, …, 8, 9, A, B, C, D, E, F) and so hex (for short) takes far fewer columns than binary, and can be thought of as a shorthand form of binary.

How to convert from binary to decimal – and back again

In binary, each position represents a power of 2. The binary value 10011001 can be written as

$2^7 = 128$	$2^6 = 64$	$2^5 = 32$	$2^4 = 16$	$2^3 = 8$	$2^2 = 4$	$2^1 = 2$	$2^0 = 1$
1	0	0	1	1	0	1	1

To convert from binary to decimal – for each 1, add its column value:

$$10011011 = 128 + 16 + 8 + 2 + 1 = 155$$

To convert from decimal to binary – there are two methods: division or subtraction:

Method 1: Division

Keep dividing by 2, noting the remainders

$155 \div 2 = 77 \ R1$
$77 \div 2 = 38 \ R1$
$38 \div 2 = 19 \ R0$
$19 \div 2 = 9 \ R1$
$9 \div 2 = 4 \ R1$
$4 \div 2 = 2 \ R0$
$2 \div 2 = 1 \ R0$
$1 \div 2 = 0 \ R1$

Working from the bottom, write the remainders:

10011011

Method 2: Subtraction

Keep subtracting powers of 2

$155 - 128 = 27$
$27 - 16 = 11$
$11 - 8 = 3$
$3 - 2 = 1$
$1 - 1 = 0$

Rewrite as a sum of powers of 2:

$155 = 128 + 16 + 8 + 2 + 1$

Use 1s to represent these powers, and space fill with 0s:

$155 = 10011011$

Converting between binary and hex is very straightforward. In hex, each column represents a power of 16. $16 = 2^4$, so each hex digit can be replaced by 4 binary digits, and vice versa (Table 1.9).

Table 1.9 Denary, hex and binary equivalents

Denary	Hex	Binary	Denary	Hex	Binary
0	0	0000	8	8	1000
1	1	0001	9	9	1001
2	2	0010	10	A	1010
3	3	0011	11	B	1011
4	4	0100	12	C	1100
5	5	0101	13	D	1101
6	6	0110	14	E	1110
7	7	0111	15	F	1111

How to convert from binary to hex – and back again

To convert from binary to hex:

1 Group the binary digits, starting from the right-hand end, into strings of 4 bits.

2 Convert each string of 4 bits into 1 hex digit (using Table 1.9):

1	0	0	1	1	0	1	1
1001				1011			
9				B			

To convert from hex to binary:

1 Convert each hex digit into 4 bits:

2 Run the bits together: 10011011.

9	B
1001	1011

So, for example, hexadecimal is used to refer to the address of some important places in memory: 02F8 is the default start address for the I/O address assignment for COM2. Read more about I/O addresses on page 78 and about logical device names such as COM2 on page 73.

You might also want to find out how much memory has been allocated for I/O addresses and so need to work out the difference between two hex addresses.

How to work out how much memory is allocated

The default I/O address for COM2 is 02F8–02FF. There are two methods: subtraction or counting addresses:

Subtract 02F8 from 02FF, and add 1

02FF
02F8
0007

Remember that the answer is still in hex and you need to convert to decimal:

7 + 1 = 8

Count, starting at 02F8 until you reach 02FF

1: 02F8
2: 02F9
3: 02FA
4: 02FB
5: 02FC
6: 02FD
7: 02FE
8: 02FF

Note: You have to 'add 1' if you subtract; this is like counting posts in a fence – you have to remember there is a post at each end! (See Figure 1.47.)

Figure 1.47
Addresses as posts

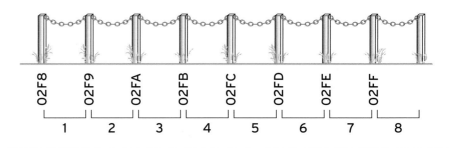

02F8	02F9	02FA	02FB	02FC	02FD	02FE	02FF
1	2	3	4	5	6	7	8

Check Your Understanding 1.20

1 Convert these numbers from decimal into binary 37 42 53 61 94 129

2 Convert these numbers from binary into decimal:

00100111 00101110 00110111 00111001 01011111 10000101

3 Convert these numbers from binary into hex:

00100111 00111000 01001001 10011100 10110111 11101011

4 Convert these numbers from hex into binary:

02EF 0EE2 2ABC 0ADD 017F 04A0

5 The default I/O address for COM1 is 0378–03FF. How much memory is allocated to this logical device?

Logical devices

COM1, COM2, ... are the logical device names given to the serial ports, assigned during the start-up boot sequence, as part of the POST process.

While you may list the items of equipment within a configuration as 'keyboard', 'mouse', 'screen', 'printer' and so on, the PC refers to these devices according to the port to which the device is attached, and assigns an IRQ (explained further on page 75) and an area within memory to be used for communication between the processor and the peripheral (also explained further on page 78). So the PC assigns logical device names as listed in Table 1.10. Figure 1.48 then shows the use of logical names within the System Properties dialogue box.

① From Control Panel, select System and then, on the Hardware tab of the Systems Properties dialogue box, select Device Manager

④ Select the Resources tab

Resource settings for COMI

② Click to reveal the list of ports

③ Right click here and select the COMI properties

Logical device names

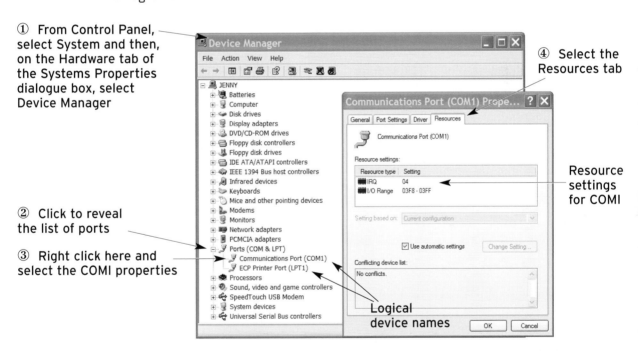

Figure 1.48   The Systems Properties dialogue box

You do need to learn the default IRQ settings and the starting I/O addresses for the serial and parallel ports. You may find it easier to learn them as presented in Table 1.10, or in the order of the IRQ (as in Table 1.11), or in the order of the I/O addresses (as in Table 1.12). Memorise whichever form of table makes most sense to you, and then make sure you can answer the questions in the following check your understanding without reference to the text.

Table 1.10 *Logical devices*

Peripheral	Logical names	Default IRQ (see page 75)	I/O address (see page 78)
Serial ports	COM1	4	03F8–03FF
	COM2	3	02F8–02FF
	COM3	4	03E8–03EF
	COM4	3	02E8–02EF
Parallel ports	LPT1	7	0378–037F
	LPT2	5	0278–027F

Table 1.11 *IRQ settings and I/O addresses for logical devices, in IRQ order*

IRQ	Logical device	I/O address
3	COM2	02F8–02FF
	COM4	02E8–02EF
4	COM1	03F8–03FF
	COM3	03E8–03EF
5	LPT2	0278–027F
7	LPT1	0378–037F

Table 1.12 *IRQ settings and I/O addresses for logical devices, in descending I/O address order*

I/O address	Logical device	IRQ
03F8–03FF	COM1	4
03E8–03EF	COM3	4
0378–037F	LPT1	7
02F8–02FF	COM2	3
02E8–02EF	COM4	3
0278–027F	LPT2	5

Note: Memory is allocated from the top down, so this order may be easier to remember.

Check Your Understanding 1.21

1 How many serial ports are there? What are their logical device names?
2 What type of port has the logical device name LPT? How many of these ports are there?
3 Which port is assigned to default IRQ7?
4 What is the default IRQ for LPT2?
5 Which device's I/O address starts at 0278?
6 Which device's I/O address starts at 0378?
7 Which two devices share default IRQ 4?
8 Which device uses I/O address 02E8?

IRQs

What does it mean?

IRQ (interrupt request): a primary system resource used to allow peripherals to interrupt processing and gain attention from the CPU.

IRQs provide a way for the CPU to stay busy while slower devices work at their own pace. The **interrupt controller** is a system component in which one bit is allocated to each device:

◆ Each IRQ bit can be set on by the device to signal that attention is needed, please.

◆ The CPU can set the IRQ bit off when the request has been dealt with.

The bits are called IRQ0, IRQ1, IRQ2, ... Originally, there were only 8 IRQ bits but, due to an increase in the number of devices supported by a PC, nowadays there are 16 bits operated through two interrupt controllers (each having 8 bits). These are **cascaded** (joined or connected) through IRQ2. Which device is assigned to which IRQ is important. Table 1.13 shows some default assignments.

Table 1.13 *Default assignments of IRQs*

IRQ	Device
0	System timer/system crystal
1	Keyboard controller
2	Bridge to IRQs 8–15
3	COM2 and COM4
4	COM1 and COM3
5	Sound card and LPT2; may also be the default for network cards
6	Floppy disk drive controller
7	LPT1
8	Real-time clock
9	Free; may be used for NICs, MPEG cards or SCSI host adaptors
10	Free; may be used for video cards or modems
11	Free; may be used for SCSI host adaptors, PCI video cards, IDE sound cards or USB controllers
12	Motherboard (PS/2) mouse connector
13	Maths coprocessor or FPU
14	Primary IDE adaptor
15	Secondary IDE adaptor

Notice that some devices, apparently, have to share an IRQ:

◆ The serial ports COM2 and COM4 share IRQ3.

◆ The sound card and second parallel port LPT2 share IRQ5.

Devices sharing IRQs can cause **IRQ conflicts** and this is to be avoided:

◆ If only one of the devices is operational at any one time, there is no conflict, but you are restricted in the range of devices that you can use simultaneously.

◆ If both devices are used, neither may work properly – or either may work occasionally – which is an unsatisfactory situation.

However, depending on the configuration and choice of connector, potential IRQ conflicts can be avoided:

◆ COM1 is normally used for the serial mouse. But having a PS/2 mouse frees up COM1 and therefore IRQ4 for use by another serial device – or some other device altogether.

◆ It would be rare to have two parallel printers, so only IRQ7 is needed for LPT1. That leaves IRQ5 free for another device.

IRQ settings are assigned during the POST process (see page 20) but you can change them once the computer has successfully booted up. There are two main methods depending on the adaptor card and the operating system installed:

◆ Early computers (e.g. DOS-based and Windows 3.X) use **jumpers**. Figure 1.30 on page 53 shows how jumpers are used.

◆ More modern computers (e.g. Windows 9X or 2000) allow you to change IRQ settings by software, e.g. using the Control Panel (Figure 1.49).

For the most modern computers, for PnP devices, assigning IRQs is done automatically for you as soon as the processor spots that the new device has been attached.

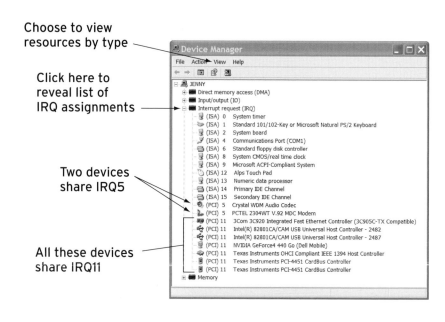

Choose to view resources by type

Click here to reveal list of IRQ assignments

Two devices share IRQ5

All these devices share IRQ11

Figure 1.49

The route to IRQ settings on Windows XP and other systems

Go and try out 1.17

Discover the IRQ settings on your computer. List them.

DMA (direct memory access)

DMA channels are one of the system resource components and allow a device to bypass the processor thus giving direct access to memory.

DMA is available for some devices (e.g. disk drives, tape drives and sound cards) but only those that have sufficient 'intelligence' to send data to memory locations and receive data from memory locations unaided. By using part of the IAS independently from the OS or the MMU, this increases the speed of access and may be used to good effect (e.g. in games) to speed up the display. The benefit of DMA is therefore faster access to memory (bypassing the CPU) and faster transfers of data.

What does it mean?

OS = operating system.

MMU = memory management unit.

A bus architecture may provide more than one DMA channel, but each one can only be used by a single device. Unlike IRQs, devices cannot share a DMA channel. One possible assignment of devices to DMA channels is shown in Figure 1.50 – but for the A+ exam you do not need to memorise the default assignment of DMA channels to devices.

Figure 1.50
DMA channels

Choose to view resources by type

Click here to reveal list of DMA assignments

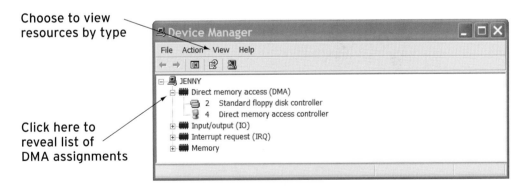

You can set the DMA channel assignments in a variety of ways:

- ◆ Accepting the preset assignments on the device's adaptor card
- ◆ Using DIP switches or jumpers on the device adaptor card
- ◆ Accepting the assignment during PnP configuration
- ◆ Using the BIOS setup utility.

Go and try out 1.18

Find out the DMA channel settings for your PC.

You may experience problems when installing a sound card, due to the difficulty in presetting its DMA channel. Other devices that you want to install may prove to be more flexible, accepting available DMA channels.

Discuss in groups how you can overcome this problem.

I/O addresses

The **I/O address** – also known as the **I/O port address** or, more simply, the **I/O port** – identifies an area in memory that the CPU can use to send messages to the device. The device can then respond using the data bus or the DMA channel. Table 1.14 shows which devices are assigned which I/O addresses (those in bold are the most important), and Figure 1.51 shows how you might access this information on your PC.

Table 1.14	*Assignment of I/O addresses to devices and ports*	
I/O address (hex)	**Number of bytes allocated**	**Device/port assigned to this address**
0000–000F	16	DMA channel 0–3 controller
0020–0021	2	IRQ 0–7 interrupt controller
0040–005F	32	System timer
0060–0061	**2**	**Keyboard**
0070–007F	16	Real-time clock
00F8–00FF	8	Maths coprocessor
0130–014F	32	SCSI host adaptor
0170–0177	8	Secondary IDE hard disk controller
01F0–01F7	8	Primary hard disk controller
0200–0207	8	Game port
0220–022F	16	Sound card(s)
0238–023F	8	Motherboard mouse
0278–027F	8	LPT2 or sound card
02E8–02EF	8	COM4
02F8–02FF	8	COM2
0300–030F	16	Network cards
03B0–03BF	16	VGA adaptor
03C0–03DF	32	VGA video adaptor
0378–037F	**8**	**LPT1** or LPT2
03E8–03EF	8	COM3
03F0–03F7	8	Floppy disk drive controller
03F8–03FF	**8**	**COM1**

Figure 1.51

The route to the I/O address list

Choose to view resources by type

Click here to reveal list of IO addresses

Keyboard IO address starts at 0060

LTPI IO address starts at 0378

COM1 IO address starts at 03F8

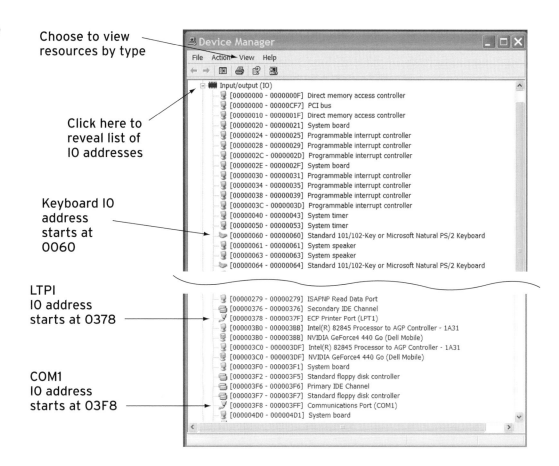

You should memorise the start addresses for common devices such as the keyboard, serial port COM1 and parallel port LPT1 [shown in bold in Table 1.14]. Notice also the amount of space that is allocated for each device – the difference between the start I/O address and the end I/O address. This can be anything from 1 byte to 32 bytes with 8 or 16 bytes being common.

Go and try out 1.19

View the I/O addresses assigned on your PC.

Modems

A modem converts signals generated by the PC, which are digital, into an analogue signal which can be sent along an analogue telephone line. In addition, a modem converts analogue telephone signals received into digital data that can be processed by the PC.

What does it mean?

Modem = modulator/demodulator.

A modem can be internal or external:

◆ An **external modem** has its own box with a power cord, and is connected to the PC via a COM port (the serial port or the USB port).

◆ An **internal modem** is an expansion board fitted into a slot on the motherboard. It may have its own speaker so that you can hear when it is dialling up.

Discuss the pros and cons of internal and external modems.
Under what circumstances might an external modem be preferred?

Figure 1.52 shows the connections needed to position a modem between the PC and the telephone line. The **RJ-11 connector** is used to link the normal phone line to the modem, and then, for an external modem, from the modem to the PC. Make sure you do not confuse the line and phone jacks.

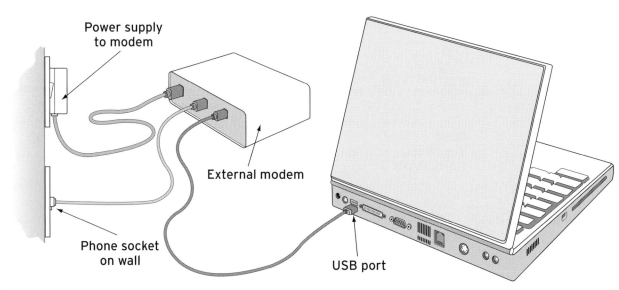

Figure 1.52   Modem connections

How to install a modem

As with any installation, you should read the instructions.

For an external modem:

1 Connect the modem's power cord to the mains supply, and into the modem itself.

2 Using an appropriate serial cable, connect the modem to one of your COM ports. This port must have an enabled IRQ; if for any reason it has been disabled, you will need to enable it (see page 75).

3 You then need to connect the telephone line to a port on the modem, and to the telephone socket on the wall.

For an internal modem, follow the same process as installing any expansion board:

1 Open the casing and identify which slot you plan to use.

2 Consult the documentation for the modem board to check what procedure you are expected to follow. This may include inserting a CD to run a setup program, before and/or after fitting the expansion board into place. You may also have to set DIP switches and/or jumpers.

3 The port for the telephone connection will protrude through the wall of the PC case (Figure 1.53). The telephone line can then be connected to the port and to the wall socket.

Figure 1.53
A modem port

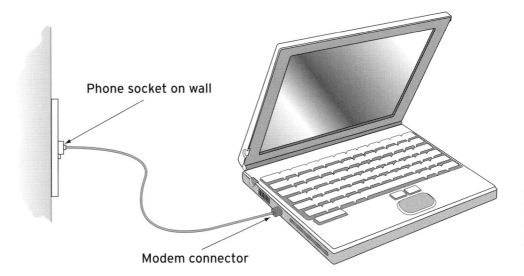

Phone socket on wall

Modem connector

Discuss how you could protect your PC from spikes that might come via a telephone connection.

A modem needs both to send and receive data, preferably at the same time:

◆ Communication that can be done in both directions, but not at the same time, is called **half-duplex** transmission.

◆ If the communications can be both ways and simultaneous, this is called **full-duplex** transmission.

When the modem first dials up, the sounds you can hear indicate that **handshaking** is taking place:

◆ When a modem answers an incoming call, it sends a **guard tone** to indicate to the caller that connection has been made with a modem, and not with a human.

◆ The caller responds – either by putting the phone down, having dialled incorrectly! – or if it is another modem, by sending a **carrier signal**.

◆ Having agreed that both ends of the line are modems, the next stage involves much buzzing to establish the quality of the line and an attempt to compensate for any noise.

◆ The speed at which transfer will happen is then agreed between the two modems.

So, during the initial handshaking stage, the two computers exchange 'rules' or 'protocols' that will determine how they communicate: at what speed the transfer of data will take place, how data might be compressed and what error checks might be incorporated. The speed at which the communication happens depends partly on the speed of the modem (given in bits per second) and on the amount of **noise** on the line, and also on what route the data is to take. If the route includes a slower patch, then the best speed will the speed across that slower link.

There are other ways of communicating between computers. Cable, DSL and satellite all offer broadband Internet access, without the need for a modem. All involve installation, according to the manufacturer's instructions, and under the control of software supplied, usually on CD-ROM. This is covered in Chapter 10 (page 350).

Modem standards

As with most equipment, if everyone works to a standard then communication between computers, and the installation of equipment within a given configuration, should be as stress-free as possible. The CCITT standards apply to various speeds of transfer of data – V.92 being the latest and fastest at 56 kbps with a variety of features supported, such as call waiting.

What does it mean?

CCITT = Comité Consultatif International Télégraphique et Téléphinique.

In the same way, there is a standard way of giving commands to the modem, although this is a de facto standard that has come about by voluntary acceptance of the first language developed by Hayes. For Hayes-compatible modems, the **Hayes Standard AT command set** is the language used by the PC to drive and configure a modem. Examples of the AT commands are listed in Table 1.15.

What does it mean?

AT = attention (not Advanced Technology).

Table 1.15 *Examples of AT commands*

AT command	Effect
AT DT 01234-123456	Dials the telephone number (01234 123456) using touch-tone dialling
AT DW	Wait for dial tone
AT HO	Hang up (end the call)
AT Ln	Set the speaker loudness to low (n = 1), medium (n = 2) or high (n = 3)
AT Mn	Sets speaker off (n = 0), on until carrier detect (n = 1) or always on (n = 2)
AT Xn	Sets response: n = 0 for blind dialling (no need to hear dial tone and does not recognise busy tone); n = 4 (the default value) for a check that there is a dial tone, and will respond to busy signal
AT Zn	Reset default settings for modem according to user profile n

1 What does 'modem' stand for?
2 What is an RJ-11 connector used for?
3 Explain the difference between half-duplex and full-duplex transmission.
4 Explain the purpose of handshaking, the guard tone and the carrier signal.

Go and
try out
1.20

1 Research on the Internet for details of internal and external modems.
2 Find out about different modem standards and how these apply to data compression
   and error correction.
3 Find out some more AT commands.

Drive controllers

There are three types of **floppy disk drive controller**:

◆ A standalone card may be installed in one of the expansion slots which acts as an
   interface for a game port, one or two serial ports, a parallel port and the floppy disk
   drive.

◆ A disk controller card may be installed in one of the expansion slots to provide an
   interface for both the hard drive and the floppy drive.

◆ Built-in controllers are the modern way. The motherboard chipset includes an interface
   adaptor to control the floppy drive (Figure 1.54).

Figure 1.54
Expansion slots

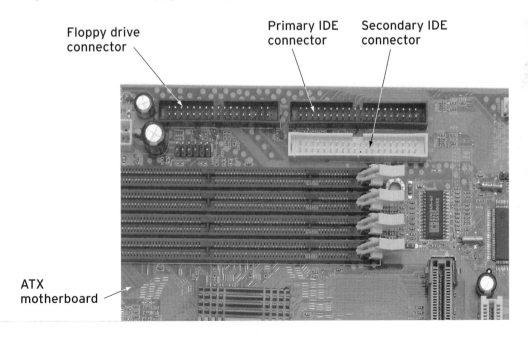

Installation of a floppy drive is explained on page 48.

Hard drives are IDE devices, controlled by an IDE controller. There are two types of IDE controller:

◆ primary IDE controller

◆ secondary IDE controller.

Each of these can support two IDE devices:

◆ a master drive

◆ a slave drive.

Assigning master/slave to the primary and secondary drives is achieved through jumper settings. Installation of IDE drives – and the installation of hard drives in particular – is covered in detail in section 5 (page 95).

Check Your Understanding 1.23

1 Explain what is meant by the PC's chipset.
2 What IRQ is used for the floppy disk drive controller?
3 What I/O addresses are assigned for the floppy disk drive?
4 What IRQ is used for the hard disk drive controller?
5 What I/O addresses are assigned for the hard disk drive?

USB ports

USB is a recent invention designed to make the installation of slow peripherals, such as the mouse, joystick, keyboard and scanners – and other devices, such as printers, digital cameras and digital telephones – as easy as possible.

What does it mean?

Remember, USB (universal serial bus) is a higher-speed serial connection standard that supports low-speed devices (mice, keyboards, scanners) and higher-speed devices (digital cameras).

On most motherboards, the USB host controller is included in the chipset. This host controller recognises when you plug in a device to a USB port and allows **hot swapping** of devices. Having recognised the device, the USB controller assigns an IRQ.

There may be as many as four USB ports supported by a motherboard (Figure 1.55). It is also possible to link the devices in a 'daisy chain' so that the PC may have many more devices attached – each device provides the USB port to the next device in the chain. Another option is to have a **hub**, into which devices can be plugged (Figure 1.56).

What does it mean?

Hot swapping means connecting (or disconnecting) a peripheral while the PC is turned on.

Figure 1.55
A USB port and
connector

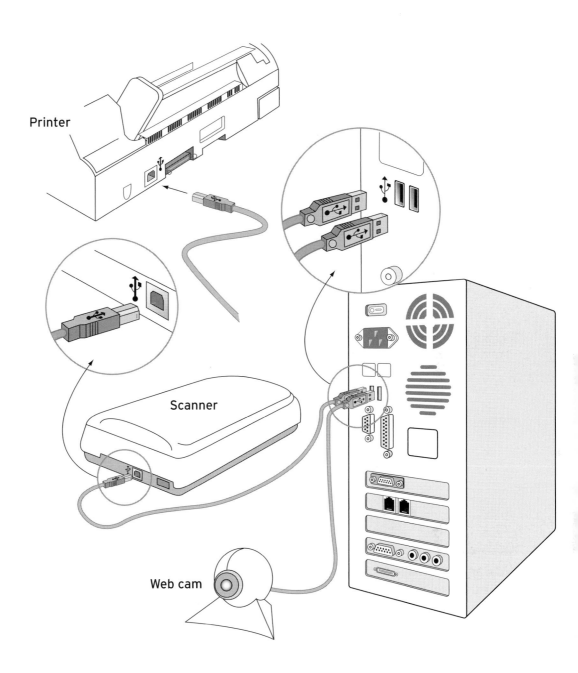

Printer

Scanner

Web cam

Check Your Understanding 1.24

1 Explain what is meant by these terms: 'hot swapping' and 'a daisy chain of USB devices'.

2 What IRQ might be used for the USB controller?

Hub with RJ45 connectors

Hub with BNC/AUI connectors

Link crossover port

RJ45 connectors

Figure 1.56   **Daisy chaining and hub options**

Infrared ports

Infrared ports are a recent invention. They are often connected to a serial port but can also be found on laptops (Figure 1.2b on page 8):

◆ The transceiver accepts infrared signals from devices such as wireless keyboards, mice and printers (Figure 1.57).

◆ The infrared device may also allow connection to a network.

Figure 1.57

The transfer of data from a wireless device to a PC via an infrared transceiver

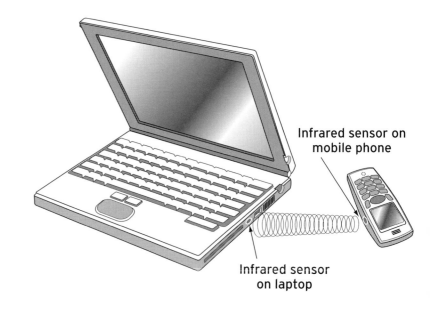

Infrared sensor on mobile phone

Infrared sensor on laptop

For the data to be transmitted successfully, the input device has to be in line of sight with the transceiver, i.e. there must be no obstruction between the two.

For PnP infrared transceivers, when you connect the device, a virtual infrared serial port and a virtual infrared parallel port are created. You will be told which ports these are and can change them if you wish. For example, if you connect the transceiver to the COM2 port, the virtual serial port will be COM4 and the virtual parallel port will be LPT3. The I/O addresses match those normally given to COM2.

For motherboards that have their own built-in transceivers, the transceiver is connected, through the casing, to a 5-pin connector on the motherboard. The COM2 port that you would normally use is disabled so that the UART chip can use those system resources (IRQ and I/O addresses) for the transceiver.

What does it mean?

The UART (universal asynchronous receiver-transmitter) chip controls all 9 pins of a serial port, converting the parallel data that arrives from the CPU into serial bits ready for transmission. Similarly, it groups incoming serial data into a parallel format before this data joins the bus on its way to the CPU.

Go and try out 1.21

1 Working in pairs, investigate which IRQs are assigned to which peripherals for a particular configuration.
2 In readiness for the work you will do in Unit 2, explore your Windows software to discover how you might alter the IRQ settings.

4 Common peripheral ports, associated cabling and their connectors

Figure 1.58 shows the rear view of a PC, with the common peripheral ports labelled.

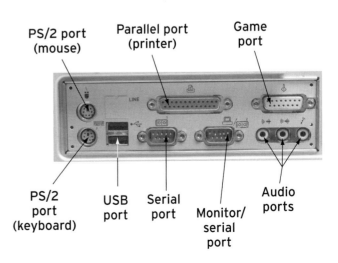

Figure 1.58
The rear view of a PC

There are two basic types of port – serial or parallel:

◆ **Serial transmission** is 1 bit at a time.
◆ **Parallel transmission** is 1 byte (8 bits) at a time.

Generally, transmission via a serial port is a slow, inexpensive method of data transfer. USB is faster than standard serial and an optical serial connection may transfer at an even faster rate, faster than a parallel connection.

What does it mean?

USB = universal serial bus.

So parallel is usually, but not always, faster than serial; its cabling is limited to a maximum 15 feet in length. It was developed for printers but is also used for CD-ROMs, external tapes and Zip drives. Each method of communication has its own standard:

◆ Serial communication adheres to the **RS232C standard**. Using the RS232C standard, a 0 bit is represented by a positive voltage of 12 V, and a 1 is represented by a negative voltage of 12 V. Therefore, to send the character B from the sending device to the receiving device, the bit stream would be signalled on the cable as shown in Figure 1.59.

What does it mean?

The RS232 standard was created by an organisation called EIA (Electronics Industry Association) and defines how two computers (or communications devices such as modems) can be connected by a serial cable.

Figure 1.59
Signalling the character B

◆ Parallel communication has the **IEEE1284** (bidirectional parallel communications) standard plus the **ECP protocol** (full duplex, i.e. simultaneous communications in both directions).

Some devices are so simple they only need serial connection: mouse and keyboard. Others benefit from the two-way communication of parallel connections: printers and much of the internal circuitry of the computer. **FireWire (IEEE1394)** was developed by Apple Computer and is ideal for connecting devices such as digital cameras, digital video cameras and external hard disks which need to transfer large files. It is similar to USB in many ways, but it is much faster, running at up to 400 Mbps.

Check Your Understanding 1.25

1 Why is parallel transmission of data generally faster than serial transmission?
2 Under what circumstances might serial transmission be faster than parallel transmission?
3 What is the name of the standard for serial communication?
4 What is the name of the standard for parallel communication?
5 What is FireWire?

CASE STUDY   Ismat, trainee technician

Ismat has joined the IT support team of a large organisation and has contacted you for some more advice. She has been asked to do some research to find out about standards used in the IT industry.

1 Prepare a list of some aspects of IT that are controlled by standards and the organisations involved in setting these standards.

2 For one particular standard, do some research yourself and provide a detailed explanation of what it entails.

Cables

A cable is used to connect a peripheral to the PC, and this can be one of several types (see Figure 1.60):

Figure 1.60
Different types of cabling

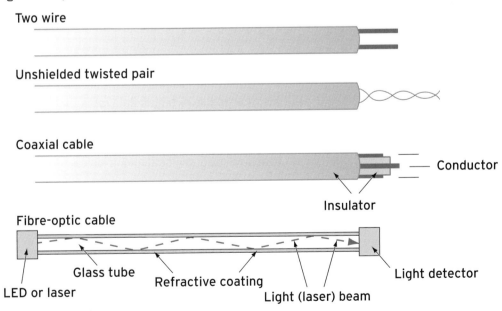

Two wire

Unshielded twisted pair

Coaxial cable — Conductor — Insulator

Fibre-optic cable — LED or laser — Glass tube — Refractive coating — Light (laser) beam — Light detector

- In **two-wire cabling**, the most basic form of electrical cabling, there are two copper wires separated by an insulator or dielectric. This can be used for low-speed transmissions but, if several of these cables are laid side by side, transmissions can suffer from interference called **cross-talk**.

What does it mean?

Cross-talk is caused when electrical signals in one pair of wires create a magnetic field, which then causes a signal to flow in another pair of wires

- **Unshielded twisted pair (UTP)** consists of pairs of insulated copper cable twisted together (the twisting reduces problems of cross-talk and noise). Various categories of UTP cable have been developed, with the main difference between them being the bandwidth available. Category 1 is normal telephone cable and only suitable for low speeds. Category 5 cable is used in network installations and has a bandwidth of up to 100 Mbps using the Ethernet LAN protocol. As the category numbers increase, so does the speed at which data can be transmitted successfully along the cable.

- **Coaxial cable** is similar to the cable used for TV aerials. It has a central copper conductor, surrounded by a thick plastic sleeve. This is then surrounded by a braided metal shield and an outer plastic insulation. This is more expensive than UTP but can achieve transmission rates of 100 Mbps.

- **Fibre-optic cable** does not use electrical currents to represent the data to be transmitted; instead, it uses light impulses. The cable is made of fine strands of glass, the light being internally refracted down the strands. Fibre-optic cable requires an optical transmitter at the sending end to convert the digital signals into light impulses, and a receiver at the other end to convert the light impulses back into digital signals.

How do you decide which cabling to use?

- Fibre-optic cables can support very high data rates and have very low error rates, as the cable is not affected by electrical noise or cross-talk. However, they are expensive and need careful installation (bending them can break the glass strands). They are generally used for network backbones (e.g. interconnecting several smaller LANs – for example, those on the separate floors of a large building).

- Coaxial cable is capable of higher data rates than UTP but is more expensive and not as easy to install (the cable does not bend easily and can be damaged by excessive bending). Coaxial cable was originally used to cable LANs but this is no longer the case.

- UTP is cheap and easy to install and is widely used in LANs.

It is important to use the correct **cable orientation**, i.e. to attach the cable the right way around. Deciding which end goes where should not be a problem, but make sure that, at each end, the cable is inserted the correct way around:

- Some connectors have an icon or some other mark to show which is the right way up.

- For some, the marking is not so obvious and you will need to take care not to force a connection.

To suit the different types of cabling, there are different types of connectors (see Figure 1.61):

- **RJ-11 connectors** are the familiar plugs and sockets used for telephone connections.

- **RJ-45** is a similar system, used in twisted pair LANs. The number refers to a standard which determines the shape and size of the plug and socket.

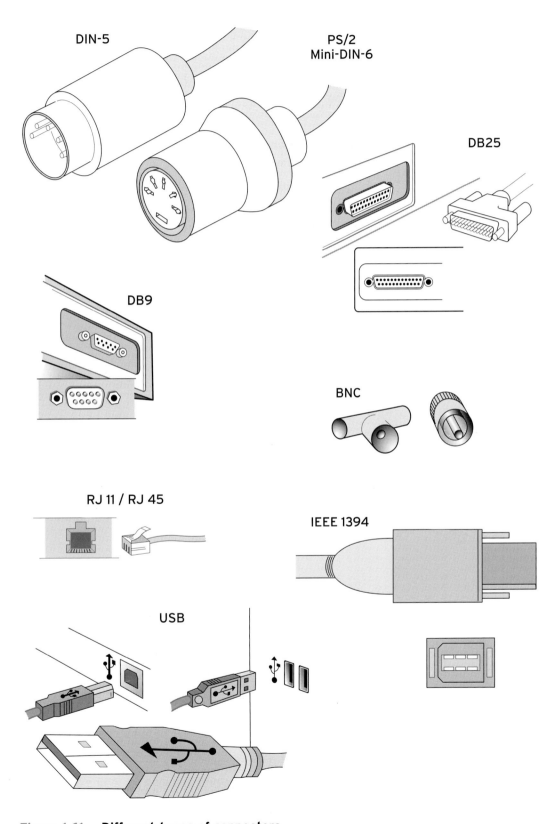

Figure 1.61   **Different types of connectors**

◆ **DB9** and **DB25 connectors** are used for the RS232 standard. The full standard has 25 lines but in practice only nine are used.

What does it mean?

RS323 is an American standard. The European equivalent is V.24. An RS323 port is a serial port.

◆ **BNC connectors** are used with coaxial cables. Computers are often connected to LANs with BNC T connectors.

◆ **USB connectors** are flatter at one end and square-ish at the other end.

◆ **PS2/mini-DIN 6-pin connectors** are circular connectors (with 6 pins!) that may be used for a keyboard or a mouse.

◆ **IEEE1394** – also known as i.Link, Lynx and FireWire – is a high-performance serial bus (HPSB). It is faster than both the USB port and any parallel port.

Check Your Understanding 1.26

1 Explain the difference between UTP cabling and fibre-optic cabling.
2 What is meant by cable orientation?
3 Explain when you would use these connectors: RJ-11, DB9, mini-DIN.
4 What is the name of the standard for parallel communication?
5 What does HPSB stand for? Give examples.

CASE STUDY

Nigel the novice PC user

Nine-year-old Nigel's new PC now has a variety of peripherals attached to it. Nigel has some questions for you to answer:

1 Why are some cables round and others flat?

2 Why can some cables be much longer than others?

3 What are all the connectors called? (For this, sketch each type of connector and label it for Nigel.)

Pin connections

Table 1.16 lists what each pin does within a 9-pin connector.

The process of communication is a conversation between the host and the peripheral called **handshaking**. The sequence of signals follows this procedure:

◆ The PC sends a signal on pin 4 (DTR) to say 'I'm ready to communicate'.

◆ The peripheral sends a signal on pin 6 (DSR) to say 'So am I'.

◆ The PC sends a signal on pin 7 (RTS) to say 'Go ahead'.

◆ The peripheral sends a signal on pin 8 (CTS) to say 'Here it comes'.

The data is then sent by the peripheral on pin 2, one bit at a time, until complete. During transmission, if there is a problem, the PC or peripheral can stop sending the signal on pin 7 (RTS) or 8 (CTS); this says 'Wait. I'm having a problem'. The flow of data can restart when the device sends a signal (on pins 7 or 8) to say 'All clear now, go ahead'.

Table 1.16 Serial connection pin assignments for a DB9

Pin	Input to PC or output from PC?	What signal does this carry?	What does this signal mean?
1	Output	CD (carrier detect)	Says that a connection has been established
2	Input	RD (receive data)	Incoming data arrives through this pin
3	Output	TD (transmit data)	Outgoing data is sent on this pin
4	Output	DTR (data terminal ready)	The host (e.g. the PC) is ready to communicate
5		Signal ground	Not used on PCs
6	Input	DSR (data set ready)	The peripheral (e.g. the modem) is able to communicate
7	Output	RTS (request to send)	The host wants to communicate
8	Input	CTS (clear to send)	The peripheral is ready to communicate
9	Input	RI (ring indicator)	The phone is ringing!

A similar process happens with parallel communication. Table 1.17 lists the functions of each pin in the 25-pin parallel connector.

CHAT *Simulate the communication between a peripheral and the PC, referring to the pin numbers that you would use.*

Table 1.17 Parallel connection pin assignments for a DB25

Pin(s)	Input to PC or output from PC?	What does this signal mean?
1	Output	Strobe
2–9	Output	Data bits 0–7
10	Input	Acknowledge
11	Input	Busy
12	Input	Out of paper
13	Input	Select
14	Output	Auto feed
15	Input	Printer error
16	Output	Initialise paper
17	Output	Select input
18–25	Input	Ground bits for bits 0–7

CASE STUDY

Nigel the novice PC user

Nine-year-old Nigel's new PC has a serial device attached using a 9-pin connector and a parallel device with a 25-pin connector. Nigel has some questions for you to answer:

1 What is the difference between a serial and parallel connection?

2 Why are there more pins on the parallel connector?

3 How does a serial device communicate with the PC and vice versa?

Wireless communications

All the peripheral communication methods described so far require cables. However, running cables in an office environment is both disruptive and expensive. It is also not very flexible; once the cabling is laid it is even more disruptive and expensive to make any changes. Wireless transmission offers the promise of connections that do not require cables and are therefore flexible and easy to install.

Two techniques have been developed for PC peripheral connections (and also for connecting mobile devices such as **personal digital assistants (PDAs)**):

◆ IrDa

◆ Bluetooth.

IrDa was formed in 1993 and, since then, the Infrared Data Association has been working to establish an open standard for short-range communication using infrared light. Communication using infrared uses similar technology to television remote controls and is limited to line of sight. Typical applications include the synchronisation of PDAs with desktop machines and connecting a laptop computer to a mobile phone to establish a dial-up connection to the Internet. IrDa has never become very popular and has a reputation of being difficult to use.

 Discuss why IrDa might be difficult to use.

Bluetooth is a low-cost radio data communication system – named after a tenth-century Danish king – that was first published in 1998. It was designed to link portable devices such as laptop computers, mobile phones and PDAs. It is restricted to a distance of only 10 metres and a speed of 1 Mbps, and so it is not intended to be a replacement for high-speed links like USB or **FireWire**. Instead, its main benefit is intended to be convenience. Bluetooth devices in the same **personal area network (PAN)** are designed automatically to recognise each other and to synchronise their databases without any complex setup.

Go and try out 1.22

Working with a friend, research the Internet to find out more about wireless communications.

5 Installing and configuring IDE/EIDE devices

IDE is one of two interfaces for hard drives that you need to study for this A+ course: IDE and SCSI. This section focuses on IDE devices and how to install and configure them. Section 6 looks at SCSI devices.

IDE is the usual interface for hard drives. The term IDE means that the drive has a built-in controller rather than a separate chip as part of the motherboard chipset. Integrating the chip within the drive leaves manufacturers free to develop the technology of IDE devices, without worrying about whether it will still be compatible with a chipset on a particular motherboard.

IDE drives are compatible with the **ATA standard**; this means you can install an old drive in a new system, and it should work!

What does it mean?

IDE = integrated drive electronics.

ATA = AT attachment.

Watch out

Installing a new IDE drive into an old PC may not be so successful.

 CHAT *Discuss with friends why it may not be sensible to install a new hard drive on an old PC.*

The ATA standards have improved with time, each new version being given a new number: ATA-1, ATA-2 and so on.

EIDE devices were so named because, at the time, they supported the ATA-2 standard rather than the original AT standard. However, since then, all IDE devices now fall into this category, so the term EIDE is often lost, and you may just refer to IDE devices.

What does it mean?

EIDE = enhanced integrated drive electronics.

ATA-4 is of particular interest: it introduced a way of increasing data transfer speed called **UltraDMA** – or UltraATA. This allowed data transfer rates of 33 MB/sec. This improvement in data transfer rates continued, with ATA-5 taking it to 66 MB/sec, and ATA-6 reaching 100 MB/sec.

The UltraDMA for the higher speeds (66 Mb/sec and 100 MB/sec) requires a double-width cable: 80 wires instead of the usual 40. There are still only 40 pins to connect, but the other 40 wires act as spacers, reducing the EMI between the more important data-carrying wires. This reduction of noise means that data can be transmitted quickly without loss of integrity.

What does it mean?

EMI = electromagnetic interference.

CHAT

Discuss with a friend how to tell the difference between a 40-pin ribbon and an 80-pin ribbon cable. (Hint: It is not twice as wide.)

Note that simply installing a new drive into an old PC may not improve data transfer speeds. The motherboard, BIOS and the operating system of the PC have to be modern enough to handle these high-speed devices:

◆ There may be a limit on the size of hard drive that can be supported by the BIOS chip, so any extra capacity would be inaccessible. For example, early BIOS chips could only support disk capacity up to 8 GB.

◆ The operating system, e.g. prior to Windows 98, may not support large disk capacity. If the operating system does not support the FAT32 system then the size of drive is limited to 2 GB per logical drive. You might dodge this problem by having more than one logical drive, but you still have the limit imposed by your BIOS.

A hard drive's specification should tell you everything you need to know about the drive's performance and this will help you to decide whether it will work on your PC:

◆ The **maximum data transfer rate** limits how quickly the drive can input and output data. This can be given as the standard that it conforms to, for example, ATA-4, and you then need to interpret this as being 33 MB/sec.

◆ **Latency** is the time it takes for the hard drive to react to a command sent to it. Latency is given in milliseconds and may be about 5 ms.

◆ **Read/seek time** measures how quickly the hard drive can find data on the hard disk within its casing. This is also given in milliseconds, e.g. 9 ms.

◆ **Write/seek time** is similar. It measures to time taken to find where to put data on the hard disk. This is usually longer, e.g. 12 ms.

Latency is a bit like the reaction time when you are driving – the time it takes for you to see a problem, realise there is a problem and hit the brake pedal. After that, the time it takes you to stop your car depends on your brakes, the condition of the road and the weather. Read and write seek times are then a measure of the mechanics of the hard drive (like the brake pads in your car). Minimal latency and quicker read/write seek times are better!

Some drives may mention the **rotational speed**: the speed at which the disk rotates within the casing. This is measured in RPM (revolutions per minute). However, it is the read/write seek times that determine how quickly data is transferred. Fortunately, the development of faster spinning drives goes hand in glove with improved read/write seek time so you can, generally, associate higher rotational speed with improved performance.

Go and try out 1.23

1 Find out what read/write seek times are quoted for two different makes of hard drive.
2 Find out what RPM might be expected on a UDMA/33 drive, or on a UltraDMA/66 drive.

Assuming that installing a new hard drive is a sensible option for a given PC, you need to be able to install and configure the IDE/EIDE device and to understand these concepts:

◆ master/slave

◆ devices per channel

◆ primary/secondary.

An IDE ribbon can support two drives and, to know what data relates to which drive, each drive is identified, either as the master drive or as the slave drive. The **master drive** is the drive that handles all the traffic on the IDE cable. Its controller retains its own data and passes on data to the slave drive. The **slave drive** – and there need not be a slave drive if there is only one drive attached to the cable – sees only the data that is passed to it by the master drive.

To identify the drives as master or slave, you need to set the jumpers for each drive, from one of four options:

◆ single   ◆ slave

◆ master   ◆ cable select.

If you only have the one drive then, although it is referred to as the master, you should opt for the **'single' jumper setting**. This may also be the factory-set default option. If you have two drives, one is designated as master and the other as slave. The **cable select** option passes the decision making as to master/slave to the cabling that you attach. You need special cabling for this – a **cable-select cable** (recognised by having a small hole in it) – but this does not work with all drives! The drive nearest the motherboard becomes the master drive, and the other the slave drive.

The drive label may tell you exactly how to set the jumpers (Figure 1.62). Otherwise, you will need to refer to documentation provided by the manufacturer, or go to the manufacturer's website for details.

Figure 1.62

A hard drive

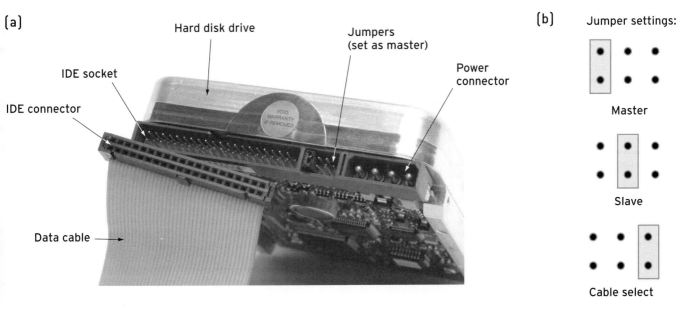

(a)   Hard disk drive   Jumpers (set as master)   Power connector

IDE socket

IDE connector

Data cable

(b)   Jumper settings:

Master

Slave

Cable select

Figure 1.63

Primary vs secondary IDE on the motherboard

IDE 1 (primary)

IDE 2 (secondary)

Etched writing on the motherboard shows which is which

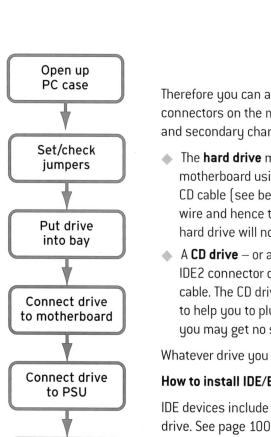

Open up PC case

↓

Set/check jumpers

↓

Put drive into bay

↓

Connect drive to motherboard

↓

Connect drive to PSU

↓

Close PC case

↓

Restart PC and check BIOS recognises drive

↓

Partition drive?

↓

Format drive

Figure 1.64

Installing a hard drive

Therefore you can attach two devices on the one channel. However, there are two connectors on the motherboard so you can attach up to four devices, called the primary and secondary channels (see Figure 1.63):

◆ The **hard drive** may be connected to the **primary channel** or IDE1 connector on the motherboard using an IDE 40-pin 80-conductor ribbon data cable. This is similar to the CD cable (see below) – and easily mistaken for it – but each conductor has a ground wire and hence there are 80 instead of 40 conductors. If you use the wrong cable, the hard drive will not work properly.

◆ A **CD drive** – or another hard drive – can then be attached to the **secondary channel** or IDE2 connector on the motherboard using an IDE 40-pin 40-conductor ribbon data cable. The CD drive is also attached via an audio cable. Audio cables are usually notched to help you to plug them in the correct way. (If you connect it the wrong way around, you may get no sound when you power up!)

Whatever drive you connect, there will also be a power cord to be connected to the PSU.

How to install IDE/EIDE devices

IDE devices include hard drives and CD-ROMS. This panel considers how to install a hard drive. See page 100 for instructions on installing a CD-ROM drive.

Installing a hard drive (see Figure 1.64) is similar to installing a **floppy** drive (see page 48), except the cover does not need to be removed:

1 Set the jumpers.

Watch out

If you are installing a second drive, you will need to check the settings for the first drive; they will need changing – e.g. from 'single' to 'master'.

2 Put the drive into the bay. You may need to screw the drive into place, or there may be mounting rails that fasten to the side of the drive so that you can click the drive into place.

3 Connect the drive to the motherboard using the ribbon cable. You need to select the correct cable: 40-wire or 80-wire, depending on the specification of the hard drive. They are the same width and both fit into the same connector! The cable has two ends: one for the motherboard and one for the drive. There is also a connector midway which you

might need to use for another device. However, if you are installing a second IDE device, and the second IDE connector is available on the motherboard, use that – you may achieve better performance if the two devices are not sharing a cable. The end that is furthest from the midway connection belongs in the motherboard. Be sure to orient the cable correctly: the red stripe along the edge of the cable indicates wire 1, and this needs to match pin 1 on the connector. The connector may have a '1' or a small triangle to show which end is pin 1.

Watch out

Be careful to connect the correct end of the cable to the motherboard, and to connect it the right way around.

4 Connect the drive to the PSU. This is more straightforward! Select a free connector from the PSU and plug it into the drive. The orientation should not be a problem: the connector is rounded on the top edge so it will only fit one way.

Your BIOS should automatically update itself when you next switch on the PC. For details of how to check the BIOS settings, see page 205.

Having installed a hard disk, though, you may decide to partition it, and you will need to format it. See page 33 for details of partitioning, and page 34 for formatting procedures.

CASE STUDY Nigel the novice PC user

Nigel has been given an older PC and he is thinking about upgrading it by installing an additional larger hard disk drive. He has looked on the Internet to find out what drives he could buy, but is not sure how, or even if, to proceed.

1 Explain the terms IDE and EIDE.

2 Why might it be impractical for Nigel to install a new disk drive on an old PC?

3 If Nigel decides to install the hard drive into the old PC, what else might he need to upgrade?

4 Explain how the new drive will work, with the old drive still in place.

Check Your Understanding 1.27

1 What does IDE stand for?
2 What is the distinction between IDE and EIDE?
3 What is the main difference between the ATA standards, e.g. from ATA-4 to ATA-6?
4 What is UltraDMA?
5 What does EMI stand for? How can this be minimised in a ribbon cable?
6 What is latency, and how is it measured?
7 Explain these terms: 'maximum data transfer rate', 'read/seek time', 'write/seek time', 'rotational speed'.
8 Distinguish between master and slave drives and primary and secondary channels.

6   Installing and configuring SCSI devices

SCSI is the second type of interface that you need to understand for the A+ course.

SCSI = small computer systems interface.

IDE interfaces are covered in section 5 (page 95). Here, the focus is on SCSI and, in particular, the installation and configuration of CD-ROM drives.

 CHAT   *With a friend, brainstorm a list of SCSI devices (apart from CD-ROM drives).*

IDE came first. It provided the in-built controller which meant that devices could be developed without worrying about the current technological breakthroughs on motherboard chipsets. The main 'problem' with IDE is the physical limitation on the number of devices that can be installed at any one time. There are two channels on the motherboard and each of these can support two IDE devices. So the total is four.

SCSI was originally devised to overcome this limitation. It involves installing an expansion card on the motherboard. This can then support more devices than the IDE channel (up to seven) – each of these devices operating through the same system resources (i.e. IRQ and I/O address), thus avoiding potential IRQ conflicts. See page 75 for details of IRQs and page 78 for I/O addresses.

The technology of SCSI then developed, and the first version was renamed SCSI-1. Table 1.18 lists the three main SCSIs.

Table 1.18   *The development of SCSI*

Type of SCSI	Expansion card	Bus speed	Notes
SCSI-1	8-bit	5 MHz	Early SCSI devices each had their own SCSI card. Result: chaos!
SCSI-2	8-bit (narrow/standard) 16-bit (wide) 32-bit (also wide!)	5 MHz (standard) 10 MHz (fast)	A standardised version of SCSI-1, offering a variety of bus width and bus speed
SCSI-3 UltraSCSI	8-bit (narrow) 16-bit (wide)	20 MHz 40 MHz 80 MHz	Same options for bus width but faster bus speed

These basic three groups of SCSI may not be referred to as such!

- An 'Ultra-40 wide SCSI' refers to the 16-bit 40 MHz SCSI-3.
- A fast wide SCSI could be the 10 MHz SCSI-2 for either 16-bit or the less common 32-bit bus width.

However, whichever SCSI technology is available, the benefit of SCSI chaining is that they usually work well together, and the cards are downward compatible. So, if you install an SCSI-3 card on your motherboard, it will support SCSI-1 devices and SCSI-2 devices as well as SCSI-3 devices. The only restriction is that the speed of each device determines the maximum speed of the data transfer along the chain beyond it (Figure 1.65). Therefore, you need to install the faster devices closer to the motherboard and work outwards with increasingly slower devices.

Figure 1.65
A chain of SCSI devices

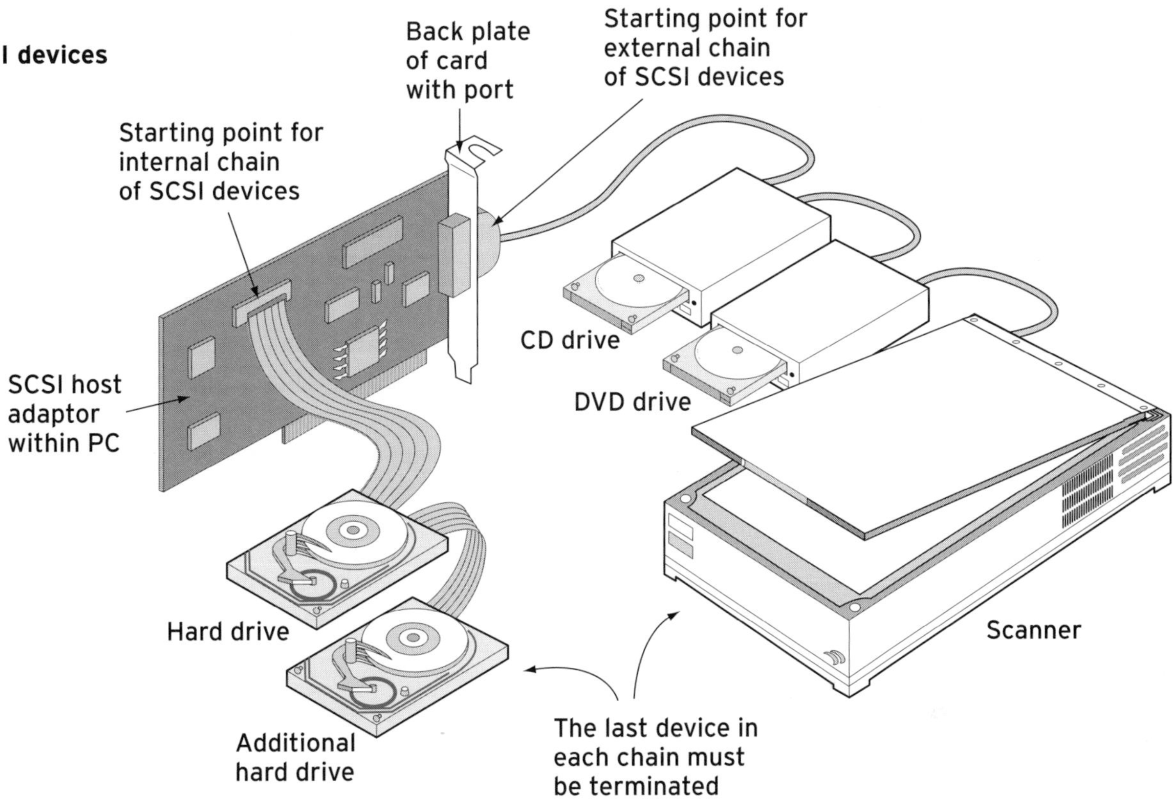

Starting point for internal chain of SCSI devices

Back plate of card with port

Starting point for external chain of SCSI devices

SCSI host adaptor within PC

CD drive

DVD drive

Hard drive

Additional hard drive

The last device in each chain must be terminated

Scanner

In the meantime, IDE technology has also moved on and, although it may still be a better option, SCSI has not been adopted as widely as might have been initially expected. So if you opt for a SCSI, you need to install the SCSI board into an available expansion slot. Each slot is connected to an expansion bus which then carries data from the board to the CPU (and vice versa). There are three types of slot on the motherboard (Figure 1.66):

◆ The **ISA slots** are the black slots. These are connected to ISA buses that move data at the slowest rate, between 3 MHz and 12 MHz, and are used for older and/or slower devices.

◆ The **PCI slots** are white and, because the PCI bus speed can be as fast as 66 MHz, these are used for high-speed I/O devices.

◆ The **AGP slot** is grey/brown and is used for a video card, its bus running at about the same speed as the system bus.

Figure 1.66
Expansion slots

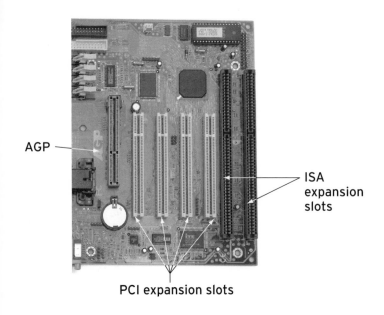

AGP

ISA expansion slots

PCI expansion slots

Table 4.8 (page 198) lists the different bus types and gives more details of these three types of slot.

Each bus has different characteristics: the bus width (8-, 16- or 32-bit) and the speed at which data can travel along the bus. In deciding which slot to use for the SCSI expansion card, you need to make sure that the bus is wide enough and can cope with the flow of data through the card. If the data arrives at the bus faster than the bus can carry it, this causes a bottleneck!

Two other buses feature in older PCs:

◆ The **VESA local bus** – also known as the VL-bus – is an extension of ISA and a forerunner of the PCI bus architecture.

◆ The **EISA (extended industry-standard architecture)** was one of several standard designs used by various types of IBM-compatible microcomputers. Its extra depth allowed for an additional set of pins, but these slots and the cards that used to fit into them are now obsolete. EISA slots look the same as ISA slots and only the motherboard documentation will tell you which are in place.

The requirements for the SCSI card will be available with the documentation supplied with it, but you can also look on the Internet for this information.

Go and try out 1.24

1 Research the Internet for details of SCSI cards.
2 Find out about the development of the PCI bus.

So, having identified which type of slot might suit the particular SCSI card, you can think about the devices that can be attached. SCSI devices may be internal devices or external SCSI devices:

◆ **Internal SCSI devices** are connected to the SCSI expansion board from inside the PC (such as disk drives).

◆ **External SCSI devices** are placed outside the PC casing and are connected, just like any other peripheral, using a connecting cable. Examples include scanners and backup tape drives. These devices have both an IN port and an OUT port; this allows them to be chained together.

The SCSI card would include both internal and external connectors so that both internal and external SCSI devices can be connected. The external connectors protrude through the wall of the PC case. The **internal SCSI connector** can be one of two types:

◆ The **SCSI A cable** is used for SCSI-1 and SCSI-2. It looks very much like the IDE ribbon cable but has 10 more wires (50 instead of 40).

◆ The **SCSI P cable** has 68 wires and a D-connector. The two rows of pins each has 34 pins, so it is not the traditional arrangement of pins you will see.

The **external SCSI connector** also comes in a variety of forms:

◆ The SCSI-1 uses the 50-pin Centronics – just like the connector for a parallel printer.

◆ The SCSI-2 has either a 25-pin, a 50-pin or a 68-pin female D-subconnector, depending on the model of card.

◆ The SCSI-3 uses a 68-pin female D-subconnector.

You need to be able to install and configure SCSI devices. When you install two disk drives on the same IDE bus, you have to identify one as the master and the other as the slave. Similarly, if you install a chain of devices on a SCSI, each device needs to be identified. Otherwise, it would not be clear which data belongs to which device. This involves assigning to the jumper block settings – or moving a thumb wheel or counter – a unique identifier for each device in the chain. If you use jumpers, you may see three pairs of pins, each pair of pins being labelled with the numbers 1, 2 and 4.

Figure 1.67 shows how to set the jumpers to assign each of the numbers from 1 to 7 to any one device in the chain. Note that if you intend to boot up from a SCSI hard drive, this device will need to be assigned the identifier '1'. The board takes the identifier '0' and the operating system will expect the next device to have the relevant information for booting up. See page 17 for details of how the boot process works.

The final device in the chain needs a special setting so that the PC knows there is nothing beyond it. The device is terminated by setting yet another jumper!

◆ When the jumper straddles the pins, the device is the terminating device.

◆ If the jumper does not straddle the pins, there is at least one more device beyond this one in the chain.

Having physically installed a SCSI device, when you turn on the PC, it should recognise the new hardware and have already configured it. There are a couple of 'extras' to remember, though:

◆ The CD-ROM installation lets you prepare a CD-R or CD-RW drive for use, but only allows you to read from it. To enable you to write to a CD-RW, you need to install a CD-writing application, such as Adaptec's Easy CD Creator, which is usually supplied with the drive or could be bought separately. This software provides a wizard to guide the user through the writing process.

CHAT *Discuss how writing to a CD-R is different from writing to a CD-RW.*

◆ If you install a **DVD drive** – or some combination drive that allows you to read/write to CD-ROMs as well as reading DVDs – you need also to have an **MPEG decoder**. Material on the DVD – sound and pictures – is compressed and has to be decompressed before you can view it. The MPEG decoder may mean another expansion board to install, or it may be done using software. If you do have a separate MPEG decoder board, this too has to be connected to the DVD drive.

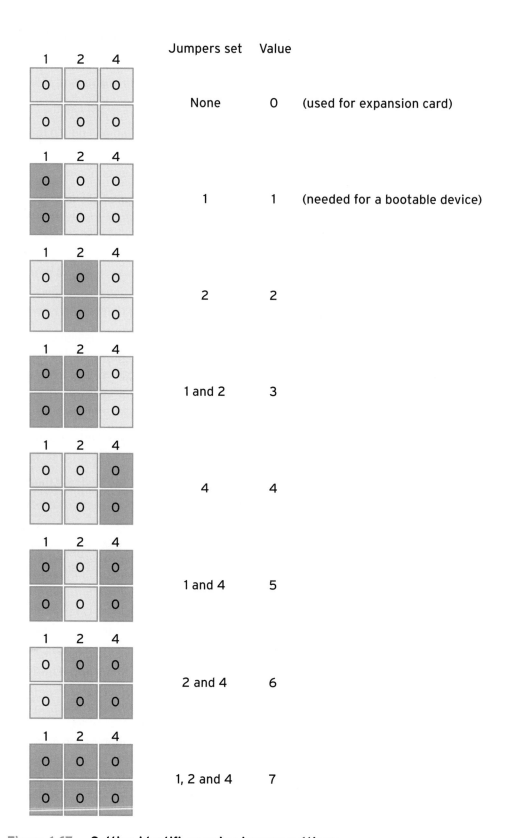

Figure 1.67   Setting identifiers using jumper settings

How to install internal SCSI devices (a CD-ROM drive)

1 Set the jumpers to assign a unique identifier to each device, and to identify the terminating device.

2 To install (or remove) an internal SCSI device, such as a CD drive, the cover does need to be removed. Slide the CD drive in from the front of the case and push it into place until the screw holes line up and it is flush with the front of the case. Don't screw it into place just yet. Wait until you are sure it is working.

3 Connect the CD-ROM drive to the SCSI card using the CD cable.

4 For a CD-ROM drive, if you intend to listen to the audio CDs, you need also to connect the drive to the sound system. An **audio cable** should run from the CD-ROM drive to the sound card on your motherboard — or direct to the motherboard if there is a built-in sound support on the motherboard. You will need to check the documentation to make sure you are using the correct cables.

5 Connect the CD drive to the PSU unit.

What does it mean? *An audio cable has three wires and runs from the CD-ROM drive to the sound card, enabling the PC to play audio CDs through the sound card and out through speakers.*

Check Your Understanding 1.28

1 Why is there a limit of seven devices that can be chained together on one SCSI card?
2 Distinguish between narrow and wide, and standard and fast SCSIs.
3 How could you make sure you could boot up from a SCSI hard drive?
4 Describe the features of a PCI bus.
5 What is the difference between an internal SCSI device and an external SCSI device?
6 How is an external SCSI device connected to the PC?
7 How is a chain of external SCSI devices attached to the PC and to each other?

CASE STUDY   Nigel the novice PC user

Nigel is thinking about installing a CD-ROM drive as a SCSI device. He has some questions he needs you to answer. Remember that Nigel is only nine years old, so keep your explanation brief and easy to follow.

1 What does SCSI stand for?

2 What is UltraSCSI?

3 Why are there different kinds of slots for the expansion boards?

4 What is meant by a terminating device?

5 If I want to write to CDs as well as listen to CDs, what else do I need to do?

6 Would it be much more difficult to install a DVD drive, one that I can play CDs on too, instead of a CD-ROM drive?

7 Installing and configuring peripheral devices

You need to be able to install and configure many different peripheral devices. You have already seen how to install some internal devices and how to connect up some external peripherals. This section looks at some more peripheral devices, including those for portable computers, and how to configure devices in general.

Depending on what peripheral you intend to attach, and depending on which port you use to attach the peripheral, apart from selecting appropriate cabling, you may also need to install an expansion board to provide the port and thus to support the peripheral. If the expansion board is already in place, you may still need to change jumper settings and/or amend the BIOS settings so that your peripheral is recognised and works as you planned. To help to establish industry standards in the development of ports and associated cabling, a committee was set up in the early 1990s, supported by the IEEE (Institute of Electrical Engineers):

◆ For serial ports, there is the **RS232c standard** and **USB**.
◆ For parallel ports, there is the **IEEE 1284**.

Attaching peripherals to serial ports

9-pin male serial port

25-pin male serial port

Figure 1.68
Serial ports

Serial ports were originally provided for all input and output devices, with parallel ports being used only for printers. The serial ports (Figure 1.68) can be identified on the back of a PC by the counting the number of pins (9 or 25) and looking for a male connector. (Parallel ports tend to be female and could have 15 or 25 pins.)

The original IEEE standard for serial ports is RS232c. This standard specified 25 pins but because PCs only use 9 of the pins it was modified to allow for this reduced size connector. Serial ports are controlled by the **UART chip**.

The UART chip controls communication between the DTE (e.g. your PC) and the DCE (e.g. your modem), converting serial streams of bits into parallel streams (on the way into your PC) and vice versa (on the way out).

What does it mean?

UART = universal asynchronous receiver-transmitter.

What does it mean?

DTE = data terminal equipment; DCE = data communication equipment.

Figure 1.69 shows how these devices are linked.

The UART chip has been developed from the initial design (8250 UART) with attempts to improve the way data is handled so that data is not lost, and that transfer is as speedy as

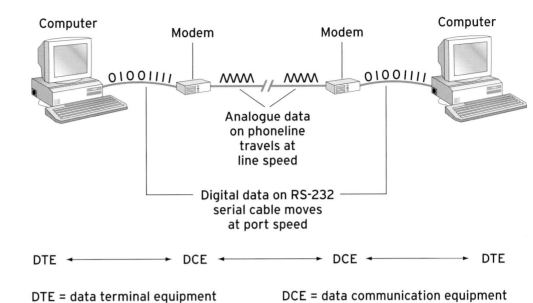

Figure 1.69
DTEs connected by
DCEs using cabling and
a telephone
communication link

possible. The chips are labelled (e.g. 16450, 16550AFN, 16750 or 16950). Higher numbers indicate a more modern version of the UART chip! Your PC may have the UART within another chip, but you can check through the Device Manager (page 132), looking at the port settings.

A **modem** can be attached to the serial port (or the USB port, see below); the installation of modems was covered in section 3 (page 79).

Check Your Understanding 1.29

1 What does modem stand for?
2 Under what circumstance might an external modem be used instead of an internal modem?
3 What type of connector is used to link a modem to the telephone socket?

Configuring a modem involves setting a number of parameters for the port, and setting other parameters for the modem. It is important that these are configured properly; otherwise they may not work well together! For the port, there are five settings to consider:

◆ The speed of transmission (in bits per second) or **port speed** needs to be about four times as fast as the modem speed. Typical values are 9600 bps and 57600 bps.

◆ The **number of data bits** used to send a single character need only be 7 (for the standard ASCII character) but in most cases you will specify 8 bits (i.e. one byte).

◆ A **parity** system within the modem should be available for checking data, so you can opt for no checking at the port. The options are none, odd or even.

◆ **Stop bits** are used to indicate that a character is starting or stopping. The options are 1, 1.5 or 2 bits, with '1' being the normal choice.

◆ **Flow control** prevents the data overflowing either at the PC or at the modem, if data is arriving faster than it can be dealt with. It can be achieved through software (Xon/Xoff) or through hardware (RTS/CTS), the later being the preferred option.

CHAT *You have met RTS and CTS before. Discuss where this fits into flow control communication.*

Installing a modem

It is important to read the documentation that comes with the modem before you start to install or configure anything! This will give you important information that you need when configuring the serial port and will help you to decide which serial port to use. See section 3 (page 80) for details of installing the modem card.

How to configure a modem

1 Use the Device Manager (page 132) to confirm that the modem card is installed. If this is not the case, you will need to install it, using the Add New Hardware wizard.

2 To configure the port, go to the Control Panel and, through the Device Manager, select the serial port that you have decided to use for the modem. Set the port settings (Figure 1.70).

Unit 2 (page 259) explains how to access the Control Panel within the Windows operating system.

3 With the PC turned off, plug in the modem. Then reboot the PC. The boot process should notice this new hardware and automatically launch the Add New Hardware wizard for you. If this does not happen, access this wizard through the Control Panel.

4 You may need to reboot your PC again so that, having identified the modem card, it now recognises the modem. The Add New Hardware wizard should load the device drivers for the modem automatically. Otherwise, you will need to use a disk supplied with the modem or go online to find the right device driver to install.

5 To configure the modem, go to the Control Panel and, through the Device Manager, select Modem and set the properties (Figure 1.71).

6 You then need to install any software to make calls through the modem, or create a dial-up networking connection. See page 352.

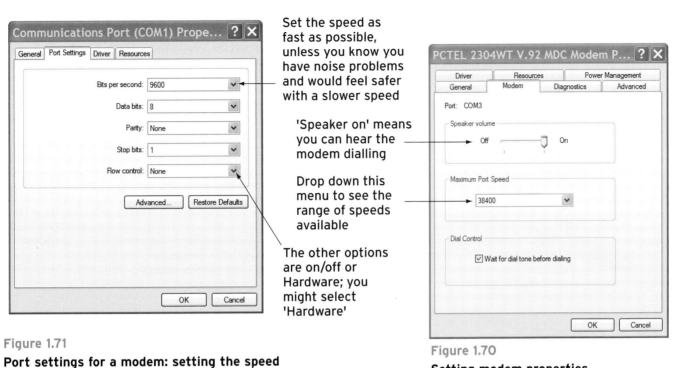

Set the speed as fast as possible, unless you know you have noise problems and would feel safer with a slower speed

'Speaker on' means you can hear the modem dialling

Drop down this menu to see the range of speeds available

The other options are on/off or Hardware; you might select 'Hardware'

Figure 1.71

Port settings for a modem: setting the speed and the port protocols

Figure 1.70

Setting modem properties

Attaching peripherals to USB ports

What does it mean? *USB (universal serial bus) is a higher-speed serial connection standard that supports low-speed devices (mice, keyboards, scanners) and higher-speed devices (digital cameras).*

You have seen how a variety of peripherals can be connected to the USB port: keyboard (page 40), printers (page 44), CD-ROM drive (page 98), LCD screens (page 65), digital camera (page 66). The USB bus type is explained in Table 4.8 on page 198.

Check Your Understanding 1.30

1 What does USB stand for?
2 Describe the USB connecting cable and its connectors.
3 What is meant by hot swapping?
4 What IRQ might be used for the USB controller?

Instead of the UART chip, for this serial port, a **USB host controller** manages the USB bus.

There may be as many as four USB ports supported by a motherboard. It is then possible to link as many as 127 devices in a 'daisy chain' so that the PC may have many more devices attached – each device providing the USB port to the next device in the chain (Figure 1.72).

SCSI devices are limited to seven in a chain. Why is seven the upper limit? Discuss why USB chains might be limited to 127 devices. (Hint: Think in binary.)

Another option is to have a **hub**, into which devices can be plugged.

The USB cable has four wires: two for data and two for power. The two power lines (one with voltage and the other acting as a ground) allow the host controller to pass power along the chain of devices. Figure 1.73 shows how the USB technology allows so many devices to be connected while using only limited systems resources.

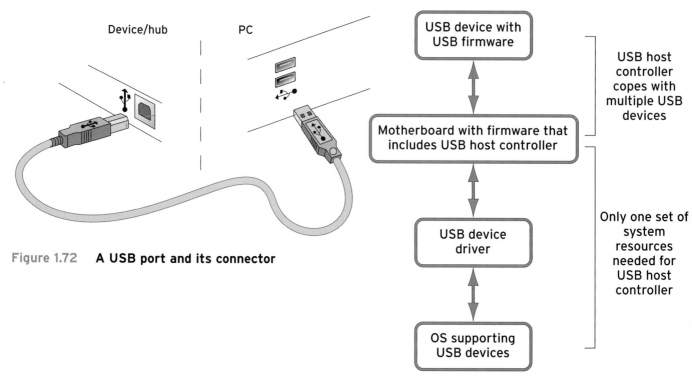

Figure 1.72   **A USB port and its connector**

Figure 1.73

Limited resource usage with USB technology

Before you can install a USB device, you need a motherboard (or expansion board) that provides the USB port, an operating system that supports USB, the USB device and a **device driver**.

What does it mean?

A device driver is a data file or program which holds information that the PC needs to be able to send data to the device and to receive data from the device, interpreting the codes used by the device correctly.

How to install and configure USB peripherals and hubs

1   Use Device Manager (page 132) to confirm that the USB host controller is installed. If this is not the case, you will need to install it using Add New Hardware.

2   With the PC turned off, plug in the USB device. Then reboot the PC. The boot process should notice this new hardware and automatically launch the Add New Hardware

wizard for you. If this does not happen, access this wizard through the Control Panel (page 259).

3   The Add New Hardware wizard should load the device drivers for you. Otherwise, you will need to use a disk supplied with the device or go online to find the right device driver to install.

4   Depending on the device, you then need to install applications software which will allow you to use the device, e.g. scanning software.

Attaching peripherals to parallel ports

Three types of parallel ports have been developed, the reason being to increase speed of data transfer:

◆   The **standard parallel port (SPP)** allows data to flow in only one direction, and it therefore provides a very slow connection. This 'normal' port is known as the Centronics port because of the 36-pin Centronics connector that fits into it.

◆   The **enhanced parallel port (EPP)** allows data to flow in both directions. This is more speedy.

◆   The **extended capabilities port (ECP)** also allows data to flow in both directions but then increases speed of transfer still further by using the DMA channel.

The **IEEE 1284** standard applies to bidirectional parallel communications (i.e. EPP and ECP ports) and requires backward compatibility so that Centronics ports will still work with modern cabling. If you are using a port that is configured as EPP or ECP, you must make sure that the cabling is IEEE 1284 compliant. Older cabling will not work.

How to install and configure parallel ports

1   If the port is on an I/O card, you need to read the documentation for the card. This will tell you how to assign the system resources (IRQ and I/O address) to the port.

2   If the port is coming straight from the motherboard, you need to look at your CMOS setup (Figure 1.74) to check the system resources and to make any necessary changes.

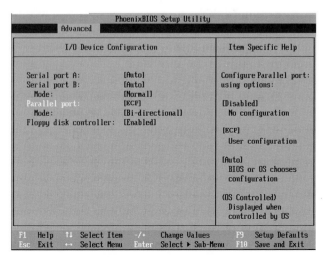

Figure 1.74

CMOs setup

3 The settings will offer you a choice of normal, EPP, ECP and EPP + ECP. If you choose ECP or EPP + ECP, you will also have to opt for ECP DMA – and this may be on channels 1 or 3.

Installing a monitor/video card

Installing a video card was used as the example for filling an expansion slot (see page 60).

Check Your Understanding 1.31

1 Which two devices are necessary before your PC can display images?
2 Which slot does the video board usually go into?
3 What information might you find on a video board?

CHAT *Discuss how to install a video card physically in an expansion slot. What safety precautions would you take during the installation?*

The monitor and video card, together, form a video subsystem. As with modems and ports, you need to match the configuration of both the modem and the video card to make them work in harmony together.

The monitor can be connected to the PC in one of three ways:

◆ The video card provides a 15-pin D-subconnector for the monitor and the monitor has a 15-pin connector that matches this, although not all 15 pins may be used on some models of monitor. So, it is possible that the monitor connector looks as if pins have broken off; this is not necessarily the case.

◆ On older PCs, there may be no video card. Instead, video support is built into the motherboard. In this situation, a cable needs to be connected to the motherboard and to the inside of the 15-pin male D-subconnector. From the outside of the PC, it looks as if there could be a separate video board.

◆ The better monitors may use a **BNC connector** instead of the standard 15-pin connector, and for these a special video card is needed so that the connector on the PC is also a BNC connector. However, this type of connection tends to be used only on the most sophisticated monitors, e.g. those used for video teleconferencing.

The monitor screen is made up of individual dots called **pixels**. The card tells the monitor what colour each pixel is to be, and this creates the image on screen. The instructions from the video card to the monitor happen frequently so the net effect on the screen is a moving picture:

◆ The **resolution** of an image is a measure of the number of pixels on the screen: the more pixels, the better the resolution. Resolution is described as width $\times$ height.

◆ The **colour depth** is the maximum number of unique colours that can be shown in a single pixel. Colour depth is measured in bits, e.g. 4-bit colour supports 16 different colours.

◆ The **refresh rate**, measured in hertz, is the frequency with which each pixel of the display is recharged. The pixel of light starts to decay as soon as it appears, and so it needs refreshing quickly enough to avoid flickering on the screen and the eye strain that would accompany this.

The monitor will have a maximum resolution, and so will the video card. To see the best possible image that your monitor can display, it is important to match these two resolutions. However, refresh rates are adversely affected by the resolution; 120 Hz rate may be achievable for 800 × 600 but it drops to 85 Hz for a higher resolution such as 1280 × 1024. If it drops below 75 Hz, there may be a noticeable flicker. So you need to decide on a resolution that is achievable without flicker.

The slot that is used for the card determines which bus is used and this affects the speed at which instructions can pass to the monitor. The AGB bus is the fastest, running at the same speed as the system bus.

The type of video card installed therefore directly affects the quality of the image displayed on the monitor. The video card has four basic functions, as described in Figure 1.75:

◆ To receive data from the CPU about what image is needed

◆ To copy this digital data into the video card memory

◆ To convert the digital data into analogue data

◆ To send this analogue data to the monitor

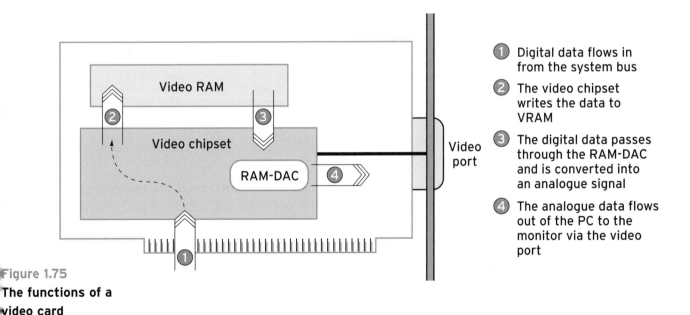

Figure 1.75
The functions of a video card

There may be three separate DACs on a video card, one for each of the colour guns (red, green, blue).

What does it mean?

DAC = digital-to-analogue converter.

113

As with all other components in a PC, the video card has developed over time:

◆ A **graphics accelerator** is a special video card that has its own in-built processor, so it can do its own calculations instead of using valuable CPU processing time.

◆ **Dual porting** allows movement of data in and out of the card simultaneously and appears on special video memory called **VRAM**.

◆ **SGRAM** synchronises the video card with the CPU clock.

◆ **WRAM** has an increased internal bus width.

What does it mean?

VRAM = video RAM.   *SGRAM = synchronous graphics RAM.*
WRAM = Windows RAM.

More colour and higher resolution both require more memory, so this can prove to be a limiting factor, and the amount of memory on a video card is an important consideration.

Just how much memory is needed?

For a resolution of 640 × 480 (minimal!) with only four colours, 256 K is needed. If the number of colours is increased to 256, this doubles to 512 K but, if you want 32-bit (24-bit true colour giving 16.7 million colours, plus an 8-bit alpha channel), you will need 2 MB! Similarly, if you increase the resolution to (say) 1600 × 1200, the memory requirement for four colours rises to 2 MB, and that for 32-bit colour jumps to 8 MB.

What does it mean?

An alpha channel is needed for 3D graphics. It controls how the three colours are displayed and is used to create effects.

The bus width on the card directly affects how much memory is needed to support the video card; less than optimum memory will adversely affect performance. Higher resolution does mean that more can be fitted on to your screen. However, this means the text appears smaller and this may not suit the user. So, a compromise needs to be made!

Check Your Understanding 1.32

1 How many bits would be needed to create 256 different colours in a pixel?
2 What is a graphics accelerator?
3 What is meant by dual porting?

Go and try out 1.25

1 Investigate different types of monitors and the connectors they use.
2 Find out the specification of a variety of video boards.
3 Find out how much memory is needed for different video resolutions and colour depths.
4 Find out what features might be available on a graphics accelerator.
5 Find out how the alpha channel works on 3D graphics.

Display Properties

Themes | Desktop | Screen Saver | Appearance | Settings

Drag the monitor icons to match the physical arrangement of your monitors.

Display:
1. (Multiple Monitors) on NVIDIA GeForce4 440 Go (Dell Mobile)

Screen resolution
Less — More
1600 by 1200 pixels

Color quality
Highest (32 bit)

☑ Use this device as the primary monitor.
☑ Extend my Windows desktop onto this monitor.

Identify | Troubleshoot... | Advanced

OK | Cancel | Apply

The Advanced settings screen allows you to
change the DPI setting; useful if your screen
resolution makes screen items too small to
view comfortably

Figure 1.76

**The settings for
configuring the video
and monitor**

How to configure a monitor/video card

1 When you install the video card and reboot the PC, it should recognise the new hardware and automatically install the video driver that matches your choice of video card.

2 From the Control Panel, choose Display and select the Settings tab to set the properties for both the monitor and the video card (Figure 1.76).

Installing external storage

External storage is generally used to back up data, e.g. an **external tape drive**. There are a number of different types of tape, DAT and DLT being the most common (Table 1.19).

Table 1.19	DAT and DTL tape drives	
Drive type	**Media size**	**Capacity**
DAT (digital audio tape) cartridge	4 mm	1 GB–20 GB
DLT (digital linear tape)	0.5 inch	10 GB–50 GB

Most tape drives are installed on the IDE/EIDE interface. (Refer to page 95 for details, and consult the documentation that is supplied with the tape device.) External hard disks may be connected via the FireWire IEEE1394 port, as discussed next.

FireWire (IEEE1394)

Images can be captured on a scanner or a digital camera and stored in **TWAIN format** for transfer and processing on a PC.

What does it mean?

TWAIN is not an acronym (according to its creators) but is taken to mean 'technology without an interesting name'.

The cable supplied with the camera or scanner may be one of four types:

◆ serial

- parallel
- USB
- FireWire.

For this fourth type, you need the IEEE1394 port to connect it to.

FireWire (IEEE1394) was developed by Apple Computer as a **high-performance serial bus (HPSB)** and is ideal for connecting devices such as external hard disks which need to transfer large files. FireWire is similar to USB in many ways, but data transfers are **isochronous**. This means they happen in real time and so the data – such as the audio and video on multimedia, which must arrive together – is co-ordinated. There is no detour via the CPU. FireWire is also much faster than USB, running at up to 400 Mbps and, unsurprisingly, more expensive.

An IEEE1394 port can support up to 63 devices and tends to be used for **consumer electronics** such as digital cameras and digital video cameras. Like USB and SCSI, it needs only one IRQ, so it does not use system resources for each of the 63 devices. It is a peer-to-peer interface, which means there is no need for a host. A video camera can support and power other FireWire devices without a PC! Figure 1.77 shows a sample IEEE1394 bus.

Figure 1.77
IEEE1394 bus

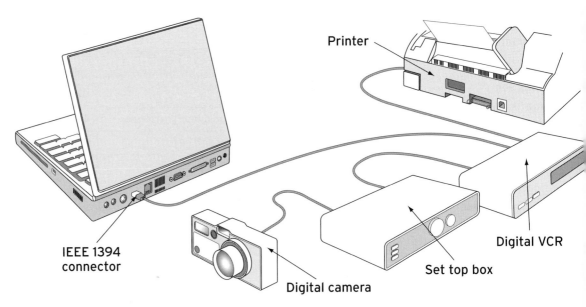

IEEE 1394 connector

Digital camera

Set top box

Digital VCR

Printer

Most operating systems support IEEE1394 but expect the controller to be an OHCI 1394 controller. Windows 2000 supports IEEE1394-compliant devices through the SBP-2 driver. Alternatively, SCSI devices can be interlaced with IEEE1394-compliant devices – this is called a **tailgate**.

What does it mean?

OHCI = open host controller interface; SBP = serial bus protocol.

How to install an IEEE1394 device

1 Check that Windows recognises that an IEEE1394 controller is present on the motherboard. Using Device Manager, check that 1394 Bus Controller is listed as an installed device. Clicking the + sign beside the 1394 entry will display the specific brand of 1394 controller. If the controller is not installed, or does not appear to be working, reinstall it using Add New Hardware. If you still have problems, check whether 1394 is enabled. If your motherboard does not support IEEE1394, you could install an adaptor card as an IEEE host into a PCI slot.

2 Connect the IEEE1394-compliant device to the 1394 port and install the device drivers for the device. You should be able to do this through Add New Hardware, without having to reboot the PC.

3 Install the software for the 1394-compliant device.

Watch out

There will be a CD and some installation instructions that are supplied with the 1394 device. Refer to these carefully.

Check Your Understanding 1.33

1 Give two examples of external devices that can be used to back up data.
2 What does DAT stand for?
3 What is TWAIN used for?
4 Which is the faster: USB or FireWire?
5 Give two examples of consumer electronic devices.
6 How many devices can an IEEE1394 port support?

Attaching peripherals to portable PCs

Portable PCs and notebooks can be configured to work with a wide range of peripherals, just like a normal PC. However, a **port replicator** (Figure 1.78) can be used to provide additional ports to extend the number and variety of peripherals that can be attached. A **docking station** (Figure 1.79) provides extra ports and additional storage media, such as a floppy disk drive for a notepad.

Figure 1.78 port replicator

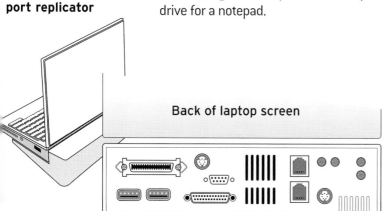

Back of laptop screen

Ports provided by the port replicator

PCMCIA cards – or PC cards for short – were originally developed for memory, but now also extend the variety of peripherals that can be attached to include USB controllers, hard disks, modems, wired networks, wireless networks, sound cards, SCSI host adaptors and IEEE1394 controllers (see the 'How to' panel in section 2, page 125). This makes up for the lack of expansion slots within a laptop!

What does it mean?

PCMCIA = Personal Computer Memory Card International Association. Chapter 4, section 3 (page 202) explains the different types of PC card.

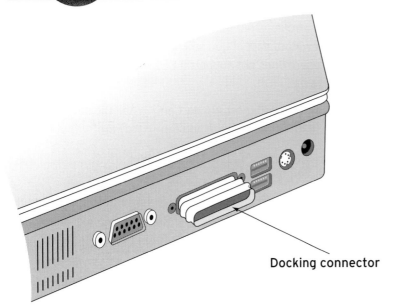

Figure 1.79
A docking station

Docking connector

The operating system provides two services to support a PC card:

◆ The **socket service** spots when the card is inserted and sets up communication between the PC card and the CPU of the laptop or notebook. It also disconnects communication when the card is removed from the slot.

◆ The **card service** provides the relevant device driver to interface with the card once communication has been established.

Cards can be changed without turning off the laptop – this is called **hot swapping**. However, you need to go through the Control Panel to Add/Remove Hardware to stop a card using Plug/Unplug a device, before you are free to take the PC card out of the slot (see Figure 1.80).

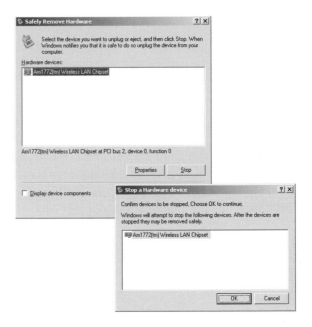

Figure 1.80
Unplugging a PC card

PC cards may also have a cable attached to them so that another device can be linked to the laptop/notebook. A PC card that is a modem card will also have a connector for the phone line. Figure 1.81 illustrates both these configurations. Section 3 explains how infrared ports work; wireless communications are discussed in section 4.

Figure 1.81

Configurations with PC cards and laptops

(a)

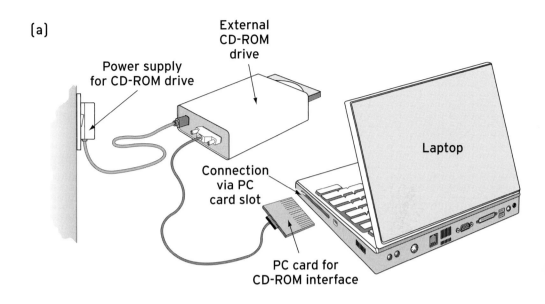

External CD-ROM drive

Power supply for CD-ROM drive

Laptop

Connection via PC card slot

PC card for CD-ROM interface

(b)

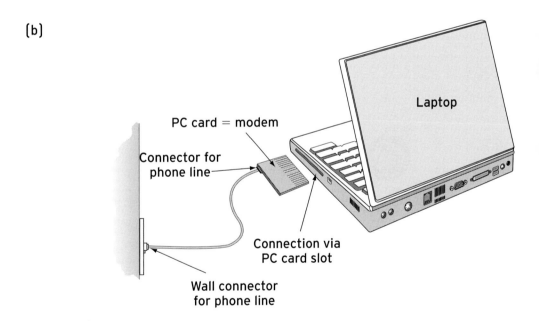

Laptop

PC card = modem

Connector for phone line

Connection via PC card slot

Wall connector for phone line

Infrared devices may also be used with laptop PCs and notebooks, such as keyboards and mice. They work in exactly the same way as on a normal PC. Chapter 6 (page 234) considers wireless networks.

Check Your Understanding 1.34

1 Explain the difference between a port replicator and a docking station.
2 What does PCMCIA stand for?
3 What does the socket service do?
4 What is hot swapping?
5 Give two examples of infrared devices.

8 Hardware methods of upgrading system performance

Systems performance is measured by how quickly the PC responds to your commands. If your PC seems too slow for you, you have two basic options: buy a newer model with more features and improved performance, or consider upgrading your current PC. Depending on what you want your PC to do, it may be cheaper to upgrade the motherboard – or to add components – than to buy a brand-new PC.

Chapter 4, section 5 (page 209) summarises what you could do to upgrade your PC, including replacing the motherboard, and the factors you would need to take into account before deciding whether to replace the PC. Here, the focus is on what you need to know about hardware methods of upgrading system performance, and the procedures for replacing basic subsystem components, unique components and when to use them.

Upgrading the BIOS

You need to know how to update the BIOS and when this should be done. If you were to interrupt the updating process, this can cause problems, and so you also need to know how to recover from this situation. Upgrading the BIOS can mean physically removing the chip and installing a new or reprogrammed one. However, BIOS is stored (nowadays) on an EEPROM. This means it can be changed (like an EPROM) but without replacement and without, therefore, risking damage to the chip, to the PC and to you.

The process of updating the BIOS is called **flashing**. Using a software utility program available from the manufacturers of flash BIOS, you can update the data held on the EEPROM, and so this is sometimes called **flash ROM**.

EEPROM chips are used in lots of other equipment, such as cars, telephones and cameras. With your friends, discuss how you can find out more about this technology.

The flashing process is speedy but needs to be carried out carefully and completely:

- If you halt the process midway, the BIOS may be unusable. So you need to be very careful to avoid accidents: turning off the power – or a power cut – may have disastrous consequences.

- Flashing the wrong BIOS, e.g. one that does not match your motherboard, will result in an unusable BIOS. So be careful to check you have selected the correct BIOS before proceeding with the flashing process.

To avoid accidental flashing – and the risk of an unusable BIOS – most PCs have a jumper block which allows you to disable flashing (see Figure 1.82). Then, when you do want to flash, you need to move the jumper into a different position before you can start the process. Using the jumper block also denies access to flashing for any computer virus which may attempt to damage your BIOS!

Go and try out 1.26

Research the Internet for suppliers of flash BIOS. Identify the software utilities available to reprogram your BIOS.

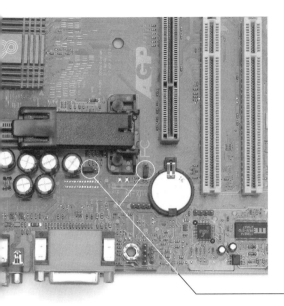

Figure 1.82

A jumper block for flashing

Here are two examples of jumper settings. Consult the motherboard documentation to locate the jumper for flashing the BIOS

What can you do if the flashing process does go wrong?

A **boot block** is an emergency program supplied with your BIOS. This will restore the BIOS from disk (floppy or CD-ROM as supplied by your BIOS manufacturer) and may involve setting a jumper on the motherboard to enable this feature.

How to upgrade BIOS

1 If you have (sensibly) set a jumper to prevent accidental flashing, reset it to allow flashing while you make the change to your BIOS. Alternatively, you may need to change a setting in CMOS to warn that a change to the BIOS is imminent.

2 Copy the upgrade BIOS software that you have downloaded from the BIOS manufacturer's website (or obtained in some other way) to a bootable disk.

Unit 2, Chapter 8 (page 306) explains how to create a bootable disk.

3 Turn of the PC and then turn it back on, booting from the disk and following the menu options to upgrade the BIOS. If you are given the option to save the old BIOS to disk do so; you may need to revert to the old BIOS if things go wrong.

4 Set the jumpers back to the 'no updating the BIOS' position.

When ought you to upgrade your BIOS?

How old the BIOS is affects which modern devices you can attach to your PC. If you install new hardware, such as a new large hard drive, you may need to replace or update your BIOS.

Discuss situations which could result in you having to upgrade the BIOS.

1 How is systems performance measured?
2 What is the process of upgrading the BIOS called?
3 How can you prevent accidental flashing?
4 What is a book block?
5 Where and how can you obtain BIOS updates?

Upgrading memory

Upgrading memory means adding more RAM to your computer. Ask yourself these questions:

◆ How much memory do I need?

◆ How much memory do I already have?

◆ How cost-effective would any additional memory be?

◆ What type and size of memory module should I buy?

Taking the last question first: you need to make sure that any extra memory you buy will be compatible with whatever is already installed – or you may need to replace memory as well as add more memory.

There are some basic rules to apply when choosing memory:

◆ Avoid low-quality memory – or expect GPF errors. Check when each chip on the RAM module was produced. Chips have a chip ID that tells you the date it was produced in the format YYMM. Look for memory modules with chips that have close dates and ones that are less than a year old.

What does it mean?

GPF = general protection fault.

◆ Buy to match your PC's hardware. Either tin or gold will have been used on the slot of each memory bank, so buy memory modules with the same finish. A mismatch can result in a chemical reaction between the tin on one and the gold on the other, which leads to corrosion and eventual failure of the module.

◆ Buy the best performance. Choose the fastest that your motherboard can support.

◆ Buy to match your current memory speed. It is possible to mix the speeds, but it is better if you don't. Certainly don't mix speeds within a bank; otherwise, the slowest speed will apply.

◆ Buy to match what is recommended. Your best source of information about what will – and what will not – work on your PC is the motherboard documentation. For example, one feature of memory is the **latency** – or CAS latency (CL) – which tells you how many clock cycles pass while data is written to memory. CL2 and CL3 are possible values (CL2 being 2 clock cycles, and faster than CL3), and you should use whichever your motherboard documentation recommends.

So, having established the basic rules of how to choose RAM, how much memory do you need? Presumably the amount you had initially was fine for the original configuration of your PC, but now you have added some additional functionality and this needs more memory. Therefore, do these checks:

◆ How much memory does your operating systems need? For example, Windows 2000 requires 64 MB of RAM.

◆ What other software have you installed and how much RAM does each package need.

◆ What devices have you attached? What RAM requirements do they have?

There is an upper limit on how much memory will fit on the motherboard, and this information will be available with your documentation for the PC. Having established the total requirement, you can check whether it is greater than the upper limit for your motherboard, in which case you need to think about upgrading the motherboard or simply replacing the PC. If the amount you need is within the scope for your motherboard, determining how much memory you have already will let you calculate the shortfall.

How to find out how much memory is installed

There are a number of ways you could find out how much RAM is installed in your PC. Here are two:

1   With the PC turned on, right click on My Computer and select Properties. The General tab describes your system in detail, including the amount of RAM.

2   With the PC turned off, open the case, locate the memory chips, read each one to see what capacity it is and add up the capacities.

Having decided how much extra memory you need, there are a variety of memory modules that you could install (SIMMs, DIMMs and RIMMs) and you would need to install the right combination of these. Chapter 4 (page 185) explains the features of the different types of RAM.

Check Your Understanding 1.36

1   If you upgrade the memory of the PC, what exactly are you adding to it?
2   What are GPF errors? How might they be avoided?
3   What metals are used for the contact between a RAM and the slot into which it fits?
4   Why is it not a good idea to mix speeds between memory modules?
5   What is latency?
6   How can you find out how much RAM is installed on your PC? Describe more than one way.

Upgrading hard drives

The hard drive of your PC holds a lot of important data and software. To upgrade the hard drive involves removing the old drive and replacing it with, presumably, a larger-capacity drive. To be able to restore the system – all software and data – you will need to back everything up from the old drive (before you remove it!) and then restore everything to the newly installed drive.

You may also have to change the BIOS if the capacity of the new drive is greater than that supported by your current BIOS.

CHAT   *Discuss the steps that you need to take to upgrade a hard drive.*

CASE STUDY Ismat, trainee technician

In Ismat's IT support team, when they need to upgrade a PC, for example to change the hard drive, they use 'ghosting' software that creates an image of the PC installation and saves it to a file. Once the replacement drive is in place, it is then simply a process of 'ghosting' the software on to the upgraded PC. This procedure is also used when an end user's computer is causing problems but the fault is difficult to trace. All the user's files are copied on to the network server for safekeeping, and then his or her PC is 'rebuilt'. All the software is reinstalled, and then the files are copied back on to the hard disk. This process is fully automated and so provides an easy way of solving some software faults.

1 Investigate the availability of 'ghosting' software on the Internet.

2 For your own PC, list the software that you might need to reinstall if you were to upgrade your hard drive.

Upgrading the CPU

If you plan to upgrade the CPU, you must ensure that the new CPU matches your motherboard, its form factor and chipset. Stepping up from one CPU to another within the same 'family' may be relatively painless, but some upgrades are not feasible. To change the CPU might then also mean changing the motherboard and the chipset, to the point where you might consider replacing the PC rather than upgrading. To find out what is feasible, you need to consult the documentation of both the manufacturer of the motherboard and of the CPU.

Check Your Understanding 1.37

1 Identify the motherboard in your PC and the CPU. (*Hint:* Turn off your PC; disconnect the keyboard; turn the PC on; it will fail with a keyboard error but the motherboard identification appears in the lower left corner and the BIOS manufacturer and version number will be at the top of the screen.)

2 Research the Internet to find out what options you would have to upgrade your CPU.

Upgrading components on a portable system

For portable systems, you might upgrade any or all of these components:

◆ battery
◆ hard drive memory
◆ types I, II and III cards.

The DC power needed for a portable PC is taken from its battery and, if you have the AC adaptor connected, the battery is recharged at the same time. The PC will automatically warn you if the battery power is becoming dangerously low, and will suspend the PC before the battery is completely drained. If you need to carry on using the portable PC, but have no mains power source available, you will need to replace the battery.

How to replace the battery

1 The battery can be released by sliding a catch to one side.

2 The replacement battery fits into the same slot (Figure 1.83).

In the same way that upgrading the hard drive memory on a non-portable PC involves taking a full backup prior to replacement and restoring the data and software afterwards, upgrading the hard drive on a laptop or on another portable PC is equally time-consuming and fraught with possible data-loss problems.

Replacement battery

Figure 1.83
The battery in a laptop

How to replace the hard drive memory

1 Back up data to another storage device, e.g. a CD.

2 Take copies of any software.

3 Turn off the PC.

4 Unscrew the drive from the PC case and replace with the new one.

5 Turn on the PC. The operating system should identify the change in hardware and install any drivers that are needed.

PC cards can be changed while the PC is still turned on; this is called **hot swapping**. Full details of the procedures to follow in replacing cards are given on page 202, so only an overview is given here.

Figure 1.84
Type I, II and III cards

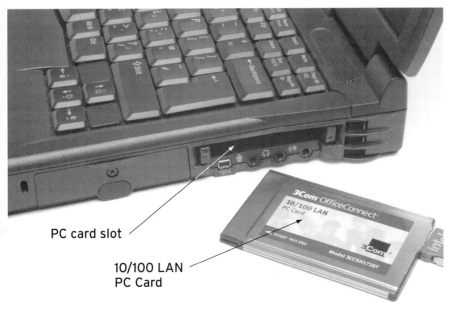

PC card slot

10/100 LAN
PC Card

How to replace PC cards

1 Go through the Control Panel and Add/Remove Hardware to reach the Plug/Unplug function. Identify the card that you want to remove and 'unplug' it (see Figure 1.84).

2 Physically remove the card, together with any other device attached to it, e.g. phone line.

3 Insert the replacement card. The operating system should automatically recognise it, 'plug' it in and load any device drivers. The first time you plug in a card you will have to provide some information but, thereafter, the PC will do everything for you.

Check Your Understanding 1.38

1 What is ghosting?
2 Give an example of a CPU upgrade that is possible.
3 Give an example of a CPU upgrade that is not possible.
4 Why might you need to replace the battery on a laptop PC?
5 What is hot swapping?

Revision 1

Remember these facts:

1 A PC needs both hardware and software to work.

2 A PC has four functions: input, processing, storage and output.

3 Peripherals: input – mouse, keyboard; output – monitor, printer.

4 External devices communicate with the PC through ports.

5 Types of ports: serial, parallel, USB, IEEE1394.

6 Inside a PC case: motherboard with the CPU chip; PSU; expansion slots.

7 CPU with internal systems bus: control unit, ALU and I/O unit, registers to hold data or instructions; a memory cache to hold data and for instructions prior to their being executed.

8 CMOS chip on motherboard holds configuration details (and is powered by the battery so is not lost when power is turned off).

9 Jumpers and DIP switches are used to set conditions manually.

10 ROM BIOS contains the jump address where the start-up instructions are stored. Flashing is the process of updating a ROM (an EEPROM) *in situ* using software.

11 Electricity is supplied to the PC as AC current. This is converted by the PSU into DC current and passed to components, directly or via other devices, e.g. in a SCSI chain. Some components have their own power supply, e.g. a printer.

12 Portable PCs operate from a (DC) battery. An AC adaptor takes AC power from the mains and uses it to recharge the battery.

13 Activity within the PC is measured in millions of cycles per second, or megahertz (MHz). Components work at different speeds (frequency), the CPU being the fastest.

14 System clock used to co-ordinate activity within PC; some components are synchronised with the system clock, e.g. SRAM. Some movement of data is asynchronous, e.g. FireWire IEEE1394 'real time'.

15 Data stored in a PC is in binary. A bit is either off or on and represents 0 or 1; 8 bits = 1 byte. Hex (short for hexadecimal) is a convenient way of writing addresses. ASCII is the standard for characters.

16 Circuit (expansion) boards can provide an interface between the motherboard and an external device.

17 Internal devices are connected to the CPU by buses.

18 Information travels within the PC on buses: data bus, address bus, control bus. Motherboard has different speed buses: ISA bus, PCI bus, AGP bus and system bus.

19 A chipset includes controllers for devices, e.g. memory controller, USB controller, IDE controller.

20 Primary storage into memory is fast but temporary. Secondary storage is on to a storage device (floppy disk, hard disk or CD-ROM), is slower but is permanent.

21 RAM is stored on SIMM, DIMM or RIMM chips.

22 Cache memory is a fast memory on the motherboard and/or very near the CPU.

23 IDE technology for disk drives allows up to four drives per PC, two per slot.

24 IRQs are assigned to devices at start up (through settings in CMOS). An IRQ line is used by the peripheral to attract the CPU's attention.

25 Software: firmware (the BIOS), operating system (e.g. Windows) and applications; device drivers control hardware.

Chapter 2 Diagnosing and troubleshooting

You need to recognise common symptoms and problems, and then know how to troubleshoot and isolate problems in a variety of components. As your experience as a technician grows, you will become more adept at recognising symptoms, identifying which components are at fault and fixing the problems that happen.

When you first start, though, where do you begin? You need a strategy for problem-solving.

In a small group, brainstorm how you solve problems at the moment.
Make notes.

A problem-solving strategy

To solve a problem, you first need to know what the problem is. This information is hidden in the mind of the user, but he or she is probably quite upset and won't be able to explain things in a cool and calm way. The user may also jump to conclusions and suggest things that are wrong with the PC, rather than just give you the facts. So, your first task is to calm the user down, bring a reassuring tone to the conversation and try to find out from him or her as much as you can about the problem. It is important that you listen carefully and ask the right questions:

◆ When did the problem start? Did the problem start just after a change in the system, e.g. just after new hardware or software had been added?

◆ Can the problem be recreated?

Figure 2.1
The jigsaw nature of problem-solving

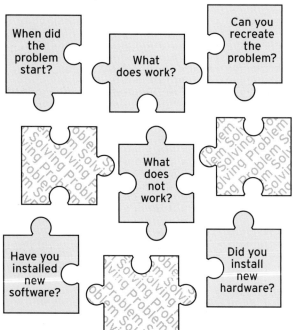

When did the problem start?

The problem started at some point in time, with or without the user noticing. If this was at the same time as some change to the system, e.g. the addition of new hardware, this suggests that the problem lies with the new hardware or its configuration. Taking the user back to a time when the PC was working will help him or her to think through the events that led up to the problem, in the right order, and exactly as it happened.

Taking notes is essential because solving problems on a PC can be a bit like putting a jigsaw together. You need all the bits – and to fit them together – before you can see the whole picture (Figure 2.1).

Thinking about the various symptoms that the user describes, you will try to match them with things that you already know about how PCs work. This may lead you to a conclusion as to what is going wrong and that can help you to solve the problem. However, you do need to find out in great detail exactly what the PC is or is not doing. PCs involve a number of interconnected parts and so, sometimes, the real challenge is to identify what does work and then, by a process of elimination, discover what does not work.

For a printer to print successfully, all components involved in the chain of action need to work and to be connected properly. Replacing components, systematically and one at a time, with components that you know work, should help you to identify the rogue component. So, if a printer will not print, what could be the source of the problem?

- The fault could lie with the PC, e.g. in the settings for using the printer.
- The cable connecting the printer to the PC could be faulty.
- The connections at either end of the print cable could be loose.
- The printer could be at fault, e.g. it has run out of paper or has been turned off.

Note that two or more of these components could coincidentally not be working, so don't assume that the fault lies just with one component! However, if the PC will print to a different printer, this would point to the cable or the printer being at fault. If the printer then works with a different PC, that just leaves the cable to be tested (see Figure 2.2).

The 'trick' is to work carefully and calmly, making notes about what combinations do work, and what combinations do not work.

Discuss problems that you have experienced with printers and how you have solved these problems. What checks did you make, and in what order?

Try not to jump to conclusions. However, if something seems obvious, just check it out. It may be that your experience with problems, or your intuition, is helping you to solve the problem. So, use this additional skill to your advantage. It will be important that your efforts result in things improving, not deteriorating! Therefore, you will need to think carefully before doing anything, and be sure to use all the skills and tools at your disposal. Some simple precautions will help you to avoid the obvious pitfalls:

- Take backups before making changes so that you can recover if things go wrong.
- Make notes, drawing sketches of how equipment was connected before you take things apart.
- Be systematic in your checking, making notes about what you have done, what worked and what did not work.

Recreating the problem

If you can recreate the problem, you could be half way to solving it. Using your knowledge of how PCs ought to work, seeing what it does at each stage leading to the fault should give good clues as to which component is not working. Replacing that component may well fix the problem.

However, sometimes, a fault is intermittent and you suspect one component but cannot be sure. In this case, you need to do lots of tests, making notes of the results and watching for signs of which component(s) may be failing.

Discuss intermittent faults that you have experienced.
How were they resolved?

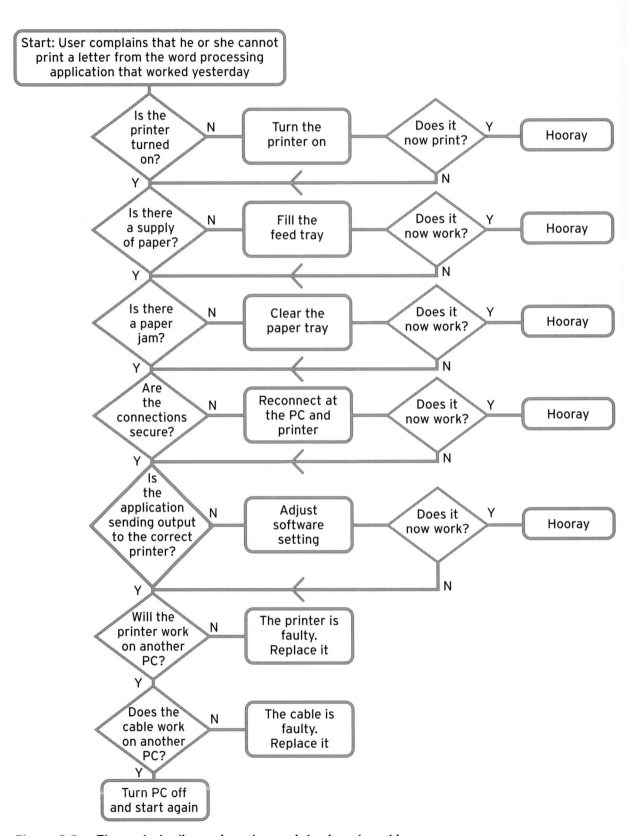

Figure 2.2 **The route to diagnosing why a printer is not working**

Your own approach to problem-solving needs to be positive:

- If you start with the assumption that you cannot imagine what the problem is, it's unlikely the solution will come into your mind.
- If you take the view that, no matter how long it takes or what it involves you will find a solution, your determination will help you to search through every possibility and arrive at the solution.

You should also look at each new problem as a welcome challenge that will help you to learn more about how a PC works and, with that extra knowledge or experience, become even better at your job.

You will most probably be working in a team. Others in your team will be able to help you and – given time – you will be able to help others.

In a small group, discuss how each of you has different experiences to bring to the whole group. Think of skills that each of you has that would help others in the group.

There are also lots of tools available to help you to find faults:

- **Software diagnostic tools** are supplied with the computer (Table 2.1). There are also others that you can buy – or license – for use on your PC (Table 2.2).

Table 2.1   *Software diagnostic tools available on a PC*

Program	Type of tool	Notes	See these pages
BIOS POST	Diagnostic tool built into a PC	Runs automatically whenever you power up; Checks all the hardware and will report any serious hardware faults	Boot process (17–24) Booting up (300–7)
DEFRAG.EXE	DOS/Windows utility	Rearranges data on a disk for more efficient I/O	Defragmentation (167) Disk defragmenter (Figure 7.15, page 263)
Dr Watson	Diagnostic tool	Useful for general protection faults; Kernel errors	
MEM.EXE	DOS utility	Reports memory configuration and usage on a PC	Memory (27–30, 49–53)
MSCONFIG	Windows tool	Useful to reconfigure system	
MSD.EXE	DOS utility supplied with earlier PCs	Creates and reports what is on a PC, i.e. its configuration; Includes BIOS, disks and memory usage Plus system resource assignments (IRQs and I/O addresses to LPT and serial ports)	IRQs (75–7); I/O addresses (78–9)
SCANDISK.EXE	Available as systems tool with Windows systems	Checks and reports problem on your hard disk; Includes any corruption of the file system and hard disk read errors; Runs automatically if you don't shut down properly!	
SYSEDIT.EXE	Windows tool	An editor that can be used to view and edit systems files, e.g. INI files, AUTOEXEC.BAT or CONFIG.SYS files	Systems files for Windows (Table 7.1, page 251)
Device Manager	Windows tool (see Figure 2.3)	Shows device driver and resource settings, etc., for individual devices; Can be used to resolve resource conflicts, e.g. IRQ, DMA channel or I/O address	Device Manager (132)
DirectX	Windows tool	Can be used to check hardware faults	Direct X (Figure 2.11, page 151)

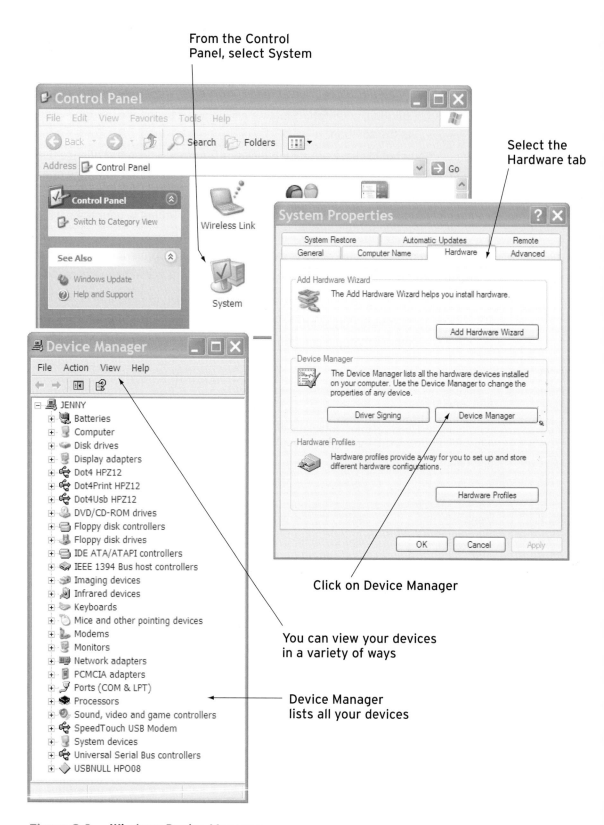

From the Control
Panel, select System

Select the
Hardware tab

Click on Device Manager

You can view your devices
in a variety of ways

Device Manager
lists all your devices

Figure 2.3   **Windows Device Manager**

Table 2.2 *Software tools that you can buy*

Type of software	Notes	See these pages
Antivirus software such as that provided by McAfee and Norton	PCs can be attacked by viruses/worms/trojans arriving with emails or during access to the Internet **Viruses** can erase data and corrupt files **Worms** – and the virus – can be sent by email to all your contacts using data from your address book **Trojans** are programs that hide a virus by pretending to be a file or program which is usually present – and harmless – on your PC Antivirus software checks for these intruders and zaps them	331–4
Diagnostic/ troubleshooting software*	Multi-purpose software utilities offer a range of diagnostic tests and reports on system status: system tune-ups: hardware diagnostics	Table 2.1, page 131
Uninstaller*	An uninstaller removes software applications that you no longer need It is useful to remove out-of-date material!	Figure 8.18, page 314

Notes: *Go to www.heinemann.co.uk/hotlinks for examples of useful websites where you can find more information.

CHAT *Unit 2 considers all the software tools listed in Table 2.1. Refer to the page number given in the last column for details of each tool.*

◆ **Hardware** such as a **multimeter** can be used to test and measure the electrical properties of your PC and its components.

Chapter 11 explains how to use a multimeter (page 364). Windows Device Manager is introduced in Unit 2 (page 132).

A **POST card** is a dedicated circuit board that is used to interpret the POST error codes which have been posted to address 80 (hex). This can save you counting the beeps given to signal an error! Table 9.1 (page 321) lists the POST error codes.

1 Common symptoms and problems; how to troubleshoot and isolate problems

As a technician, in your job, you may be presented with problems to fix that point to any one of many components of a PC:

◆ After turning on the PC power, nothing happens!

◆ The power light is off.

◆ The fan is not blowing out air.

◆ The floppy disk cannot be read.

◆ The paper fails to print.

During booting up the PC may report errors:

◆ No beep or a continuous beep, or a repeating short beep

◆ A POST error

◆ A parity error

 Discuss problems that you have experienced within your group.

Regardless of how the problem arises, you need to apply your problem-solving strategy:

◆ Calm the user – this may be yourself!

◆ Find out from the user when the problem started. If you are the user, you may find that talking to yourself – daft as it sounds – can actually help.

◆ Ask questions to check the details of the problem.

◆ Make notes.

◆ Try to recreate the problem.

Then, according to the problem and what the PC seems to be doing, you will start checking what does – and what does not – work.

For any device that is not working as you would like, you need to isolate the fault:

◆ There may be a problem with the cabling used to connect it to the PC.

◆ You may not have the correct hardware settings for any jumpers, or incorrect software settings on CMOS.

◆ There may be a conflict between two devices that is causing one or both of them not to work properly. You can find out more about **IRQ conflicts** and how to resolve them on page 76.

◆ Or the problem may be related to the device itself.

With a friend, discuss how you might identify an IRQ conflict and how you might resolve it.

Cables are an essential part of the PC system, connecting external peripherals to the ports. They are also used inside the PC case to connect devices to the PSU or to the motherboard. So, if any device is not working, the first thing to check is the cabling for that device.

What can go wrong?

◆ The wire within the cable may be damaged. You can test for connectivity using a multimeter. (See page 364 for details of how to use a multimeter.)

◆ You could choose the wrong type of cable. For each peripheral device that you plan to attach, there may be a choice of cabling and connector that would work – you need to make sure you choose the correct one. For different ways of connecting keyboards and mice to a PC, see pages 40 and 41.)

◆ If the cable is too long, this can cause data-corruption problems.

◆ You might use the wrong port for the connection. You may have to choose between a serial port or a parallel port, and configure the software accordingly.

◆ You may fail to fit the connection firmly into the port so that it is loose and not all pins make contact. If you move a PC, a loosely fitting connection may come adrift if any tension is put on the cable.

◆ One or more pins could be damaged. This can be avoided by careful handing, and taking care not to misorientate the connection.

◆ You might misorientate the connector, i.e. connect it the wrong way round.

How would you know there might be a problem with the cabling?

◆ One sure-fire indication that the cabling is incorrect is if the lights stay on, e.g. for the floppy drive or the hard drive.

◆ Another indication would be a POST error message suggesting that you have no boot device available. (For the beep error codes and other start-up messages that the POST may give you, see pages 321–3.).

Share with friends details of situations where you investigated a PC fault and the cabling was the cause

Jumper settings and **CMOS settings** are specified in the documentation supplied with any device, so a quick check of this should solve any problems that relate to this aspect of the installation. **IRQ conflicts** tend to happen just after a new item of equipment is installed; its settings clash with another peripheral that was working fine until you changed the configuration, and now neither peripheral functions properly. You can find out more about IRQ conflicts and how to resolve them on page 76.

1 Write down your problem-solving strategy.
2 Explain how you might isolate a fault.
3 Give two examples of how cabling might be the source of a fault.
4 What is a jumper setting?
5 What is an IRQ conflict?

This section now considers all the components that you have already met and lists what might go wrong with each of them. The components are considered in alphabetical order here to help you find the relevant section, once you have isolated which component might be at fault.

BIOS

Unless there is a power cut when you are in the process of flashing the BIOS, there should not be a problem from the BIOS. It is important, though, that any upgrades are made as necessary, e.g. to fix a compatibility problem that has been identified by the manufacturer.

If you make changes to the BIOS setup that causes the PC to stop responding, you will need to use the Restore Defaults command to erase your settings and go back to the original factory settings (see Figure 2.4). You ought to have kept a note of settings that have been done – ones that worked – since you obtained the PC, and be able to return to where you were before you tried to make the changes to the BIOS.

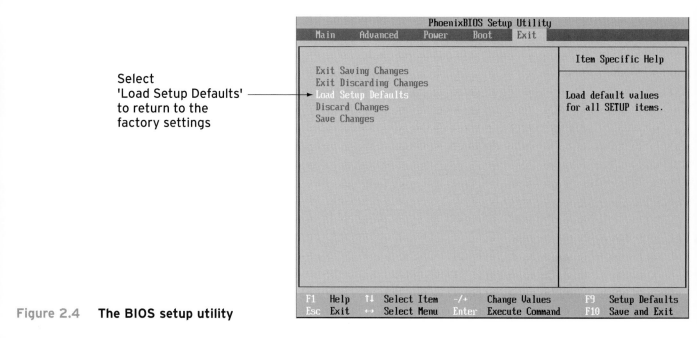

Select
'Load Setup Defaults'
to return to the
factory settings

Figure 2.4   **The BIOS setup utility**

For Windows 2000, the BIOS must be compliant to the ACPI (advanced configuration and power interface). If you have a BIOS which is not ACPI compliant, you may experience boot errors and your PC may crash frequently. The ACPI includes the OnNow standard without which the Windows 2000 Setup program cannot communicate with hardware devices.

What does it mean?   *The OnNow standard can start the PC with a single key stroke.*

Go and try out 2.1

For a given PC, check whether the BIOS is ACPI compliant by:

1   referring to the documentation supplied with your BIOS and/or your motherboard
2   referring to the HCL (hardware compatibility list), and
3   accessing the PC manufacturer's website.

If your BIOS is the most up-to-date version and is compatible for your PC, there should be no problems, but if there is a problem it is most likely to happen during the boot process. Chapter 1 (page 17) and Unit 2, Chapter 8 (page 300) explain the boot process in detail. Unit 2, Chapter 9 (page 321) gives full information about the error codes that might be generated during the boot process.

CD-ROM drives

You may have a variety of problems with CD-ROM drives:

◆ The BIOS may not 'see' the CD-ROM drive.

◆ You cannot see any files on the CD-ROM drive.

◆ There are data transfer problems, i.e. the CD-ROM drive is not writing to or not reading correctly from the disk.

In a small group, discuss problems that you have experienced with CD-ROM drives, and how these were resolved.

If the BIOS does not recognise that you have a CD-ROM drive attached, the problem is probably to do with your installation:

◆ There is a faulty connection. Check the connection to the motherboard and to the PSU.

◆ If the CD-ROM is an IDE device, you may have an incorrect jumper setting, e.g. of master/slave. If you have signalled two masters, or two slaves, on any one connection, the BIOS will not recognise the presence of any of them. If there is only one device, it should be set to 'single'. (Chapter 1 (page 95) explains how to install and configure IDE devices).

◆ If the CD-ROM drive is an SCSI device, check the ID assignment as well as the jumper settings. If the last device in the chain is not set correctly as the terminator, or an earlier device in the chain is set as terminator, this will cause recognition problems for the PC. (Chapter 1 (page 100) explains how to install and configure SCSI devices.)

If the BIOS still does not recognise the drive, you may have a boot virus. So, run a virus scan program to eliminate this possibility. If you cannot write to a CD-R, this may be because it has already been written to, and this is only allowed the once, and even then requires a special CD writing application. If you cannot read from or write to a CD-RW disk, it may be because the packet-writing software needed for this has not been installed, or is not installed correctly.

1 Give examples of two problems you might have with a CD-ROM drive.
2 What is meant by master and slave drive?
3 What is an SCSI device ID?

CPU

Any problem with the CPU is easily fixed: you replace it. However, what may appear to be a problem with the CPU might well be caused by some other component:

◆ An overheated CPU will fail, but the fault lies with the cooling system.

◆ An underpowered CPU will not perform well, but the fault lies with the PSU.

◆ A CPU which is not compatible with the motherboard and/or its chipset will not work as planned.

Simply replacing a failed CPU with a newer version will not solve the problem. The root cause of the problem needs to be fixed, too. It may be that the CPU is just not seated properly. If a **ZIF (zero insertion force)** socket is being used, make sure that it is truly locked into place.

How can you tell that the CPU is going to fail?

Several conditions would suggest that the CPU is likely to fail, and you should therefore look for the cause of these problems to protect the CPU:

- The PC fails to boot.
- The PC will boot, but the operating system does not start.
- The PC gives parity errors during the POST process, and for more than just one device.
- The PC locks within minutes of booting up.
- The PC crashes either at start up or when you are running applications.

Looking at the last problem first, the fault could lie with the CPU or the motherboard or the chipset, or it may be due to a corrupted file within the applications software. You could – and may be should – go through the process of checking the CPU, motherboard and chipset, but it may be wiser simply to try reinstalling the applications software. Companies that have many computer users to support tend to use ghosting to reinstate an employee's PC as a first attempt to fix a problem. A note is kept of what was going wrong so that the IT support team can watch for patterns and may be identify the source of the fault at some later date, but this very quick process is the most painless way of getting an employee back to work on his or her PC.

What does it mean?

Ghosting software creates an image of a PC installation that can then be copied to another PC.

A PC that boots okay but freezes soon after may be overheating. To check this, turn the PC off and wait long enough for the CPU to cool down. If you turn on and it boots okay but then crashes again in about the same time frame, overheating is your problem.

Why should a CPU overheat?

The cooling system relies on a heat sink and/or a cooling fan plus a good supply of cool air to take the heat away:

- If the CPU and heat sink have parted company, the air gap between them will prevent the heat sink doing its job, and the CPU will overheat. In fixing this, use plenty of thermal paste to glue the two together again.
- If the PC case is not closed properly, the flow of air to cool the CPU is not as effective as it ought to be, and overheating of the CPU may result.
- **Expansion slot covers** are part of the cooling system (Figure 2.5). If an expansion slot is not being used, it is important to use its cover so that the case does not have huge holes through which air can enter or leave and ruin the planned route of air to cool the CPU.

Figure 2.5
Expansion slot covers

Unused expansion slots need covers to ensure correct airflow within PC case

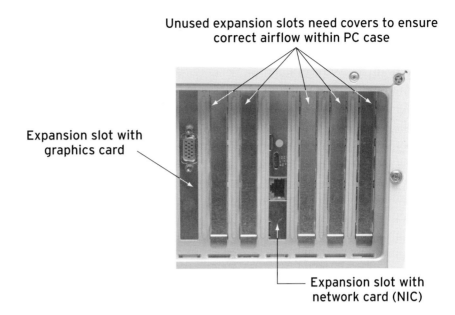

Expansion slot with graphics card

Expansion slot with network card (NIC)

If the faults suggest an overheating problem, but you find nothing wrong with the cooling system, the problem may lie with synchronisation between the CPU and the motherboard. If they are not using the same settings for the system clock, this can result in their being so out of tune that that system crashes.

◆ *Check:* the motherboard documentation to find out what settings should have been used.

◆ *Check:* system clock jumper settings on the motherboard.

◆ *Check:* BIOS settings for the system timers.

What happens when the CPU is not being powered correctly?

If, during the POST process, you hear a beep code to indicate a CPU fault, check first whether the CPU is powered at all. See Unit 2, Chapter 9 (page 321) for details of the beep error codes and other start-up messages that the POST may give you. Use a multimeter (page 364) to do this.

◆ If any leads are dead – or even just low – you will need to replace the PSU.

◆ If the power supply is okay, the problem lies with the CPU and you need to replace it.

If you do replace the CPU and the problems persist, the next culprit to consider is the motherboard itself (see page 364).

Check Your Understanding 2.3

1 What is a ZIF socket?
2 How can you tell that the CPU is going to fail? Give three examples.
3 What is meant by ghosting?
4 In what circumstances might a CPU overheat?
5 Explain the importance of expansion slot covers in the cooling system.
6 How can a multimeter be used to check whether the CPU is receiving power?

DVD

Like the CD drive, the DVD drive is also an optical disk storage device. While the same size physically, it is double sided so it holds at least twice the data that you can fit on to a CD-ROM. It may hold 25 times as much, depending on the format used. A DVD drive can be used to read CDs, read DVD-ROMs and play DVD-video movies. An internal DVD may use the IDE interface, but external DVDs will be on the SCSI interface. Like the CD-ROM drive, sound is through the sound card. In addition, video is through the video card.

Problems for DVDs are very similar to those for CD-ROMs (page 136), plus those for the sound card (page 154) and the video card (page 148).

Discuss with friends any problems you may have experienced while playing DVDs – and how you solved them.

Floppy disk drives

You may have a variety of problems with floppy drives:

◆ The BIOS may not 'see' the floppy drive.

◆ The floppy light won't go off, or there is no light.

◆ The PC will not boot from the floppy disk drive.

◆ There are data transfer problems, i.e. the floppy drive is not writing or not reading correctly to the floppy disk.

Floppy drives are relatively inexpensive and so, if the fault can be identified as being with the drive, the drive is simply replaced.

In a small group, discuss problems you have experienced with floppy disks and how you have resolved them.

If the BIOS does not recognise that you have a floppy drive attached, the problem is probably to do with your installation (see page 48):

◆ There is a faulty connection. Check the connection to the motherboard – does the red stripe line up with pin 1? – and to the PSU.

◆ Check the position of the twist in the ribbon cable.

◆ Check that the BIOS has the correct setting for the size and capacity of floppy drive (Figure 2.6).

If the BIOS still does not recognise the floppy drive, you may have a boot virus. So run a virus scan program to eliminate this possibility.

Figure 2.6
This 3.5" floppy disc has a capacity of 1.44/1.25MB

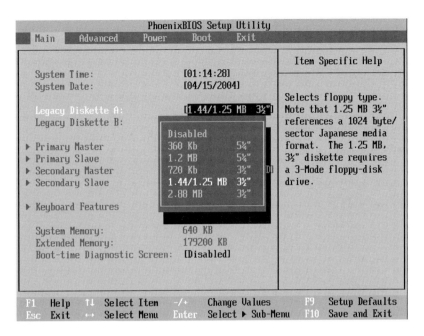

If the floppy drive light stays on, you have incorrect orientation with the ribbon cable. Check that the ribbon is connected with the red stripe lining up with pin 1 on the floppy drive slot.

If there is no light, the problem is with the power supply; check the connection with the PSU.

You may only need to boot from the floppy drive in exceptional circumstances but, if you cannot do so, your PC becomes inoperable. Failure to boot from the floppy drive could be for one of three reasons:

- Your A: drive may not be listed as the first boot drive – or your floppy drive may not be listed at all – in the CMOS settings.
- The floppy disk may not be bootable, i.e. it does not contain the requisite files. (For details of the files that are needed for a boot, see page 252.)
- There may be a problem with the drive itself, as detailed above, and the BIOS cannot see it.

Floppy disks can become damaged through mishandling or poor storage so, if you experience error messages reporting a failure to read or write, this would indicate physical damage to the disk surface – or a problem with the drive:

- If the drive is at fault, you may have misaligned read/write heads – and the solution is to replace the floppy disk drive.
- However, before discarding the drive, check that it is not the floppy disk that is the problem by trying another floppy disk – one that you know is okay. If the drive reads another disk with a problem then the fault lies with the original floppy disk. Scandisk/Check Disk is the utility to use to check the surface of the floppy disk – or you simply discard the floppy disk! (See page 131 for more details of ScanDisk and other utility programs that you can use to check your floppy disk.)

If you cannot read from a floppy disk, it may be that it has not been formatted for the PC you are working on (see page 34).

If you cannot write to a floppy disk, it may just be that the disk is write-protected. This can be fixed – if you really do want to write to the disk, and it is not just your mistake in picking up the wrong floppy disk – by sliding the write-protect tab across on the disk (Figure 2.7). You will also not be able to write to a floppy disk if it is full, but an error message will let you know if this is the case.

Figure 2.7
The write-protect tab on a floppy disk

Floppy disk

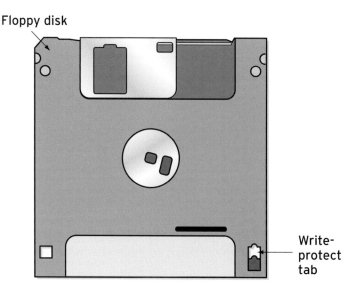

Write-protect tab

1   What is the significance of the red stripe along the side of the ribbon cabling for a floppy drive?
2   What is the significance of the twist in the cabling for a floppy drive?
3   What is a boot virus?
4   Why might you not be able to read data from a floppy disk?
5   Why might you not be able to write data to a floppy disk?

Hard drives

Make sure you take a full backup of the hard disk before making any changes or dismantling equipment.

You may have a variety of problems with hard drives:

◆ The BIOS may not 'see' the hard drive.

◆ At the command prompt, no letter (for the logical drive) may appear.

◆ You cannot see any files on the hard drive.

◆ There are data-transfer problems, i.e. the hard drive is not writing or not reading correctly to the disk.

In a small group, discuss problems you have experienced with floppy disks and how you have resolved them.

If the BIOS does not recognise that you have a hard drive attached, the problem is probably to do with your installation (see page 95):

◆ There is a faulty connection. Check the connection to the motherboard and to the PSU.

◆ There is an incorrect jumper setting, e.g. of master/slave. If you have signalled two masters, or two slaves, on any one connection, the BIOS will not recognise the presence of any of them.

Clean booting from a floppy disk may indicate that you have a conflict between your hard drives, so this is the first thing to do.

What does it mean? *A clean boot involves booting your PC using a floppy disk that has minimal files – as required for booting up – and no other complications.*

If the hard drive is an SCSI device (see page 100), and you are experiencing problems, make these checks:

◆ Are you using the correct ID assignment as well as the correct jumper settings? If the last device in the chain is not set correctly as the terminator, or an earlier device in the chain is set as terminator, this will cause recognition problems for the PC.

◆ Is the CMOS setting for the hard drive None or Auto-detect?

◆ Is the most up-to-date device driver installed?

If the BIOS still does not recognise the hard drive, you may have a **boot virus**. So run a virus scan program to eliminate this possibility. (See page 331 for details of how to protect against viruses and how to remove them.)

The lack of a logical device letter at the prompt would suggest that the hard disk has yet to be partitioned – or, if it has, then the operating system does not recognise this. Such a situation could arise if you have partitioned with one operating system (e.g. using Dynamic Disk for disk management improvements in XP) but then try to use the disk on an earlier version of Windows.

If you cannot see any files on the hard disk, it probably has not been formatted. Or, if it has been formatted, it is not using a filing system recognised by the operating system. For example, Windows 98 does not recognise NTFS.

If you experience error messages reporting a failure to read or write, this would indicate physical damage to the disk surface. Scandisk/Check Disk is a utility that allows you to check the surface of the hard disk. See Table 2.1 (page 131) for more details of ScanDisk and other utility programs that you can use to check your hard disk.

Finally, you should accept that a hard drive has moving parts and these wear out in time. So, if your hard drive action becomes louder over time, this is an indication that its bearings are wearing and it may fail soon.

Check Your Understanding 2.5

1 As a safety precaution, what should you do before investigating any fault related to the hard drive?
2 What is clean booting?
3 What CMOS settings should be used for an SCSI hard drive?
4 Briefly explain what is meant by partitioning and formatting a hard drive.

Keyboard

Keyboards are relatively cheap components so, if you have a problem, it is usually more cost-effective to replace than to attempt a repair. Faults tend to be from one of two sources:

◆ The cable may be defective. This can result in characters appearing on the screen that bear no resemblance to what you keyed in.

◆ A key may be stuck, due to being accidentally held down, e.g. if you have a book resting on the keyboard – or there may be dirt beneath the key which is making the contact constant. Releasing a stuck key from under a book is easy and only takes a few seconds once you realise the problem. If it is jammed down you could try prising it free gently.

If fluid is split on the keyboard causing stuck keys and any other problems, you might consider washing the keyboard – in a dishwasher on the top tray with a 'not heated dry' option – and leaving it to dry out completely for several days before trying it out. In the mean time, you need a replacement keyboard!

In a small group, share experiences of attempting to clean a keyboard. How successful were you?

Memory

See Chapter 1 (page 27) to find out more about memory, cache memory and storage devices. Chapter 4 (page 181) focuses on memory in greater detail.

Table 8.1 (page 286) lists the minimum memory requirements for a range of operating systems. Memory requirements will also be increased depending on the peripherals that you have in the configuration, and what applications software is installed.

If you have insufficient RAM installed, your PC will use space on the hard disk to create a virtual memory. (Unit 2, Chapter 7 (page 268) explains memory management and virtual memory.) However, this means your system is working more slowly than it might. Adding more memory may fix this problem. Chapter 1 (page 49) looks at adding and removing memory, and considers upgrading memory (page 122).

Memory problems may be disguised as problems with the motherboard or other components, so they are difficult to isolate. There are a variety of sources of memory problems:

◆ You have installed more memory than your PC can handle, or installed incompatible memory modules. (See page 49 for details of how to select memory and how to install the correct amount to meet your needs.)

◆ You have incorrect BIOS CMOS settings.

◆ The memory module is damaged.

◆ The memory module is not seated properly.

When the fault arises, this can indicate the source of the problem:

◆ If problems arise just after new software has been installed, then perhaps you have insufficient memory. Check the memory requirements; it is bound to be higher than earlier versions of the same software.

◆ New software may well have a bug which causes memory problems, so check the vendor's website to see if this error has been reported and whether there is a fix that needs to be done.

◆ If problems arise just after you have installed new hardware – or even after just removing hardware – then you may have dislodged a connector in the process. So, double check all connections. Also check whether any new hardware needs more memory than you have available.

If there seems to be no reason for the memory failure, it may be the memory module is at fault.

◆ Check for corrosion. When buying memory it is important to match tin with tin and gold with gold on the contacts (see page 122).

◆ Check for signs of overheating.

◆ Check the power supply.

So, how do you know if there is a memory problem?

There are lots of situations which could point to a problem with memory:

◆ Your PC won't boot and you hear a beep.

◆ Your PC boots but the screen stays blank. Putting non-parity RAM in a PC that has ECC memory, or SDRAM in one that supports only EDO, will prevent the boot process completing and results in the blank screen. So check the specification for your PC and what memory is installed.

What does it mean?

ECC = error correcting code; EDO = extended data output.

◆ Your PC boots but the memory count is incorrect. It will be less than the actual amount because there is some memory that it has not been recognised. Check that you don't have the wrong type of memory installed. For example, if you have dual-bank memory added to a single bank, the PC will count only half of the dual-bank memory. There may also be more memory than the upper limit visible to your PC.

◆ Your PC gives you an error message.

Memory error messages can take many forms:

◆ Memory failure at xxx, read xxxx, expecting xxxx.

◆ Memory address error at xxxx.

◆ Memory parity interrupt at xxxx.

◆ Memory verify error at xxxx.

◆ Memory mismatch error.

Here, xxxx is the hexadecimal address of the memory where the fault lies. (See page 70 for an explanation of how memory is addressed using the hexadecimal system of numbers.)

Any such message can indicate a failing memory module – or a problem between old memory and new memory:

◆ If removing a newly installed memory module removes the fault, replace the old memory with the new memory.

◆ If this does not solve the problem, there is a problem with the new memory: it is either defective or it is not compatible with your system.

However, memory errors can show up when the problem is actually with the motherboard. Equally, many situations can be caused by a memory problem – e.g. if the PC crashes or reboots itself for no apparent reason – but you will try other devices first to isolate them. Only when you have checked that all other devices are working, should you consider whether defective memory might be the cause.

Memory problems need not even be hardware related. Software errors can happen but rebooting may well solve these problems:

◆ Windows may write part of its registry to a part of RAM which is defective. Unit 2 (page 261) explains the role of the registry.

◆ There may be bugs within software which cause general protection faults and exception reports, such as page faults. Unit 2 (page 328) looks at how to solve general protection faults.

Check Your Understanding 2.6

1 How might corrosion happen in a memory module?
2 Give two examples of situations which suggest a fault with the memory.
3 Give one example of a software-related memory fault.

Modems

Modems and Internet access problems provide the source of the most common faults that technicians face on a daily basis:

◆ Windows does not 'see' the modem.

◆ The **ISP (Internet service provider)** software does not 'see' the modem.

◆ The modem achieves a connection, but it is poor quality and/or it then disconnects.

◆ No dial tone found.

In a small group, discuss problems you have had with modems, and how you have solved them.

If Windows does not see the modem, there may be a conflict between the jumper settings on the modem and the settings that Windows is assuming for Plug and Play. (Chapter 1, page 80, explains how to install a modem.)

◆ Check the documentation for both.

◆ You can use Device Manager to find out what Windows thinks is attached to the port that is being used by the modem, and whether this presents a problem (Figure 2.8). (See Unit 2 (page 132) for details of how to use Device Manager.)

◆ The Control Panel also offers a modem diagnostics option. This sends test AT commands to the modem to see what happens. See Chapter 1 (page 79) and, in particular, Table 1.15 (page 82) for details of AT commands.

If the ISP software does not see the modem, this may be because you have changed modems and the ISP software has not noticed:

◆ Delete all modem device drivers apart from the one that you need for the new modem and then rerun the setup software for the ISP.

◆ Check also that the correct COM port has been identified for the modem.

You may have a dial tone but experience a noisy connection. This may be due to an overlong telephone cable or a mistake in the connectors. Figure 1.52 (page 80) shows how the modem ought to be connected to the phone line.

Figure 2.8
The Diagnostics tab within the Modem Options of the Control Panel

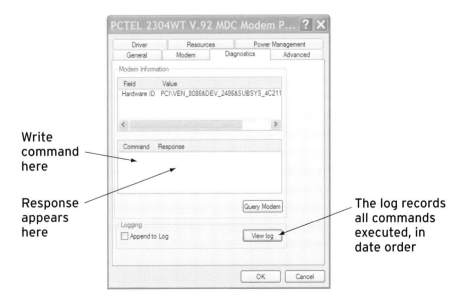

Write command here

Response appears here

The log records all commands executed, in date order

If the modem is connected to the Internet, but then the connection fails, it may be a problem with the ISP. If you try again later and get the same problem, it may still be a problem at the ISP end. However, it would be worth checking that dial-up networking and TCP/IP have been correctly installed as networking options. Unit 2 explains dial-up networking (page 352) and TCP/IP protocols (page 346).

If the modem complains that there is no dial tone, then there is none – and you need to check the connections to the phone line:

◆ Is there a loose connection?

◆ Is the phone line connected to the correct jack on the modem?

◆ Does the phone company have a fault on the line? Check the existence of a phone line by plugging in an ordinary telephone – or opting to hear the dial tone through your internal modem.

If the modem seems okay, and the card appears to be working, you may simply need to reset your modem, using the AT command ATZ. Table 1.15 (page 82) lists the AT commands.

Check Your Understanding 2.7

1 What does ISP stand for?
2 What may explain a noisy connection?
3 How might you check that there is a dial tone on a phone line?

Monitor/video

Chapter 1 (page 42) describes monitors in some detail, and tells you how to install a video card (page 60).

Check Your Understanding 2.8

1 What three ways might be used to connect a monitor to a PC?
2 How do you set the resolution and colour depth for a monitor?

If the monitor is displaying nothing at all – just a black screen – ask yourself these questions to narrow down the source of the problem:

◆ Is the power light on? If not, it could need connecting to the PC, plugging in or turning on!

◆ What are the settings for contrast and brightness? Are they high enough? If not, adjust these using the controls on the monitor casing.

◆ Is the video card slotted in properly? See Chapter 1 (page 9) to identify the location of the video board within the PC casing, and page 60 for installing the video card.

◆ Does the video work during the boot process, displaying the usual text messages, but then fail? This would indicate a problem with Windows rather than a hardware fault.

◆ Does the monitor work if you start in safe mode? If so, it is probably the video driver that is at fault. (See Unit 2 (page 306) for details of how to start in safe mode.)

If the screen does display something, but just garbage, check out the device driver; it will either be corrupted or the wrong one.

If the screen image looks strange in that it is too red or too green or too blue, the problem is probably with the monitor hardware:

◆ Check that the cabling is securely connected; a loose cable can result in one of the three colours (RGB) not firing properly.

◆ Check for bent pins.

◆ Check the contrast and brightness controls on the monitor.

If you see a black ring on the screen, you need to adjust the screen size so that it is centred and large enough to fill the screen. If the picture is clearly recognisable but there are perhaps black specs in certain situations, or red or green or blue patches on what should be a white area, these are hardware faults.

CASE STUDY   Nigel the novice PC user

Nigel has found this explanation of how a monitor creates coloured dots on the screen:

The way the monitor displays colour is through a rectangular surface with coloured phosphors on it. When the CRT is heated, it emits negatively charge electrons which are attracted to the positively charged front of the CRT where they strike the phosphors and cause them to light up momentarily. The RBG guns within the CRT direct the electrons through the triad of phosphors that will generate a single pixel, in such a way as to create exactly the colour mix of red, green and blue that is needed for that dot (see Figure 2.9).

1 What does CRT stand for?
2 What does RGB stand for?
3 Find out the dot pitch of a monitor.

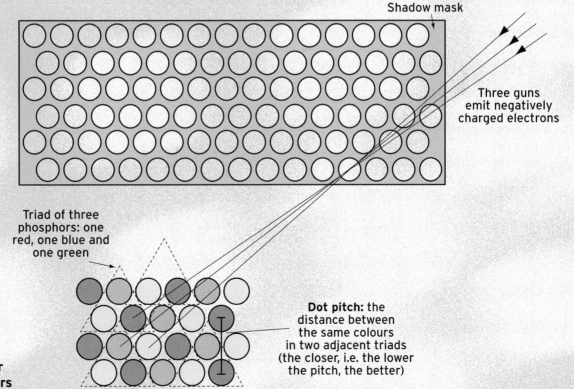

Figure 2.9
How a monitor displays colours

To investigate the possibility of hardware faults with a monitor, you might use a **monitor-testing program**. This identifies damaged phosphors, convergence problems or other faults that you cannot fix, and any of which may mean the monitor needs to be replaced.

What does it mean?

Convergence problems happen when the dots in a triad are misaligned in some way.

Go and try out 2.2

1 Research the Internet for monitor-testing programs.
2 With the permission of the owner of your PC, download a free monitor-testing program, and try it out.

Monitor problems may be software related. An application may have a problem running through your video card to create the graphics on screen:

◆ The software may have a troubleshooting option to help you to overcome any problems and that should be your first line of attack.

◆ If that does not improve the situation, you could try turning down the acceleration setting in Windows (Figure 2.10).

Figure 2.10
The Monitor Troubleshooting tab

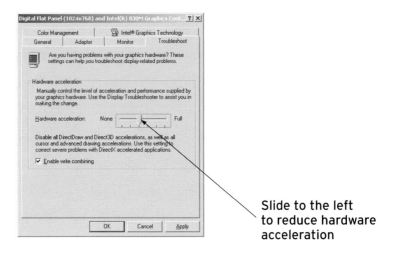

Slide to the left to reduce hardware acceleration

◆ If the problem is still not solved, you may run the DirectX troubleshooter (Figure 2.11).

It may simply be that your device driver is out of date, so check that it is the most up-to-date version available.

If you have made changes to settings and the net result is an unreadable image, reboot your PC in safe mode (page 306), and choose a lower setting, e.g. a lower refresh rate or lower resolution. When you reboot in normal mode, all should be well!

(a)

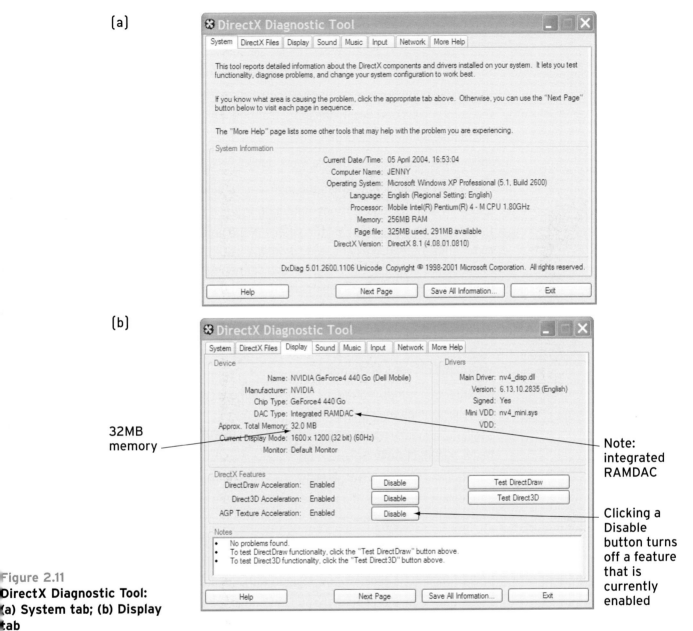

32MB
memory

Note:
integrated
RAMDAC

Clicking a
Disable
button turns
off a feature
that is
currently
enabled

(b)

Figure 2.11
DirectX Diagnostic Tool:
(a) System tab; (b) Display
tab

Motherboards

Chapter 4 (page 181) focuses on the motherboard, so only brief details are given here.

The motherboard is the most important component in the PC. If you have a problem and have exhausted the testing of all other devices that might be to blame, you will need to consider whether the fault lies with the motherboard. The POST reports will give the best clue as to the source of the problem. The meanings of the POST audible/visual error codes are given on page 321.

Before replacing the motherboard, though, make sure that no other device is causing the motherboard to fail. If it is, it will damage the replacement motherboard as well. Check in particular whether the PSU is producing too much power.

Mouse

Problems with the mouse fall into these groups:

◆ Windows does not see the mouse and gives an error message at start up.

◆ The mouse pointer leaps about on screen and is difficult to control.

◆ The pointer will not move in one particular direction.

◆ The mouse pointer freezes on screen.

If Windows does not see the mouse, work out which part may be at fault:

◆ Check the connection between the mouse and the port.

◆ Establish that the mouse is not at fault by trying it on a different PC.

◆ To isolate the mouse as being the source of the problem, you can use keyboard commands instead. If a keyboard command works, such as opening the Windows Start menu by pressing the Start key, but you cannot give the same command by a click of the mouse, then it really is the mouse that is the problem.

Like keyboards, mice are relatively cheap components and it may be more cost-effective to replace a mouse than to spend a lot of time trying to work out what is wrong. However, many problems with a mouse are due to poor maintenance and a thorough clean will transform the mouse's performance:

◆ A pointer that jumps around the screen is almost certainly due to a build-up of dirt on the rollers inside the mouse.

◆ Similarly, a mouse that refuses to go in one direction probably has one roller so dirty that it no longer rotates.

If cleaning does not solve the problem, the contacts or rollers may be so worn that it is time to replace the mouse. If a mouse pointer freezes on screen, however, there are several possibilities to consider:

◆ It may be that the current application is at fault and is 'not responding' and, with that condition, the mouse has no effect. So there may be nothing wrong with the mouse. Unit 2 (page 303) explains how to cope with a system lock-out.

◆ There may be an IRQ conflict that you will need to resolve, perhaps by changing jumper settings. Chapter 1 (page 75) explains IRQs, with Figure 1.49 (page 76) illustrating how to change an IRQ using software through the Control Panel.

Check Your Understanding 2.9

1 Why might a mouse pointer become difficult to control?

2 You think a mouse is working but it does not work on this PC.
   How might you check that the fault does not lie with the mouse?

3 You are running Word and the mouse seems to have stopped working.
   How can you check whether the mouse is at fault or the software?

4 How might a mouse perform if you do not clean it regularly?

NIC

Problems that might arise with networks are discussed in Chapters 6 (page 227) and 10 (page 339).

Power supply

If you get an electrical shock from the case (other than ESD), there is a problem with the PSU, and one that can be dangerous. It is unlikely that you can fix it, so you should replace the PSU. Other situations can indicate problems with the PSU:

◆ After turning on the PC power, nothing happens!
◆ The power light is off.
◆ The fan is not blowing out air.
◆ There is no beep or a continuous beep or a repeating short beep.
◆ A POST error in the 020–029 range.
◆ A parity error.

In trying to locate the source of the problem, make these checks:

◆ Is there power to the wall socket?
◆ Is the power cord plugged into the wall socket?
◆ Is the power cord plugged into the surge suppressor?
◆ Is the surge suppressor switched on and working?

If the power is available and plugged in and the surge suppressor is working, the fault lies with the power switch or the PSU. Either way, you may need to replace the PSU! Trying a replacement PSU should confirm that the old one is not functioning properly.

If the PSU is 'dead', the replacement should solve the problem. However, problems can arise when a PSU begins to fail and starts to cause intermittent errors which make you think another component is at fault:

◆ If a memory problem is reported but cites a different address, it may be the PSU that is faulty rather than the memory.
◆ If the PC reboots itself after a random amount of time, there could be a problem with the PSU.

Problems with the PSU fall into three groups:

◆ **Physical failure** means the PSU is not generating the right voltages on the right wires. This usually means the PC does not even boot up. Table 1.2 (page 14) lists the correct voltages needed by various components. You can check the voltages using a multimeter (see page 364). A replacement PSU is usually the most cost-effective solution – and the safest option.
◆ **Overloading** can happen if you have too many devices configured with your PC. You will notice problems at start up when the drives use a lot of power to spin up, or while working if you try to access the hard drive, e.g. to save a file. The replacement PSU will need a higher wattage if you are to see a solution to this problem.

◆ **Overheating** is caused either by the passage of air being blocked, or – and it may seem strange – by not having the case closed. Like any air-conditioning system, the cooling system in a PC relies on a clear airway, and one that directs air where it is needed, i.e. across those components that need the most cooling. So, if you leave the case open, or fail to fit expansion slot covers the flow of air is not so cleverly directed and important components may overheat and, eventually, fail.

Check Your Understanding 2.10

1 What does ESD stand for?
2 How could you check whether the PSU has failed physically?
3 How can overloading happen?
4 How can overheating happen?

Printers

Chapter 5 (page 214) is devoted to printers and includes a subsection which looks at common problems with printers.

SCSI devices

If one or more devices within – or more likely at the end of – a chain of devices is not working properly, check your installation of each individual device:

◆ Are you using the correct ID assignment as well as the jumper settings?
◆ Is the last device in the chain set correctly as the terminator?

See the entries for hard drives (page 142) and CD-ROMs (page 136).

Sound card/audio

Installing a sound card is the same as installing any other expansion card (page 60), except there are some extra connections to worry about (see Figure 2.12):

◆ Sound cards can be affected by EMF (electromagnetic field) emissions from other components, so the sound card needs to be placed in a slot as far away as possible from the PSU and any disk drives.

◆ You will probably have two speakers, but there is only one speaker jack on the sound card, labelled as SPK (short for speaker) or simply 'Output'. So one speaker is attached to this jack and then the other speaker is connected to the first speaker, as in a chain. The speakers may be battery operated but it is more likely there will be an AC adaptor you need to connect to a power source – and to turn on.

◆ The microphone has to be connected to the MIC (short for microphone) port on the sound card.

◆ The next two connections on the sound card are called the 'Line out' and 'Line in' ports. Line out is for an external recording device or could be used for a different set of speakers. 'Line in' may or may not be present but is for taking sound from elsewhere, e.g. from your stereo system.

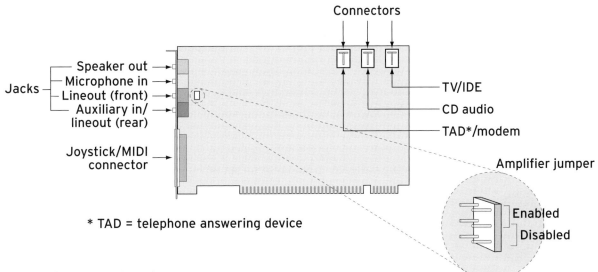

Figure 2.12   **Connecting a sound system**

CHAT   *Discuss how you might use the 'Line in' port to copy music from vinyl to CD.*

◆ The last connector is a 15-pin female plug for a joystick or MIDI instrument. This connector has two rows of pins which distinguishes it from the video connector that also has 15-pins but arranged in three rows (Figure 2.13).

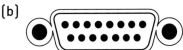

For a particular PC, investigate its sound system:

1 How many speakers are used, and how are they connected to the sound card?
2 What colour coding, if any, is used to identify the ports on the sound card: SPK and MIC, Line in and Line out?

Sound card problems fall into these categories:

◆ Windows does not 'see' the sound card.
◆ There is no sound coming out of the speakers.
◆ There is no sound going in through the microphone.
◆ The quality of sound is poor, with crackling noises.

Figure 2.13
15-pin female
connectors:
a) for a joystick;
b) for video

CHAT   *In a small group, discuss problems that you have experienced with sound cards, and how you resolved them.*

If Windows does not see the sound card, then there is some problem with the installation of the sound card, so check using Device Manager to see what Windows thinks is installed. See Unit 2 (page 137) for details of how to use Device Manager.

◆ If Windows thinks there is no card in the slot where your sound card is positioned, the card may not be slotted in properly, or it may be a defective card.

◆ If Windows knows there is something in place but cannot recognise it, there will be an exclamation mark (!) beside the entry – or it may appear in the category called 'Other Devices'. Refer to the documentation that was supplied with the card, and rerun the Setup program so that the correct drivers are installed.

Watch out

Always make sure that the most up-to-date drivers are installed – for every device that needs one.

If Windows recognises the sound card, it displays a speaker icon (Figure 2.14).

However, its not being there does not necessarily mean there is no sound card! A simpler reason could be that the icon's display has been turned off.

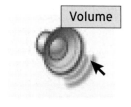

Figure 2.14
The Speaker icon on the Task bar

How to turn on the Speaker icon display

1 Go to the Control Panel and select Multimedia or Sounds and Multimedia or Sounds and audio devices, according to the version of Windows you are using.

2 Select the option to display volume control on the Task bar and click on OK (Figure 2.15).

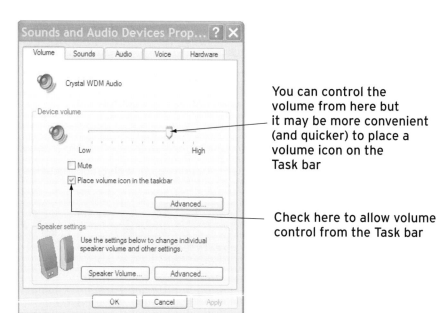

You can control the volume from here but it may be more convenient (and quicker) to place a volume icon on the Task bar

Check here to allow volume control from the Task bar

Figure 2.15
Opting to show the volume control on the Task bar

If you have no sound, it may be that the volume is turned down too low for you to hear anything, or it may be that the volume has been set as **mute**:

◆ Single clicking on the Speaker icon in the Task bar brings up the **master volume** and shows whether the sound is on mute (Figure 2.16a).

◆ Double clicking on the Speaker icon brings up the full **volume properties box** which gives you greater control over the output of sound (Figure 2.16b).

Clear any mute check boxes by clicking on them, and drag the sliders upwards to increase the volume. If you can hear sound coming from the system, e.g. Windows beeping when you have new incoming emails but cannot hear sound that is taken in via the microphone, the problem lies with the connection of the MIC jack on the sound card – or you may simply need to turn on the microphone, if it is one that has an on/off switch.

In the same way as the volume of sound output is controlled through the Play Control volume properties box, there is a Record Control volume properties box accessible from the Options menu of the Play Control box. Selecting Properties offers the choice of Playback or Recording (Figure 2.17). Notice the Select box; this has to be checked for any device that you want to use as input.

Any poor-quality sound – e.g. crackling from the speakers – may be a sign that the recording device is enabled and is picking up ambient static. This is easily fixed by unchecking all the Select boxes on the Recording properties screen – but remember to reselect when you want to use a recording device.

(a)

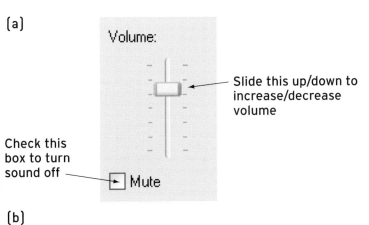

(b)

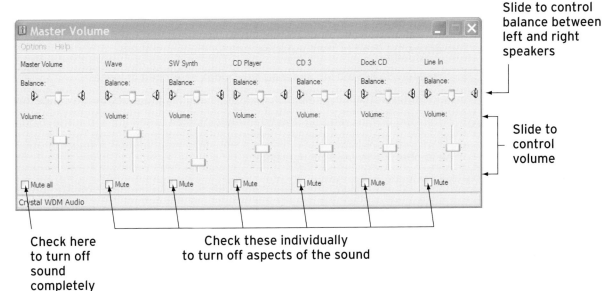

Figure 2.16   The Play Control volume indicators obtained by: (a) single clicking; or (b) double clicking the Speaker icon on the Task bar

Choose Options on the Master Volume menu bar and select Properties

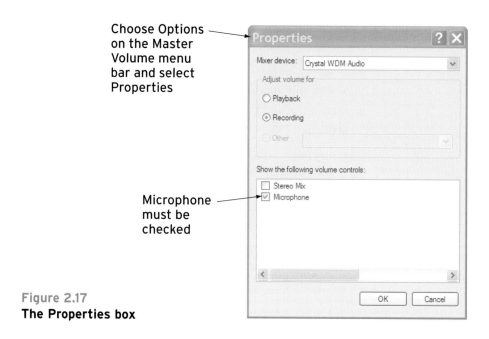

Microphone must be checked

Figure 2.17
The Properties box

Check Your Understanding 2.11

1 What does EMF stand for?
2 What are SPK and MIC?
3 What are the Line-in and Line-out ports used for?
4 What will happen if you double click the Speaker icon on the Task bar?
5 What is meant by a mute setting?
6 How can you access the Recording box to select the microphone as an input device?

Tape drives

Tape drives are used to read and write data on mini-cartridges:

◆ These have a limited life and may fail if worn, stretched or loose.

◆ The formatting process takes an hour or so and is necessary before a tape can be used.

◆ If the tape is removed from the drive while its light is still on, it is in the middle of a data transfer, writing data to the tape. This can cause corruption of the data and it will then be impossible to read the data back.

Problems that happen when trying to use a tape drive fall into four broad groups:

◆ Windows does not recognise the tape drive.

◆ You cannot write to the mini-cartridge.

◆ Writing to the mini-cartridge and/or reading from it is too slow.

◆ The drive fails intermittently or reports errors in reading/writing.

If Windows does not recognise that you have a tape drive attached, the problem is probably to do with your installation:

◆ Is there is a faulty connection? Check the connection and the orientation of the cabling.

◆ Check the system resources for a possible conflict. Tape drives normally require an IRQ, DMA channel and an I/O address.

If you cannot write to the mini-cartridge, make these checks:

◆ Are you using the correct type of tape according to the manufacturer's instructions?

◆ Have you put the cartridge in the right way around?

◆ Has the mini-cartridge been formatted?

◆ Is the tape write-enabled?

◆ Does the tape need retensioning?

What does it mean?

Retensioning involves fast forwarding a tape and then rewinding it to eliminate loose spots.

If this does not fix the problem, take the mini-cartridge out, reboot the PC and try again. If the data transfer is too slow for you, ask yourself these questions:

◆ Is there enough memory on my PC for this software to run?

◆ Should I replace this mini-cartridge with a new one?

◆ Would erasing the tape and then reformatting it help? Check that the software can do this before proceeding.

◆ Is there an option within the software to optimise the speed of data transfer? Data compression may affect the data transfer rate and turning this off – or on – may solve the problem.

◆ Could you install an accelerator card to speed up transfer? Check the manufacturer's instructions for this option.

If you are experiencing intermittent errors, the fault is tricky to locate:

◆ Make sure you are using the correct tape type and format for your tape drive.

◆ The tape may simply be too worn and needs to be replaced.

◆ You could clean the read/write head, following the manufacturer's instructions as to how this should be done.

◆ You could reformat the tape – and retension it.

◆ Make sure that the tape drive, assuming it is an external tape drive, is as far away from both the monitor and the PC case as is possible.

Check Your Understanding 2.12

1 What might happen if you were to remove a tape cartridge while the light is still on?
2 What does retensioning involve?
3 What is an accelerator card?

USB

Like the SCSI chain of devices, USB devices can be linked though hub(s) and are assigned unique address IDs during the process called **enumeration**. When the new device is recognised, the host asks the device to identify itself, in terms of its type, manufacturer, the bandwidth it requires and so on. Using this data, the operating system automatically loads the appropriate device drivers, or asks the user to insert the disk as supplied by the manufacturer. Any potential resource conflicts are dealt with by the host and you do not need to configure IRQS, I/O addresses or DMA channels.

When a device is unplugged, the host spots there has been a change in voltage, notes the address ID as now being free and lets the operating system know to unload the device driver. So, apart from perhaps the cable slipping loose, nothing should go wrong with a USB device. If it does not work, there must be something wrong with the device and you will need to replace it.

Discuss with friends any problems you have had with USB devices, and how you have resolved these problems.

2 Eliciting problem symptoms from customers

Basic troubleshooting procedures rely on applying good practices for eliciting problem symptoms from the user.

What is the problem?

For users, the problem is the failure of the PC to do what they want it to do!

◆ A user may complain that the printer is not working, when actually the problem lies with the printer driver.

◆ A user may complain that the CD drive is not working and you find that the user has inserted the CD upside down.

As part of your problem-solving strategy you need to encourage the user to describe the problem as he or she sees it, but ignore – or at least set aside – the interpretation given as to what is causing the problem. If it turns out that the user is the problem, you will need to use your communication skills to explain the correct procedures so that the user understands what happened and knows enough to prevent it happening again. Diplomacy and tact will be essentials tools!

Working in groups of four, split into two teams:

1   In your team, plan a hardware fault that you will present to the other pair, e.g. disconnected cabling, unseated expansion board. Agree between you what symptoms your PC would show if this fault were to happen.

2   Taking turns, act as user pair and technician pair. The technician pair ask questions to try to find out what the problem is. The user pair answer these questions (honestly!).

3 Write down what you, as the technician pair, would do to isolate the fault, and hopefully fix it.

4 With the permission of your tutor, as the user pair, and out of sight of the technician pair, set up a PC with the fault as planned.

5 As the technician pair, follow your plan to isolate the fault and then fix it.

6 Discuss what you found difficult about this process, and what you found easy.

7 Repeat the activity, choosing different hardware faults.

Software or hardware?

If the problem lies with the hardware, the easy option is to replace it. It may not be economical to repair a damaged component.

◆ Using your knowledge of PC equipment, you can check devices to see whether they are the source of the fault.

◆ You can check the media and how they are being used with the device to make sure this is not the cause of any problem.

If the problem lies with the software, there are a number of possibilities:

◆ The settings on the software need to be changed, e.g. to recognise a peripheral or load a different device driver.

◆ What the user wants to do cannot be done using the software currently installed on the PC. New software may have to be purchased, and the PC may need to be upgraded in some way to support this software.

Working in groups of four again, split into two teams:

1 In your team, plan a software fault that you will present to the other pair, e.g. the wrong setting for a monitor. Agree between you what symptoms your PC would show if this fault were to happen.

2 Take turns as in the previous activity to act as user pair and technician pair.

3 Write down what you, as the technician pair, would do to isolate the fault, and hopefully fix it.

4 With the permission of your tutor, as the user pair, and out of sight of the technician pair, set up a PC with the fault as planned.

5 As the technician pair, follow your plan to isolate the fault and then fix it.

6 Discuss what you found difficult about this process, and what you found easy.

7 Repeat the activity, choosing different software faults.

Information gathering

Note-taking is an essential part of diagnosing and troubleshooting. Collect as many details as you can:

◆ The customer environment

◆ Symptoms noted

◆ Error codes

◆ The situation when the problem occurred

You may be issued with a form to complete, to log details of the fault. Or you may have to enter these details on an on-screen form to add to a database of reported faults (Figure 2.18). Figure 2.19 shows a form you might complete to list important information about the PC you are trying to fix.

Discuss with a friend the PC identification form. Do you understand all the entries? Could you complete this form for your own PC?

1 Complete a PC identification form for a given PC.
2 Swap PC identification forms with a friend and check the entries he or she has made.
3 Discuss any discrepancies.

ERROR LOG (FRMCallLog)

CallID	AutoNumber
DateOfInitialCall	
TimeOfInitialCall	
WhoCalled	
EngineerAllocated	0
DatePassedToEngineer	
TimePassedToEngineer	
ReportFromEngineer	
ErrorDiagnosis	
Cost£	£0.00
CostTime	0
Recommendations	

Figure 2.18
An error log form

You will need to ask questions to encourage the user to describe the circumstances immediately before the problem was noticed:

◆ What error messages were given?

◆ What were you doing when the problem happened?

◆ Which application were you using?

◆ Can you show me what happened?

PC Identification Form

Name .... Number ....

CASE Manufacturer: .... No of bays: 3.5 inch .... 5.25 inch ....

MOTHERBOARD   Form factor? AT/ATX

Manufacturer: .... Model: .... Bus speed: .... MHz

CHIPSET   Manufacturer: .... Model: ....

BIOS   Manufacturer: .... Model: ....

CPU   Manufacturer: .... Model: .... Speed: .... MHz

Socket/Slot?   No of CPU socket/slots: ....

PSU   AT/ATX/Other .... Wattage: ....

EXPANSION SLOTS

No of ISA slots: .... No of PCI slots ....

No of EIDE connectors: .... AGP slot?   YES/NO

No of floppy connectors: .... No of serial ports: ....

No of parallel ports: .... No of USB ports: ....

Any other ports or slots: ....

MEMORY   No of memory slots: .... Max memory supported: ....

Fastest memory supported: ....

MEMORY INSTALLED

30-pin SIMMs: .... 72-pin SIMMs: ....

168-pin DIMMs: .... 160-pin RIMMs: ....

184-pin RIMMs: .... Other: ....

HARD DRIVE   Manufacturer: .... Model: .... Size: ....

Cylinders: .... Heads: .... Interface type: IDE/SCSI

CD-ROM   Manufacturer: .... Model: .... Speed: ....

Interface type: IDE/SCSI

FLOPPY DRIVE Manufacturer: ....

MONITOR   Manufacturer: .... Model: ....

VIDEO CARD   Manufacturer: .... Model: ....

Memory: .... MB   ISA/PCI/On board

SOUND CARD   Manufacturer: .... Model: ....

ISA/PCI/On board

MOUSE   Type: PS/2/Serial/USB

KEYBOARD   Connector: 5-pin DIN/6-pin mini DIN/USB

Matches connector on motherboard? YES/NO

Figure 2.19   **A PC identification form**

Ask also about events prior to the problem:

◆ Have you moved this PC recently?

◆ Have you had any power cuts or electrical problems recently?

◆ Have you added new hardware or software to this PC configuration recently?

◆ Has someone else been using your PC recently?

Your task is to fix the PC, not assign blame. So avoid questions which suggest that the fault is entirely that of the user:

◆ Did you drop the PC?

◆ Have you spilt tea over this keyboard?

Instead, offer these possibilities as being non-attributable:

◆ Do you think the PC might have been dropped?

◆ Is there any chance this keyboard has had tea spilt over it?

Remember that your role as technician puts you in a supporting role. So show respect for the user:

◆ Don't talk jargon to impress the user, or talk down to him or her.

◆ Don't pile your tools on top of working papers on the user's desk.

◆ Don't use his or her telephone.

◆ Don't take over the mouse while he or she is using it.

◆ Accept that the user also has work to do, and you need to fit your task around this.

Your next source of information is the output from POST, so you then need to try to boot the PC to see what happens. Chapter 1 (page 17) describes the boot process, and Unit 2 (page 321) lists the errors message and POST codes that you might see.

While you are with the user and/or working on the PC, behave in a professional way:

◆ Before you start to test equipment, make sure that you have the permission of the user to proceed.

◆ Explain to the user what you plan to do, and justify why this is so.

◆ Do not repartition or reformat a disk without first making sure that data has been backed up.

◆ Be aware of the confidentiality of the data you may be handling.

◆ Do not pass comment on the user's choice of equipment, or software, or how he or she has been using it.

◆ If you cannot solve the problem and need to refer to someone more experienced, be honest with the user.

◆ If you make a mistake which results in some corruption of data, for example, again, be honest.

 In a small group, share experiences of working with users.

You may find that part of your role as a technician includes training users in the correct use of hardware and software. This may involve you in guiding a user through the steps needed to perform some function. While it might have been quicker to do it yourself, the time spent training the user may save you time in the future, due to a reduction in the number of callouts from this particular user.

Go and try out 2.7

Your tutor will present you with a PC that has a fault:

1 Ask questions to elicit as much information as you can, and make notes of the answers received.
2 Think about how you might isolate the fault and devise a plan of what you will check and in what order. Write this down and obtain approval from your tutor before proceeding.
3 Follow your plan to solve the fault. Present your findings to your tutor.

Revision 2

Remember these facts:

1 To protect the components within a PC from ESD, use an ESD wrist strap and a grounding mat when you are repairing the PC, and an anti-static bag for storing components while they are out of the PC.
2 To protect a PC from EMI, cover expansion slots that are not in use, and keep the PC as far away as possible from high-powered electrical equipment.
3 To protect a PC from electrical damage, use surge suppressors, line conditioners and a UPS.
4 A technician's toolkit includes conventional tools (such as screwdrivers), a bootable disk, diagnostic hardware and software, plus access to manufacturer's specifications of hardware and software (online or hard copy manuals).
5 A multimeter can measure volts, amps, ohms and continuity, and can therefore be used to check the condition of cabling and whether power is reaching components.
6 PC failure can be the result of human error but is more likely to be caused by build-up of dust, overheating, power supply problems, EMI, ESD, virus attack or accidental spillage of drinks.
7 Keeping a log helps to track problems and identify possible sources of faults.
8 Keeping a written record of CMOS settings may allow you to revert to current settings, rather than the factory-set settings, in the event of disaster.
9 Taking backups before investigating faults on a PC will allow you to recover data files in the event of disaster.
10 Problems with the PSU can cause a PC to crash or reboot, or result in memory or data errors, and can damage the motherboard and other components.

11 Troubleshooting involves finding out what works and then, by a process of elimination, finding out what does not work.

12 Temporarily replacing a suspect component with one that is known to be working can confirm the component's state.

13 Using a single suspect component on a system that is otherwise known to be working can confirm the component's state.

14 A user whose PC has just failed needs gentle handling, if you are to elicit enough information to be able to fix the problem.

15 Asking the right questions and writing notes are essential skills of a technician.

Chapter 3 Preventive maintenance

Preventive maintenance is an essential part of running a computer system. It aims to prevent problems arising, saving time in diagnosing and fixing faults. It can also extend the life of your PC. Like any machine, a PC needs some attention on a regular basis if only to keep it clean. Computers attract a lot of dust:

◆ If it settles on the outside, it soon forms a grimy layer of dirt, which is unsightly.

◆ If it settles on the inside, dust can block airways, preventing the cooling mechanism from working properly. Overheated components may then fail.

Just how regular the maintenance tasks are performed depends on the task. It could be daily, weekly, monthly or annually, or just when necessary, as suggested in Table 3.1. If the air in which the PC operates is dusty or smoky, even more frequent cleaning will be necessary.

What does it mean?

Fragmentation happens when files have to split up into sections and saved in separate locations on the disk because there is no contiguous space available that is big enough to hold the entire file.

Defragmentation tidies up the disk, making available clusters that are no longer needed (because files have been deleted) and collecting the separate elements of fragmented files together.

Table 3.1 *Preventive maintenance schedule*

Frequency	Maintenance task	See these pages
Daily	Virus scan of memory and your hard disk Take backup of changed data files	Antivirus software, Table 2.2 page 133 Backing up, page 31
Weekly	Clean mouse (ball and rollers) and check for wear Clean keyboard, checking for stuck keys Clean monitor screen Clean printer Delete temporary files (disk clean) Defrag hard disk and recover lost clusters	How to clean mouse, page 171 How to clean keyboard, page 171 How to clean monitor screen, page 172 How to clean printers, page 222 Disk defragmenter, Figure 7.15, page 263
Monthly	Clean outside of case Take complete backup of data files*	Backing up, page 31
Annually	Check motherboard: reseat chips if necessary Clean adaptor card contacts with contact cleaner and reseat	Motherboard, pages 53–7, 181–213
As required	Clean floppy disk drive if it fails, using a proprietary disk-drive cleaning kit to clean the read/write heads Record and back up CMOS setup configuration Keep written record of hardware and software configuration	CMOS settings, page 204

Note: *The frequency of backups is dependent on the volume of transactions and the importance of the material; it may be that full backups are required weekly or even daily.

For some routine maintenance tasks, the computer can remain powered up (e.g. cleaning the mouse), or must be powered up (e.g. to do a virus check). For others, it is necessary to switch off (e.g. cleaning the monitor). As soon as you have completed the maintenance task, make sure that the PC still works!

Discuss with a friend – for which tasks should the PC be turned off?

Some hardware can – and needs to be – cleaned (casings, mouse rollers, etc.) but some hardware is sealed so your maintenance is restricted to 'cleaning' using software (e.g. deleting temporary files off the hard disk).

Which hardware is sealed and how might you maintain it?

Remember to keep a record of what maintenance has been done, any faults found and what you have done to fix these faults.

In small groups, discuss which maintenance tasks you consider to be essential, and how often you think they need to be done.

1   Preventive maintenance products and procedures

You need to be able to identify the various types of preventive maintenance products and procedures, and know when to use/perform them. This section looks at these topics.

◆ Liquid cleaning compounds
◆ Types of materials to clean contacts and connections
◆ Non-static vacuums (chassis/power supplies/fans)

In choosing maintenance products, you should be aware of potential health risks to you in using these products, as well as selecting the right type of product for the task in hand. For example, many of the chemical solvents are poisonous and may need special handling.

When you buy any chemical product, you should find a **material safety data sheet (MSDS)** – or something similar, e.g. as part of the label – that lists important data to help you to handle and use it correctly and safely.

◆ The toxicity of the product
◆ Any health effects
◆ First aid measures, e.g. if you were to ingest some accidentally
◆ How to store the product
◆ How to dispose of the product
◆ What to do if the chemical is spilt

Information about the hazards of chemical cleaners are also available on the Internet. Visit www.heinemann.co.uk/hotlinks to see examples of these sites and make notes.

Liquid cleaning compounds

The cheapest liquid cleaning compound is **water**. Used carefully, it can be used to clean cases, but you must be sure not to wet the electronic parts of the PC.

Watch out

Water conducts electricity so water on a circuit board can cause a short circuit.

Water can be mixed with a **general-purpose cleaner**, and this may be necessary if the casing has not been cleaned for some time and dirt has built up (Figure 3.1). The most expensive option, but the safest for your PC, is **isopropyl alcohol**. This chemical can be used to clean the PC case, the keyboard case and keys, and any other similar casing on your PC. It removes dirt and then evaporates so the equipment does not become wet. Because it is a chemical, it can harm you, though. So read the instructions carefully, and follow them!

CASE STUDY   Nigel the novice PC user

Nigel realises that he has to keep his PC clean and has been investigating liquid cleaning compounds. He has read somewhere that 'rubbing alcohol should not be used'.

1 Use the Internet or other sources to find out whether it is correct that rubbing alcohol should not be used and, if so, find out why.

2 Find out what dangers lie in using isopropyl alcohol.

3 Write notes for Nigel as to what products he might consider using.

Cleaning materials

The most essential item would appear to be a **soft lint-free cloth**. This can be used as a dry duster for the screen, or with a cleaning fluid to clean casings. **Paper towels** may also be useful, especially to mop up any spillages. **Cotton buds** or swabs may also be considered

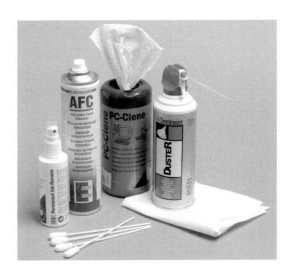

Figure 3.1
PC cleaning products

– especially for cleaning the contact points inside a mouse – but take care they do not leave deposits. You may also need a **non-static brush** or probe, and/or a small **flat-bladed screwdriver** to dislodge stubborn bits of dirt, e.g. on the mouse rollers.

Dust can be blown off the fan and power supply grill using **compressed air**. Compressed air is also good for cleaning the 'gills' on a heat sink. (There may be one on the CPU.) Compressed air is sold in a can with a long thin nozzle extension to reach into the smallest crevice. Because of its cooling properties, it may be used to cool an overheated component.

Watch out

Compressed air is very, very, cold so do not direct it on to your skin.

Non-static vacuums

Vacuuming the inside of a PC can remove a lot of the dust that collects. Some small cleaners include brush heads, which are ideal for the purpose. However, it is important to use non-static vacuum cleaners. These ionise the air and therefore produce no harmful charge.

What does it mean?

Ionise = to make the air a conducting material.

Watch out

Do not use a vacuum cleaner to try to clean a laser printer. The toner would clog the vacuum unless it has specifically designed to handle it.

Go and try out 3.2

For a given PC, you are going to give it a spring clean and time how long this takes you.

1 Examine the PC to see what you think needs cleaning.
2 Make a list of the tasks you intend to do, and obtain approval from your tutor.
3 Assemble the cleaning materials that you plan to use. Check these also with your tutor.
4 Clean each component separately and then check that the PC still works before moving on to clean the next component. (Refer to the 'How to' panels that follow, if you need to.)
5 Tick each item on your task list, noting how long it took you to do.
6 When you have finished, draw up a maintenance list for future cleaning of this PC, and estimate how much time per week will be needed.

Watch out

Remember to apply the safety rules while completing the maintenance tasks.

How to clean a mouse

1 Make sure there are no applications running before opening the mouse.

2 Turn the mouse over and remove the cover. This may involve rotating or sliding the cover to free it.

3 Using clean hands, remove the ball and examine it for cracks or problems with its shape. (If there are problems with the ball, you need to replace it or, preferably, the entire mouse.)

4 Use a soft lint-free cloth to clean the mouse ball. There is no need to use cleaning fluid for this stage.

5 Use compressed air to blow out any loose dust and dirt.

6 Inspect the rollers inside the mouse. There may be three in total and all may show signs of dirt wrapped around them. You can use a small flat-bladed screwdriver to scrape the dirt off gently, or a cotton bud or foam wand soaked in a cleaning solution (Figure 3.2). Be sure to remove any debris that falls off the rollers.

7 Wait until any chemical solvents that you have used have evaporated and then replace the ball and the cover.

8 To clean the outside of the mouse, use a soft lint-free cloth with either isopropyl alcohol or a non-sudsing general-purpose cleaner.

9 Check also the mouse pad. If it is worn, replace it. If it is dirty, wipe it clean to prevent the dirt being transferred to the mouse.

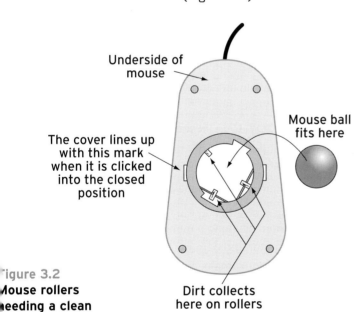

Underside of mouse

The cover lines up with this mark when it is clicked into the closed position

Mouse ball fits here

Dirt collects here on rollers

Figure 3.2
Mouse rollers needing a clean

How to clean a keyboard

1 Disconnect the keyboard and/or turn off the power.

2 Turn the keyboard upside down. This should dislodge any large dirt particles!

3 Non-static brushes or probes may be needed to loosen any large or stubborn bits of dirt from between the keys. You might also use a folded paper towel, very slightly moistened. It will slip and slide easily between the rows of keys.

4 Then use compressed air to blow out smaller dust/dirt particles, or use a keyboard vacuum.

5 Clean the keys and case, using a soft lint-free cloth, with either isopropyl alcohol or a non-sudsing general-purpose cleaner.

6 If the cleaner contains any water, be sure that the keyboard is completely dry before powering up again.

How to clean a monitor

1 Make sure the screen is off, has been disconnected and has cooled down. This will reduce the risk of static electricity.

Watch out

Do not wear an ESD wrist strap while cleaning the monitor.

2 For the outer casing, especially the top, use compressed air to remove dust. Be careful not to blow dust into the monitor vents. You could use a slightly damp lint-free cloth – with either water or a general-purpose cleaner or isopropyl alcohol to clean stubborn dirt marks. If you use water-based cleaners, make sure none drips inside the monitor through the vents.

3 You can buy anti-static cleaners especially designed for use with monitors, or you can use a soft lint-free cloth to dry dust the screen.

Things to avoid

Remembering what to do almost becomes second nature, the more times you clean your PC. For the A+ examination, don't forget what not to do, though!

◆ Blowing away dust by blowing with your mouth may seem effective and is much cheaper than buying cans of compressed air, but you risk introducing your own spit into the equipment – and getting dust in your eyes.

◆ Using water-based cleaners may be cheaper than alcohol-based ones, but the alcohol-based ones will evaporate, leaving the equipment safe to turn on. Using water anywhere near a computer is asking for trouble.

◆ Don't use alcohol-based products to clean the mouse ball. It affects the rubber and can shrink the ball or make it lopsided.

◆ Be sure to use the correct solutions when cleaning a monitor. Otherwise you may dissolve any special coating on the monitor and damage the display. Ammonia-based products such as regular glass cleaner, for example, can be harmful; it can affect the anti-glare coating used on some screens. Soap-based products will leave smears, and the monitor will not look clean at all.

Watch out

Do not open the cover of a monitor to clean it.

CHAT *In small groups, discuss your experiences with the maintenance of PCs and share ideas about things that you think should be avoided.*

2 Issues, procedures and devices for protection

You need to identify issues, procedures and devices for protection within a computing environment. This section looks at these topics:

◆ UPS and suppressors.

◆ Determining the signs of power issues.

◆ Proper methods of storage of components for future use.

UPS and suppressors

A **UPS (uninterruptible power supply)** [Figure 3.3] aims to provide just that: an uninterrupted power supply! The UPS has two circuits:

◆ An AC circuit acts as a surge suppressor, protecting the PC against spikes and other fluctuations.

◆ A battery with a DC to AC converter provides a backup store of energy so that, if there is a brownout, the battery power can be converted into AC power and supplied to the PSU.

There are two types of UPS:

◆ **Standby UPS** operates from the AC but switches to battery operated if the power supply drops too low.

◆ **Inline UPS** operates from the battery and only switches to the AC if there is a problem with the battery.

Watch out

Do not plug a laser printer into a UPS; it uses too much power at start up and again during fusing processes. The laser can also create noise for the UPS or surge suppressor.

CHAT

Discuss with friends whether you should unplug a PC before working on it.

UPS is not to be confused with **SPS (standby power supply)** or **battery backup** (which supplies power when none is available but has no power-conditioning feature).

There is a way of protecting your PC against problems with the external supply: a **power strip** – or **surge suppressor** – protects the PC by taking the hit from any voltage spike:

Figure 3.3   **A UPS**

◆ A **MOV (metal oxide varistor)** within the suppressor absorbs the spike, but can also be knocked out by it. An LED will indicate the level of protection; if this LED fails the suppressor needs to be replaced!

◆ A surge suppressor's **clamping voltage** is the voltage at which the suppressor is set to kick into action.

◆ The **clamping speed** is the reaction time of the suppressor – a bit like the thinking speed when you have to hit the brakes on a car.

The specification for a surge suppressor includes its **energy absorption rate** (in Joules) and the **level of protection** offered, given by the number of watts that will pass through the suppressor:

◆ The higher the energy absorption rate the better: 200 Joules is okay, 400 Joules is good protection but 600 Joules will give the best protection.

◆ The lower the watts, the higher the protection: 500 watts is okay, 400 watts is better but 330 watts is best.

A surge suppressor may also smooth out line noise by filtering the incoming power stream. This is called **line conditioning** and is measured in decibels. Apart from the power source, power faults may enter the PC via the telephone connecting line, so the surge protector should include a phone-line protection. Alternatively, you might install a separate phone/modem isolator.

As ever, the more you pay, the better the product. UL (Underwriters Laboratories) standard UL1449 covers surge suppressors. Any product with that has met this standard should protect your PC adequately.

Check Your Understanding 3.1

1 Distinguish between UPS, PSU and SPS.
2 What is line conditioning?
3 Name two types of UPS.

Determining signs of power issues

Chapter 2 (page 153) considers in more detail things that can go wrong with the PSU. Here, only a brief overview is given.

If the power supply is faulty and/or the PSU is not working properly, how will you know? There are a number of signs that all is not well:

◆ You receive an electrical shock from the case (other than ESD)!

◆ After turning on the PC power, nothing happens ...

◆ The power light is off.

◆ The fan is not blowing out air.

◆ You hear no beep or a continuous beep or a repeating short beep.

◆ A POST error in the 020–029 range is reported.

◆ A parity error is reported.

Any of these could indicate that there is a power issue. If you receive a shock, you will most probably have to replace the PSU. If there is no sign of life in the PC, you might make some checks:

◆ Is there power to the wall socket?

◆ Is the power cord plugged into the wall socket?

◆ Is the power cord plugged into the surge suppressor?

◆ Is the surge suppressor switched on and working?

If the power is available and plugged in – and the surge suppressor is working – then the fault lies with the power switch or the PSU. Either way, you probably need to replace the PSU.

Discuss with a friend how you can tell when a problem is caused by the PSU.

Storing components for future use

New components are shipped in **anti-static bags**. This is to protect them against accidental damage by ESD (see page 178). Save these anti-static bags to store components such as cards and small FRMs (field replaceable modules) when they are not within the PC (Figure 3.4). This will protect the components from a build-up of static.

Components that you do not intend to keep can be disposed of. However, there are procedures to follow. See page 177 for details of components that represent a hazard and require special disposal procedures.

What does it mean?

FRM = field-replaceable module

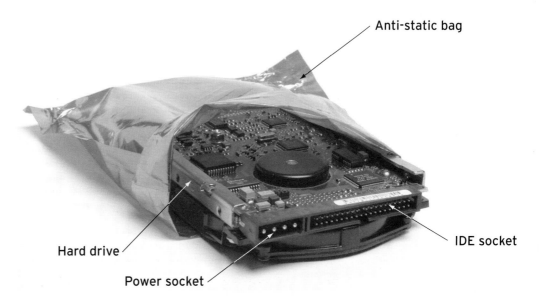

Anti-static bag

IDE socket

Hard drive

Power socket

Figure 3.4
An anti-static bag

3 Potential hazards and proper safety procedures relating to lasers

A PC is powered by electricity, and that presents a hazard. (See page 358 for an introduction to electricity, electronics and ESD.) When working with PCs, you must recognise potential hazards and adopt proper safety procedures; otherwise you are putting yourself, and possibly others, at risk.

CASE STUDY — Nigel the novice PC user

Nigel is keen to work on the inside of his PC, maintaining it and upgrading it, but is worried about harming himself.

1 In simple terms, explain how electricity works. The analogy between electricity flow and water flow may help him to understand the concepts.

2 Explain the risks of Nigel giving himself a shock.

3 List potential sources of danger, and explain why they are particularly hazardous.

4 Explain why, although a wire carries electricity and is potentially dangerous, if it is surrounded by rubber to form a cable, Nigel should not get a shock from it.

Check Your Understanding 3.2

1 There are three 'types' of electricity: AC, DC and static. Distinguish between these three forms.
2 Distinguish between a conductor and an insulator, and give examples of each.
3 Explain the terms 'transistor', 'diode', 'resistor' and 'capacitor'.

The **power supply** carries with it all the dangers of any electrical supply. At 230 V AC, the mains power is the most dangerous voltage in the computer. You can electrocute yourself if you touch a live wire.

Voltage measures the electrical pressure in a circuit. **High-voltage equipment** has, as its name suggests, a higher voltage going through it than other equipment. This makes it a greater source of danger. Monitors use high voltages. Within a PC, the voltages needed for components are given in Table 1.2 (page 14). These look quite low but could still give you a nasty shock.

The CRT (monitor) – like the PSU – contains a **capacitor**. This component is a dump spot for electrical charge, used to smooth out the flow of electricity in a circuit. It holds the charge even when there is no power supply attached to the CRT and can be lethal if you touch it.

Watch out

Never wear a grounding strap when opening a monitor. The capacitor holds an enormous charge, and wearing the strap offers a short cut – straight through you – to ground.

The cable for an optical device contains a laser beam instead of a current of electricity. This makes for much cleaner and quicker transfer of data. With it, it brings risks. Never look into a laser beam – it will burn the retina of your eye and blind you.

Check Your Understanding 3.3

1 Which components need voltages as low as 3.3 V?
2 How high a voltage does a disk drive need?
3 Give an example of a high-voltage item of equipment.
4 What makes the CRT so dangerous?

4 Special disposal procedures; environmental guidelines

Some items require special disposal procedures. You need to know the environmental guidelines that are to be followed. Table 3.2 gives all the relevant details for batteries and CRTs.

Table 3.2 *Environmental guidelines for special disposal procedures*

Item for disposal	Hazard	Environmental guidelines
Batteries	PC batteries are usually lithium batteries for powering the CMOS memory, but can include lead, nickel-cadmium and/or mercury. All these chemicals present risk to humans. Leaking batteries pose a greater hazard.	Lithium batteries must not be disposed of in a fire or in water. If sent to a landfill, these chemicals can seep into the environment through groundwater. Take care not to get the **electrolyte** (the fluid within the battery) in your eyes. Dispose of batteries as per local regulations.
CRTs	CRTs contain acids, aluminium, ammonia, deionised water, metal (including a high level of lead), mercury oxidisers, phosphorous, photo-resist materials, solvents (and their vapour) and many other harmful chemicals.	Monitors take up valuable space in landfill sites and contain chemicals that can seep into the environment through groundwater. Special disposal services cater for monitors.*

Note: *Disposal procedures are explained in the MSDS for a product.

Go and try out 3.3

1 Visit the EPA (Environmental Protection Agency) website (follow the links from www.heinemann.co.uk/hotlinks) to see what products are covered by regulations. Make notes.
2 Find out how you should dispose of spent toner kits and cartridges.
3 Read the label on a can of chemical solvent and make notes on its safe use and disposal.

Even circuit boards contain a small amount of lead in the soldering so, in disposing of a PC or any part of a PC, be sure to follow the regulations imposed by the government and local authorities.

5 ESD precautions and procedures

What does it mean?

ESD (electrostatic discharge) = an electrical shock caused when two objects (you and the PC!) of uneven charge make contact. Electricity flows from high voltage to low voltage so, if you are carrying a build-up of static electricity, you can give your PC a shock.

This section looks at three important safety topics.

◆ What ESD can do, and how it may be apparent or hidden
◆ Common ESD protection devices
◆ Situations that could present a danger or hazard

Watch out

Follow the safety rules whenever working on a PC

1 Be prepared: have the right tools to hand.
2 Obey the dress code: nothing dangling that will trap you.
3 Wear your ESD wrist band . . .!
4 Before starting, turn off the PC and disconnect the AC power cord.
5 Read the manual – don't do things from memory.
6 Ground yourself by touching the chassis to discharge any static electricity that has accumulated on your clothing or body.
7 Handle all parts gently, holding components by their edges, not by the connector.
8 Remember that some components may be too hot to touch safely.
9 Have a 'buddy' – someone nearby who can call an ambulance if things go horribly wrong!
10 Take your time and think carefully before acting.

Your safety – and that of the PC – should be top of your priority list when working on a PC:

◆ Turn off the PC at the power switch and check that the power does go off (e.g. the power light goes out). The mains supply at 230 V AC is the most dangerous voltage in the computer. Conventional monitor screens also use high voltages and can be very dangerous.
◆ Unplug the PC power cord.
◆ Place the computer on a flat surface and make sure it is free of metallic objects, electrical chords and power supplies.
◆ Make sure that you and the PC are not in contact with any other grounded objects. In particular, make sure that the PC is not touching another PC or electrical device which is plugged into an electrical socket.

When opening a computer, before you touch anything, you must make sure you are not carrying any **static electricity**. For details on static electricity, look in the background information section under electricity.

ESD will happen if there is a potential difference between you and the PC. If so, current will flow between you, and may damage the components within the PC. So you must be sure to discharge any electricity that you are carrying safely, before risking discharging it on the PC:

◆ Wear an ESD grounding strap on your wrist (or ankle) and, while working on the inside of the PC, connect this strap either to the chassis of the PC or to a grounding mat (Figure 3.5).

Watch out | Never wear a grounding strap when operating a monitor. The capacitor holds an enormous, charge, and wearing the strap offers a shortcut – straight through you – to ground.

◆ Fit a grounded pad beneath the PC. Touching this pad before touching the PC will discharge any build-up of static electricity.

Some techniques aim to reduce static electricity:

◆ Apply an anti-static treatment to carpets so as to reduce static build-up.
◆ Store any electrical components in anti-static bags until needed.
◆ Since dry air can cause static electricity, installing humidifiers which replace moisture in the air and aiming for a humidity level of greater than 50% should reduce the risk of static electricity build-up.

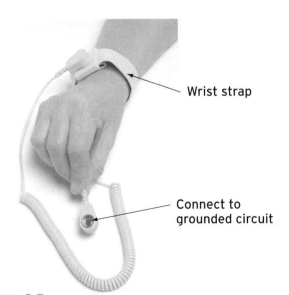

Wrist strap

Connect to grounded circuit

Figure 3.5
An ESD wrist strap

Is there any good news about ESD? Yes!

◆ ESD is used to apply toner to paper in photocopy machines and laser printers.
◆ ESD is used to clean up the air, removing pollen and dust to create a healthier environment.

Want to find out more about ESD? Visit www.heinemann.co.uk/hotlinks and follow the links from there.

179

CASE STUDY

Nigel the novice PC user

Nigel has realised that he is more of a danger to the PC than the other way around.

1 Explain how static electricity is a source of harm for a PC.

2 Explain what can be done to minimise this risk.

Revision 3

Remember these facts:

1 Preventive maintenance is an essential part of running a computer system.

2 Defragmentation tidies up the files on a hard disk.

3 A material data safety sheet gives important information about the safe handling and storage of a product.

4 A non-static vacuum ionises the air and therefore produces no harmful charge that might damage a component.

5 Wattage is a measure of electrical power.

6 Electrical voltage measures the potential difference between two points in an electrical system.

7 Current is measured in amps.

8 Resistance is measured in ohms.

9 Wattage is calculated as volts times amps.

10 One volt drives a current of one amp through a resistance of one ohm, which is one watt of power.

11 PCs run on DC power, and this is converted from the AC supplied in the mains by the PSU

12 A conductor is a material that allows current to flow through it.

13 An insulator is a material that does not allow current through it.

14 A surge suppressor protects a computer against spikes in the power supply, which can damage components.

15 A line conditioner is used to smooth the incoming power supply, thus reducing brownouts and spikes.

16 An anti-static bag can protect a component from static build-up.

17 High-voltage equipment, such as that used in monitors, presents a hazard to users.

18 The CRT contains a capacitor which holds electrical charge, even when the source of power is turned off – and hence is too dangerous to touch in any circumstances.

19 Batteries need special disposal procedures.

20 Static electricity can be reduced by installing a humidifier.

Chapter 4 Motherboard/processors/memory

Before looking in detail at motherboards, there are two important components on a motherboard that you have met already and that you need to understand:

- ◆ The CPU (central processing unit) - or microprocessor - or processor (page 182).
- ◆ The memory which comprises various types of RAM (page 185).

Check Your Understanding 4.1

1 What is the most important part of the CPU?
2 What does the BUI do?
3 Explain the terms ALU and FPU.
4 What does the MMU do?
5 What does the PTU do?
6 Explain the terms DIPP, PGA, SEC and ZIF.
7 List the various types of RAM.
8 Explain what is meant by volatile.
9 Explain the terms DIP, SIMM and DIMM.
10 What is cache memory?

You need to be able to distinguish between the popular CPU chips by making comparisons between their basic characteristics:

- ◆ physical size
- ◆ voltage
- ◆ caching abilities
- ◆ socket or slot used for mounting on the motherboard.

You also need to know other details, such as the number of pins on a chip's packaging, and what special features such as multimedia they support. You need to know the answers to questions like these:

- ◆ Which CPU supports multimedia? *Answer:* Pentium MMX.
- ◆ Which processors have MMX support? *Answer:* Pentium Pro.

You also need to know about the various types of RAM: their characteristics and hence to what use they are put in a PC. So, the next two sections look at CPU chips and their characteristics, and then the categories of RAM, before focusing on motherboards (page 191).

In a small group, discuss which processors are installed on PCs that you use. How old are these processors?

1   Popular CPU chips and their basic characteristics

You should be aware of the history of CPUs (see Figure 4.1) and important milestones in the development of the CPU.

As each new processor was developed, the density of semiconductors increased. This allowed more tasks to be carried out in the same timeframe, thus speeding up processing on the PC.

Check Your Understanding 4.2

1. When did the 486 processor first appear?
2. When did the first Pentium appear?
3. Which processor doubled the internal clock speed?
4. Which processor trebled the internal clock speed?
5. Which processor included pipelining?
6. Which processor took the number of transistors past 5 million?

Go and try out 4.1

1. Research the Internet to follow the development of processor in the last few years and extend Table 4.1 to bring it up to date.
2. Draw a time line to mark the important developments.

Intel manufacture **Pentium processors**, the most popular chips in PCs nowadays. It is a true multiprocessor because it has two ALUs (arithmetic and logic unit) and so can do two calculations at the same time.

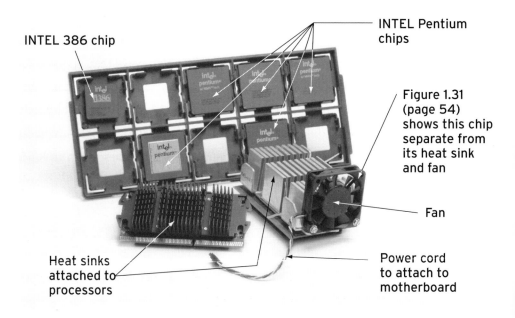

INTEL 386 chip

INTEL Pentium chips

Figure 1.31 (page 54) shows this chip separate from its heat sink and fan

Fan

Power cord to attach to motherboard

Heat sinks attached to processors

Figure 4.1
Popular CPU chips

You need to know the fine details of the evolution of Intel processors and their characteristics in terms of physical size, voltage, speeds, onboard cache or not, sockets and SEC.

What does it mean?

SEC (single-edge connector) = a type of module that has connectors only along one edge.

Table 4.1 presents some of these facts for you, focusing on the Pentium processors.

MMX (multimedia extensions) technology provides additional features for Pentium processors:

◆ Additional 57 instructions for improved audio, graphic and video capabilities

◆ SIMD (single-instruction multiple data) technology

◆ Double-sized cache (to 32 K)

Go and try out 4.2

Research the Internet to follow the development of the Pentium beyond the Pentium III and extend Table 4.1 to bring it up to date.

Table 4.1   *Intel processors**

CPU	Packaging	Voltage	MHz	Memory (MB)	Cache (K)	Notes
Pentium	PGA	5	60–200	4 K	16	32-bit **multi-tasking** with RISC design techniques Superscalar architecture (executes two instructions per clock cycle)
Pentium	PGA	5	166–233	4 K	32 MMX	
Pentium	PGA	1.5	150–200	64 K	1000 Pro	Developed as a network server, e.g. for Windows NT; used in configurations with 1, 2, 4 processors; 1 MB L2 cache
Celeron	PGA, SEC	1.5	266, 600	4 K	128	Developed for desktop and portable PCs; a low-cost version of the Pentium II, but still with MMX technology
Pentium II	SEC	1.5	233–450	64 K	512	Equivalent to Pentium Pro but with MMX technology, so excellent for full-motion video and 3D imaging
Pentium II Xeon**	SEC	1.5	400–450	64 K	512–1000	Xeon enables 4–8 CPUs in one server
Pentium III	SEC, FC-PGA	1.5	450–1 GHz	64 K	256	9.5 million transistors 32 K L1 cache, 512 L2 cache
Pentium III Xeon**	SEC	1.5	500–1 GHz	64 K	256	Xeon enables 4–8 CPUs in one server

Notes: *All CPUs listed have a 64-bit data bus. **Xeon processors succeeded the Pentium Pro (network server).

What does it mean?

Multi-tasking = the operating system supports more than one program at a time.

You should be aware of other manufacturers of processor chips, although you do not need to memorise the fine detail. So this section looks at two other popular CPU chips (AMD and Cyrix) and lists some facts about their range of processors.

CASE STUDY — AMD and Cyrix

Jared has done some research into AMD (Advanced Micro Devices) and produced these notes:

Since AMD (Advanced Micro Devices) released its 75 Mhz 5x86 microprocessor, it has provided some competition for Intel:

◆ AMD's 5x86 processor was compatible with 486 motherboards but with more power (similar to early Pentium processors).

◆ The K6 (including 3DNow, AMD's own set of multimedia commands) outperformed the Pentium MMX on speed and price.

◆ The K6-2+ has more L2 cache and advanced power control features.

◆ The K6-III has 256 K of L2 cache and clock speeds of 400-600 Mhz.

◆ The K6-III+ offers an additional 1 MB of cache.

◆ The 1 GHz Athlon processor supports Intel's MMX as well as its own 3DNow and improved FPU functions. With 256 K L2 cache and 128 KB L1 cache, it outperforms the Pentium III. The Athlon plug is designed for AMD's Slot A bus (speeds of 200-400 MHz) and is compatible with the Slot 1 connector.

◆ The 700 MHz Duron processor is targeted at business and home users as well as portable applications.

Ahktar has investigated these Cyrix, and produced these notes:

Cyrix (now owned by VIA Technologies) cloned the Pentium to create the 6x86-P series, each one being given a number to show which Pentium processor it matched, e.g. the 6x86-P200 had the performance of a Pentium 200 MHz processor:

◆ The series (6x86-P120 to 6x86-P200) had compatibility problems and also suffered from overheating.

◆ Cyrix then developed a lower-power and hence lower-temperature version: 6x86L.

◆ The MII (or Cyrix 6x86MX) had an MMX set of instructions and a Pentium rating of 166-433.

◆ The VIA Cyrix III matches the Intel Pentium II Celeron processor

Check that you understand the terms Jared and Ahktar have used in their notes:

1 Explain what is meant by L2 cache.
2 What are 'power control features'?
3 What does MHz represent as a measure?
4 What are FPU functions?
5 What is a Slot 1 connector?
6 Why should a processor suffer from overheating problems?
7 What does MMX stand for?

Apart from being able to interpret the 'jargon', you must be able to identify the ROM and BIOS chips installed within a given PC.

Go and try out 4.3

For this activity you will need a complete motherboard (in or out of a PC, working or otherwise), the manuals that go with the motherboard and access to the Internet.

Watch out

Watch out If you use a working motherboard within a PC for this activity, make sure you observe all safety rules.

Go and try out 4.4

Your task is to determine whether the BIOS on the motherboard will support an expansion card that you might install into the PC so that you can edit videos:

1 Find the BIOS chip and draw a sketch to show where it is located on the motherboard.
2 Looking at the chip, describe its physical appearance.
3 Still looking at the chip, write down the manufacturer and its version number.
4 What is the battery type?
5 Is it a rewritable BIOS?
6 Visit the manufacturer's website to see what features are supported by your version of the BIOS.
7 Research the BIOS manufacturer's website to see if a newer version of this BIOS is available, and what features the newer BIOS supports.
8 Can the BIOS be upgraded?
9 What are the steps that must be taken to upgrade the BIOS?

2 Categories of RAM: terminology, their locations and physical characteristics

ROM and RAM (see Figure 4.2) are the two basic type of memory used on a computer:

◆ Read-only memory – in theory – can be read from but not written to. (See Chapter 1 (page 27) for more details on the types of ROM.)
◆ Random access memory can be written to and read from.

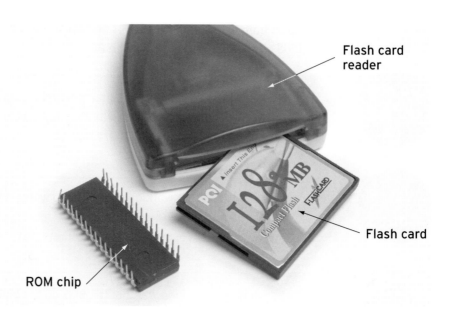

Flash card reader

Flash card

ROM chip

Figure 4.2   A ROM chip

CHAT

Remind yourself about the different ROM: PROM, EPROM and EEPROM. Research the Internet to discover how technology has developed to make it possible for ROM to be written to, instead of just read from.

RAM is either static (SRAM) or dynamic (DRAM). Table 4.2 compares the two types.

Table 4.2   *SRAM and DRAM*

SRAM	DRAM
Holds its content, for as long as it has a power stream	Has to be **refreshed** every 2 milliseconds, even if the content of the RAM has not changed in the mean time
Very fast access times of 2 ns (or less)	Slower access times: 50–120 ns
*Larger (two more pins than DIP RAM)	Smaller
*Due to the complexity of its circuitry, is more expensive	Simple and hence relatively cheap
Used for cache memory rather than primary memory	

Note: *It is because SRAM is larger than DRAM and much more expensive that it is used for L2 cache memory on the motherboard.

What does it mean?

Refreshing = a special logic circuit reads the content of the memory location and then rewrites it.

SRAM is available in two packagings in a variety of increments.

◆ A single DIP chip
◆ A COAST module (cache on a stick)

The type and amount of memory that a motherboard can support depends on the motherboard, so refer to the motherboard documentation for details. SRAM may be synchronous or asynchronous:

◆ **Synchronous SRAM** uses the system clock to co-ordinate the timing of its signals with the CPU.

◆ **Asynchronous SRAM** does not!

DRAM comes in many forms, as shown in Figure 4.4, and is measured in megahertz.

What does it mean?

Pipelining = a technique to speed up the execution of instructions. The microprocessor starts executing a second instruction before the first one has been completed. Then several instructions – as many as six at a time – are in the 'pipeline'.

DRAM is available in three packagings (see Figure 4.3), as described in Table 4.3.

Rambus DRAM, developed by Rambus Inc is packaged as a RIMM (RAMbus inline memory module). This is similar to the DIMM but has 184 connecting pins. The RIMM memories are 16-bit and are packaged inside a **heat spreader**, an aluminium sheath that protects the RIMM from overheating (Figure 4.5). There is also a SORIMM (small outline RIMM) like the DORIMM.

(c)
DIMM in situ
DIMM has either
SOJ or TSOP
soldered on
two sides

(a)

The DIP form is used
to install memory
directly onto the
motherboard

(b)

SIMMs are either
surface mounted
SOJ (small outline
J-lead) or TSOP
(thin small outline
package) soldered
on one side

Figure 4.3   **DRAM packaging:**
(a) DIP; (b) SIMM; (c) DIMM

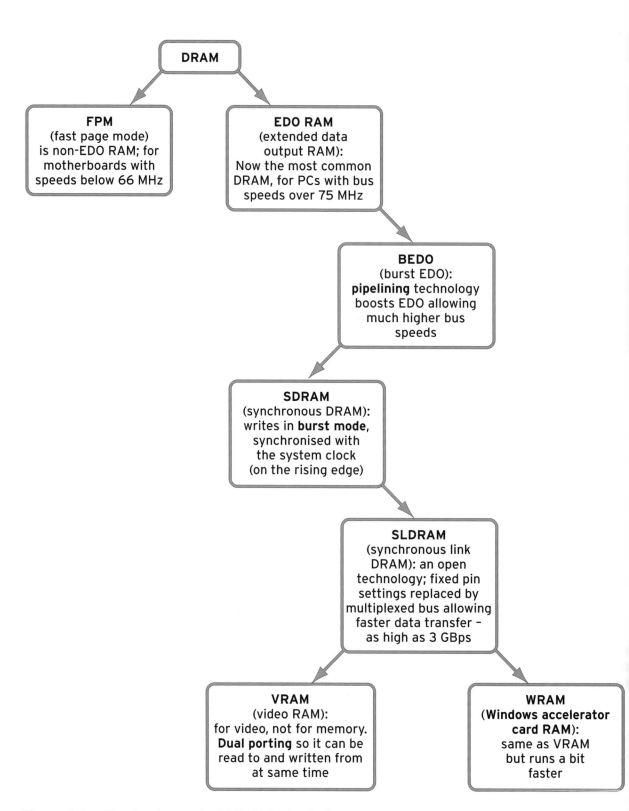

Figure 4.4   **The development of DRAM technologies**

Table 4.3 *RAM packaging options*

Packaging	Notes	See these pages
DIP (dual in-line packaging)	Through-hole electronic component fits through holes in the motherboard Arranged in rows called **banks**	Figure 1.26, page 51 Figure 4.4, page 187
SIMM (single in-line memory module)	Small circuit board of 8 (Macintoshes) or 9 (PCs) RAM chips, the 9th being used for **parity checking** Memory standard for 486 and early Pentiums 32-bit bus 30 or 72 contact pins Capacity of 1–16 MB (NB: measured in bytes) Installed in vertical sockets	Figure 1.3, page 9 Figure 4.4, page 187 Parity checking, page 190
DIMM (dual in-line memory module)	Small circuit board holding memory chips Memory standard for most recent Pentiums 64-bit bus 168 contact pins Available as 3.3 V or 5.0 V, and buffered or unbuffered giving four versions of DIMM*	Figure 1.3, page 9 Figure 4.4, page 187

Note: *Also available as SODIMM (small outline DIMM).

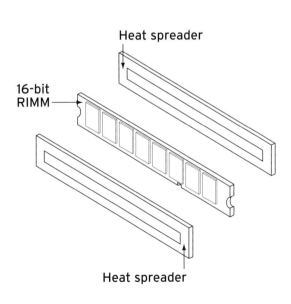

Heat spreader

16-bit RIMM

Figure 4.5
RIMM module within its heat spreader

Heat spreader

VRAM (video RAM) is a special type of RAM, a separate high-speed memory used to store screen data ready for display, thus avoiding using main memory to hold screen data. To calculate the amount of VRAM needed, multiply the resolution by the number of colours, e.g. for 1024×768 with 16-bit colour, you need $1024 \times 768 \times 16$ bits. To turn this into megabytes, divide by 8 (to turn bits into bytes) and then by 1000000 (to turn bytes into megabytes). **WRAM (Windows accelerator card RAM)** is another special type of RAM, also used on video cards. Chapter 1 (page 114) explains how VRAM and WRAM are used to improve the display of video material.

Check Your Understanding 4.3

1 Distinguish between ROM and RAM.
2 What does the D in DRAM mean? How is this different from SRAM?
3 How do SRAM and DRAM compare for speed of access?
4 How do SRAM and DRAM compare for cost?
5 What does COAST stand for?
6 What is meant by 'asynchronous'?
7 What is the benefit of pipelining?
8 Which type of DRAM is based on the Rambus technology?
9 List three types of DRAM packaging.
10 How can you calculate how much memory you need for VRAM?
11 What is WRAM?

Memory integrity

SRAM holds its data and DRAM is refreshed, so does this mean that data is always correct? Well, no! Data can 'leak' and bits change from 0 to 1 (and vice versa). There are two ways that this problem can be addressed:

◆ **Parity checks** can identify if there has been some corruption of data in memory. Parity can be either odd or even. Both forms of parity checking work in the same way: with **odd parity**, for every 8 bits of data, one is used as a parity bit. It is set to 1 to make the number of 1s within those 8 bits odd (or even, if it is **even parity**), or left as 0 if there are already an odd number of bits. When parity is checked, the number of bits set on is expected to be odd (for odd parity, and even for even parity). If it is not, a **parity error** is flagged and the data is known to have been corrupted in some way.

◆ **ECC (error correction code)** identifies and fixes some data corruption. ECC memory can detect up to a 4-bit memory error, and will correct 1-bit errors but report an error for anything more serious.

The **memory controller** supervises the movement of data into and from memory and, in the process, determines which method (if any!) is used to check the integrity of the data:

◆ **Non-parity memory systems** do not check memory using either of the two systems described. You cannot install this form of memory within a parity system; it will fail as soon as you try to boot up.

◆ **Parity memory** will work within a non-parity system; the extra parity bit is simply ignored.

Discuss with a friend and explore how you might check whether there is an option to turn off parity checking within the BIOS setup on your PC.

Check Your Understanding 4.4

1 What is meant by data integrity?
2 Explain what is meant by even parity.
3 What type of memory can detect and correct 1-bit parity errors?
4 What will happen if you install non-parity memory into a parity-checking system?

3 Motherboards, their components and their architecture

The motherboard is the most important piece of equipment within a PC system. It is a PCB (printed circuit board) that houses many of the essential parts of the PC and all connections between the PC and the peripherals go through it. The **form factor** (see Figure 4.6) defines the shape and size of the motherboard, and how it is mounted within the chassis.

Figure 4.6 **Form factors**

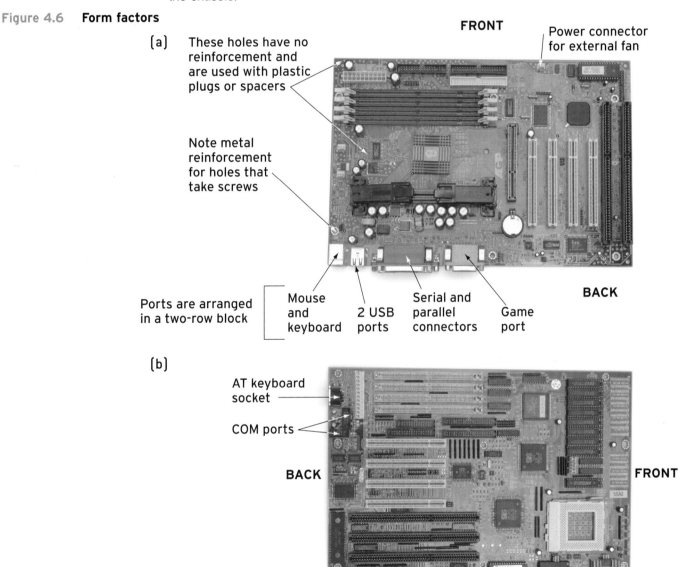

(a)

These holes have no reinforcement and are used with plastic plugs or spacers

Note metal reinforcement for holes that take screws

Ports are arranged in a two-row block

FRONT

Power connector for external fan

BACK

Mouse and keyboard

2 USB ports

Serial and parallel connectors

Game port

(b)

AT keyboard socket

COM ports

BACK

FRONT

Reinforced hole for screwing motherboard into place

Two form factors types are considered in some detail – AT (Full and Baby) and the ATX – see Table 4.4 for a comparison of these motherboards.

191

Table 4.4   *Types of motherboard*

Make	Width (inches)	Length (inches)	Orientation of expansion slots	Extra notes
AT (Full)	12	13	Parallel to longer edge	Same as original IMB PC AT motherboard; now obsolete
Baby AT	8.5	9.5–13	Parallel to longer edge	A smaller version of AT
ATX	7.5	12	Parallel to shorter edge	Similar size to Baby AT

 CHAT *The size of a motherboard is given in inches (Imperial measure). Discuss why this might be so, and calculate the metric equivalents for each of three different form factors.*

There are other form factors (Table 4.5) and, while you do not need to learn these in detail, note the variety of form factors that have been developed in the past.

Table 4.5   *The wide variety of form factors*

Size (inches)	Form factors
8.5 by 8.5	Micro-AT
8.5 by 13	IBM PC; IBM PC XT
8.5 by 10–13	Baby AT
8–9 by 10–11	Mini-LPX*
8–9 by 10–13.6	NLX*
9 by 7.5	Flex-ATX
9 by 11–13	LPX*
9.6 by 9.6	Micro ATX
11.2 by 8.2	Mini ATX
12 by 9.6	ATX
12 by 11–13	AT

*Note: *Backplane design rather than motherboard.*

While Table 4.5 gives the essential information about form factor, other factors also need to be noted when choosing a motherboard:

◆ *Type, placement and size of the power supply.* Is its position convenient for access to other components?

◆ *Power requirements of the system.* Will it supply the required amount of wattage to support your planned configuration?

◆ *Location and type of external connectors.* Will it support everything that you plan to install?

◆ *Airflow and cooling systems.* Will these be powerful enough to protect your system from overheating?

Newer designs of PC – incorporating the ATX motherboard – include an automatic shutdown/restart facility. This **soft switching** means the motherboard controls the power on/off functions. The ATX form also provides **split voltage** to the motherboard. Previously, a voltage regulator was needed to provide the various voltages required from one power source: 3.3 V, ± 5 V and ± 12 V according to the component's needs.

 What does it mean? *Soft switching = the computer turns itself off and restarts itself.*

Split voltage is a way of supplying several different voltages, according to requirements.

The **airflow and cooling system** may seem a minor design point but, like a car engine, if the chips within the PC become overheated, they may fail (see Figure 4.7). Some

Figure 4.7
The effects of overheating

components generate a lot of heat (3D video cards, multiple hard drives, etc.) and these can affect other chips close to them. So, the placement of essential chips (like the CPU!) has to be carefully decided, all within a limited amount of space on the motherboard.

Early PCs (before the 486) were cooled by airflow within the case created by a fan in the PSU. This **radiant cooling** relied on cool air being sucked into the case by the fan. For later models of PC, a **processor cooling fan** or a **heat sink** (or both) were attached to the CPU (Figure 4.8). To make the system even more efficient, the PSU fan was reversed so that it acted as an extractor, pulling hot air out of the PC case.

Figure 4.8   **A heat sink**

Fins on heat sinks
allow heat to pass
to air efficiently

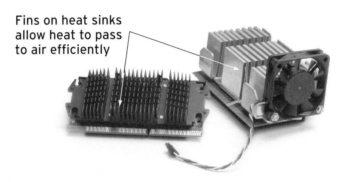

What does it mean?

Heat within any hot material passes to the cooler air around it. A heat sink has lots of fins so that its surface area is maximised and the heat transfer is maximised.

The Pentium processor presents special problems: it runs much hotter than previous designs of chip and so needs a careful heat dissipation system; otherwise it can overheat and fail. The heat sink and/or fan is moulded on to the chip and attached with a **thermal grease**.

What does it mean?

Thermal grease – also known as thermal gunk/compound/goo or heat-sink jelly – is a dialectic gel, i.e. it improves heat conductivity between the two materials it joins.

Watch out

Thermal grease may be mercury based, so avoid contact with your skin.

193

Dust is another problem. Early motherboard designs actually drew cold air (with its dust particles) into the computer, and across the CPU on its way out of the computer. Newer designs take the warm air around the CPU and suck it out of the machine. Laptops are particularly prone to overheating and may need two fans to control the temperature of the chips.

CHAT *Brainstorm with friends: how many different terms are used to describe a motherboard?*

Go and try out 4.5

Research the Internet to find out how the various terms for a motherboard developed.

There are families of motherboard:

◆ A **motherboard-style mainboard** puts all a PC's primary component on single PCB. Being on a single PCB makes it 'motherboard' style.

◆ A **backplane mainboard** provides a number of card slots into which other cards – called **daughterboards** – can be fitted. This allows processors and memory circuit cards to be put together to create particular capability.

There are two types of backplane mainboard:

◆ A **passive backplane** provides a simple bus structure and limited data buffering. This allows the daughterboards to interconnect.

◆ An **active backplane** is more complex and provides extra 'intelligence' to help the daughterboards.

Motherboards may also be integrated or non-integrated:

◆ An **integrated motherboard** provides nearly everything on the one PCB: this includes things which would otherwise be added using expansion cards, such as video and disk controllers.

◆ A **non-integrated motherboard** requires all the extra facilities to be achieved through expansion boards.

Integrated motherboards seem a good idea – everything in one place. That's fine until something goes wrong and the complete motherboard has to be replaced, not just one expansion card. However, the norm is now for integrated motherboards (Figure 4.9).

A motherboard houses many components (Table 4.6). How these components – and other peripherals – relate to each other via the motherboard is determined by **protocols**. Chapter 1 discusses IDE devices (page 95), and SCSI (page 100).

Table 4.6 *Components of a motherboard*

Component	See elsewhere in this book
BIOS and CMOS	18, 204
Bus architectures: ISA, PCI, IDE, SCSI, PCMCIA, USB, AGP, VESA local bus	197–9
Cache memory	28–30
Microprocessor	24–6
Memory: SIMMs and DIMMs	27–30, 49–53
Power supply	11–17
I/O ports including communication ports	Figure 1.2, pages 8–9

Figure 4.9
An integrated motherboard

FRONT

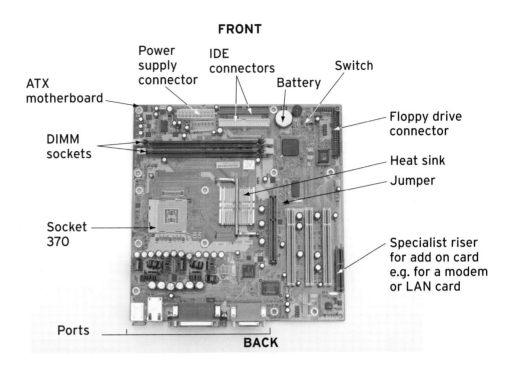

Power supply connector
IDE connectors
Battery
Switch
ATX motherboard
DIMM sockets
Socket 370
Ports
Floppy drive connector
Heat sink
Jumper
Specialist riser for add on card e.g. for a modem or LAN card
BACK

Check Your Understanding 4.5

1 Explain these terms: 'form factor', 'soft switching', 'split voltage'.
2 Explain how a Pentium processor is kept at the optimum temperature.
3 What is thermal grease used for?
4 What is meant by an integrated motherboard?

As an IT technician, you need to be competent at removing and installing motherboards. Chapter 1 includes a how-to panel for installing a motherboard (page 57).

The ability to identify all the components of a motherboard properly should help you when troubleshooting.

Go and try out 4.6

For this activity, you will identify the components on a given motherboard and will need access to manuals for the motherboard as well as access to the Internet.

1 Open the PC case so that you can see the motherboard.
2 Record the information listed in Table 4.7.

Watch out

Check that the systems power supply is disconnected at the wall, that the PC is on an anti-static mat and that you are wearing your ESD wrist strap.

Table 4.7   Components on a motherboard

Components	Available? (Y/N)	Write notes here
Motherboard manufacturer		Name:
Motherboard model number		
Form factor		Physical size and layout:
Type of CPU installed		
Types of CPUs supported		Socket? Slot?
Chipset		
BIOS manufacturer		Name:
BIOS battery		Type:
ISA or EISA		Number and type:
PCI		Number and type:
AGP or AGP Pro		Number and type:
DIP settings		
Jumpers		

Chipsets

The chipset is a group of chips that control the flow (of data, instructions and control signals along the various buses) between the CPU and the memory. It enables communication between the processor and all the peripheral devices connected to the motherboard and contains enough instructions – but only just enough – to issue control commands to device drivers; each driver then controls a particular peripheral device. The chipset also supports extras such as the expansion cards and power management features (see page 208).

A chipset tends to be integrated within the motherboard so – to upgrade – you have to upgrade the complete motherboard. This is important to note: for example, the chipset decides the limit for the amount of memory that a PC can cache. Chipsets can be divided into two:

◆ The larger chip (called the **North Bridge**) looks after main memory, cache memory and the PCI bus controllers.

◆ The smaller chip (called the **South Bridge**) controls peripherals and non-essential functions such as the serial port controller.

Chipsets are matched to a processor (although some support more than one processor) and to the motherboard type. For this reason, they are often named after how they are mounted on the motherboard, by the number or name of the slot/socket. There are other **controller sets** on a motherboard:

◆ The keyboard controller

◆ I/O device controller

CHAT *Discuss with a friend: what other controller sets might be found on a motherboard?*

If a motherboard does not support a particular device within its chipset, or via other controllers, you need to add a card to control the device – or you may purchase an IDE device, in which the controller chip is incorporated. This is an option with many high-end devices.

 What does it mean?

IDE = a generic term to describe any drive that has a built-in controller.

Go and try out 4.7

Visit Intel's websites to find out more about their chip technology. Follow the links from www.heinemann.co.uk/hotlinks.

Make notes on their range of processors and any interesting facts that you discover about the history of the development of their chips.

Bus architecture

The **bus** is a communication link that connects the CPU to the main memory, and allows data and instructions to travel within the computer. There are lots of bus types (Table 4.8).

 CHAT *Brainstorm with friends everything you know about USB.*

Go and try out 4.8

Check out www.heinemann.co.uk/hotlinks and follow the links to find out more about USB.

Buses vary in size: 8-bit, 16-bit, 32-bit or 64-bit:

◆ 8-bit is now outdated.

◆ ISA architecture provides a 16-bit bus.

◆ MCS was the first 32-bit bus.

What does it mean?

A bus is a group of thin wires – electronic transmissions lines – that are used to carry information around the computer.

The more bits supported by the bus, the more data that can be carried at any instant in time. The speed at which the data travels along the bus, though, is determined by the PC clock speed, measured in megahertz. So, it is a combination of bus width and clock speed that determines the processing power of a PC (Figure 4.10).

There are two main types of bus:

◆ The **internal bus** (or **system bus**) connects the main memory, the CPU and all other main components on the motherboard. On Pentium motherboards, the **system chipset** provides this communication link.

Table 4.8 Bus types

Bus type	Notes	See these pages
ISA (industry-standard architecture)	Now outdated and supported by a limited number of motherboards. Originally used in IBM PC/XT and PC/AT. Since 1990s has been replaced by PCI. In 1993, Intel and Microsoft introduced PnP ISA; this enabled the operating system to configure the expansion board automatically, instead of the user setting DIP switches and/or jumpers.	Jumpers, Figure 1.30, page 53
PCI (peripheral component interface)	Local bus standard developed by Intel Corp. A 64-bit bus that may be implemented as a 32-bit bus. Runs at clock speeds of 33 MHz or 66 MHz. With 32-bits and 33 MHz, it yields a throughput rate of 133 MBps.	Clock speed, Figure 1.9, page 22
IDE (integrated drive electronics)	The controller chip WD1003 is mounted on the hard disk, not on an adaptor. Thus the conversion to parallel data is already done on the disk, and transfer speed is increased significantly. The adaptor contains only amplifying circuits to/from the I/O bus and is simple and cheap.	Installing and configuring IDE devices, pages 95–9
SCSI (small computer system interface)	A parallel interface used by Apple Mac, PCs and UNIX systems. Faster data transmission (up to 80 MBps) than standard serial and parallel ports, and allows more than one device to be attached to a single SCSI port. Lack of a single SCSI standard means some devices may not work on some SCSI boards.	Installing and configuring SCSI devices, pages 100–5
PCMCIA	This standard for PC cards was originally designed to add memory to portable computers. There are three different sizes, suitable for a range of devices, and three sizes of slot into which they variously fit.	PC cards and PCMCIA slot, see page 202
USB (universal serial bus)	This PnP interface supports a data speed of 12 Mbps, and accommodates a wide range of devices, such as MPEG video devices, data gloves and digitisers. USB is not vendor specific and is managed by an independent organisation. Full-speed USB devices signal at 12 Mbps, and slow ones use a 1.5 Mbps subchannel.	USB ports, pages 84–6
AGP (accelerated graphics port)	Developed by Intel and based on PCI, this is designed specifically for 3D graphics. It gives direct access to the memory for the graphics controller, speeding up access and allowing 3D textures to be stored in main memory rather than video memory.	AGP graphics card in AGP slot, Figure 1.38, page 60

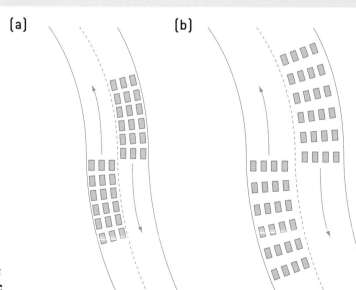

Figure 4.10
The M25 motorway with (a) stationary traffic; and (b) fast-moving traffic

◆ The **external bus** (or **expansion bus**) connects peripherals, i.e. devices outside the PC case, to the motherboard.

There are four types of 'passenger' on a bus, according to the bus:

◆ The **address bus** carries addresses, e.g. of instructions and data, so that the PC can find the next instruction to be executed and find the data to work on, and know where to put the results of any calculation. The width of the address bus determines the highest address in memory that can be directly accessed.

◆ The **control bus** carries control signals! These are used to synchronise movement around the motherboard and to co-ordinate activity within the PC. Control signals give the status of each device attached to the CPU, e.g. the RTS signal meaning 'ready to send'.

◆ The **data bus** is the busiest channel because most data processing involves moving data to/from peripherals. It carries data to and from the CPU, main memory and all the peripherals.

◆ The **power bus** supplies power to each component on the motherboard. The PSU provides power to the motherboard and this is then passed on to other devices that require it.

Check Your Understanding 4.6

1   Distinguish between the internal bus and the external bus.
2   Name the four types of bus according to the data that is carried.

Expansion buses

When you connect a peripheral using an expansion slot, you set up channels through which information can pass:

◆ Some of these channels carry power to the peripheral.
◆ Some connect to the internal address and data buses.
◆ Others are used for **system resources**.

System resources provide the interface for communication and control of individual device adaptors and the serial, parallel and mouse ports. These systems resources vary for each peripheral device but they share common features:

◆ *Timing:* the **clock signal** feeds the expansion card with the bus clock so that the card can synchronise its signals with that of the motherboard.

◆ *Communication from the device to the CPU:* the **IRQ** allows the device to interrupt the CPU and gain attention. There are many devices attached at any one time, so each is given a distinct IRQ number. The CPU then knows which device needs attention and can interpret the other signals accordingly. If two devices share the same IRQ number, this will cause a problem – an **IRQ conflict** – if they are both active at the same time! See Table 1.11 on page 74.

◆ *Communication from the CPU to the device:* the I/O address for each device determines an area within memory where the CPU can leave a message for a device. See Table 1.12 on page 74.

◆ *Direct access to main memory, bypassing the processor* may be an option via a **DMA channel** (page 77).

◆ *Communication between devices, bypassing the processor* may be an option via **bus mastering**. This feature can improve performance of a PC, freeing up the processor for other work.

Table 4.9 shows the progression in development of expansion buses over time, and Figure 4.11 shows examples of these architectures.

The **SCSI** (pronounced skuzzy), although not an architecture, is used to connect internal and external devices. Up to eight such devices (printers, scanners, CD-ROM devices) can be linked in a daisy chain to one **host adaptor card** in the SCSI slot. The SCSI card can be ISA, EISA, VLB or PCI – with features as per Table 4.9.

Table 4.9 *Expansion bus development*

Bus width (bits)	Bus architecture	Notes	Speed (MHz)	Configuration used to designate IRQ or DMA numbers
8		Now out-of-date architecture	Bus speed = 8	Jumpers and DIP switches
16	ISA on 286, 386, 486 and some Pentium PCs	ISA was introduced with the IBM AT and was known as the AT bus; 8-bit architecture extended to include 8 more IRQs and twice as many DMA channels. The bus clock was separate from the CPU clock – allowing the slower data bus to operate at its own pace	Bus speed = 8	Jumpers and DIP switches
32	MCA	MCA was introduced with IBM PS/2; the first 32-bit bus width. Included **bus mastering**. Same size as ISA slot, but twice as many channels	Bus speed = 10	Jumpers and DIP switches replaced by software designation of IRQ and DMA numbers
32	EISA	An improved version of ISA and challenging MCA: backward compatible with ISA due to 8 MHz bus clock; increased number of I/O channels	Bus speed = 8	Software designation of IRQ and DMA numbers
32	VLB on 486s	VESA local bus was developed to provide a slot – called the **bus slot** or **processor direct slot** – which ran at the same speed as the CPU	Processor speed up to 40 MHz	Jumpers and DIP switches
32 or 64	PCI on the Pentium	A processor independent bus with bus speed of 33 MHz	Processor speed up to 33 MHz	PnP devices so automatically configures own IRQ, DMA and I/O port addresses
32	AGP	Based on the PCI, AGP was developed as a high-performance bus for graphics and video. Not backward compatible with PCI	Bus speed = 66 MHz	PnP

Figure 4.11
**Expansion slot
(a) ATX motherboard
expansion slots
AGP, PCI and ISA;
(b) AT motherboard
expansion slots PCI
and ISA**

(a)

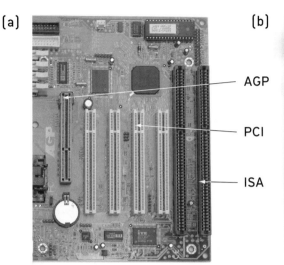

(b)

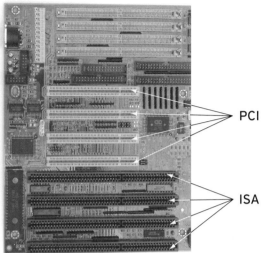

AGP

PCI

ISA

PCI

ISA

Buses of different types can be connected so that devices on one bus can communicate with devices on the other bus (as in a network). The connection is called a **bridge**. For example, in Pentium systems, there may be a PCI-ISA bridge within the chipset. Figure 4.12 shows a bridge that is a normal network connection.

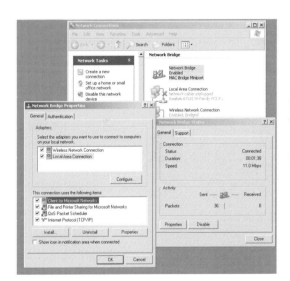

Figure 4.12 **A bridge that is a normal network connection**

Check Your Understanding 4.7

1 Why are expansion buses needed?
2 What name is given to the type of resource used to control individual device adaptors?
3 How is the synchronisation of signals between devices achieved?
4 Explain the meaning of the term 'interrupt'.
5 What is an IRQ conflict?
6 What channel allows a device to access memory directly, bypassing the CPU?
7 What is bus mastering?

Expansion buses for portable devices

On a notebook computer, upgrade slots are usually on the side (Figure 4.13).

PC card slot
allows an 'expansion'
card to be inserted

Figure 4.13
Laptop expansion slots

The PC card – slotted into the PCMCIA bus – is used to add memory, modems, NICs and hard disks to portable computers. Each card is 85.6 mm by 54 mm (3.4 by 2.1 inches!) and there are three thicknesses of PC card:

◆ Type I cards are up to 3.3 mm thick with a single row of connectors (used primarily for RAM or ROM memory).

◆ Type II cards are up to 5 mm thick with two rows of connectors (used for I/O devices such as NICs, data/fax modems and mass storage devices).

◆ Type III cards are up to 10.5 mm thick with four rows of connectors (used for rotating mass storage devices such as an external hard disk for a notebook computer).

These cards fit into one or more of three sizes of slot:

◆ A Type I slot can hold one Type I card.

◆ A Type II slot can hold one Type II card or two Type I cards.

◆ A Type III slot can hold one Type III card or a Type I card and a Type II card.

PC cards can be removed and replaced while the computer is powered up – called **hot-swapping**. This means you can insert a fax modem card to send a fax and then remove it, replacing it with a memory card.

Check Your Understanding 4.8

1 What devices are Type II PC cards used to add to portable computers?
2 Explain the meaning of the term 'hot-swapping'.

Sockets and slots

Table 4.10 lists the socket types used for the Pentium processors. Notice that the number of pins (almost) increases with each new socket type. Figure 4.14 illustrates some of these socket types.

Table 4.10 *Socket types used for Pentium processors*

Socket	Number of pins	Packaging	Processor
Socket 4	274	PGA	Pentium 60; Pentium 66
Socket 5	320	SPGA	3v
Socket 7	321	SPGA	Super 7 socket is used for AMD K6 processors
Socket 8	386	SPGA/ZIF	Pentium Pro
Socket 370	370	PPGA	Celeron; name confirms the number of pins!

Sockets 0–3 and 6 were used on the 486 processor, and are not important for this course. Table 4.11 shows the slot types that are used to mount microprocessors on to motherboards.

Figure 4.14
Socket types: (a) Slot 1 on ATX motherboard; (b) Socket 5 on AT motherboard; and (c) Socket 370Z1F on ATX motherboard

(a)

Slot 1 with supports retracted

(b)

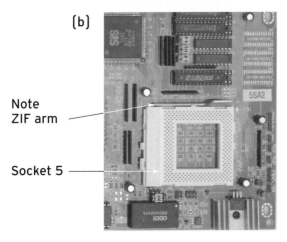

Note ZIF arm

Socket 5

(c)

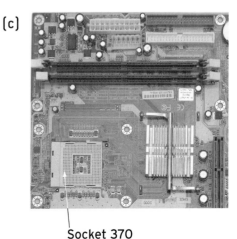

Socket 370

203

Table 4.11 *Slot types*

Slot	Notes
Slot 1	AKA SC-242 connector: Intel's connector for Celeron, Pentium I and Pentium II processors
Slot 2	AKA SC-330 connector: Intel's connector for Pentium II Xeon and Pentium III Xeon; helps multiple processors to work together in the same PC
Slot A	Physically the same as Slot 1, but with different pin assignment making it unusable with Intel processors. Used by AMD Athlon
Slot M	For 64-bit Intel Ithanium processor

Check Your Understanding 4.9

1 Which socket type is used for the Pentium Pro?
2 Which slot type is used for AMD Athlon?

4 CMOS

CMOS (complementary metal-oxide semiconductor, pronounced sea-moss) is a form of memory that uses IC semiconductor chips. It enjoys the benefits of semiconductor memory:

◆ The storage capacity is high.
◆ The time to read data is very short.
◆ Access is direct.
◆ CMOS requires little power to retain their content; with small batteries to power them, they provide non-volatile memory (which does not lose its data when the power is switched off).

So CMOS is a special type of non-volatile memory. Needing only 1 millionth of an amp of electrical power, it can be powered using a low-voltage dry cell or lithium battery. The CMOS battery (Figure 4.15) is located on the motherboard (or on older systems, in a battery pack attached to the PC case).

CMOS was originally used to store the configuration data for a PC, but is now used in nearly all memory and processor chips. At start up, during the boot sequence, the BIOS runs the POST program which verifies the configuration data in the CMOS for any physical devices that are detected.

The CMOS contains details of all the peripheral devices and system settings for a PC. When you buy a new PC, the CMOS will have standard settings, but these can be changed to suit each individual user. You may also want to change the CMOS settings if you are upgrading your PC and/or adding new peripherals.

To view the current CMOS settings, you need to interrupt the boot process. Each make of PC has a particular key (or combination of keys) that allows you to do this. To stop the

Figure 4.15
A CMOS battery

CMOS battery

boot up, you have a short time span when you can interrupt the process and enter the **setup program** (Table 4.12).

Table 4.12	*BIOS Setup Program access keys*
Key	**BIOS**
F1	IBM Aptiva
F1 or F2	Phoenix BIOS
F10	Compaq
Delete	AMI, Award
Ctrl + Alt + Esc	Award

The key that you need to use is shown during the on-screen sequence during the booting up. If you miss interrupting the boot process the first time, make a note of the relevant key and restart your computer, pressing the key before it starts to load up your operating system.

 Discuss with your friends how you can access the current CMOS settings on each of your PCs.

Having interrupted the booting-up process, you can access the configuration menu and change the settings to suit your own requirements. You would be wise to take a backup of your PC's hard disk before making any changes to the BIOS – just in case! There are two levels of settings:

◆ Standard settings (Table 4.13) cover the basic data for your system (such as the clock) and peripherals.

◆ Advanced settings cover more complex settings, e.g. for the motherboard, processor and chipset.

 With a friend, discuss under what circumstances you might need to change the date and time through the Control Panel.

205

Table 4.13 Standard CMOS settings

Setting	Example	Notes
System clock (date and time)	MM/DD/YY HH:MM	The current time may also be altered through the Control Panel
IDE primary and secondary masters		Default setting is 'Auto', i.e. the system relies on auto-detection
Floppy disk drives (A and B)		Type of disk: default may be 1.44 MB in drive A and drive B 'Not installed' (see Table 4.14 and Figure 4.16 for a full list of disk types)
Video display	VGA/EGA	
Halt on		May be three levels: halt on no errors; halt on all but . . .; halt on all errors

Table 4.14 Floppy disk types

Capacity	3.5-inch	5.25-inch
360 KB		Low-density 5.25-inch disk (now obsolete?)
720 KB	Low-density 3.5-inch floppy disk	
1.2 MB		'Normal' 5.25-inch floppy disk
1.44 MB	'Normal' (default) 3.5-inch floppy disk	
2.88 MB	High-density 3.5-inch floppy disk	

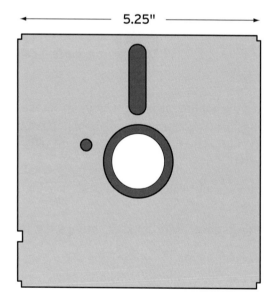
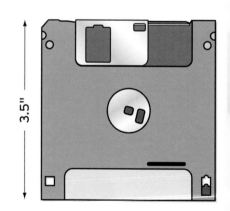

Figure 4.16   **Floppy disks**

Go and try out 4.9

Complete this activity, working in pairs. Make notes as you explore the CMOS setting options.

1 Turn on the PC and interrupt the boot sequence (Figure 4.17).

Figure 4.17
The opening start-up screen

Award Modular BIOS v6.00PG, An Energy Star Ally
Copyright (C) 1984-99, Award Software, Inc

26167MS V.13 122999

Main Processor : AMD Athlon(TM) 1000MHz
Memory Testing : 131072K OK

Award Plug and Play BIOS Extension v1.0A
Copyright (C) 1999, Award Software, Inc.

Interrupt the boot sequence by pressing a key

Press DEL to enter setup
2/29/199-AMD-72M-23296-7878DA343DC-OB

2 Explore the settings that you might change and look, in particular, for these options (Figure 4.18):

Explore the Advanced menu, Power menu and Boot menu

The Exit menu is shown in Figure 2.4 on page 136

On the main menu you can amend the system time and date

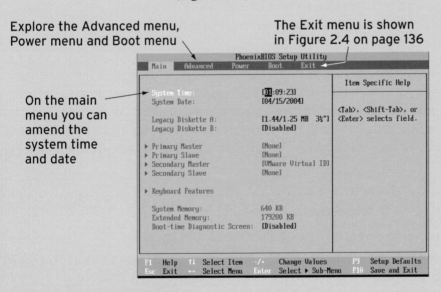

PhoenixBIOS Setup Utility

| Main | Advanced | Power | Boot | Exit |

System Time: [01:09:23]
System Date: [04/15/2004]

Legacy Diskette A: [1.44/1.25 MB 3½"]
Legacy Diskette B: [Disabled]

▶ Primary Master   [None]
▶ Primary Slave   [None]
▶ Secondary Master   [VMware Virtual ID]
▶ Secondary Slave   [None]

▶ Keyboard Features

System Memory: 640 KB
Extended Memory: 179200 KB
Boot-time Diagnostic Screen: [Disabled]

Item Specific Help

<Tab>, <Shift-Tab>, or <Enter> selects field.

F1 Help   ↑↓ Select Item   -/+   Change Values   F9   Setup Defaults
Esc Exit   ←→ Select Menu   Enter Select ▶ Sub-Menu   F10 Save and Exit

- COM/serial port: memory address, interrupt request, disable.
- Printer parallel port: uni, bidirectional, disable/enable, ECP, EPP.
- Floppy drive: enable/disable drive or boot, speed, density.
- Hard drive: size/drive type.
- Memory: parity, non-parity.

Figure 4.18   **Screens at setup**

3 Note any other options.

There may also be settings for PnP. If PnP is not supported on your system, the BIOS start-up program will store an ESCD in CMOS to assign the system resources for your PnP devices.

What does it mean?

EPP (enhanced parallel port) allows bidirectional communication, but only one way at a time, i.e. half duplex.

SPP (standard parallel port) allows one-way communication between a computer and a printer, i.e. simplex.

PnP (Plug and Play) is a configuration standard that allows the BIOS and your operating system to recognise and automatically configure a peripheral as soon as you plug it into your computer.

ESCD (extended system configuration data) serves as the link between the BIOS and the operating system for PnP devices.

Depending on your BIOS, there may be additional start-up menus:

◆ The **power management** menu allows you to set options to be used when the system automatically powers down.

◆ The **integrated peripherals** menu relates to those peripherals that are part of – i.e. integrated into – the motherboard, e.g. USB, audio and serial and parallel ports.

Go and try out 4.10

1 Turn on your PC and interrupt the boot sequence.
2 Go to Advanced settings and list the options open to you.

You should keep a hard copy of your current CMOS settings, and date this. Then, when you make a change, note and date the changes. This 'audit trail' of your customisation of the CMOS may prove very useful if something goes wrong with your PC. For example, if you were to remove the CMOS battery from the PC (for any reason!), settings – such as the user and supervisor passwords – will automatically be reset to the original factory default settings.

Passwords

You have the option to set passwords at two levels:

◆ The **user-level** password is needed before the PC will boot up.

◆ The higher level is **supervisor level**. Without this password, you cannot access the BIOS settings.

If you set up both passwords but forget one or both of them, what will happen?

◆ If you forget the user password but can remember the supervisor password, you can turn on the PC and interrupt the boot process before it reaches the point of asking for the user password. You can then use the supervisor password to reset the user password (and then make a point to remember it!).

◆ If you forget the supervisor password but can remember the user password, you can use the PC but you cannot make any further changes to the BIOS settings.

◆ If you forget both passwords, you have problems!

You can temporarily bypass the password-checking process. To do this, you need to use the password-clear jumper (Figure 4.19). However, unless you recall the supervisor password, you cannot reset the user password.

All is not lost though – provided you kept track of the BIOS settings that you have made to your PC. You can remove the CMOS battery so that these two passwords are reset to the factory default settings – and then configure the CMOS settings from scratch again.

Figure 4.19
A password-clear jumper

BIOS CMOS
clear jumper

5 Upgrade or replace?

If your PC seems too slow for you, or you want to install new software or new peripheral devices, you may need to think about upgrading.

Should you upgrade by making changes to your current PC or should you buy a new one? The decision is yours – but these questions may help you to decide:

◆ *How old is your current PC?* If your PC is very old, developments in technology may well have overtaken it, and you may need to think seriously about replacing it, simply to take advantage of new products (hardware and software).

◆ *What specification are you aiming for?* Be quite clear in your own mind what you are trying to achieve. What is essential? What might be considered an optional extra? If someone else is paying for this new PC, they might have different ideas about what is, and what is not, an essential feature.

◆ *How much do you have to spend?* You will want to get the best value for your money, but you may be limited in your choice by how much you can afford. If you do decide to buy a new PC, you might be wise to spend up to your limit and to purchase a PC with the best spec available, even if right now it seems to supersede your requirements. In a year's time, it may look quite old hat!

Having established the parameters of your own requirements, consider the choices open to you for each component of the PC. Think first about the motherboard and its form factor, and then be sure to choose a motherboard that is well supported by documentation! Table 4.15 summarises your options.

You will also have to spend time considering alternative suppliers. This is beyond the scope of this course, but you will find almost everything you need to know on the Internet.

Discuss with others in your group what they have done in the past: upgraded or bought new. What lessons have you learnt between you?

Figure 4.20   **To upgrade or replace?**

Table 4.15 *Thinking about upgrading*

Component	Things to think about	Sources of information
Motherboard	Form factor: you are limited by the PC case as to what would physically fit. The power supply must match the form factor – and changing the form factor may mean you have to change this. Similarly, if you change the case so as to change the form factor, you might have to purchase a new power supply.	Check the supplier documentation and your own documentation.
	BIOS: choose the best! You will want to take advantage of newer technologies.	See flash ROM (page 27), PnP (page 208), and ATA standard (page 95).
	If you are looking to increase the number of devices supported, look in particular at the number and type of slots and sockets provided.	Sockets/slots (pages 203–4).
	It may be that some devices, for which you currently have expansion boards, are supported on the new motherboard via built-in connectors. This would leave you even more room for expansion in the future.	Check the supplier information for what devices have in-built controllers.
	The bus speed of the motherboard (and its chipset) must be compatible with your CPU. Otherwise, you'll need to replace the CPU too. The chipset is likely to be integrated into the motherboard; any change to the chipset means a new motherboard.	Check the supplier documentation and your own documentation.
CPU	Whether you can even think about upgrading depends on your current motherboard (its form factor and chipset).	Check the documentation supplied with your motherboard.
	Some upgrade options may have a knock-on effect and mean you also have to change other components (like the PSU).	Check the specification for each CPU you are considering and check its compatibility with your current PC specification.
	Your choice of CPU also depends on the CPU socket provided on your motherboard.	Identify the CPU mounting type; this should also be clear from your documentation.
	Should you keep to the same manufacturer? Upgrades within a series of processors from one manufacturer may be more viable than trying to change manufacturer.	Check the supplier's documentation. Ideally this should be done when you initially buy a PC, but then you would probably choose the latest version provided by a particular manufacturer and not know what future developments are likely.
Cache memory	Any additional L2 cache memory must match the motherboard bus speed. Take care not to add too much; it may actually reduce performance.	
Memory	Check how much memory your motherboard will support before buying extra memory cards.	Types of memory (pages 27–30).

Revision 4

Remember these facts:

1   The motherboard contains the CPU, power supply connections, ROM BIOS, CMOS chip and chipset, RAM and RAM cache, jumpers, expansion slots, I/O ports including communication ports and real-time clock.

2   Chips have basic characteristics: physical size, voltage, caching ability, the socket/slot used for mounting on the motherboard.

3   ROM is read-only memory. It can be read but not written to. RAM (random access memory) can be read from and written to.

4   Dynamic RAM needs to be refreshed.

5   Synchronous SRAM uses the system clock to co-ordinate the timing of its signals with the CPU.

6   RAM is packaged in DIPs, SIMMs and DIMMs.

7   Parity checks can identify if there has been some corruption of data in memory. ECC (error correction code) identifies and fixes some data corruption.

8   The memory controller supervises the movement of data into and from memory and, in the process, determines which method is used to check the integrity of the data.

9   The form factor defines the shape and size of the motherboard, and how it is mounted within the chassis.

10   Soft switching means the motherboard controls the power on/off functions.

11   The CPU performance is measured by its speed, the efficiency of its programming code, the size of its L1 cache, word size, data bus size, the maximum memory address that can be accessed and any multiprocessing abilities.

12   CPUs need cooling and may have a heat sink and/or fan attached using thermal grease to prevent an air gap between the CPU and the cooling device.

13   CPUs fit into slots (1, A, 2) or sockets (7, 370, 423, 603).

14   The chipset is a group of chips that control the flow (of data, instructions and control signals along the various buses) between the CPU and the memory.

15   A ROM chip contains the code to manage the POST and system BIOS and to let you make changes to the CMOS settings.

16   The bus is a communication link that connects CPU to the main memory, and allows data and instructions travel within the computer. Buses vary in size: 8-bit, 16-bit, 32-bit or 64-bit.

17   The SCSI (pronounced skuzzy), although not an architecture, is used to connect internal and external devices.

18 Buses of different types can be connected by a bridge, so that devices on one bus can communicate with devices on the other bus (as in a network).

19 The PC card – slotted into the PCMCIA bus – is used to add memory, modems, NICs and hard disks to portable computers. PC cards can be removed and replaced while the computer is powered up – called hot-swapping.

20 Passwords can be set at user level (to block booting up by unauthorised users) and supervisor level (to control access to BIOS settings).

Chapter 5 **Printers**

1 **Basic concepts: printer operations and printer components**

Printers are peripheral devices, attached to the processor by a port, and they have a certain amount of intelligence: to receive commands and data from the processor, and to send signals back to the processor. Details of the various printer connections and configurations are covered in this chapter (page 224) and information on the logical device names for printer connections, IRQs and I/O addresses is on page 74.

This section concentrates on the different types of printers and how they work. Table 5.1 summarises the information, but the sections that follow give more detail.

Table 5.1	*Categories of printer*				
Category	**Impact printer?**	**Feed mechanism**	**Printer type**	**Resolution**	**Speed**
Dot matrix	Yes	Continuous	Character	9-, 18-, 24-pin (NLQ)	32–72 CPS
Inkjet	No	Sheet	Line	150–1400 dpi	2–9 PPM
Laser	No	Sheet	Page		

Printers produce output on paper, and all printers have a mechanism for pulling in paper and pushing it out after the printing has been completed. Basically, there are two options for paper feeder mechanisms:

◆ **Sheet feed** (see Figure 5.1) prints on single sheets of paper, usually A4. These may be taken from an in-tray and then deposited in an out-tray.

◆ **Continuous stationery** can be fed through a printer by rotating sprocket bands (see Figure 5.2). The two outer edges of the paper have sprocket holes which fit on to the sprocket bands, and are clipped into place. The position of the rotating bands on the platen can be moved to accommodate different widths of continuous stationery.

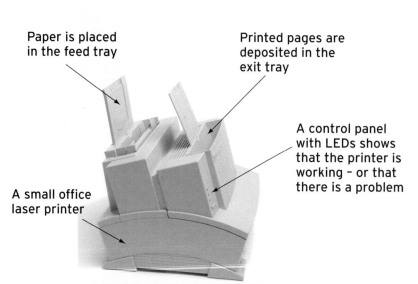

Paper is placed in the feed tray

Printed pages are deposited in the exit tray

A control panel with LEDs shows that the printer is working – or that there is a problem

A small office laser printer

Figure 5.1
Sheet paper feed

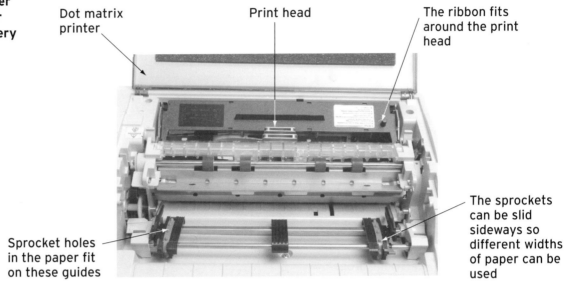

Figure 5.2   A paper feed mechanism for continuous stationery

Dot matrix printer

Print head

The ribbon fits around the print head

The sprockets can be slid sideways so different widths of paper can be used

Sprocket holes in the paper fit on these guides

The marks are made on the paper by a printing process and these vary according to how the printing is achieved.

Go and try out 5.1

Older technologies of printers involved burning the characters on to the page, and/or using special types of paper. Research the Internet to find out more about these alternative printing options. Are any still in use today?

Dot matrix printers

A dot matrix printer has a moving ribbon through which pins are hammered to create dots of ink on the paper, which is held in place on the rolling platen.

What does it mean?

The platen is the rubberised roller against which characters are printed in an impact printer.

Each pin makes a single dot and the number of pins that are used is a measure of the resolution of the printer, in dpi (dots per square inch). It may be 9, 18 or 24 pins. The 9- and 18-pin versions can only produce draft quality output; the 24-pin version is called **NLQ (near-letter quality)**. However, none of these is as good as can be produced on the inkjet or laser printers.

Dot matrix printers are examples of **impact printers** – and the impact is noisy! However, the pressure of the impact means that this type of printer is good for printing on to multi-part documents. Neither laser printers nor inkjet printers can be used for this purpose.

Paper is usually continuously fed, and the colour of the print is limited by the ribbon. Often this is only black, but it is possible to have two colours: black and red. The ribbon can be messy to replace (see Figure 5.3)! Wash your hands as soon as you have done it, to avoid leaving inky fingerprints wherever you go.

Figure 5.3 **The ribbon for a dot matrix printer**

The ribbon has to be fitted around the print head

The ribbon needs to be taut. This allows adjustment

The cartridge drops into place on a dot matrix printer

The speed of the printing is measured in characters per second (CPS). Typical speeds are 32-72 CPS but can depend on the mode being used:

- **Font mode** creates one character at a time: text, numbers or symbols.
- **Dot-addressable mode** is used for graphics and charts.

Watch out

Do not touch the print head of a dot matrix printer; it may be hot. Clumsy handling of the print head – when cold – can damage the fragile pin wires.

Go and try out 5.2

1 You may not meet a dot matrix. They are relatively old technology. Research the Internet for details of dot matrix printers and even earlier technologies.
2 Nowadays, printers are combined with other features, such as scanning and photocopying. Research the Internet for such combination products.

Inkjet printers

An inkjet printer squirts ionised ink on to the paper where it cools and dries. As many as 50 tiny nozzles may be used in the ink stream. Magnetised plates in the ink's path direct the ink on to the paper in the desired shapes. **Bubble-jet printers** work in much the same way.

Most inkjets use thermal technology, whereby heat is used to fire the ink on to the paper. The squirt is initiated by heating ink to create a bubble; pressure then forces it to burst and hit the paper. Because heat is involved, there has to be a cooling process and this slows down the process. Another method uses a piezo crystal at the back of the ink reservoir. Like a loudspeaker cone, this flexes when an electric current flows through it. So, when a dot is required, a current is applied to the piezo element; the element flexes and forces a drop of ink out of the nozzle.

There are advantages of the piezo method:

◆ There is greater control over the shape and size of ink droplet.

◆ The ink does not have to be heated, so there is no need for ink that can withstand high temperatures.

◆ There is no heating and so no need for a cooling process, saving time.

The ink is bought in cartridge form and is clean to replace. Black cartridges can be used for bulk text printing but colour cartridges are also available, offering a spectrum of colours from three separate jets of colour. The print mechanism is also within the cartridge so this is replaced each time you install a new cartridge.

Like dot matrix printers, the resolution is measured in dpi, but you would expect 150–1400 dpi to give much better quality printing.

These printers do not rely on impact to create a character and so – apart from the print head moving to and fro – they are quiet.

Paper is fed in one sheet at a time. The next sheet is sucked into its starting position. Then rollers are used to clamp the sheet in place while the printing takes place. The paper moves on, synchronised with the movement of the print head until a complete sheet has been printed. The sheet is then ejected to be retained in a tray.

The speed is measured in pages per minute (PPM) because the CPM measure is not applicable. Lines of print are created in several passes and then a complete line of characters appears, before the process moves on to create the next line of characters. An inkjet printer is an example of a **line printer**. Typical speeds are 2-9 PPM.

One drawback of inkjet printers is that they require a special type of ink that is apt to smudge on inexpensive copier paper (see Figure 5.4), so you really ought to use a higher-quality paper. Despite the need for more expensive paper, inkjet printers are generally not as expensive as laser printers, but they will be considerably slower.

CASE STUDY   Nigel the novice PC user

Nigel has an inkjet printer.

1 Explain how the printer puts ink on to the paper.

2 Explain why there are two (or more) different cartridges to install.

3 Explain the characteristics of inkjet printers – resolution and printing speed – giving the units used to measure these.

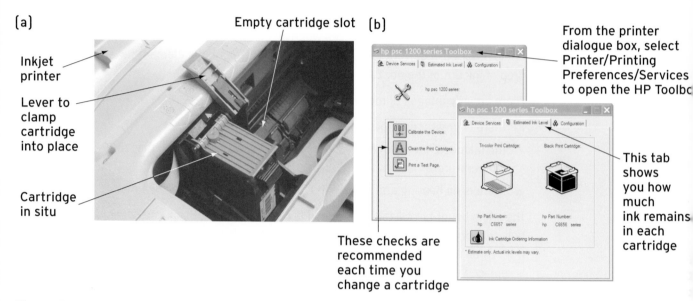

Figure 5.4
(a) Changing cartridges on an inkjet printer; (b) the software cleaning option

Laser printers

A laser printer is an example of a **page printer**. The paper is fed through rollers but the image for a complete page is created in one go.

The process of printing a page – called the **EP (electrophotographic) process**, first developed by Xerox and Canon – uses a laser beam to produce an electrostatic charge and then a dry toner to create the printed image. Hewlett Packard then developed a similar process, called the **HP process**. Later, the **LED (light-emitting diode) process** was developed; this replaces the laser with an array of LEDs and, for 600 dpi resolution, it needs 600 LEDs per inch.

Toner is made from fine iron particles coated in a plastic resin. When heated, the plastic melts and the toner sticks to – or bonds with – the paper. The toner is supplied within a cartridge, so replacing the toner should be a clean process (Figure 5.5). However, if you do spill toner, refer to page 223 for details of what action to take.

Within the cartridge, as well as the toner, there are also two other component parts of the process:

◆ A **photosensitive drum** holds an electrical charge, apart from where light has been shone on to it.

◆ A **roller** is used to develop the final image on the paper.

Within the printer itself, there are then other essential components, starting with the power supply:

◆ A **high-power voltage supply** converts the AC current into higher voltages needed by the printer to charge the drum and transfer and hold the toner on the paper surface.

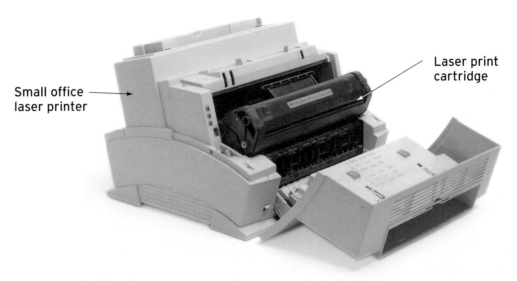

Small office laser printer

Laser print cartridge

Figure 5.5
Changing ink cartridges on a laser printer

◆ A **DC power supply** is used to run the logic circuitry (± 5 V), the paper transport motors (24 V) and a cooling fan.

Moving paper in and out of the laser printer involves four types of rollers, each having its own motor:

◆ The **feed roller** picks up the paper from the input tray and feeds it into the printer.

◆ The **registration roller** lines up the page at the correct position, ready for the writing stage of the printing process.

◆ The **fuser rollers** apply pressure to the paper – and heat it to 165–180°C – so that the plastic resin within the toner melts and the iron particles stick to the paper. These rollers are Teflon coated and treated with an oil to stop the paper sticking to them as it passes.

◆ The **exit roller** deposits the printed page in the out-tray.

Watch out

The heat within a laser printer is from the fusing process – not from the laser beam itself.

Most printer problems happen in the paper transport area of the printer. See page 223 for common problems with printers.

The electronics of the laser printer may rely on two corona wires:

◆ The **primary corona** – also known as the **main corona** or the **primary grid** – creates an electrical field to charge the photosensitive drum uniformly to -600 V. This corona is inside the cartridge and prepares the drum to receive the image.

◆ The **transfer corona** creates a charge on the paper, to which toner will be drawn by the magnetic properties of the iron within the toner. The paper passes across the transfer corona and then on to a **static charge eliminator strip** which reduces the charge so that the toner will not stick to the drum. (Some printers use a transfer roller instead of a transfer corona wire.)

The **controller** of the printer is its own motherboard, similar to the motherboard of a PC:

- The controller communicates with the PC.
- It has a memory to hold details of what is to be printed.
- It controls the other parts of the printer, thus creating a printed page.

As with the memory of a PC, the size of the memory of a printer can be increased to allow larger documents to the printed, and to generate high-resolution graphics.

Having met all the component parts, Table 5.2 lists the essential stages in printing a page and Figure 5.6 illustrates it. Note that the first four stages take place inside a removable toner cartridge.

The standard toner is black, but colour laser printers are also available, at even greater cost.

Table 5.2 *Printing a page on a laser printer*

Step	Stage	Notes
1	Cleaning	A fluorescent light is shone on the drum to remove any electrical charge. Any toner left over from the previous printing will become unstuck and a rubber blade is used to clear it off the drum. This toner is not recycled but goes into a separate compartment reserved for such used toner particles.
2	Conditioning	The primary corona conditions the drum by creating an electrical field so that the drum is uniformly charged to -600 V.
3	Writing	A laser beam and a series of mirrors are used to trace an image on the drum. The laser bean is turned on and off and where the light shines on the drum, its charge is reduced to about -100 V. The paper is then brought into position, held by the registration rollers.
4	Developing	The magnet within the developing roller within the toner cartridge attracts the iron particles of the toner. As the developing roller rotates near the drum, the toner is attracted to the areas of the drum that have lower voltages, thus creating the required image on the drum.
5	Transferring	The back side of the paper is given a positive charge and, as it passes by the drum, this attracts the negatively charged toner from the drum on to the paper. The toner is then in the correct position but needs to be fixed into place.
6	Fusing	The paper passes between the fusing rollers and the combination of pressure and heat bonds the toner to the paper.

Check Your Understanding 5.1

1. Give an example of a page printer.
2. Give an example of a printer that has a continuous paper feed mechanism.
3. What is meant by NLQ?
4. What is an impact printer? Give an example.
5. What is a platen?
6. Where would a piezo crystal be used? What are the advantages of using a piezo crystal?
7. What voltages are used within a printer, and how are these supplied?
8. Name the four types of roller within a laser printer.
9. Distinguish between the primary corona and the transfer corona.
10. List the five stages in the EP/HP process, in the correct order.

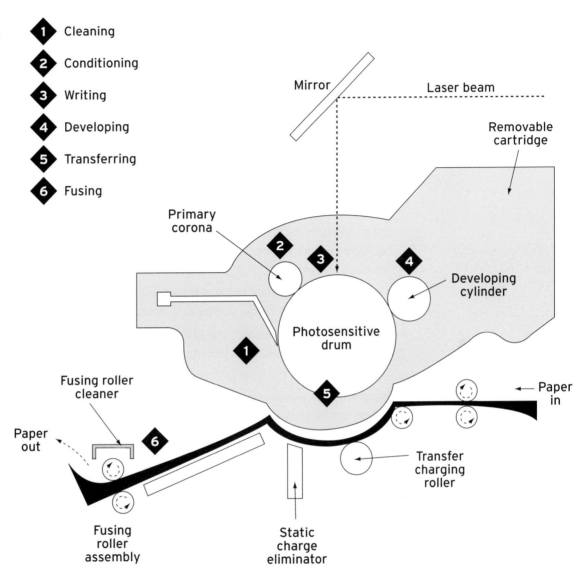

Figure 5.6
The stages of EP

1 Cleaning
2 Conditioning
3 Writing
4 Developing
5 Transferring
6 Fusing

2 Care and service techniques, and common problems

Printers are an essential part of most computers. It is therefore important that you can care for a printer, applying service techniques and solving common problems.

Following the manufacturer's recommendations

To ensure good feed of paper and output of printed pages, always use the correct weight and type of paper as per the printer manufacturer's recommendations. Some lasers print best on special laser paper, which is finished on one side.

 To save money, some people buy refilled ink cartridges. Is this a good idea?

Keeping the printer clean

One way of keeping a printer clean is to avoid introducing dirt into it:

◆ With a laser printer that has a transfer roller, do not touch the roller. The natural oils on your skin will permanently mark the roller.

◆ If you have a paper jam, remove any torn paper carefully, as per the manufacturer's recommendations.

You then need to clean the printer regularly as part of your maintenance program:

◆ The fuser rollers can become dirty and leave residue on the paper. Clean these printer parts as necessary to maintain print quality.

◆ Dot matrix printers can be vacuum cleaned, or any dust blown out with compressed air. For laser printers, special vacuum cleaners are required; otherwise, the toner can ruin the vacuum cleaner.

◆ A wire brush can be used to clean the paper transport of an inkjet or laser printer. Rubber-conditioning products may also be used.

◆ The laser printer produces ozone gas and may have an ozone filter to trap this gas and any paper dust. Replace this filter as per the manufacturer's recommendations.

◆ The mirrors inside the laser printer can be cleaned with a lint-free cloth.

◆ The printer may have a head-cleaning sequence. For example, an inkjet printer will have a head-cleaning utility so, if you don't use the printer for some time and the ink dries out, you can refresh the nozzles. Figure 5.4 on page 218 shows the software used to clean an inkjet printer.

◆ Some printers provide a utility to check the quality of the print, e.g. for alignment of the colour guns. The software provided with the printer will guide you on how to use this.

Go and try out 5.3

For this activity, work in groups of three, with three printers: a dot matrix printer, a laser printer and an inkjet printer. Select one printer each.

1 Examine the printer to see what might need cleaning. Do a sample print to check the quality of printing.
2 Consult the user documentation for cleaning and maintenance recommendations.
3 Decide what cleaning you will do, and what products you need. See page 168 to check the purpose of various types of preventive maintenance products.
4 Clean the printer.
5 Explain to your two friends what you did, and compare notes with each other as to the differences between the cleaning done for the three types of printer.

CHAT   *Discuss how often a printer should be cleaned.*

Avoiding accidents

As with other PC equipment there are a few safety rules to follow:

◆ For most printers, plug it into a surge protector or UPS. However, do not plug a laser printer into a conventional PC UPS, unless the UPS can handle the peak loading of the laser printer.

◆ Remember that the fusing rollers of a laser can be hot.

◆ If you spill toner on your skin, brush it off carefully. Do not use hot water; this may cause the toner to fuse with your skin! Instead, use cold water, if necessary, to wash the affected area.

◆ Never look directly at the laser; it would burn your eye.

 What other safety advice can you give? Hint: think clothing.

Common problems

Printers have moving parts which finely co-ordinate movement of the paper with that of the printing mechanism, so there is much that can go wrong. You may have made the 'usual' mistakes during installation:

◆ Have you securely connected the correct cabling to the correct port using the correct orientation?

◆ Have you installed a printer driver that is appropriate for your type of printer?

◆ If you have several printers set up, are you sending the printout to the printer that is connected, and/or have you set the printer up as the default printer?

Unit 2 (page 309) focuses on the software aspects of using printers. Table 5.3 identifies common hardware-related problems that you need to be able to address.

Even the cheapest of printers (at under £100) will have software to help you to troubleshoot printing problems, so this is a useful source of help (Figure 5.7).

Figure 5.7   The help screen for the HP psc1210 printer/scanner/copier

Table 5.3 *Common printer problems*

Problem	What to check	Notes
Paper fails to print	Is the printer power cable plugged into the wall socket? Is the cable the correct type? Is each end of the cable well connected? Is the printer turned on? Is there a supply of paper in the in-tray? Has there been a paper jam? Is the port working?	To check the port, use loopback plugs. Diagnostic software may also report printer errors during the POST process. Your application software may have stopped responding. If it is a software error, closing down and restarting the system may solve the problem.
Printer memory overflow errors	Is the memory board working? Has the memory board been installed correctly?	If the memory board is working correctly, you may need to install additional memory.
Paper jam	Are you using the correct weight of paper? Does the printer need cleaning? Is humidity causing the sheets of paper to stick together? Is there a thickness control mechanism which is not set correctly?	In clearing a paper jam, take care when removing torn pieces of paper. None must remain. Fanning the paper before putting it into the feed tray helps to separate the sheets. Some printers have a thickness control which means it grips more (or less) tightly to the paper as it passes by.
Poor print quality	Is the toner running low? Is the lightness/darkness setting correct?	Taking the toner cartridge out of a laser printer and shaking it (gently) will give you some more printing before you have to replace the cartridge. If you have black smudges then you may have a problem with the rollers; clean the printer.

Go and try out 5.4

For this activity, work in pairs, taking it in turns to be the user and the technician.

1 On your own, plan a hardware fault that you will present to the other person, e.g. disconnected cabling, paper jam, blotchy printing. Decide on a type of printer and what symptoms that your printer and/or PC would show if this fault were to happen.
2 Taking turns, act as user and technician pair. The technician asks questions to try to find out what the problem is. The user answers these questions (honestly!).
3 Then the technician of the pair suggests what to do to isolate the fault, and hopefully fix it.
4 The user can then reveal the actual source of the problem. Discuss whether the technician in your pair would have found the fault, and anything that might have improved the troubleshooting technique.
5 Repeat the activity, choosing different printer faults.

3 Printer connections and configurations

Printers are peripheral devices; they are attached to the processor by a port, e.g. a serial or parallel port, a USB or an IrDa interface. How to connect a printer is covered in Chapter 1 (page 43).

What does it mean?

USB (universal serial bus) is a higher-speed serial connection standard that supports low-speed devices (mice, keyboards, scanners) and higher-speed devices (digital cameras).

CHAT *Identify the cables in Figure 5.8. Are they the same as the ones used on your printer?*

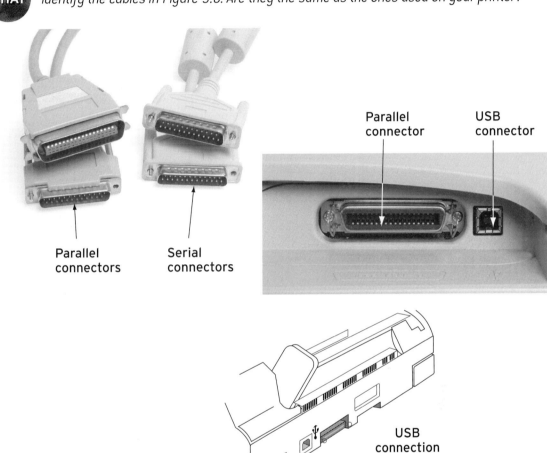

Parallel connector

USB connector

Parallel connectors

Serial connectors

USB connection

Figure 5.8
Different printer-connecting cables

If a parallel cable is used, to protect data integrity during transfer, the maximum length of cable should be 15 feet, although 9–12 feet is even better. Newer IEEE-1284 cables could be 30 feet in length (see IEEE1284 standards on page 111), and 50-foot high-end cables are also available. However, if you need to be more than 10 feet from a printer, you should have a networked configuration.

Using a **switchbox** (manual or automatic), it is possible to connect more than one printer through the same port on a PC, or to have more than one PC share the same printer. Manually, a dial is set to link the required PC and printer. With an automatic switchbox, activity on the line is identified.

Connecting a printer to a network so that this valuable resource can be shared is relatively simple to do (see Figure 5.9):

◆ Printers that are network-ready have a NIC (network interface card) into which an RJ-45 connector can be inserted.

◆ For printers that are not network-ready, a network printer interface device (such as HP's Jetdirect) can be used to connect one or more printers to the network. These devices connect to the parallel port of the printer and provide a built-in NIC that will then connect to the network, probably via an RJ-45.

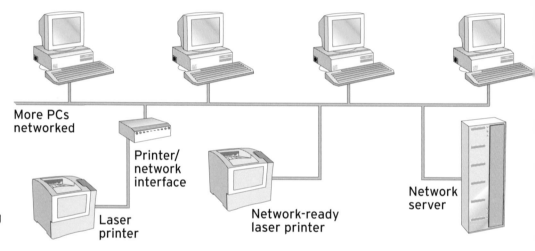

More PCs networked

Printer/ network interface

Laser printer

Network-ready laser printer

Network server

Figure 5.9 Connecting a printer to a network

Check Your Understanding 5.2

1 How might a printer be connected to a PC?
2 What restrictions are there on the length of cabling to be used for a printer?
3 How can you have more than one printer connected to the same standalone PC?
4 How can printers be shared between different users?

Revision 5

1 There are three main types of printer: dot matrix, inkjet and laser.

2 Dot matrix printers are impact printers and expect continuous stationery. They can be used for multi-part stationery. Ink is provided on a ribbon.

3 Inkjet printers shoot a squirt of ink on to the page. Clogged nozzles can be cleaned using a software utility.

4 Lasers printers produce the highest-quality print in a six-stage process: cleaning, conditioning, writing, developing, transferring and fusing.

Chapter 6   Basic networking

This section looks at basic networking concepts: how a network works, how to network a PC and the effect of making changes to or repairing a network.

> **What does it mean?**
>
> *A network is two or more computers connected together so that they can share resources.*

1   Basic networking concepts: how a network works

Accessing a network involves logging on to a PC that is part of a network:

◆ In a **LAN (local area network)**, all the resources are very close to each other, e.g. in the same room or on the same floor of an office building.

◆ In a **WAN (wide area network)**, the resources can be in separate buildings, even separate towns or countries (Figure 6.1).

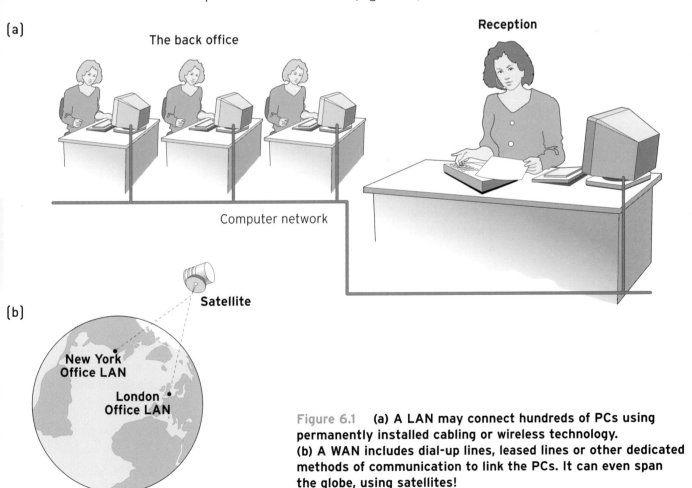

(a) The back office

Reception

Computer network

Satellite

(b)

New York Office LAN

London Office LAN

Figure 6.1   **(a) A LAN may connect hundreds of PCs using permanently installed cabling or wireless technology. (b) A WAN includes dial-up lines, leased lines or other dedicated methods of communication to link the PCs. It can even span the globe, using satellites!**

IP addresses are used to identify nodes on both LANs and WANs (see Figure 6.2).

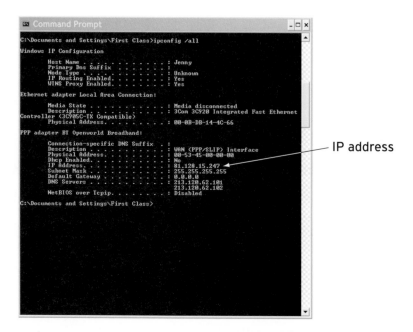

IP address

Figure 6.2
IPCONFIG/ALL

What does it mean?

IP = Internet protocol. Chapter 10 (page 340) explains the need for an Internet protocol.

There are two basic network architectures (see Figure 6.3):

◆ In a **client/server network**, one PC is set aside as the **server**. The software that masterminds the networking activity is a network operating system (NOS), one especially designed to cope with the extra demands of having more than one PC (**client**) to look after, and the communication between PCs and the sharing of resources such as hard disks and printers. The servers and clients are classified into **domains** according to their role within the network. (Chapter 10, page 341 explains what is meant by a domain and tells you all about domain names.)

◆ In a **peer-to-peer network**, no one PC is set aside for special duties and there is no need for a special NOS. Each PC shares part of the overhead of managing the network, and shared files reside on hard drives within the network. All PCs can still share resources, but data has to travel back and forth between the PCs. This is okay for a few PCs but beyond five PCs it makes sense to set one PC aside as a server and to have a NOS managing all the traffic.

Larger networks have more than the one server. Servers can also focus on one task alone:

◆ The **file server** holds all the files for all the clients on the network.

Figure 6.3
Network architectures

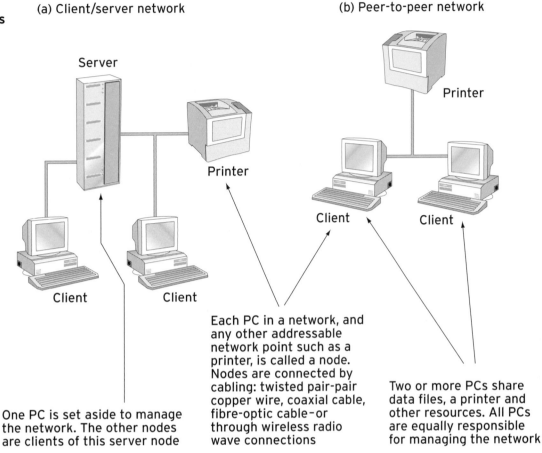

(a) Client/server network

(b) Peer-to-peer network

Server

Printer

Client   Client

Printer

Client   Client

One PC is set aside to manage the network. The other nodes are clients of this server node

Each PC in a network, and any other addressable network point such as a printer, is called a node. Nodes are connected by cabling: twisted pair-pair copper wire, coaxial cable, fibre-optic cable–or through wireless radio wave connections

Two or more PCs share data files, a printer and other resources. All PCs are equally responsible for managing the network

◆ An **application server** may be assigned to hold a copy of commonly used software applications centrally, relieving individual PCs of the need to hold a copy of every piece of software that may be needed.

◆ A **database server** may be assigned to hold a database which can then be accessed by others on the network.

◆ The **communications server** handles the interface with the outside world, e.g. for email, fax and Internet services. This server may also be called the **Internet host server**.

◆ The **printer server** manages the printers and the queues of documents being sent by clients, spooling the files ready for printing.

Check Your Understanding 6.1

1 Explain these terms: 'LAN', 'WAN', 'client', 'server'.
2 What is an IP address used for?
3 Give three examples of the tasks a server might be assigned.

How PCs are physically joined together to create a network is called the **topology** of the network (Figure 6.4).

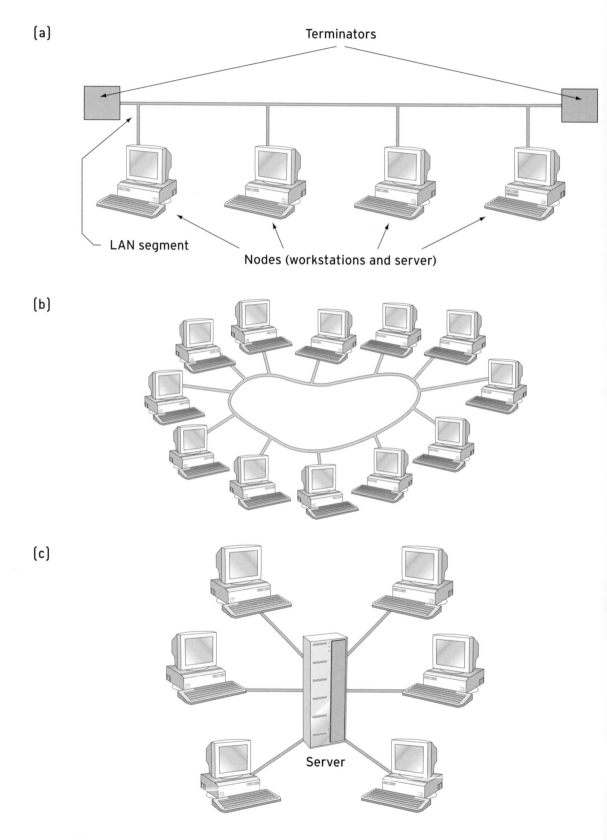

Figure 6.4   Network topologies: (a) bus (b) ring (c) star

- In a **bus** topology, the PCs form a single chain.
- In a **ring** topology, the single chain of PCs is connected to form a closed loop.
- In a **star** topology, the PCs are all linked to a central point, e.g. at a **hub** (Figure 6.5).

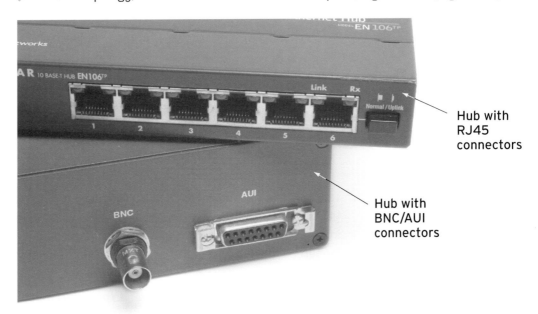

Hub with RJ45 connectors

Hub with BNC/AUI connectors

Figure 6.5   **A hub**

Networks can also be analysed by type:

- **Ethernet** is a bus topology that uses copper or fibre-optic cabling and operates at either 10 Mbps or 100 Mbps. Ethernet devices are connected by a hub or switch.
- **Token ring** is a ring topology that uses copper or fibre-optic cabling and operates at either 4 Mbps or 16 Mbps. Token rings can support as many as 250 nodes.
- **FDDI** is the standard for ANSI and ISO for ring topologies of data networks using speeds of 100 Mbps. The FDDI NIC converts digital data from the PC into light that can be transmitted on fibre-optic cabling, and into digital data for incoming data.

What does it mean?

FDDI = fibre-distributed data interface; ANSI = American National Standards Institute; ISO = International Standards Organisation.

There is an important distinction between **physical topology** and **logical topology**:

- A token ring is physically connected to form a star; each PC is connected to the hub. However, logically, data travels as if in a ring, going to each of the networked PCs one at a time, systematically, albeit via the hub each time (see Figure 6.6).
- The FDDI system actually has the PCs linked in a ring, does not have a hub and uses tokens that are passed around the ring. So its topology, physically and logically, is that of a ring (see Figure 6.7).

The type of network determines the speed at which data will travel and this is dependent on the type of cabling used in the network and the method of transmission:

Figure 6.6
Data packet flow through a hub – data from one PC (e.g. A) is passed to all other PCs (i.e. B and C and D)

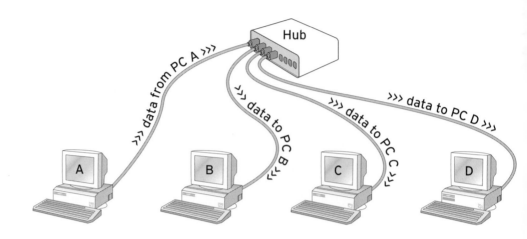

- There are a variety of cables that could be used to carry the data – **twisted pair** (shielded or unshielded, i.e. UTP), **coaxial** or **fibre optic** – or the network may rely on infrared transmission so that cabling is not necessary. Each type of cable has properties which lend it to the fast transmission and/or safe transmission of data.

What does it mean?

UTP = unshielded twisted pair. Chapter 1 (page 89) discusses the different types of cabling.

- Communication that can be done in both directions, but not at the same time, is called **half-duplex** transmission. If the communications can be both ways and simultaneous, this is called **full-duplex** transmission.

Discuss situations in real-life communications where half-duplex is acceptable and/or necessary. (Hint: Think classrooms!)

Whichever cabling and communication are decided, standards have to be followed:

- Serial communication adheres to the **RS232C standard** (see Chapter 1, page 88).
- Parallel communication has the **IEEE1284** (bidirectional parallel communications) standard plus the **ECP protocol** (full duplex, i.e. simultaneous communications in both directions).
- **Wireless Ethernet** is another standard: IEEE802.11 (Figure 6.8).

If there are too many PCs to be linked, a hub is insufficient. Also, since networks can only connect with other networks of the same type, and there are lots of different network types in existence, there is a general communication problem. To solve these problems, smaller groups of PCs are linked (of one network type), and then these groups are linked to other networks (which can have a different network type). Two items of equipment are needed to achieve this:

- The hub is replaced by a **switch**. Instead of sending all the data to all the PCs in the hub's network, the switch has extra intelligence so that it can route data direct to the P for which it is intended. It therefore segments the network.

Figure 6.7
Hubs used to create (a) a star bus network or (b) a token ring

(a)

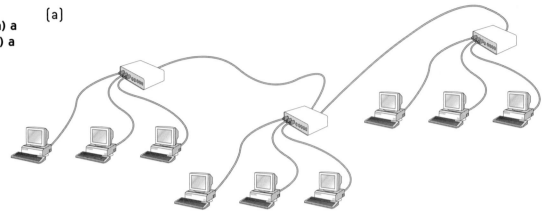

(b)

Token ring cable

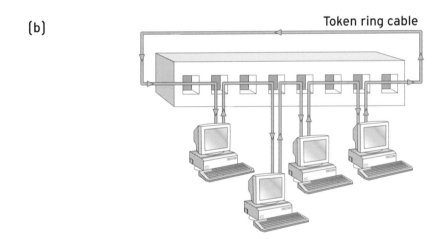

◆ A **gateway** is used to link networks of a different type; it translates between the various protocols being used within each network.

Gateways are a combination of hardware and software and may be a dedicated server on the network:

◆ The **protocol gateway** is the most common and is needed for networks that have different protocols.

◆ An **address gateway** is needed for networks that have different directory structures and file management techniques.

◆ A **format gateway** would be needed to link networks that use different data format schemes, e.g. to link a network using ASCII with one using EBCDIC.

What does it mean?

ASCII = American Standard Code for Information Interchange; EBCDIC = Extended Binary-Coded Decimal Interchange Code.

Figure 6.8
Wireless LAN

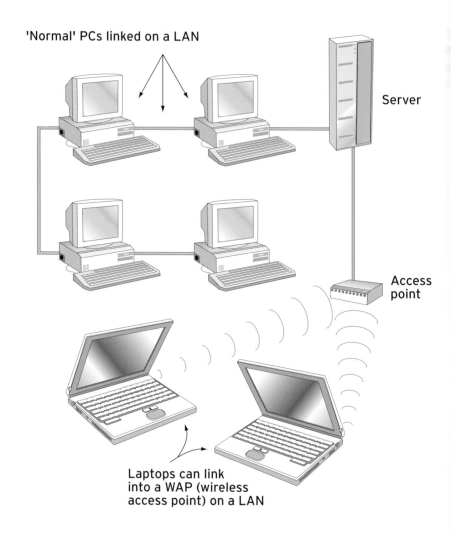

'Normal' PCs linked on a LAN

Server

Access point

Laptops can link into a WAP (wireless access point) on a LAN

Some other items of equipment may also be found in a network:

◆ Data that travels from one node to another can only travel so far without risk of corruption. A **repeater** (Figure 6.9) can be used to increase this distance; it retransmits whatever it receives.

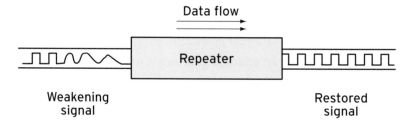

Data flow

Repeater

Figure 6.9 **How a repeater works**

Weakening signal

Restored signal

◆ A **bridge** can be used to link two LANs so they can operate as one single network. Looking at it another way, a bridge can be used to segment a large network into smaller, more manageable groups of PCs (see Figure 6.10). A bridge that is connected to several networks identifies whether an incoming packet is for its own network. If it is not, the bridge sends it to all other networks to which it is connected.

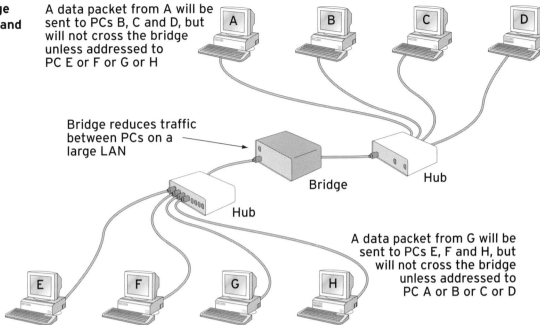

Figure 6.10 **A bridge segments a network and connects networks**

A data packet from A will be sent to PCs B, C and D, but will not cross the bridge unless addressed to PC E or F or G or H

Bridge reduces traffic between PCs on a large LAN

Bridge

Hub

Hub

A data packet from G will be sent to PCs E, F and H, but will not cross the bridge unless addressed to PC A or B or C or D

◆ A **router** is used to connect networks and can belong to more than one network. It uses the network address of a destination node to work out what route the data could best take (Figure 6.11).

Networks of any size and type can also be linked to other resources, such as the Internet.

For the user, access to the whole network is made by working at one of the PCs within the network. In deciding on a network, the network manager needs to select a NOS, a network architecture and a network topology and type that will work together, plus the right cabling and connectors.

Check Your Understanding 6.2

1 Ethernet is one type of network. Name two other types of network.
2 Explain these terms: 'FDDI', 'ANSI', 'ISO'.
3 Which provides the fastest transmission rates: UTP or fibre optic?
4 Distinguish between full duplex and half-duplex.
5 Name the standard for serial communication and the two standards for parallel communication.

Go and try out 6.1

1 Research the Internet to find out about Ethernet.
2 What network operating systems are compatible with Ethernet?
3 What topologies are compatible with the NOSs that are compatible with Ethernet?
4 What cabling might you use with an Ethernet network?

Figure 6.11 **A router directs traffic across networks**

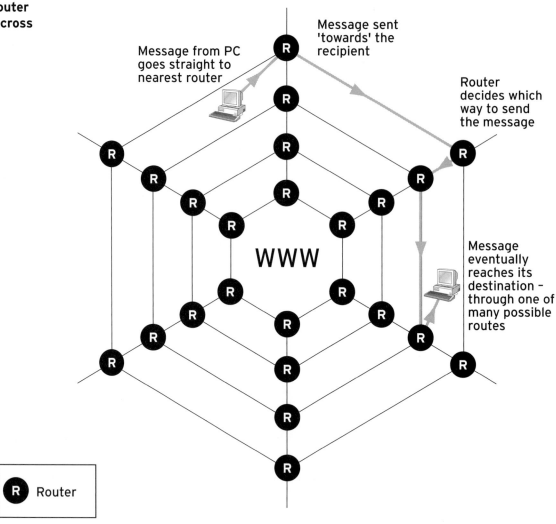

Message from PC goes straight to nearest router

Message sent 'towards' the recipient

Router decides which way to send the message

Message eventually reaches its destination – through one of many possible routes

R Router

CASE STUDY   Nigel the novice PC user

Ismat has been offered a promotion within the IT support team. It will involve working on networks.

1 Explain the different network topologies: bus, ring and star.

2 Briefly describe how these devices are used in networks: bridge, switch, router, gateway.

3 Give examples of differing gateways.

4 Explain in what circumstances a repeater would be used.

Hardware protocols

Data is packaged before being sent over a network. It is split into separate **packets** of data:

- At the start of the packet, there is a **header**.
- Then there is the data.
- At the end of the packet, there is a **trailer**.

Each packet is sent separately and may take a different route from other packets, so they may not arrive in the same order that they left.

On arrival, the header (which says something like '3 of 7' so the receiving PC can reconstruct the complete message) is stripped off, as is the trailer. That just leaves the data.

Brainstorm with friends what information you think the header needs to contain so that the right PC receives it, and knows where it has come from. (Hint: Think about what information accompanies an email.)

The exact size of the packets of data depends on the NOS and is one of the **network protocols** for communication.

For each type of network (Ethernet, token ring, FDDI), protocols determine the 'rules' that the data will follow while on route:

- The **error-checking method** that will be applied on receipt to make sure there has been no corruption during the transfer.
- Any data compression techniques that will be applied to the data.
- What data will indicate that the end of the packet has been received, i.e. what is in the trailer.
- How the receiver will let the sender know that the packet has been received safely.

With a friend, recall the handshaking protocols used by a modem. This is the same concept as with any networking communication.

Three particular protocols are worthy of note:

- **TCP/IP** is much used on Windows-based networking and is the most popular on the Internet.
- **IPX/SPX** is used on Novell networks.
- **NetBEUI** is an older network and is not found in modern systems.

Other protocols you may meet on the Internet are discussed in Chapter 10 (page 346).

What does it mean?

TCP = transmission control protocol; IP = Internet protocol.

IPX/SPX = Internet packet exchange/sequence packet exchange.

NetBEUI (NetBIOS-extended user interface) is a network protocol used only by Windows systems for LANs with no external connections. It does not support routing, i.e. addressing through a router to other networks.

NICs (network interface cards)

Every PC in the network has to have a NIC. The main purpose of the NIC is to receive data from other NICs on the network, and to send data to them.

During the manufacturing process, each NIC is physically encoded with an address which uniquely identifies it: its **MAC address**. The MAC address is a 48-bit address (but written as 6 pairs of hex digits).

CHAT

Discuss with a friend how you might find out the MAC address of the NIC card on your PC. (Hint: Look for the GETMAC or WINIPCFG commands in your Help system.)

What does it mean?

MAC = media access control.

So, what happens when you connect a PC to an existing network?

◆ When you connect an extra PC to an Ethernet network, it identifies itself by its MAC address and its network name to the rest of the PCs on the network. Devices such as switches and hubs need to retain this data so that they can direct incoming data to this PC when necessary.

◆ When you connect an extra PC to a token ring network, it needs to be assigned a unique address. The PC sends out test frames with its ID address and the system sends test frames back – this checks that communication between the two works. If there is a duplication of addresses, you will need to adjust the jumper or DIP switches to alter the address.

The important thing to remember is that each PC on a network has to be uniquely addressable, not how this is actually achieved.

Recall also that each NIC is given an IRQ (usually IRQ3, IRQ5 or IRQ10), an I/O address (usually 0300) and a DMA channel by way of system resources. (See page 75 for more information on IFRQs, I/O addresses and DMA channels.)

The NIC type has to match the expansion bus for the slot (PCI or, on older systems, ISA), but it must also match the network type and, in particular, the data speed of the network. So, for example, on an Ethernet network, you must install an Ethernet NIC. Ethernet has different subtypes of Ethernet according to the maximum speed of data transfer that they support:

◆ Ethernet 10BaseT has a top speed of 10 MB/sec.
◆ Ethernet 100BaseT has a top speed of 100 MB/sec.

You can buy a 10/100BaseT NIC which will work on either of these two subtypes.

There are several different ways of providing a NIC (see Figure 6.12):

◈ You can install a NIC in an open expansion slot on the motherboard and then connect the cabling to the NIC port. (See page 61 to find out about adding/removing a NIC panel.)

Figure 6.12 **An NIC**

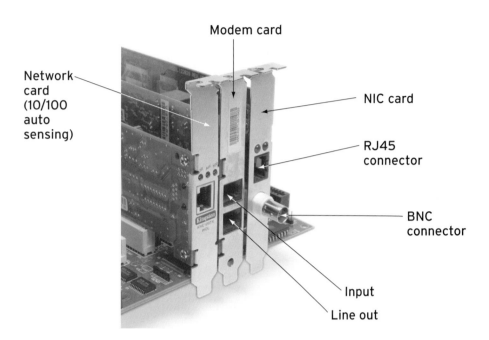

- The PC can be connected through a device, such as a modem, attached to the USB port.
- You can use a PC card as a network card for a portable computer, i.e. a laptop or notepad.

Note that the NIC connectors will determine the type of cabling that can be used on the network and vice versa. Cabling was discussed earlier in this section; see page 232.

Having installed cards in expansion slots or completed the hardware installation in some other way, you will need to complete the installation using software. How to configure the software for a modem is covered in Chapter 1 (page 108).

Check Your Understanding 6.3

1 Describe what is in a data packet.
2 What is a protocol? Give two examples of what a protocol may determine.
3 Name the protocol that is used on Windows-based networks and is most popular on the Internet.
4 What is a MAC address?
5 How might you provide a NIC on a portable PC? Suggest two ways.

Setting up a network

There are two stages to setting up a network:

- The physical installation of the hardware
- Configuring the software

The physical installation is explained in the 'How to' panel below. Note that, if a standalone PC already has a NIC installed, this has to be reinstalled for it to work in a network environment. Configuring the software is covered in Chapter 10 (page 347).

How to connect a peer-to-peer network

1 For each PC, install a NIC.
2 Connect each NIC to the hub using an appropriate cable.
3 Connect the power cable of the hub to the wall socket.

If you are planning to share a printer on the network, it has to be installed on your PC as a network printer. So, when you go through the Add Printer wizard, instead of checking the 'local printer' box, you will need to check the 'networked printer' radio button instead (Figure 6.13).

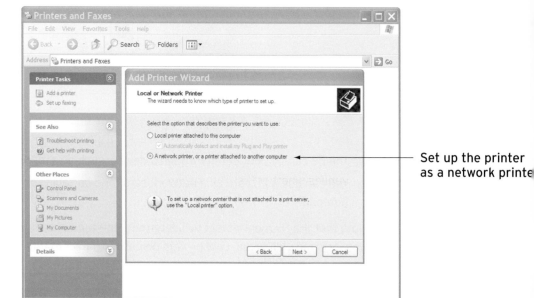

Set up the printer as a network printe

Figure 6.13
Setting up a shared printer

Also, you need to install a device driver for the printer, even if the printer is already installed on another PC in the network and that PC has a device driver for it. Device drivers for printers vary according to the operating system, and your device driver must match your operating system. PCs in a network can work under different versions of Windows, so long as each has its own device driver for the shared printer.

In a small group, discuss your experiences of installing networks. What problems did you encounter? How did you resolve these problems?

2 Ramifications of repairs on the network

When working on a PC, it is essential that you know whether the PC is networked or standalone. If you assume a networked PC is standalone, you may damage the PC and ma even cause damage to the whole network. For example, on a peer-to-peer network, if the data another PC is using were to be on the PC that you turn off, the network connection would be broken and the data lost to the other PC. You would not be popular.

So, how can you tell if a PC is networked?

◆ The cabling at the back of the PC should tell you straightaway whether the PC is part of a network – at least, one that is not using wireless technology. However, the PC user may have disconnected the PC before you arrived, so check with the user to make sure.

◆ Whether or not there is network cabling, you should still check to see if a NIC has been installed. If there is no NIC, there can be no networking.

◆ My Computer or Windows Explorer may show networked drives as E:, F: or higher letters.

◆ The hard disk can also tell you whether the PC is involved in networking. There may be a folder called NWCLIENT. The AUTOEXEC.BAT and CONFIG.SYS files will also show commands that relate to networking activity.

If the PC is networked, some precautions are necessary before you start troubleshooting to repair the PC:

◆ Make sure the PC is logged off the network. If you try to open a shared folder on the network, you should not be able to do so. If you can, then you are still logged on.

◆ Make a backup of all data on the hard disk before working on the hard disk at all. (This applies whether the PC is networked or standalone.)

◆ Disconnect the network cable from the NIC.

You can then proceed with your troubleshooting. When you are finished, make sure you reconnect the NIC cabling. Then ask the user to log on, just to make sure that the PC link to the network has not been affected by the repairs you have done.

There can be knock-on effects of making repairs on the network: effect on bandwidth, loss of data, and network slowdown.

◆ **Bandwidth** is a measure of the data transmission capacity and hence the capability of the network. If a NIC is sending out a faulty signal or is set up incorrectly, this can reduce the bandwidth, to the detriment of all other users on the network.

◆ A breakdown on the network can result in a **loss of data**, or at least a loss of access to data, depending on where the data is stored and what was happening when the breakdown occurred.

◆ Problems on the network can slow everything down, to the point that it is not providing acceptable service to some or all users. This is called **network slowdown**.

Revision 6

1 A LAN may connect hundreds of PCs using permanently installed cabling or wireless technology.

2 A WAN includes dial-up lines, leased lines or other dedicated method of communication to link the PCs.

3 Networks fall into two classes: client/server or peer-to-peer.

4 Large networks have servers: a file server, an application server, a database server, a communications server, a printer server.

5 Network topologies: bus, ring, star.

6 A hub is used to connect all PCs in a star network and sends all data to all PCs.

7 The physical topology of a token ring is a star; the logical topology is that of a ring.

8 For LANs, the four physical network architectures are Ethernet, token ring, FDDI and wireless LAN.

9 Wireless networks need a wireless NIC, including an infrared port, or an antenna, to send and receive signals.

10 Communication that can be done in both directions, but not at the same time, is called half-duplex transmission. If the communications can be both ways and simultaneous, this is called full-duplex transmission.

11 Cabling meets standards: RS232C for serial transmission; IEEE1284 and ECP for parallel transmission.

12 A PC is connected to a network using a NIC which communicates with NICs in other PCs on the network.

13 Communication on a network is standardised: hardware protocols such as Ethernet and token ring are supported by operating systems adopting protocols such as NetBEUI or TCP/IP.

14 Networks of different types can be linked, so a wired LAN can be linked to a wireless LAN.

15 NICs and their device drivers must match the network type and work with the bus of the slot into which the NIC will fit.

16 The MAC address uniquely identifies a NIC and, hence, a connection to/from a networked PC.

17 Communication between TCP/IP networked PCs uses the IP address rather than the MAC address.

18 Bridges and switches are used to segment large networks, reducing the overall amount of traffic and making the network more manageable.

19 A gateway is used to link networks of a different type: different protocol, different address, different data representation format.

20 TCP/IP and IPX/SPX are routable networking protocols. NetBEUI is not a routable networking protocol.

21 A repeater retransmits whatever it receives, extending the distance possible between nodes.

22 Data is sent in packets with a header and trailer.

23 Network protocols determine the error-checking method to be used and whether compression is permitted.

24 Bandwidth is a measure of the data transmission capacity and hence the capability of the network.

Unit 2
Operating System Technologies Concepts

This unit focuses on specific areas of knowledge and understanding required of a technician working in a Windows environment. There are four elements in this unit, each one contributing to the test questions:

Element	Topic	Marks in test (%)
2.1	Operating system fundamentals	30
2.2	Installation, configuration and upgrading	15
2.3	Diagnosing and troubleshooting	40
2.4	Networks	15
Total		100

Unit 1 has involved you in lots of reading, lots of concepts to understand and terminology to learn, and some practical work on PCs. This unit is completely different. Instead of reading and thinking about hardware, you will spend nearly all your time using the software.

The chapters in this unit guide you through what you need to know and present you with screen shots that you can compare with those on your own PC screen. You need to be able to recognise a dialogue box when presented with it in an exam question, and to know what options you would select in given circumstances. This will only happen if you have worked your way through all the dialogue boxes and explored the operating system fully. So, in the same way that a taxi driver has to learn the 'knowledge' of London, you have to learn the menus and options available on the Windows family of operating systems.

Which operating system should you study?

Well, in an ideal world, you will be familiar with all operating systems. However, there is a limit to the resources available to you, and a limit of your time so, if you make sure you are familiar with at least two operating systems this should be enough to pass the A+ examination.

Screen grabs in this book are mostly from Windows XP. You should have access to two or three other operating systems so, in total, you should have gained exposure to enough examples.

1 Operating system functions, structure and major system files

While a PC is turned off, it is just a collection of hardware. Turn it on and the system BIOS boots up the computer and then all communication between peripherals and the processor is via device drivers. The next layer up is the operating system – and this supports the applications software that you have installed on the PC (Figure 7.1).

This course focuses on the Windows operating system and you need to be aware of the development of this software. The history section (see www.heinemann.co.uk) presents this background material, in case you need to refer to it.

Check Your Understanding 7.1

1 Which operating system is most commonly used?
2 Name three non-Windows operating systems.
3 What type of user interface is used with a Windows operating system?

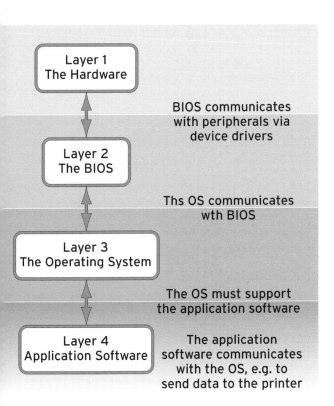

Figure 7.1   **The four-layer model of a PC**

Operating system functions

All operating systems offer much the same basic system functions and these are discussed in this chapter.

◆ To provide an interface between the user and the PC – see page 245
◆ To manage memory – see page 268
◆ To provide the software interface between the PC and its peripherals.

You need to focus on the functions of Windows 9X (see page 270) and Windows 2000 (see page 272). Windows XP is the operating system used for many of the screen shots in this unit. So, this gives you an insight into a third, and more modern, operating system.

Discuss with friends which operating systems you have installed on your PCs. Between you, you should have a variety.

Over time, operating systems have evolved to provide better and better facilities for the user:

◆ Backward compatibility

◆ Multitasking and time sharing

◆ Clipboard facilities

See also other features of operating systems: virtual memory (page 268) and PnP (page 208).

Backward compatibility

Backward compatibility means the operating system will support applications software and data file formats from earlier versions of the operating system. It cannot support ones that are to be invented in the future, precisely because they have not yet been invented! So, if you try to run modern software on an older PC, you might run into difficulty, not least because of memory requirements.

However, the early operating systems were not even backward compatible. Each time an operating system was released, it bore no resemblance to earlier ones. So, the provision of backward compatibility is a definite plus point.

Discuss with friends any problems that you have experienced due to a lack of compatibility.

Multitasking and time sharing

Multitasking means the operating system can cope with more than one program at a time.

A virtual machine is a simulated 8086 CPU operating in its own separate address space.

Windows 3.1 could run in standard mode or enhanced mode. In enhanced mode, it could run more than one program at a time and this was done by creating **virtual machines**.

An 8086 CPU can only execute one task at a time, but multiple virtual machines running at the same time means more than one program can run at a time, i.e. **multitasking**.

Multitasking means that more than one program is sharing the use of the CPU: this is called **time sharing**. How that time is shared is decided by the operating system:

◆ Windows 3.X supports **co-operative multitasking** in which programs give way when another program requests use of a resource; the program lets the operating system know when it has finished using the CPU.

◆ Windows 9X supports **pre-emptive multitasking** which means the operating system controls the timesharing and can suspend a program that is monopolising a resource.

Because Windows supports multitasking, you can have several windows open at the same time:

◆ One will be the **active window** (usually shown by having a brighter colouring in the strip at the top of the window).

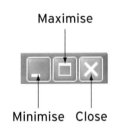

Figure 7.2   **Minimise, maximise, close**

◆ Other windows will be behind the active window, and will become visible and thus accessible if you close or minimise the active window.

◆ Windows that have been **minimised** (Figure 7.2) appear in the taskbar at the bottom of the screen. Clicking on one of these tasks maximises the task and makes it the active window.

Because you can control the size of the windows on your desktop, you can arrange the windows so that more than one can be viewed at any one time (Figure 7.3).

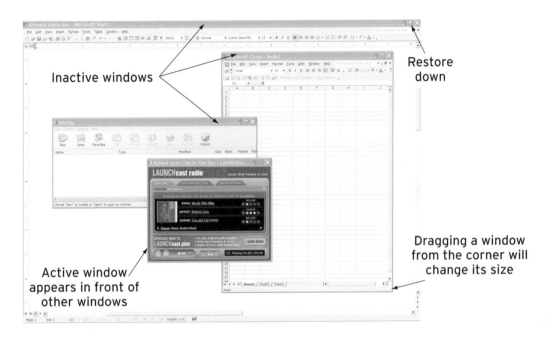

Figure 7.3   **Multiple screens on the same desktop**

Multitasking is not to be confused with **multiprocessing**, in which the PC has more than one processor working at the same time, or with **multithreading** – a program spawns several activities under its control and these all run concurrently.

Multiprocessing can be achieved in one of two ways:

◆ **Asymmetrical multiprocessing (ASMP)** assigns the work of a particular program to a particular processor, which then runs the program until it is completed. This is like having separate PCs within the same PC casing; at any one time, a processor may be idle.

◆ **Symmetrical multiprocessing (SMP)** divides the work from all the programs and assigns tasks to each of the available processors, making better use of all processors.

Clipboard facilities

One of the great benefits of the early Windows operating systems over DOS is the **clipboard**: a facility for data sharing between applications.

DDE (dynamic data exchange) enables users to cut and paste data from one application into another. Windows 9X improved this facility by including **OLE (object linking and**

embedding) which, instead of just copying data, created dynamic links between applications so that, if the data changed in one, it was changed in the other at the same time.

Copying or cutting from one application and pasting into another means you have to move between the two applications.

How to use the clipboard to data share between applications

1 In one application, with that window active, highlight the material that you want to share with another application. Right-click and select Copy – or use shortcut key Ctrl-C – to copy the selected text to the clipboard.
2 Access the other application. This may involve minimising the first application, or you may need only to click on the other window to make that application the active window.
3 Position the cursor where you want the shared data to appear. Right-click and select Paste – or use the shortcut key Ctrl-V – to paste the clipboard contents into place.

1 What are the main functions of an operating system?
2 What is meant by backward compatibility?
3 Explain the difference between multitasking and multiprocessing.
4 What is an active window?
5 What is dynamic data exchange used for?
6 What is a clipboard?

Experiment with copying and pasting:

1 Copy a range of cells from an *Excel* spreadsheet into a *Word* document. What does it create in *Word*?
2 Copy a table from a *Word* document into a blank spreadsheet in *Excel*.
3 How could you use a table of data in a *Word* document to create a database in *Access*?
4 Experiment with moving other forms of data from and to other applications, and share your results with friends.

The structure of an operating system

An operating system is a collection of software utilities, developed over a long time, that, between them, provide the functionality of the operating system as a whole.

Major systems files

Table 7.1 lists the major system files that are essential to the running of the operating system.

Table 7.1 System files for Windows

Program filename	Notes	See
AUTOEXEC.BAT	This file, with CONFIG.SYS, is used by MS-DOS and other operating systems at startup. It does not have to be present but, if it is, its commands are used when the computer goes through the startup process. It contains the instructions to run any programs that you have decided ought to run automatically at startup, e.g. MSCDEX.EXE, PROMPT and MOUSE.COM (which loads a mouse driver). It runs during the boot process but you can also run it at any other time, by keying AUTOEXEC at the MS-DOS prompt and pressing Return. Modern operating systems use IO.SYS instead.	MSCDEX.EXE (page 273) PROMPT (page 273)
BOOT.INI	This hidden file is in the root directory of the primary partition. It contains the menu that appears each time the PC is started. If the user does not react within 30 seconds then the PC automatically boots to the default OS. BOOT.INI can be accessed using *Notepad*, but a better way of controlling options for the Startup menu is through System Properties.	Dual booting (page 300)
COMMAND.COM	This command-line processor interprets commands for interactions with the user.	
CONFIG.SYS	This file, with AUTOEXEC.BAT, is used by MS-DOS and other operating systems at startup. It can only be run during the boot process. It does not have to be present but, if it is, its commands are used when the computer goes through the startup process. It contains instructions to load device drivers (e.g. for a CD-ROM drive) and to real/protected set environmental settings. It loads HIMEM.SYS and EMM386.EXE. This file is used to load real-mode drivers when a protected mode driver is not available. Modern operating systems use IO.SYS instead.	HIMEM (page 268); EMM386 (page 268); real/protected mode (page 268)
IO.SYS	This file is one of the three essential files to boot MS-DOS. This file replaced the four DOS files (IO.SYS, MSDOS.SYS, CONFIG.SYS, AUTOEXEC.BAT) for Windows 9X systems. It is replaced by NTLDR for Windows 2000.	Booting up (page 300–7)
MSDOS.SYS	This program is the controller for software interaction including the MS-DOS kernel. It is one of the three files needed to boot MS-DOS.	
WIN.COM	This file loads the GUI for Windows 9X by loading three files: KRNL32.DLL, GDI.EXE and USER.EXE.	Windows 9X boot process (page 301)

Note: *SCANDISK is called Check Disk in Windows 2000 and XP.

What does it mean?

MS-DOS, originally written by Microsoft for the IBM PC, is an operating system for the Intel 80806, 186, 286, 386, 486 and Pentium processors.

The **COMMAND.COM file** is the command-line processor which interprets commands for interactions with the user:

◆ In a DOS-based OS, the user inputs commands at the prompt. See page 273 for some commands that might be input; Chapter 8 (page 306) explains MS-DOS mode.

◆ In a GUI, the user makes selections using a mouse (a pointing device to control the cursor on screen), clicking on objects on the screen (buttons and hotlinks) and entering text into text boxes.

Apart from the essential files, there are other important files in the OS:

◆ The **LOGO.SYS graphic file** contains the logo that is displayed on the screen during the boot process.

◆ Table 7.2 lists some examples of **log files** created by Windows. These keep track of what is happening and can be useful when troubleshooting.

Table 7.2	*Log files for Windows*
Program filename	**Notes**
BOOTLOG.TXT	If a logged boot is requested (by keying WIN/B), the PC starts in **logged mode**. This file is then created to record the boot sequence.
DETLOG.TXT	This file is used to keep track of the hardware.
SCANDISK.LOG	SCANDISK* performs checks on the integrity of the data on a disk, looking for logical errors in the FAT file and physically checks the surface of the disk for imperfections that would affect its performance. This file records the findings of the checking process.
SETUPLOG.TXT	This file records all the actions taken to install files on the PC. The installation process may only take 30 minutes or so, but the entries on this file run to many hundreds (see Figure 7.4).

Check Your Understanding 7.3

1 Name the major systems files that are essential to the running of an operating system.
2 BOOT.INI is a hidden file. What does this mean? How can you change the attributes of a file to hide it?
3 What is the purpose of the COMMAND.COM file?
4 What is a log file?

Go and try out 7.2

1 Locate the Startup and Recovery options screen. (*Hint:* Right-click on My Computer and select Properties.) What happens if you opt to edit the options manually?
2 Using the Search option on the Start menu, locate a log file and see what it has in it. (*Hint:* Search on *log.txt and include hidden files.)
3 Using the WIN command at the DOS prompt, opt for a logged boot, boot up and then check the contents of BOOTLOG.TXT.

Files used during the boot process

Three major systems files are used during the **MS-DOS boot process**:

◆ IO.SYS
◆ MSDOS.SYS
◆ COMMAND.COM

On a bootable disk there may be two startup configuration files:

```
SETUPLOG.TXT - Notepad                                                          _ □ X
File  Edit  Format  View  Help
Time,File,Line,Tag,Message
09/03/2002 13:23:39,d:\xpsp1\base\ntsetup\syssetup\syssetup.c,6018,BEGIN_SECTION,Installing windows NT
09/03/2002 13:23:41,d:\xpsp1\base\ntsetup\syssetup\wizard.c,1568,,SETUP: Calculating registery size
09/03/2002 13:23:41,d:\xpsp1\base\ntsetup\syssetup\wizard.c,1599,,SETUP: Calculated time for win9x migration = 120 seconds
09/03/2002 13:23:41,d:\xpsp1\base\ntsetup\syssetup\syssetup.c,6049,BEGIN_SECTION,Initialization
09/03/2002 13:23:41,d:\xpsp1\base\ntsetup\syssetup\syssetup.c,6169,BEGIN_SECTION,Common Initialiazation
09/03/2002 13:23:41,d:\xpsp1\base\ntsetup\syssetup\syssetup.c,1616,BEGIN_SECTION,Initializing action log
09/03/2002 13:23:41,d:\xpsp1\base\ntsetup\syssetup\log.c,133,,GUI mode Setup has started.

09/03/2002 13:23:41,d:\xpsp1\base\ntsetup\syssetup\syssetup.c,1621,END_SECTION,Initializing action log
09/03/2002 13:23:41,d:\xpsp1\base\ntsetup\syssetup\syssetup.c,1706,BEGIN_SECTION,Creating setup background window
09/03/2002 13:23:41,d:\xpsp1\base\ntsetup\syssetup\syssetup.c,1717,END_SECTION,Creating setup background window
09/03/2002 13:23:41,d:\xpsp1\base\ntsetup\syssetup\syssetup.c,1768,BEGIN_SECTION,Initializing SMS support
09/03/2002 13:23:41,d:\xpsp1\base\ntsetup\syssetup\syssetup.c,1777,,Setup: (non-critical error): Failed load of ismif32.dll.
09/03/2002 13:23:41,d:\xpsp1\base\ntsetup\syssetup\syssetup.c,1779,END_SECTION,Initializing SMS support
09/03/2002 13:23:41,d:\xpsp1\base\ntsetup\syssetup\syssetup.c,1810,BEGIN_SECTION,Shutting down power management
09/03/2002 13:23:41,d:\xpsp1\base\ntsetup\syssetup\syssetup.c,1813,END_SECTION,Shutting down power management
09/03/2002 13:23:41,d:\xpsp1\base\ntsetup\syssetup\syssetup.c,1892,BEGIN_SECTION,Processing parameters from sif

0x00010201 (0x00000000)
03/03/2003 11:42:09,d:\xpsp1\base\ntsetup\oobe\msobmain\msobmain.cpp,6079,,NetUserGetInfo First Class (0x00000000)
03/03/2003 11:42:09,d:\xpsp1\base\ntsetup\oobe\msobmain\msobmain.cpp,6103,,Change First Class password property from 0x00000201 to 0x00010201
(0x00000000)
03/03/2003 11:42:09,d:\xpsp1\base\ntsetup\oobe\msobmain\msobmain.cpp,6079,,NetUserGetInfo Les Lawson (0x00000000)
03/03/2003 11:42:09,d:\xpsp1\base\ntsetup\oobe\msobmain\msobmain.cpp,6103,,Change Les Lawson password property from 0x00000201 to 0x00010201
(0x00000000)
03/03/2003 11:42:09,d:\xpsp1\base\ntsetup\oobe\msobmain\msobmain.cpp,7996,,CobMain::SetComputerDescription()
03/03/2003 11:42:09,d:\xpsp1\base\ntsetup\oobe\msobmain\msobmain.cpp,8003,,SetComputerDescription to: Laptop 1
03/03/2003 11:42:10,d:\xpsp1\base\ntsetup\oobe\msobmain\msobmain.cpp,3066,,START m_pobCommunicationManager->DoFinalTasks
03/03/2003 11:42:10,d:\xpsp1\base\ntsetup\oobe\msobmain\msobmain.cpp,3068,,FINISH m_pobCommunicationManager->DoFinalTasks
03/03/2003 11:42:10,d:\xpsp1\base\ntsetup\oobe\msobmain\msobmain.cpp,3080,,CMP_GetServerSideDeviceInstallFlags returned 0x00000000
03/03/2003 11:42:10,d:\xpsp1\base\ntsetup\oobe\msobmain\sysclock.cpp,825,,DISPID_SYSTEMCLOCK_SETAUTODAYLIGHT□
03/03/2003 11:42:10,d:\xpsp1\base\ntsetup\oobe\msobmain\sysclock.cpp,725,,DISPID_SYSTEMCLOCK_SETTIMEZONEIDX□
03/03/2003 11:42:10,d:\xpsp1\base\ntsetup\oobe\msobmain\msobmain.cpp,6028,,MainWndProc called PostQuitMessage().
03/03/2003 11:42:10,d:\xpsp1\base\ntsetup\oobe\msobmain\msobmain.cpp,1578,,RunOOBE - message loop finished
03/03/2003 11:42:10,d:\xpsp1\base\ntsetup\oobe\msobmain\main.cpp,513,,Starting AutoActivation
03/03/2003 11:42:10,d:\xpsp1\base\ntsetup\oobe\msobmain\main.cpp,516,,GetCanonicalizedPath: C:\WINDOWS\System32\oobe\OOBEINFO.INI
03/03/2003 11:42:10,d:\xpsp1\base\ntsetup\oobe\msobmain\main.cpp,540,,AutoActivation done
03/03/2003 11:42:11,d:\xpclient\base\ntsetup\oobe\common\cunknown.cpp,60,,FinalRelease□
03/03/2003 11:42:11,d:\xpclient\base\ntsetup\oobe\common\cunknown.cpp,60,,FinalRelease□
03/03/2003 11:42:11,d:\xpsp1\base\ntsetup\oobe\common\cunknown.cpp,60,,FinalRelease□
03/03/2003 11:42:11,d:\xpsp1\base\ntsetup\oobe\msobmain\main.cpp,921,,OOBE has finished.
```

Figure 7.4   The SETUPLOG.TXT file

◆ CONFIG.SYS

◆ AUTOEXEC.BAT

MS-DOS can start up without these files, so they are optional.

CONFIG.SYS and AUTOEXEC.BAT are text files, so they can be edited using a text editor such as EDIT. However, there are other less dangerous ways of changing the settings held in these files.

CHAT *With a friend, think how you might change a setting in CONFIG.SYS or AUTOEXEC.BAT, without directly using a text editor.*

What is the difference between system files used by MS-DOS, Windows 9X and Windows 2000?

◆ In Windows 9X, the IO.SYS file combines the role of MSDOS.SYS with that of IO.SYS, and IO.SYS therefore retains control during the boot process for a bit longer. WINCOM then provides a GUI and loads many more files, e.g. to manage virtual memory, to let the user log on and check their details, and to run any programs that you have asked to be run at Startup, before presenting the desktop screen. (See page 300 for details of the Windows 9X boot up.)

◆ Windows 2000 is based on Windows NT and much of the boot process revolves around

What does it mean?   *NTLDR = NT loader.*

253

the NTLDR. Because dual booting is an option, the BOOT.INI file may have a role to play in displaying a menu of OSs to the user. (See page 302 for details of the Windows 2000 boot up, page 300 for dual booting and page 307 for BOOT.INI.)

The three OSs – MS-DOS, Windows 9X and Windows 2000 – are very different in way the software is built into the OS:

◆ MS-DOS is just DOS with its command-line interpreter. There is no GUI.

◆ Windows 9X incorporates both the DPMI and a GUI so that the user can use DOS commands but the GUI presents a more user-friendly interface.

What does it mean?

DPMI = DOS-protected mode interface; GUI = graphical user interface.

◆ Windows 2000 loses the underlying DOS structure and is built on Windows NT instead. This means that settings are stored in the Registry, and that you can make changes to these settings using the Control Panel. See page 261 to find out how the Registry works.

Check Your Understanding 7.4

1 Explain the purpose of the IO.SYS, MSDOS.SYS and COMMAND.COM files.
2 What is held in the CONFIG.SYS and AUTOEXEC.BAT files?
3 What is the main difference between MS-DOS-based systems and Windows systems?
4 Explain the terms: 'DPMI', 'GUI' and 'NTLDR'.

2 Navigating the operating system

To find the technical information that you need, you have to navigate the operating system The Windows operating system is based, not surprisingly, on 'windows'. These windows are linked in a tree-like structure. To locate a particular window – and so to gain access to the technical information that it provides – you will need to know where this window sits within the tree structure.

Navigating through Windows involves three skills:

◆ *Locating information:* to move through screens, you need to double-click on an option, or single-click to select it and then click on OK.

◆ *Accessing information:* if you right-click on an option, a menu will appear, suited to where you chose to right-click

◆ *Retrieving information:* you can open files in a variety of ways.

With Windows, there is usually at least two ways of doing anything. This section now looks at *Explorer*, My Computer and the Control Panel – for Windows XP – to find alternative ways of doing some basic tasks. You need to explore these three topics on at least two other operating systems.

Explorer

Windows *Explorer* is a program supplied as one of the Accessories (Figure 7.5).

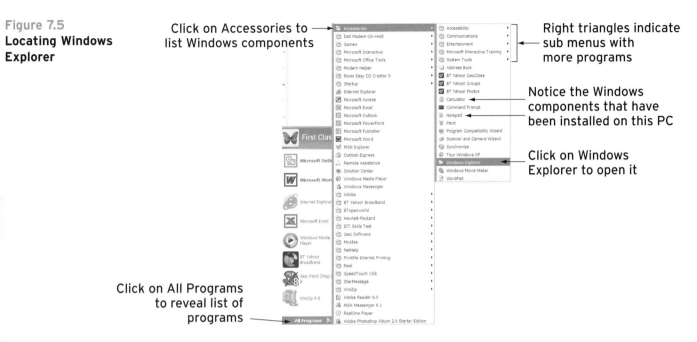

Figure 7.5
Locating Windows Explorer

Click on Accessories to → list Windows components

Right triangles indicate ← sub menus with more programs

Notice the Windows components that have been installed on this PC

Click on Windows Explorer to open it

Click on All Programs to reveal list of programs

Once selected, *Explorer* presents you with the directory/folder structure for your desktop. If the View Folders option has been selected, a left-hand pane shows that the Desktop has four elements (Figure 7.6):

◆ My Documents (below)
◆ My Computer (page 257)

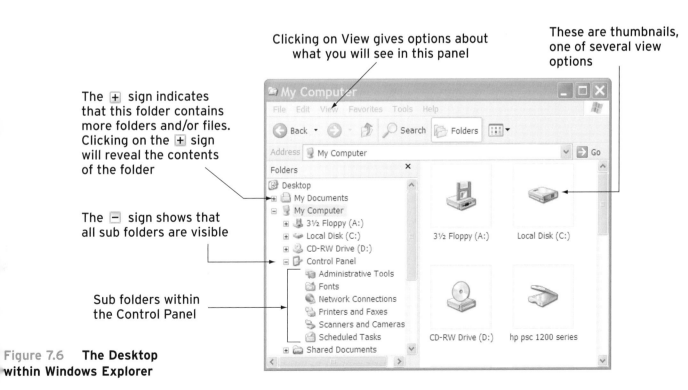

Clicking on View gives options about what you will see in this panel

These are thumbnails, one of several view options

The ⊞ sign indicates that this folder contains more folders and/or files. Clicking on the ⊞ sign will reveal the contents of the folder

The ⊟ sign shows that all sub folders are visible

Sub folders within the Control Panel

Figure 7.6   **The Desktop within Windows Explorer**

255

◆ My Network Places (page 345)

◆ Recycle Bin

Depending which of these four are highlighted, the right-hand panel displays the folders within that element.

My Documents

The My Documents folder contains – you guessed it! – your documents. This includes spreadsheet files and database files, not just *Word* documents.

By clicking on any folder, you can navigate your PC until you find the file you want to access, or the folder you want to work with:

◆ If you double-click on a file, Windows will try to open that file. According to the file extension, Windows will 'guess' which application created the file and, if you have that software installed, it will open the application and open the file within it. If you don't have the software that Windows thinks you need, you will be asked to suggest an application that can be used to open the file.

◆ If you open two windows in Windows *Explorer*, you can move files from one folder in one window to another folder in the other window, or you can move an entire folder (Figure 7.7).

Files can be
listed in detail
(View menu)

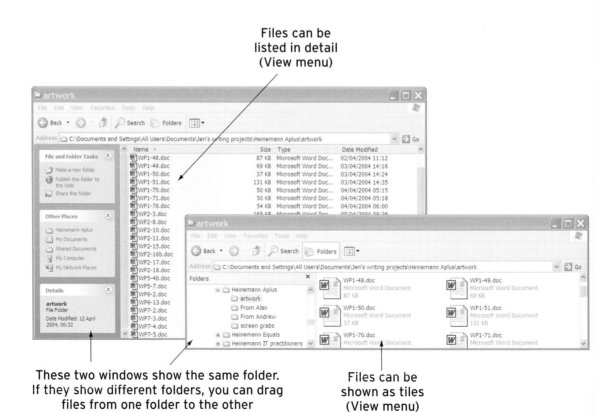

These two windows show the same folder.
If they show different folders, you can drag
files from one folder to the other

Files can be
shown as tiles
(View menu)

Figure 7.7   **Two windows open at the same time to facilitate file management**

Complete these activities using one particular operating system and make notes. Repeat for another operating system, and identify any major differences between the two.

1 Open Windows *Explorer* and explore the options available on the toolbar.
2 In the Tools drop-down menu, select Folder options and find out how to reveal the extensions for known file types.
3 Use Windows *Explorer* to open a file. How else could you have opened the same file, by another route? Compare your method with others.
   How many different methods can you identify?

My Computer

You can access the My Computer folder through Windows *Explorer* (Figure 7.6), or you can click on Start and select it from there (Figure 7.8).

The My Computer folder gives you access in the same way as Windows *Explorer* does:

◆ to all drives
◆ to the documents for each use on the system
◆ to the Shared Document folder, and
◆ to the Control Panel (see page 259).

However, there are differences in the order of options that you are offered when you right-click on an entry. This is because the right-click produces options that are sensible considering where you are and Windows takes into account the route taken to an entry (Figure 7.9).

Figure 7.8 **Click on Start to see what programs to run or files to open**

My Recent Documents offers you a list of files you have worked on recently

In the same way that you can copy and/or move files between folders in the My Documents folder, you can copy and/or move files between drives.

CHAT *Discuss how you could use the My Computer folder to manage floppy disks and CDs. (Hint: Try right-clicking on the entry for the drive and note the various options.)*

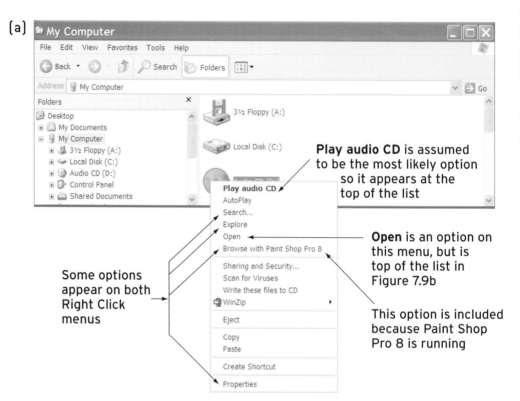

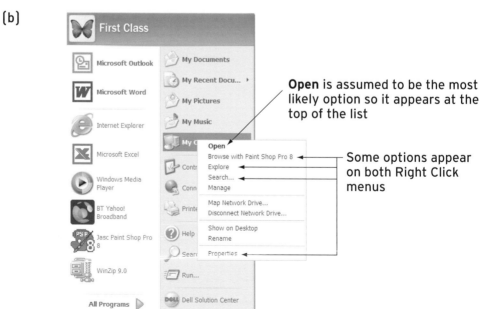

Figure 7.9 **Right-clicking on the A: or D: drive from Explorer, and from My Computer**

As with the previous activity, compare how to do these things on one operating system with another.

1 Open the My Computer folder through the Start key and explore the options available on the toolbar.

2 In the Tools drop-down menu, select Folder Options and find out how many file extensions Windows recognises. For a few extensions, find out which application is used to open any file with that extension.

3 Select the C: drive and navigate to locate a file that you have recently worked on. Clicking on the filename should open the file. From this window, how else might you have opened this file? With a friend, list the options found so far to open a file.

4 Open two windows: one from My Computer for the CD drive; the other through Explorer for My Documents. Experiment with copying files to a CD-RW and copying from a CD-R.

Control Panel

The Control Panel (Figure 7.10) can be accessed through Windows Explorer, My Computer or by clicking on Start and selecting it (Figure 7.8, page 257).

The Control Panel gives you access to everything you need to control your PC: from adding a new piece of hardware to setting the time, from choosing your Internet options to setting power options.

You will need to visit every location on the Control Panel and become familiar with every dialogue box, and every option available. On the one shown in Figure 7.10, there are 21 icons with some being more important than others. Your Control Panel may have a different set of icons – it depends on your OS.

However, it is not quite as big a task as you might think, becoming familiar with every route through the Control Panel. Many of them lead to the same place; what you need to learn is which route is best for you:

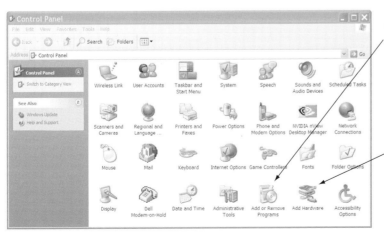

Add or Remove Programs lists the software installed on your PC and reports how often you use it. You can then decide which, if any, to delete

Add Hardware leads to a wizard which guides you through installing the device driver for a new piece of equipment. It also offers a troubleshooting service

Figure 7.10   **Control Panel**

◆ In Windows XP, the Administrative Tools icon on the Control Panel leads to seven more icons (Figure 7.11). The Computer Management icon then leads to the Device Manager (Figure 7.12). Alternatively, the System Properties panel (Figure 7.13) has seven tabs and the Hardware tab provides a link to the Device Manager.

◆ The Computer Management window offers Performance Logs and Alerts, but these are also available via the Performance icon (Figure 7.14) on the Administrative Tools window.

*Under Storage, the Computer Management icon leads you to an option called **Disk Defragmenter** (Figure 7.15). Discuss with a friend: how else can you locate the Disk Defragmenter utility?*

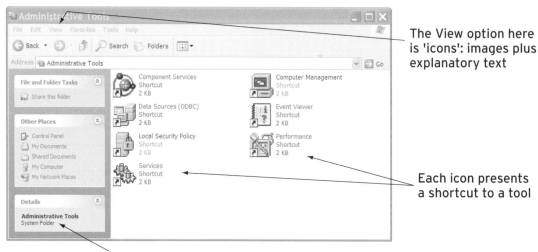

The View option here is 'icons': images plus explanatory text

Each icon presents a shortcut to a tool

This screen shows the Administrative Tools available in Windows XP. Different tools are available in other versions of Windows

Figure 7.11
Administrative tools

Figure 7.12
Device Manager

Figure 7.13 General and Hardware tabs for System Properties

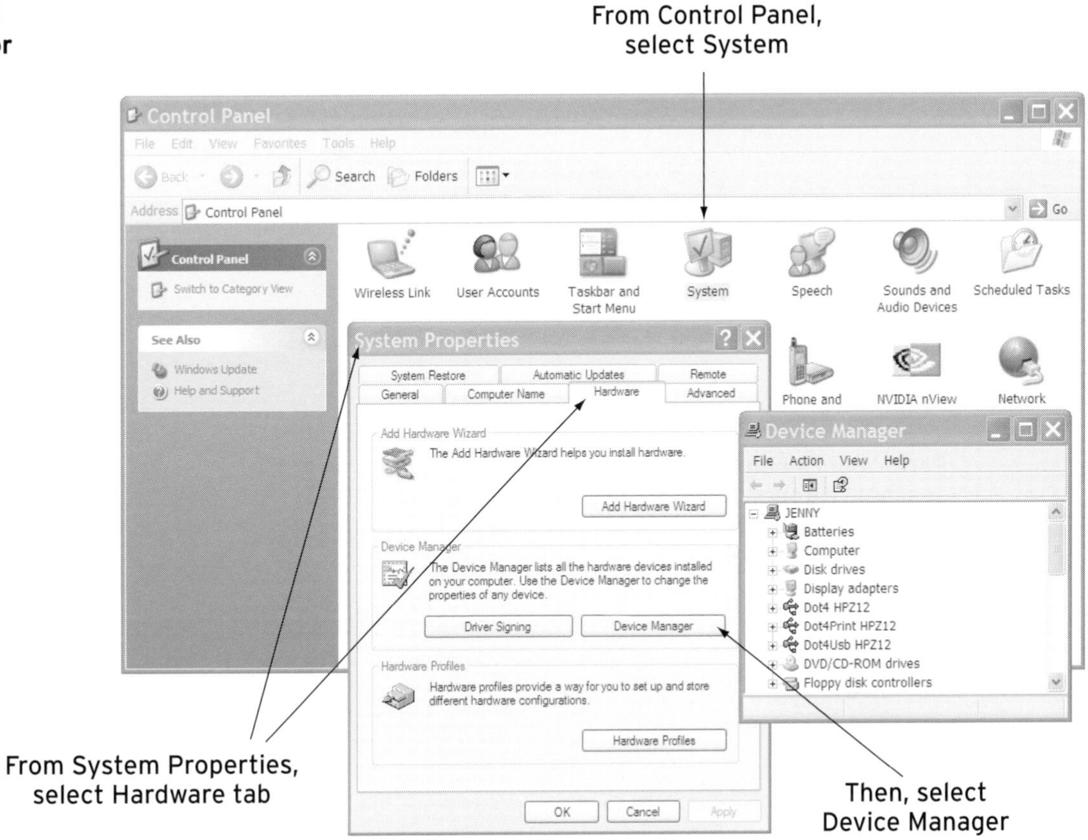

From Control Panel, select System

From System Properties, select Hardware tab

Then, select Device Manager

Go and try out 7.5

1 Working with two friends, share the list of icons on the Control Panel. Of your share, select two or three that interest you.
2 Explore each of your chosen icons in detail. Make notes so that you can remember what you have discovered and be able to explain it to your two friends.
3 Take it in turns to present your findings to each other.

The settings that you change through the Control Panel are stored in the **Registry**. So, each time you turn on your PC, the operating system 'knows' the settings that you want to use:

◆ The hardware attached to your PC
◆ The applications that you have installed
◆ The machine's IP address
◆ Details of your user account
◆ The colour settings of your desktop

Windows 3X stored these settings in .INI files (win.ini, system.ini). (See page 280 for more details about .INI files.)

(a)

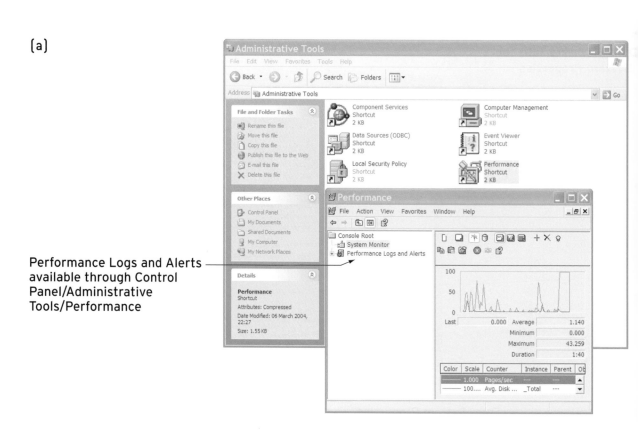

Performance Logs and Alerts available through Control Panel/Administrative Tools/Performance

(b)

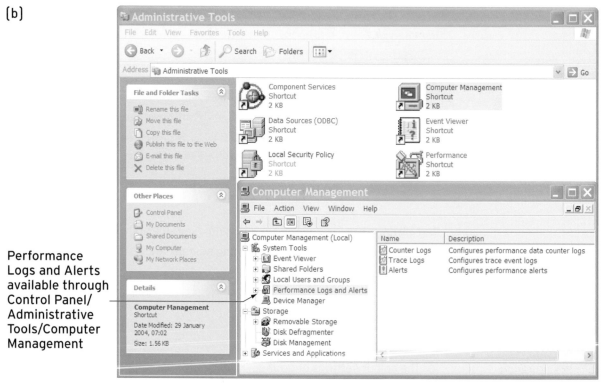

Performance Logs and Alerts available through Control Panel/Administrative Tools/Computer Management

Figure 7.14   **Performance icon**

Figure 7.15
Disk Defragmenter

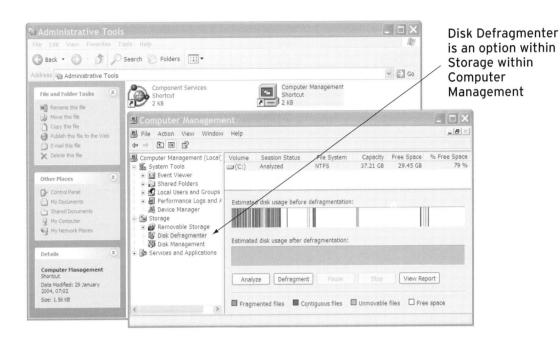

Disk Defragmenter
is an option within
Storage within
Computer
Management

Starting with Windows NT v3.1, these settings were stored in the Registry, a hierarchical database. Windows 2000 is based on Windows NT so it too has a Registry, as does Windows XP:

◆ The Registry stores settings that Windows makes itself, e.g. the hardware configuration identified during the boot process.

◆ Whenever you make a change to your settings, e.g. using the Control Panel, it is recorded in the Registry.

You should not experiment with the Registry – and never use the Registry to change a setting that you can change elsewhere, e.g. within the Control Panel.

Watch out

If you want to change a setting, do so using the Control Panel. This is the safest option.

You need to be able to find data within the Registry and to understand what effect it is having, if only to make sense of Microsoft Knowledge base articles or other technical information that refers to the Registry and tells you how to solve a particular problem by editing a certain **registry key**.

Registry keys point to data held within the Registry database hierarchy, of which there are many levels. First, the configuration data is divided into five **subtrees** as described in Table 7.3.

What does it mean?

A subtree is a subsection of a tree, containing one node and all nodes 'beneath' that node (Figure 7.16). HKEY = handle for a key.

Table 7.3 Registry subtrees

Subtree	Notes
HKEY_LOCAL_MACHINE	Settings for the hardware currently installed in the machine
HKEY_CURRENT_USER	The user profile for the person currently logged on to the machine
HKEY_USERS	A DEFAULT profile which describes how the machine behaves when no one is logged on
HKEY_CLASSES_ROOT	File association information and the OLE registration database
HKEY_CURRENT_CONFIG	The hardware configuration at boot-up time

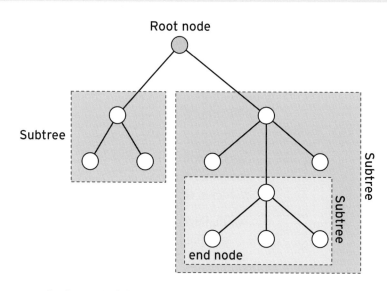

Figure 7.16
A tree structure

Then these five keys are further subdivided into subkeys. For example, within HKEY_LOCAL_MACHINE, there are five keys (Table 7.4).

Table 7.4 Registry subtrees of HKEY_LOCAL_MACHINE

Subtree	Notes
HKEY_LOCAL_MACHINE\Hardware	
HKEY_LOCAL_MACHINE\SAM	Contains the user database
HKEY_LOCAL_MACHINE\Security	Contains information like the name of the domain
HKEY_LOCAL_MACHINE\Software	Contains configuration data such as software modules
HKEY_LOCAL_MACHINE\System	Contains configuration data such as drivers

The HKEY_LOCAL_MACHINE\System key is further subdivided into a number of subkeys:

◆ HKEY_LOCAL_MACHINE\System\System ControlSet001

◆ HKEY_LOCAL_MACHINE\System\ControlSet002

◆ HKEY_LOCAL_MACHINE\System\CurrentControlSet

and so on. CurrentControlSet is then further subkeyed:

◆ HKEY_LOCAL_MACHINE\System\CurrentControlSet\Control

◆ HKEY_LOCAL_MACHINE\System\CurrentControlSet\Services

Although this results in a lot of keys, every detail is neatly filed away ready for use during the booting-up process or at any other time.

Notice that each level of key is separated by a backslash (\).

The Registry (Figure 7.17) is mostly contained in a set of binary files called **hives**, as listed in Table 7.5. The core of the Registry is held in four hives, SAM, Security, Systems and Software:

◆ SAM contains the user database.

◆ Security contains information like the name of the domain.

◆ System contains configuration information such as drivers, etc.

◆ Software contains configuration information about the software modules.

All the Registry hives have backup copies, with the .LOG extension. These are actually journal files, which record the changes made to the primary file. If the system crashes during a hive write operation, the LOG file is used to 'roll-back' the hive file to its original condition:

◆ Machine-specific hives are in the /WINNT/SYSTEM32/CONFIG folder.

◆ User-specific hives are in the /WINNT/PROFILES directories (Win NT) or /WINNT/DOCUMENTS AND SETTINGS/USER ID directories (Win 2000).

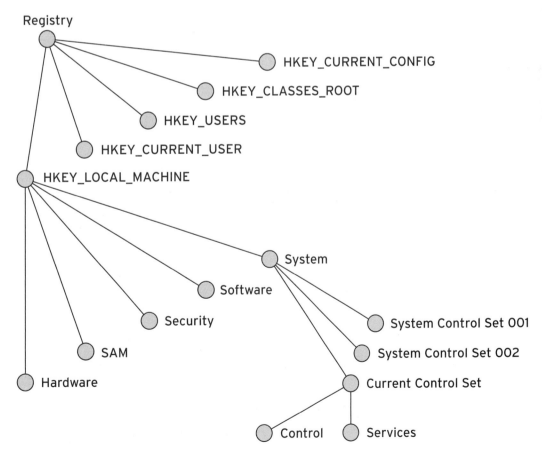

Figure 7.17
The structure of the registry

Table 7.5 *Hives*

Subtree/key	Filename
HKEY_LOCAL_MACHINE\SAM	SAM (primary) and SAM.LOG (backup)
HKEY_LOCAL_MACHINE\SECURITY	SECURITY (primary) and SECURITY (backup)
HKEY_LOCAL_MACHINE\SOFTWARE	SOFTWARE (primary) and SOFTWARE.LOG (backup)
HKEY_LOCAL_MACHINE\SYSTEM	SYSTEM (primary) and SYSTEM.ALT (backup)
HKEY_USERS\DEFAULT	DEFAULT (primary) and DEFAULT.LOG (backup)
HKEY_CURRENT_USER	NTUSER.DAT
HKEY_CLASSES_ROOT	(Created from current control set at boot time)

Having located the required registry key, what will you find?

When you access the registry key, you will find a **value entry**, which is made up of a name a data type and a value. There are five **data types** in the Registry (Table 7.6).

Table 7.6 *Data types*

Data type	Notes
REG_BINARY	Normally shown as a hexadecimal value. Not very easy to understand or edit!
REG_DWORD	Also binary but 4 bytes long
REG_EXPAND_SZ	A character string of variable size
REG_MULTI_SZ	String data, but a number of parameters can be entered as 1 value separated by nulls
REG_SZ	A simple string

What should you do if you have tried to edit the Registry and things have gone horribly wrong? Windows maintains a copy of the CurrentControlSet key – the **LKG (last known good) configuration** – which you can load if you seriously mess up. Otherwise, you will need to keep the installation CD handy!

Each time Windows boots and the first logon is successfully completed, it saves a copy of the hardware configuration from the Registry. This LKG configuration is stored in HKEY_LOCAL_MACHINE\HARDWARE. If Windows detects a hardware problem, it adds the LKG option to the startup menu. Choose this option if you have had boot problems, for example after installing a new device driver.

Watch out

If you are having trouble with booting, don't log on as, if you do, you will lose the LKG configuration.

Go and try out 7.6

The place to go for the full set of definitions for the Registry is the Windows 2000 resource kit. Working with two friends, find some definitions and share them.

CASE STUDY   The computer's name

Jenny has a laptop and she has decided to call it Laptop 1. This data is stored in the Registry at:

My Computer\HKEY_LOCAL_MACHINE\SYSTEM\ CurrentControlSet\ComputerName\Active ComputerName

Figure 7.18 shows the entry in the Registry.

1 Using the Control Panel, check the name of your PC. If it does not have one, choose one.

2 Open the Registry to check the entry for your PC's name.

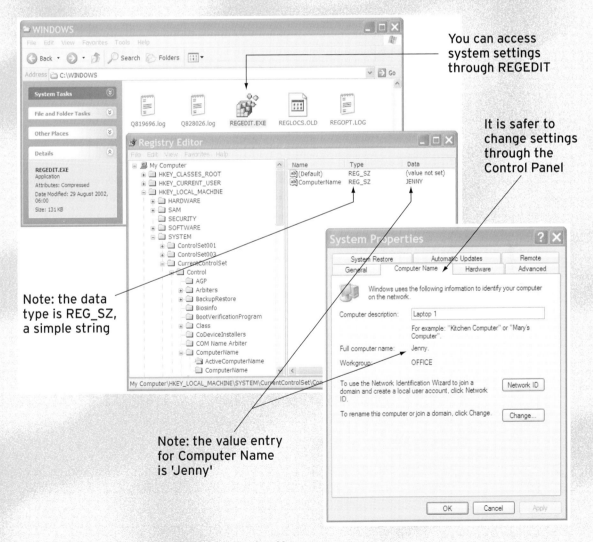

You can access system settings through REGEDIT

It is safer to change settings through the Control Panel

Note: the data type is REG_SZ, a simple string

Note: the value entry for Computer Name is 'Jenny'

Figure 7.18   The Registry entry for Computer Name

3 Memory management

There are two basic ways of addressing memory:

- With **real-mode memory addressing** (the default for DOS applications), the PC acts like an 8086 processor, and is limited to accessing just the first 1 MB of RAM.

- With **protected-mode memory addressing** (used by operating systems apart from DOS), a program is allocated its own memory space, which can be above the 1 MB limit of real-mode memory addressing. This protects the program from other applications wanting to use its memory space. It also limits an application to its own memory space although this can include memory located above the 1 MB barrier of real mode.

Note: All Windows versions after *3.X* run in protected mode.

If you boot up from DOS, the default will be real-mode memory addressing. DOS cannot access the protected-mode drivers for peripherals such as your sound card, so these drivers need to be loaded to real mode, and you can very quickly run out of memory.

Without **virtual memory**, few present-day applications would run on a PC. The capacity of a PC may be 64 MB, but an application may demand 100 MB of RAM. To cope with this, the memory management system uses space on the hard disk – called **swap space** – to make up the shortfall, e.g. another 36 MB of memory. Data is swapped in and out of RAM from this swap space, so that the CPU has access to the data it needs. In the background, the memory manager pulls in blocks that are needed in RAM and moves inactive blocks out of RAM. Windows 3.X, 9X and 2000 Pro implement virtual memory in **swap files**.

> **What does it mean?**
>
> *Virtual memory is storage space on the hard disk that is used to supplement real memory (physical memory within the PC) so as to accommodate data manipulation requirements that exceed the memory capacity of the PC.*

Memory is divided logically into four basic divisions as shown in Figure 7.19.

> **What does it mean?**
>
> *TSR = terminate and stay resident (see Chapter 9, page 329).*

Why is conventional memory only 640 K in size?

- Early processors were limited to addressing 1 MB of the RAM (due to the number of bits available for the addressing of data and instructions).

- IBM decided that 384 K of memory was needed for its BIOS and utility programs, leaving only 640 K of RAM for the operating system and the user.

Device drivers are needed to access the upper areas of memory:

- EMM386.EXE is the primary memory manager. This special driver frees up conventional memory by letting unused areas within the usually reserved area to be used for DOS drivers and memory resident programs.

- HIMEM.SYS is a memory manager that allows Windows 3.X and Windows 9X, EMM386.EXE and other operating system utilities, to access memory above 1 MB. HIMEM.SYS creates XMS (extended memory standard) memory.

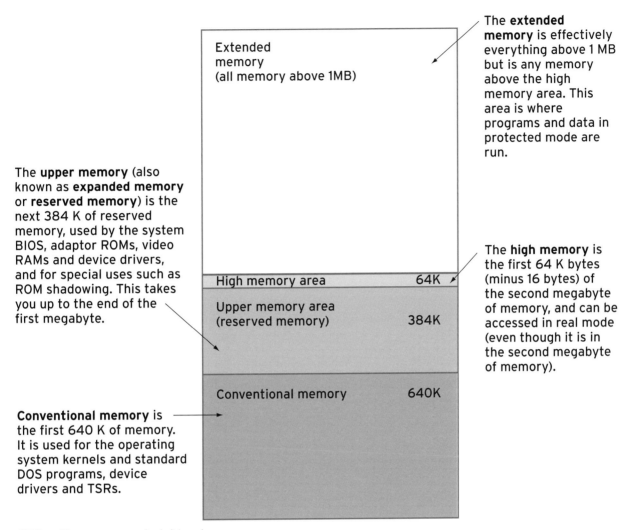

The **extended memory** is effectively everything above 1 MB but is any memory above the high memory area. This area is where programs and data in protected mode are run.

The **upper memory** (also known as **expanded memory** or **reserved memory**) is the next 384 K of reserved memory, used by the system BIOS, adaptor ROMs, video RAMs and device drivers, and for special uses such as ROM shadowing. This takes you up to the end of the first megabyte.

The **high memory** is the first 64 K bytes (minus 16 bytes) of the second megabyte of memory, and can be accessed in real mode (even though it is in the second megabyte of memory).

Conventional memory is the first 640 K of memory. It is used for the operating system kernels and standard DOS programs, device drivers and TSRs.

Figure 7.19 **How memory is laid out**

Without HIMEM.SYS (or another XMS manager) running, Windows cannot detect extended memory. Table 7.7 shows the code that you may need in your CONFIG.SYS file.

Table 7.7 *CONFIG.SYS file coding to utilise memory in upper memory and high memory*

Your aim	Code for CONFIG.SYS	Notes
To add expanded memory emulation	DEVICE = HIMEM.SYS	HIMEM.SYS converts extended memory into XMS memory, and is essential for Windows 3.X and Windows 9X
To implement EMM386 with EMS simulation	DEVICE = C:\DOS\EMM386.EXE	EMM386.EXE manipulates the XMS memory
To use EMM386 without the EMS emulation	DEVICE = C:\DOS\EMM386.EXE NOEMS	NOEMS means 'no EMS'
To load drivers, TSRs, etc., to upper memory	DOS = UMB	UMB means 'upper memory block'
To use high memory rather than upper memory	DOS = HIGH	

Using the high memory can save 45 K of space in conventional memory. More modern operating systems take care of all the memory management for you.

Check Your Understanding 7.5

1 What mechanism allows virtual memory to be implemented in a Windows system?
2 What is the first 640 K of memory called?
3 What is the memory above 1 MB called?

4 Windows 9X terminology

Windows 9X terminology relates to both the Windows 95 and Windows 98 operating systems. You need to be familiar with every part of both operating systems, so the more time you spend onscreen, for example, looking at the options within the Control Panel, the better. Table 7.8 lists files that you need to be familiar with.

Table 7.8   Windows 9X files

Filename	Notes	See
COMMAND.COM	An essential system file	Table 7.1, page 251
DOSSTART.BAT	A graphical DOS environment for launching programs and managing files	**www.heinemann.co.uk/hotlinks**
IO.SYS	An essential system file	Table 7.1, page 251
MSCONFIG	A Windows 98 file	
REGEDIT.EXE	This file lets you edit the Registry	Registry (page 261)
SETVER.EXE	Lists the version numbers of software	Figure 7.20, page 271
SMARTDRV.EXE	Utility that creates a disk cache in conventional memory or extended memory	**www.heinemann.co.uk/hotlinks**
SYSEDIT	This editor lets you edit system files	See below
SYSTEM.DAT	One of the two registry files	Registry (page 261)
SYSTEM.INI	A store for settings; replaced in Windows 95 by SYSTEM.DAT in the Registry	
USER.DAT	One of the two registry files	Registry (page 261)
WIN.INI	A store for settings; replaced in Windows 95 by USER.DAT in the Registry	

These files have to be opened through the **Run Command** because they are not available on any Windows menus. Access the Run command (Figure 7.20) by clicking on Start or go to the DOS Command Prompt through Accessories.

SYSEDIT is one such file. When you Run SYSEDIT, the four systems files AUTOEXEC.BAT, CONFIG.SYS, WIN.INI and SYSTEM.INI are all opened so you can conveniently edit all of them at the same time (Figure 7.21).

Figure 7.20　**The Start menu, the Run dialogue box and SETVER**

Choose Run from the Start menu

Type in the name of the program . . .

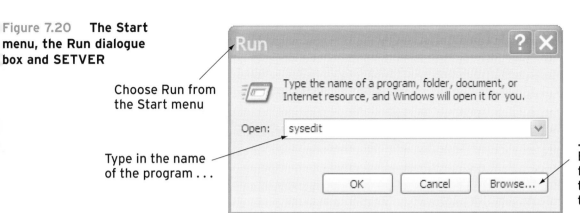

. . . or use the Browse option to find the program that you want to run

SYSEDIT opens with all four files open, ready for editing

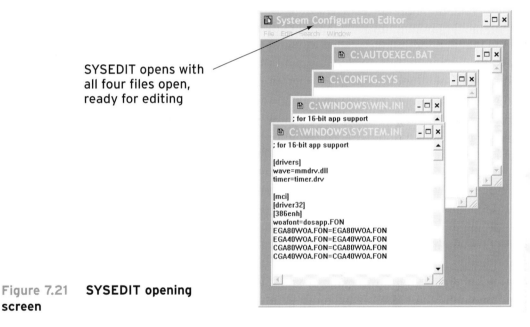

Figure 7.21　**SYSEDIT opening screen**

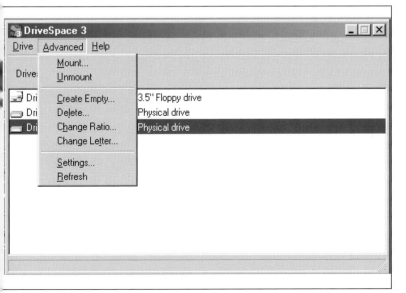

Figure 7.22　**DriveSpace**

DriveSpace

DriveSpace is a method of increasing the storage capacity of a disk. It was popular when disks were expensive, but the fall in price has resulted in much larger disk capacities and there is now no real need for it.

Window 9X has a Windows interface for managing DriveSpace available as a system tool within the Accessories folder (Figure 7.22).

5   Windows 2000 terminology

The introduction of Windows 2000 brought with it new terminology, not least because it is based on Windows NT. Table 7.9 lists the terms that you should be familiar with.

Table 7.9   *Windows 2000 files*

Filename	Notes	See
BOOT.INI	An essential system file	Table 7.1, page 251
NTBOOTDD.SYS	Used to boot SCSI devices when no SCSI BIOS is available	
NTDETECT.COM	Detects installed hardware and sends the information to the registry	Installing Windows 2000 (page 297); the Windows 2000 boot process (page 302)
NTLDR	NT loader	Windows 2000 boot process (page 302)
REGEDIT	This file lets you edit the Registry	Registry (page 261)
REGEDT32	The configuration editor for Windows NT; this can be used to modify the Windows NT configuration database, or the Windows NTregistry	

Computer Management (Figure 7.23) is a collection of Windows administrative tools that you can use to manage a local or remote computer. A Computer Management console will present information (usually in the left pane of your window) related to a console tree:

◆ *System tools:* event viewer, shared folders, local users and groups, performance logs and alerts, device manager

◆ *Storage:* removable storage, disk defragmenter, disk management (e.g. formatting)

◆ *Services and applications:* start, stop, pause, resume or disable a service

The right pane then gives the details so that you can decide how to continue.

To use Computer Management tools, you must be logged on as the administrator of the network; no other users should have access to these tools.

Go and try out 7.7

1   Working in pairs, compare how REGEDIT works in Windows 9X and in Windows 2000.
2   Explore the Computer Management tools available on your PC.

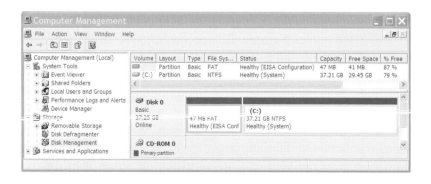

Figure 7.23
Computer Management

6 Command prompt procedures (command syntax)

Instead of going through Windows menu selections, you can enter commands directly into the command – or CMD – prompt. You can boot straight to the **Command Prompt** using **Restart in MS-DOS mode**, or it is available through the Accessories Folder (Figure 7.24).

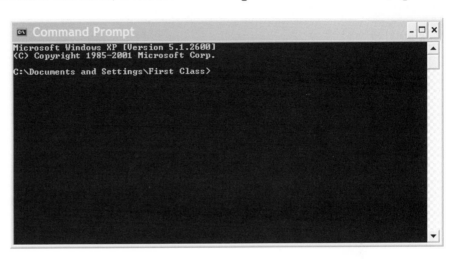

Figure 7.24 Accessing the Command Prompt

The command line prompt for DOS is

C:\WINDOWS>_

The underscore at the end is called the **prompt**. It flashes to attract the user's attention and indicates that the operating system is expecting some input from the user. You can control the appearance of the prompt using PROMPT.

At the start of the command line, the letter C followed by the colon indicates the active disk drive. The backslash and the name WINDOWS indicate the active directory.

What does it mean?

Directory: a logical division of the disk within a tree structure, nowadays called a folder.

Further backslashes are used to indicate subdirectories:

C:\WINDOWS\COMMAND

At the prompt, the user has two types of command that can be keyed in:

◆ **Internal DOS commands** are built into the DOS kernel and are therefore available at all times. This includes commands like those listed in Table 8.6 (page 303).

◆ **External DOS commands** refer to programs that are stored on the DOS folder, such as FORMAT and FDISK.

At the prompt, you can use commands, such as the ones listed in the A+ examination specification:

ATTRIB	FDISK	MSCDEX	SCANREG
DEFRAG	FORMAT	SCANDISK	VER
EDIT	MEM	SETVER	XCOPY

Most of them share names with the Windows-based utilities as listed in Table 7.11 on page 282. Make sure that you are familiar with them all, in what they do and how to access these functions via DOS as well as via Windows.

Go and try out 7.8

1 Working with a friend, copy the list of commands above in a column. Beside each one, write what you think the command will do.
2 Compare the list of commands with the utilities in Table 7.11. Fill in some gaps.
3 Using a DOS manual, look up any remaining commands to see what they do.
4 Use the Help option within Windows *Explorer* to find out which of these commands can be done using Windows. Keep your findings safe for a later activity.
5 Find out how to use the PROMPT command.

Each DOS command has a **syntax** that you have to follow. Otherwise, the command-line interpreter will not understand what you want done:

◆ To specify a setting, you may need to include a **switch**. For example: FORMAT A:/Q means 'format drive A using the quick formatting option'. Notice the forward slash; this indicates a switch will follow.

Discuss with a friend how you would do a quick format of a floppy disk in drive A:, using Windows menus. (Chapter 1, page 34, explains quick formatting.)

◆ You can use a **wild card** in a DOS command. For example, COPY A:*.doc D: will copy all the files with a .doc file extension from a floppy disk in drive A: to drive D:.

What does it mean?

A wild card is a character that is used in place of one or more characters. An asterisk (*) is a wild card for any number of characters. A question mark (?) is a wild card for a single character.

With a friend, discuss which Windows feature allows you to copy files and folders from one place to another, without having to use DOS commands.

Go and try out 7.9

You are to use DOS commands for this activity and time how long it takes you. You are to create a directory called C:\APLUS and save within this folder a test file called GOATO1 that is read-only.

1 Start your stopwatch. Access the DOS prompt. Write down how you did this.
2 At the C: prompt, use the DIR command to list the directories on the C: drive. Write down the total number of files and directories on the C: drive and make a note of the amount of free space.
3 Use the MD command to create a directory called C:\APLUS.
4 Display the contents of the APLUS directory. Note any files that are listed and any other information given.

5 Use the CD command to go back to the C: directory.

6 To create the test file, use the command COPY CON FILENAME which will copy a file from the console (i.e. the screen) and put it in a file called FILENAME. Replace 'FILENAME' with 'GOATO1'.

7 When you press Return, you will be on a blank line, so key in a message such as 'This is a test for GOATO1'. End your message with the key combination Ctrl-Z.

8 DOS should confirm: 1 file(s) copied. Check that the newly created file is in the C: directory by using DIR.

9 Copy the file from the C: directory to the C:\APLUS directory. Confirm that it has been copied correctly by displaying the directory for C:\APLUS.

10 Delete the file GOATO1 from the C: directory. Confirm by displaying the directory for C:.

11 Refer to your DOS manual – or to the onscreen help available through Windows *Explorer* – to check the syntax needed for the ATTRIB command and then use it to display the attribute of the file GOATO1 (Figure 7.25).

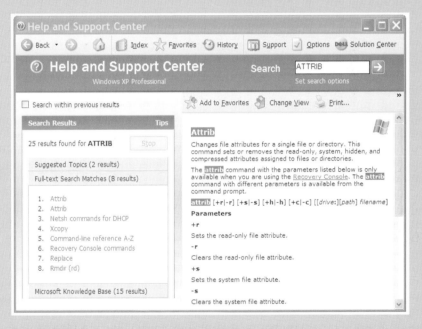

Figure 7.25
The Help screen for ATTRIB

12 Change the attribute so that the file becomes read-only. View the attributes to make sure you have set the attribute correctly.

13 Stop the stopwatch. How long did this activity take you?

14 Repeat the activity using Windows, and using an application to create the test document. Compare how long it takes you to do.

CHAT *Discuss with friends how you can print out a list of the contents of a folder on a printer.*

7 File management

You need to have file management skills.

- Creating new folders and files
- Finding files and folders
- Moving files from one folder to another
- Deleting files and folders
- Renaming files and folders
- Setting file management options

A **file** is a collection of data stored under a single filename:

- Each file has a **file extension** (see page 279) which indicates which software application was used to create it, and therefore what applications might be used to open it.
- Each file has a **file attribute** (see page 278) which determines what access is allowed.

A **folder** contains files and/or or more folders. You can create new folders in many different ways:

- Within My Computer, the main menu File option includes New Folder.
- Within an application, during Save As, you have an option to create a new folder in which to save the file (Figure 7.26).

There are also several options when trying to locate a file or a folder:

- The Search option from the Start will help you to trace a file or folder.
- Within an application, during Open, you have an option in Tools to search for the file you want to open (Figure 7.27).

The search can be done based on whatever information you want to supply.

- Filename
- Date of creation
- File extension
- A character string within the file, or within its filename

Moving, deleting and renaming files can also be done at various points using Windows – or using DOS commands. Table 8.6 (page 303) lists the internal DOS commands for file and directory management.

Deleted files are placed in the Recycle Bin, but are not fully deleted until you use DiskClear to remove these – and other files – permanently. Table 3.1 (page 167) includes disk cleaning as part of a regular maintenance programme.

There are also options to help you to control the file management windows:

- You can switch between Classic view and other views such as Web view (Figure 7.28).
- You can decide exactly what information to display for each file, and hide files if you do not want them listed within *Explorer*.

(a)

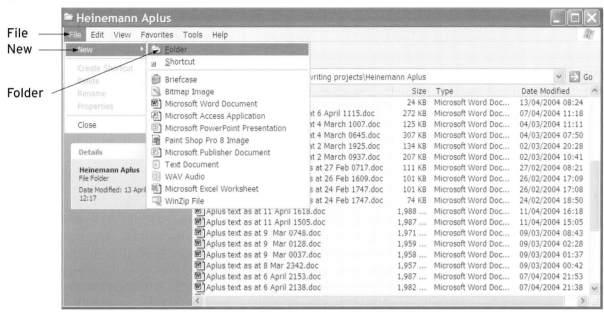

(b)

New Folder icon

Figure 7.26
Creating folders

Go and try out 7.10

1 In a small group, brainstorm ways of deleting files – on purpose, not accidentally! Make a list.

2 Repeat, with a different group of friends, to create a list of ways of renaming files and folders. Be sure to include using a function key: F2.

3 Look for similarities between the lists created.

4 Explore the File Management options screens.

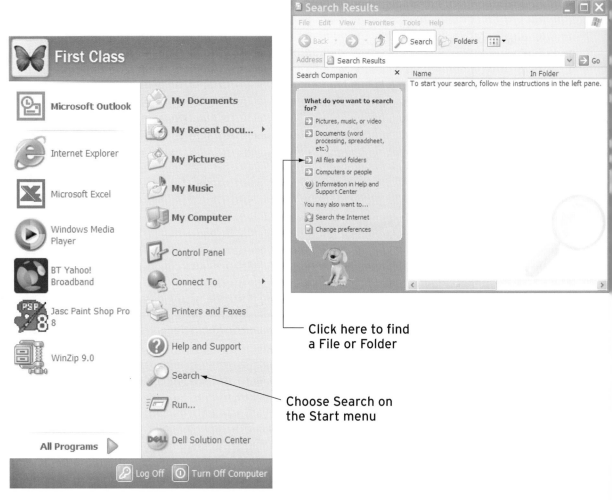

Figure 7.27   **Searching**

File attributes

So that files may be protected from unauthorised access, each file has an attribute which determines what access is allowed:

- **A (archive) files** are available for backup and will be recognised as such by any backup utility program at backup time.

- **H (hidden) files** do not appear on *Explorer* directory listings, so unless you knew they were there they remain hidden.

- **R (read-only) files** can be opened and read but not overwritten. Nor can they be deleted. To use the material in a read-only file, you would need to use Save As and save it under a different name.

- **S (system) files** can be overwritten but, because they are used by the operating system, you should do so with great care. This attribute marker identifies them as important files, to be treated with care.

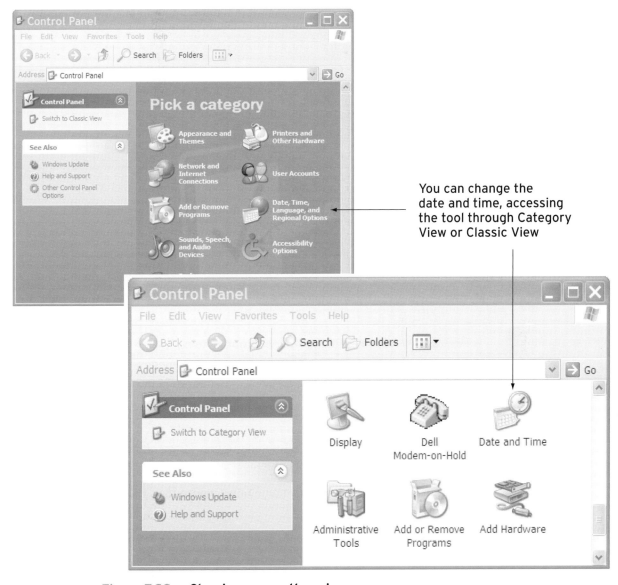

You can change the date and time, accessing the tool through Category View or Classic View

Figure 7.28   **Classic versus other views**

What does it mean?

The ATTRIB command can be used to set or alter an attribute to a file – A (archive/backup), H (hidden), R (read-only) or S (system) – or to display the current attribute of a file.

File extensions

File extensions indicate the type of information within a file.

CHAT *Discuss with friends the file extensions used in software applications such as Word, Excel and Access.*

279

Table 7.10 lists the most common ones that are found in operating systems software.

Table 7.10	File extensions	
Extension	**File content**	**Example**
.BAT	A batch file	AUTOEXEC.BAT
.COM	A command file	COMMAND.COM
.DAT	File extension which holds data	USER.DAT
.EXE	An executable file	ATTRIB.EXE
.INI	Initial values	WIN.INI
.SYS	A system file	C+ONFIG.SYS

Discuss other situations where naming conventions are recommended, e.g. in the naming of tables, queries, forms and reports within Microsoft Access.

Compression and encryption

Using Windows 2000, you can **encrypt a file** by setting a file property.

What does it mean?

Encrypt: encode so that the data in a file cannot be understood with the key to the encryption.

Windows uses a standard 56-bit encryption. Microsoft recommends that you create an NTFS folder in which to place the files, and mark the folder for encryption.

You may also, but not at the same time, choose to compress a file, making it take up less memory or disk space.

With friends, discuss why you might want to compress a file.

Go and try out 7.11

1 Select a folder to encrypt. Right-click and choose Properties. Under Attributes, select Advanced, and check the box for 'Encrypt contents to secure data' (Figure 7.29). Click OK to close the dialogue box.
2 Select a folder to compress. Make a note of its size. Follow the same route and choose 'Compress contents to save disk space'. Check the size of the folder after compression. What space saving did you achieve?
3 What other options do you have for compressing files? List some suitable software applications.

File systems

After partitioning but during high-level formatting, a disk is prepared by creating the operating system's file system and management tables and files. (See page 34 for

Figure 7.29
Advanced attributes

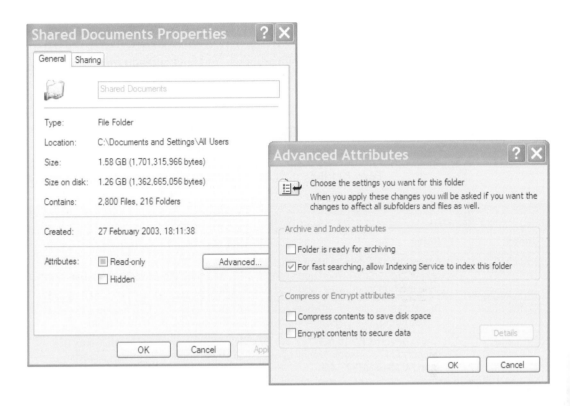

details of the geometry of a disk and how to format a disk.) Table 7.1 (page 251) lists which primary files are created during the formatting process.

A **FAT (file allocation table)** is stored on a storage device which keeps track of where files are stored on that backing storage device. It is created during formatting. Because the FAT is so important, two copies of it are kept and they are synchronised with each other. If your PC crashes, it may happen midway through saving a file, and there may be a discrepancy between the two FAT files. Utilities such as ScanDisk check for this.

FAT 16 was originally just called FAT, but it was renamed to distinguish it from FAT32; the 16 and 32 refers to the bus width: 16-bit or 32-bit. FAT16 is used on DOS and Windows 95; FAT32 on Windows 98 and Windows 2000.

NTFS is the file used on Windows NT; NTFS5 is a more up-to-date version than NTFS4 and can be used with Windows 2000. NTFS has additional file management features like being able to assign **permissions to individual files**. It also offers dual booting (see page 300).

HPFS (high-performance file system) is used on IBM's OS/2 operating system and can co-exist on a system with an existing FAT file system.

Optical disks have their own filing systems, and Windows 98 and 2000 support both these:

◆ **CDFS (compact disk file system)** is used for optical disk files.
◆ **UDF (universal disk format)** is one of several Windows files systems and is replacing CDFS.

Windows-based utilities

A **utility** is a useful program. You have already met some through your exploration of the Control Panel:

◆ Device Manager

◆ System Manager

◆ Computer Manager

Table 7.11 lists the other ones that you need to know about for the A+ examination.

Table 7.11	*Windows-based utilities*	
Utility	**Notes**	**See these pages**
ASD.EXE	Automatic skip device: Identifies devices that can cause Windows 98 to stop responding (hang) when you start your PC, and then disables them so that they are bypassed when you next restart your PC.	
ATTRIB.EXE	Used to set or alter an attribute to a file – A (archive/backup), H (hidden), R (read-only) or S (system) – or to display the current attribute of a file.	File attributes pages 278–9
Cvt1.EXE	Drive Converter FAT16 to FAT32. Windows 95 only supported FAT16 while later OSs support FAT32. To avoid having to repartition, this Windows 98 utility converts from FAT16 to FAT32.	FAT, pages 281, 289
DEFRAG.EXE	Used to defragment a hard disk, rearranging data on the disk, making more space available for files to be stored and improving the efficiency of I/O operations.	Defragmentation, page 167; Disk Defragmenter, Figure 7.15, page 263
EDIT.COM	A text editor that is not Windows-based.	Command prompt procedures, page 273
EXTRACT.EXE	Extracts files from compressed archives as on the startup disk.	Start-Up disk, page 306
FDISK.EXE	The Fixed Disk Management partitioning utility is used to create and delete partitions.	Partitioning a hard disk, page 33
FORMAT	Prepares a disk so that you can write to it.	Formatting a disk (page 34)
HWINFO.EXE	This utility deals with hardware information, e.g. the date and clock.	
MSCONFIG.EXE	This utility will only run from Start/Run: lets you decide how Windows should start up, so you can turn off selected drivers in an attempt to isolate a problem.	
REGEDIT.EXE	This utility will only run from Start/Run: an *Explorer*-type program that lets you view information and/or back up the Registry.	Explorer, pages 254–6
REGEDT32.EXE	The configuration editor for Windows NT, this can be used to modify the Windows NT configuration database, or the Windows NTregistry.	
ScanDisk/Check Disk	ScanDisk is called Check Disk in Windows 2000 and Windows XP. It checks a disk logically (for errors in the FAT) and physically (for surface errors).	FAT, pages 281, 289
SCANREG	When you start your computer successfully, the Windows Registry Checker tool (Scanreg.exe) creates a backup of system files such as System.dat, User.dat, System.ini and Win.ini once daily.	Registry, page 261
SYSEDIT.EXE	This utility will only run from Start/Run: an editor that can be used to view and edit systems files, e.g. INI files, AUTOEXEC.BAT or CONFIG.SYS files.	Systems files for Windows, Table 7.1, page 251
WSCRIPT.EXE	A Windows Script Host that can be used to run scripts in Visual Basic or JavaScript.	

Go and try out 7.12

1 Working with a friend, for each of the utilities listed in Table 7.11, make notes as to how you would access the utility using Windows.
2 Look back at your notes from Activity 7.8 on page 274, and fill in any gaps.
3 Select two utilities that you have not used before and experiment with them. Use the Windows Help facility to find out about them (Figure 7.30).

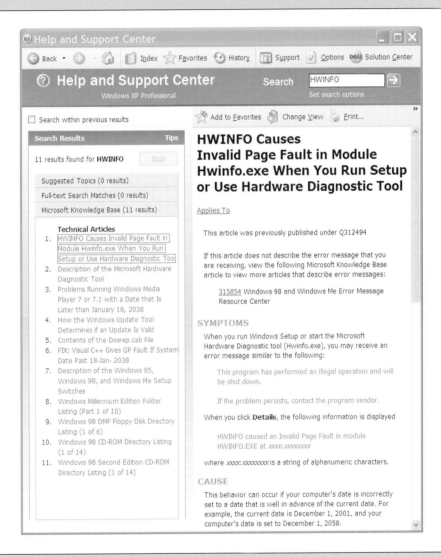

Figure 7.30
The HWINFO Help screen

Check Your Understanding 7.6

1 List the skills of file management that you should have.
2 Distinguish between the terms: 'drive', 'folder' and 'file'.
3 What criteria could you use to search for a file?
4 What is Classic view?
5 List the four file attributes. How can you change this for a file?
6 What is the purpose of a file extension?
7 What is utility? Give four examples, explaining what purpose they serve.

Revision 7

Remember these facts:

1   An operating system provides an interface between the user and the PC.

2   An operating system manages memory and provides the interface between the PC and its peripherals.

3   Backward compatibility means the operating system will support applications software and data file formats from earlier versions of the operating system.

4   Multitasking means the operating system can cope with more than one program at a time.

5   A virtual machine is a simulated 8086 CPU operating in its own separate address space.

6   Multitasking means that more than one program is sharing the use of the CPU: this is called time sharing. How that time is shared is decided by the operating system.

7   With co-operative multitasking, programs give way when another program requests use of a resource; the program lets the operating system know when it has finished using the CPU.

8   With pre-emptive multitasking, the operating system controls the timesharing and can suspend a program that is monopolising a resource.

9   Because Windows supports multitasking, you can have several windows open at the same time. The active window has a brighter colouring in the strip at the top of the window.

10 Windows can be minimised (sent to the taskbar), maximised (making it the active window) or closed.

11 With multiprocessing, the PC has more than one processor working at the same time.

12 With multithreading, a program spawns several activities under its control and these all run concurrently.

13 Asymmetrical multiprocessing (ASMP) assigns the work of a particular program to a particular processor, which then runs the program until it is completed. Symmetrical multiprocessing (SMP) divides the work from all of the programs, and assigns tasks to each of the available processors, making better use of all processors.

14 DDE (dynamic data exchange) enables users to cut and paste data from one application into another, using a clipboard.

15 The COMMAND.COM file is the command-line processor which interprets commands for interactions with the user.

16 The LOGO.SYS graphic file contains the logo that is displayed on the screen during the boot process.

17 Log files are created by Windows to keep track of what is happening and can be useful when troubleshooting.

18 Three major systems files are used during the MS-DOS boot process: IO.SYS, MSDOS.SYS and COMMAND.COM.

19 There are two optional startup configuration files: CONFIG.SYS and AUTOEXEC.BAT.

20 Navigating through Windows involves three skills: locating information, accessing information and retrieving information.

21 The Control Panel gives you access to everything you need to control your PC: from adding a new piece of hardware to setting the time, from choosing your Internet options to setting power options.

22 The settings that you change through the Control Panel are stored in the Registry.

23 Windows maintains a copy of the CurrentControlSet key – the LKG (last known good) configuration – which you can load if you seriously mess up.

24 There are two basic ways of addressing memory: real-mode memory addressing and protected-mode memory addressing.

25 Memory is divided logically into four basic divisions: conventional memory, upper memory (also known as expanded memory or reserved memory), high memory and extended memory.

26 Computer Management is a collection of Windows administrative tools that you can use to manage a local or remote computer.

27 At the command prompt, the user has two types of command that can be keyed: internal DOS commands are built into the DOS kernel and are therefore available at all times. External DOS commands refer to programs that are stored on the DOS folder, such as FORMAT and FDISK.

28 Each DOS command has a syntax that you have to follow. To specify a setting, you may need to include a switch. You can use a wild card in a DOS command.

29 A folder contains files and/or or more folders.

30 A file is a collection of data stored under a single filename, including a file extension which indicates which software application was used to create it, and therefore what applications might be used to open it.

31 Each file has a file attribute which determines what access is allowed: Archive, Hidden, Read-only or System.

32 A FAT (file allocation table) is created during formatting and stored on a storage device, to keep track of where files are stored on that backing storage device.

Chapter 8 Installation, configuration and upgrading

1 Installing Windows 9X/Windows 2000

Whichever operating system you decide to install, you need to make sure that your PC has the minimum requirements for installation to be achievable, and that it will be compatible with your hardware and applications software.

First though, will the operating system fit on your PC? Table 8.1 lists the minimum (Min) requirements. Note also the recommended (Rec) requirements. A PC starved of memory, for example, will run more slowly than one with lots of spare capacity. The ones shown in bold (for Windows 98 and Windows 2000) are the most important ones to be able to recall.

Table 8.1 *Making sure the operating system will fit*

Operating system	Processor	Memory	Hard drive space
Windows 95	Min 386DX/20 Rec 486DX/66	Min 4 MB Rec 16 MB	Min 10 MB Rec 50 MB
Windows 98	**Min 486DX/66** **Rec Pentium**	**Min 16 MB** **Rec 24 MB**	**Min 180 MB** **Rec 295 MB**
Windows ME	Pentium/150	32 MB	Min 480 MB Rec 645 MB
Windows 2000 Professional	**133 MHz or higher-Pentium-compatible**	**Min 64 MB RAM. Up to a max of 4 GB**	**2 GB hard drive** **Free space of 650 MB**
Windows 2000 Server	133 MHz or higher-Pentium-compatible CPU	Min 128 MB RAM Rec 256 MB RAM. Up to a max of 4 GB	2 GB hard drive Free space of 1 GB
Windows XP	Min 233 MHz Rec 300 MHz	Min 64 MB Rec 128MB	1.5 GB

Check Your Understanding 8.1

Surely the speed of a PC depends on its clock speed? Why, then, should a PC run more slowly, just because it has insufficient memory?
(*Hint:* Look at how virtual memory works.)

The hardware configuration of peripherals has to be adequate, too:

◆ A mouse is essential for all Windows operating systems.

◆ You would expect to have a VGA video card or, preferably, a SVGA video card.

◆ For Windows 95, the CD-ROM is optional, but for 2X CD drives are required for all others, not least because the operating system is supplied on CD.

It is also important to check that the operating system will support all the peripherals that you have – or plan to have – on the system. For operating systems supplied on CD-ROM, the CD will include a **hardware compatibility list (HCL)**. For an operating system that is already installed – and on which there are incompatibility problems – this is a useful source of information. However, if deciding whether to upgrade, it is more sensible to visit the Microsoft website to check before you buy (Figure 8.1).

Go and try out 8.1

Visit the Microsoft website and check for scanners that are compatible with Windows 2000.

You will want to run applications software on the PC – and not all applications software is compatible with all operating systems, so this needs checking too.

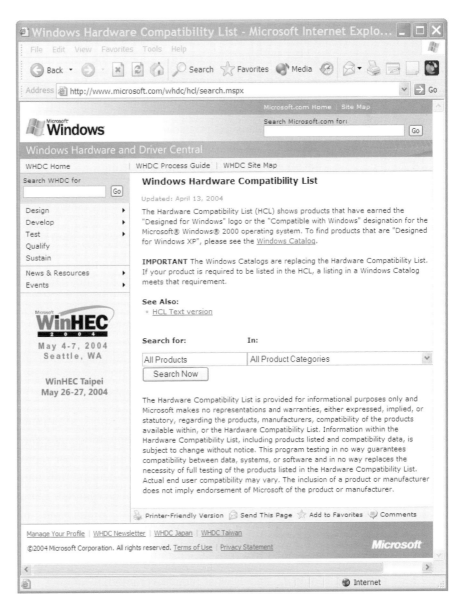

Figure 8.1
A Microsoft website

Next, you need to consider your device drivers. The hardware may be compatible with the new operating system, but the device driver may not. You can download the drivers that will be compatible, but you need to do this *before* you upgrade.

Go and try out 8.2

Revisit the Microsoft site and check out compatibility problems for applications software and for device drivers.

Finally, it is important that your BIOS is compatible with the operating system. This too can be checked in the documentation or online.

So, to summarise:

◆ Is the PC big enough/fast enough/have all the right bits to cope with the operating system?

◆ Will the operating system support all the peripherals?

◆ Will the operating system support the applications software?

◆ Are the device drivers compatible?

◆ Is the PC's BIOS compatible with the operating system?

If an upgrade is not possible, then the installation has to be done from a **clean start**, i.e. the disk has to be partitioned afresh and the hard drives formatted. See page 33 for partitioning and page 34 for formatting.

If you do decide to go ahead, make sure that you have fall-back plans in case things go wrong during installation of the operating system:

◆ Take a full backup of everything on your hard drive, just in case recovery requires you to make a clean start.

◆ Note all system settings so that you can reset them if necessary.

In a group, share your experiences of installing a new system or upgrading. What went wrong? How could you have prevented any disasters?

If you are upgrading from one operating system to another, you may be able to uninstall the old one. For example, Windows 98 includes an uninstall option. However, if this goes wrong, you will need to make a clean start.

You need to make sure that no applications are running before you start the installation, including anti-virus software. The operating system will want to write to the master boot record in the hard disk and this is one area that is protected by the anti-virus software. If you forget to do this, the installation process will warn you and you can respond to let it past the anti-virus software protection routines. See page 133 for details of anti-virus software.

You will follow instructions according to the particular operating system that you are installing. This may involve five stages (Table 8.2).

Table 8.3 shows what files are created.

Table 8.2   Installing an operating system

Stage	Notes	See these pages
1 Partition	Partitioning and formatting the drive are necessary if the upgrade is not available automatically	Partitioning a hard disk, page 33
2 Format drive		Formatting a disk, page 34
3 Run appropriate setup utility	The setup utility will be on the CD-ROM and you may only need to place that in the CD drive to start the utility	Setup program, page 205
4 Loading drivers	Loading drivers may be from CDs supplied with the peripherals, or by downloading from the Internet	Device drivers pages 110, 307
5 Start up	Start-up procedures include creating start-up disks, just in case the system fails at a later date	Start-up disk, page 306

Table 8.3   Files created during formatting

Operating system	Primary files	Notes	See these pages
DOS	FAT16	This was originally just FAT but, to distinguish it from FAT32, the 16 refers to the 16-bit bus	FAT, page 281
OS/2	HPFS (high-performance file system)	Supports drives up to 2 TB and file system) individual files up to 2 GB with LFN (long filenames, up to 256 characters) Can co-exist with a FAT16 file system	
Windows 3.X	VFAT (virtual FAT)	VFAT, while included in the list of several Windows files systems, is actually a file management overlay that enhances the FAT file system, e.g. by allowing LFNs	
Windows 9X	FAT32	Supports larger disk capacity (up to 2 TB) and uses a smaller **cluster** size for more efficient storage utilisation	Cluster, page 34
Windows NT	NTFS (NT file system)	Transaction logs assist in disk recovery procedures Can set permissions at directory and individual file level Fragmented files can span physical disks Can co-exist with FAT files	Log files, Table 7.2, page 252
Windows 2000	FAT32 NTFS5.0	FAT32 supports drives up to 32 GB Windows supports both FAT 32 and NTFS	NTFS, page 281

How you partition a hard disk depends on which operating system is installed:

◆ MS-DOS/Windows 9X – use the FDISK utility.

◆ Windows 2000 and XP – go through Windows Setup, or the Disk Management utility.

How to partition a hard disk using FDISK

This process will wipe the contents of the hard disk. Take a full backup before you start!

You need – an operational PC; a bootable floppy disk with DOS FDISK; and FORMAT commands:

1 Boot up the computer using the bootable floppy disk.

2 At the DOS prompt, key in FDISK and press ENTER. (You can reach the command prompt for DOS from Windows. Select Start – Programs – Accessories – MS-DOS prompt.)

3 Select option 4 (Figure 8.2) so that you can check and confirm current partitions. If there are partitions already set up, you will need to delete them. Note that you need to delete logical drives in the Extended partition before you can delete the Extended partition itself.

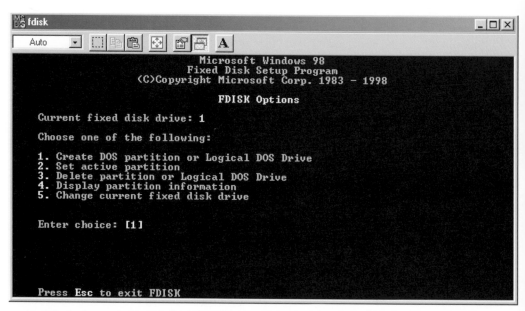

Figure 8.2
The FDISK options

4 To delete a partition, choose the type of partition you want to delete: Primary DOS, Extended DOS, Logical DOS drives in the Extended partition, a Non-DOS partition, and then follow the on-screen instructions to complete the deletion.

5 Once all the partitions have been cleared, you can choose 1 from the menu to create a DOS partition (Figure 8.2). You will want to create a Primary DOS partition before any others, so select this and follow the on-screen instructions for the creation stage.

6 You should now exit FDISK (by pressing ESC as given in Figure 8.2), reboot the computer with the floppy still in the drive and check (as at step 3 above) that the partition has been set up correctly. Make sure, in particular, that the primary partition is set to 'active'.

How to partition a hard disk using Windows 2000 or XP

This process will wipe the contents of the hard disk. Take a full backup before you start!

When you first install Windows 2000, as part of the Setup program, you are offered the option to partition your hard disk and to install Windows on that drive. If you have already installed Windows 2000 on your PC, the Disk Management utility can be used to partition the drive (and to format it too):

1 Access the Disk Management utility by selecting Start – Settings – Control Panel – Administrative Tools – Computer Management (Figure 8.3).

Figure 8.3
The Computer Management screen

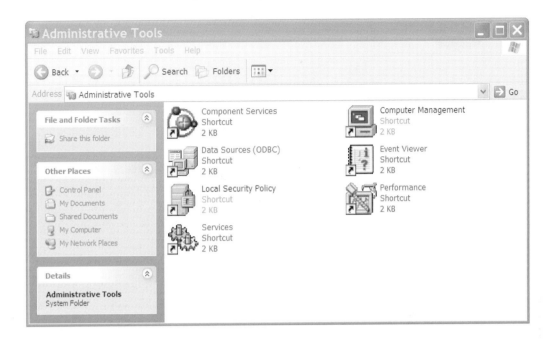

2 Click on Disk Management to see how your storage is currently partitioned (Figure 8.4).

Figure 8.4
Computer Management setup screen

This drive shows the partitions that are set up. Yours will have unallocated space on it.

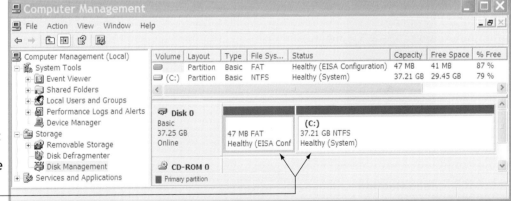

3 Right-click on the unallocated space available on your drive and select New Partition.

4 Following the on-screen instructions of the New Partition wizard (Figure 8.5), choose Primary Partition and enter the amount of space that you want to allocate to this partition. The default option will be the maximum allowed but you can make it smaller.

5 You can then allocate the drive letter for this partition – from the list provided (Figure 8.5e).

6 You are then ready to partition the drive, so select Format This Partition with the Following Settings, complete the dialogue box (Figure 8.5f) with your choices and click on Next.

7 You will be told when the partitioning is complete.

Watch out

You will need to restart your computer for the partitioning to become operational.

(a)
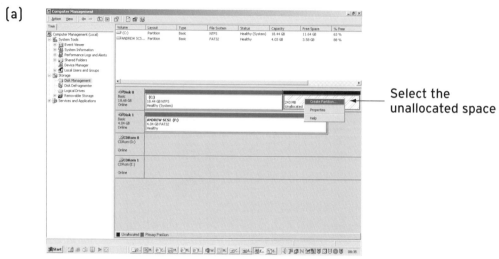
Select the unallocated space

(b)

(c)
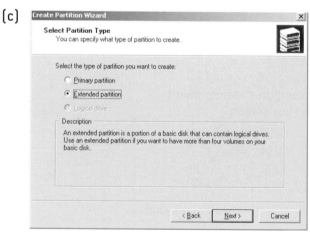

(d)
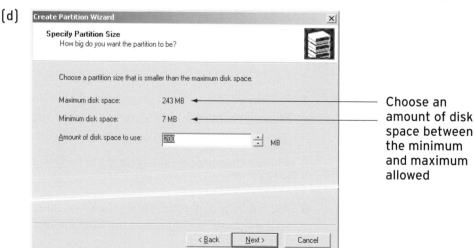

Choose an amount of disk space between the minimum and maximum allowed

Figure 8.5 **(a) Selecting the unallocated space to create a partition (b) The Create Partition Wizard (c) Selecting the partition type: extended (d) Specifying the partition size (e) Assigning the drive letter (f) Deciding on a name (g) Checking that the details are correct (h) Waiting for completion (i) All done! (j) The drive can now be accessed.**

(e)
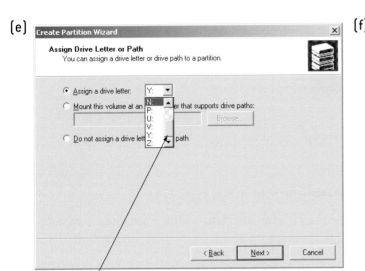

The early letters in the alphabet are already assigned, so choose a letter further down the alphabet

(f)
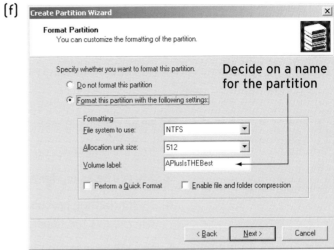

Decide on a name for the partition

(g)
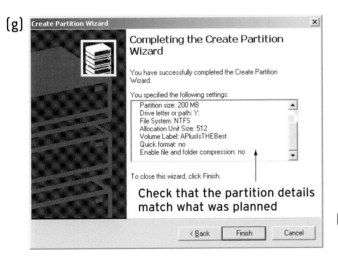

Check that the partition details match what was planned

(h)
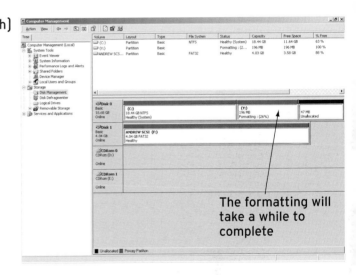

The formatting will take a while to complete

(i)
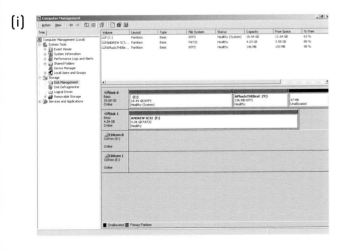

(j)
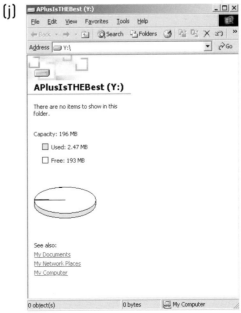

How to format a floppy disk

You can buy floppy disks that have already been formatted. In this case, you have to do nothing to make them usable on your PC. You can format using the DOS command FORMAT, or using the formatting tools available within Windows.

Using DOS

1 Place the floppy disk in drive A: and click it into place.

2 Key in FORMAT A: and press Enter.

3 You will be asked for a **volume label**. Key one in and press Enter.

4 The formatting process will then start – and may take a little while. Once complete you can remove the floppy disk from the drive.

5 You will be given the option to format another disk, but can stop as soon as you have formatted all the disks that you need.

Using Windows

1 Place the floppy disk in drive A: and click it into place.

2 From the Start menu, select My Computer.

3 Right-click on the entry for drive A: and select the Format option.

4 The Format dialogue box summarises everything the computer needs to know about what type of format you want. It also offers you default options which will work for you without you changing anything.

5 Complete the entries for the Format dialogue box (Figure 8.6), including the volume label and checking the Quick Format box if you are reformatting the disk. Then click on Start.

Choose Quick Format if you are reformatting the disk

The volume label is optional but if you label each floppy disk in this way – and handwrite the same information on a label on the floppy disk – this will help to keep track of what data is where on your disks.

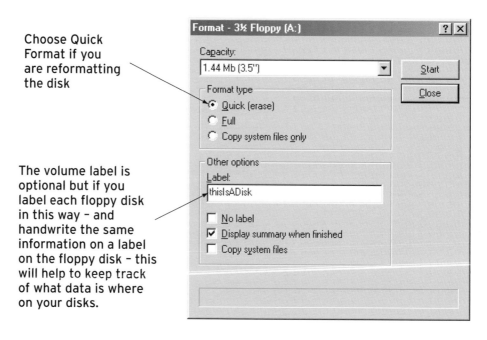

Figure 8.6
The Format dialogue box

6 A warning message will appear. Do check that you have the right floppy disk in the drive, and that you are formatting the correct drive. Once you click on OK, you cannot undo this operation.

7 You will be told when formatting is complete and can then remove the floppy disk from the drive and exit from the Format dialogue box.

There are lots of options when formatting a disk using DOS. From the Command prompt, keying FORMAT /? and pressing Enter will display the full list. Compare this with the options available within Windows.

If you suspect that a floppy disk is damaged, reformatting will check for physically unusable sectors. Don't use the Quick Format option for this type of formatting, because it skips these physical checks.

How to format a hard disk

1 Formatting a hard disk follows on from partitioning it. Having reached the point where the Primary DOS partition has been created, exit FDISK and then restart the PC with the floppy disk in the drive. Make sure you set the Primary drive to 'Active'.

2 To format the partition that was just created, key in format C: /s from the Command prompt. The C: tells the format program to make the C drive usable for DOS. The /s switch results in system files being copied to the hard drive during formatting, so that it is bootable.

3 The program then asks if you want to format the drive. This will erase anything that is on the drive, but your drive is empty anyway, so key Y for 'Yes' and press Return to continue.

4 When the format is complete, enter your name as the 'volume label'.

5 When the Command prompt is returned, restart the computer without the bootable floppy inserted, just to make sure that the computer will boot from the hard drive.

Details that apply to Windows 9X and Windows 2000 are now given here.

Installing Windows 9X

The process for installing Windows 9X involves several stages:

◆ Partition the hard drive.

◆ Format the hard drive.

◆ Run appropriate setup utility.

◆ Load drivers.

◆ Start up.

How to install Windows 98

For this activity, you need a PC with a partitioned and formatted hard drive, a bootable floppy disk with CD-ROM drivers or a bootable CD-ROM drive and Windows 98 Second Edition Install CD:

1. There are two ways of booting up and reaching the Setup program stage. If you using a bootable floppy with CD-ROM support, put it in the floppy drive and start up the PC. If a message says 'Press any key in order to boot from the CD' then do so. If you have to boot from the floppy disk, insert the disk and turn the computer on. At the DOS prompt, change the directory from A: to the CD-ROM drive by keying 'D:' and pressing Return. Then key 'setup' and press Return to start the installation.

2. The Microsoft Windows 98 Setup screen will display some options:

   - To set up Windows now press Enter.
   - To learn more about Setup before continuing, press F1.
   - To quit Setup without installing Windows, press F3.
   - Press Enter to install Windows 98.

3. First, before you install, Windows Setup needs to run ScanDisk to make sure that there are no problems with the hard drive.

4. Press Enter to continue. The graphical setup interface will be displayed.

5. After this, the Setup process is automated and you will be asked for minimal input:

   - The directory where Windows 98 is be installed.
   - Which Setup option is to be used – 'Typical' is the one that is typically used!
   - Which components are to be installed at this time.
   - How is the computer to be identified – you can enter a name here.
   - Where is the computer located?
   - Just follow the on-screen instructions.

6. Having taken all the user input, the serious copying of files starts. To show progress, a percentage is shown.

7. As with all installations, you will be asked to confirm that you have read the software licence and to check a box to confirm your agreement with it. You have no real option here. If you want to continue with the installation, you have to agree to the terms of the licence.

8. As a further check, you have to key in the CD-KEY. This information is on the Certificate of Authenticity on the CD case.

9. Clicking finish will leave you ready to start using Windows 98. The OS will automatically detect hardware and then ask you for the date and time.

10. When prompted, reboot the machine; Windows 98 should be installed successfully.

You are going to install Windows 95 or Windows 98 on a PC. Collect together all the documentation that you think you will need. Read through the instructions given in the 'How to' panels above and check that you understand them.

Refer to your notes throughout this activity. Make further notes about what happens at each stage.

Go and try out 8.4

1 Partition and format the hard drive.
2 Run the Setup utility and load device drivers.
3 Start up the PC to make sure the installation has worked.

Discuss how your installation went, and compare notes.

Installing Windows 2000

To upgrade a PC from one Windows operating system to Windows 2000, first it is important to check that the upgrade is possible. For example, it is not possible to upgrade from Windows 3.X or Windows Me to Windows 2000. The documentation with Windows 2000 spells out what can and cannot be done by way of an upgrade.

The documentation is supplied on the CD and includes tools to help you to check for compatibility (Table 8.4).

So, either your system will be upgradable or you will have prepared it for a clean start. See pages 143 and 288 for details of preparing a PC for a clean start, and partitioning and formatting the hard drive.

When you are ready to start, you will need to run the appropriate **setup utility**. As with most things on a PC, there is more than one way of accessing the setup program:

◆ From the command line for DOS or Windows 9X, key in EXECUTE WINNT.EXE.
◆ From the Start Run dialogue box in Windows 9X or Windows NT, key in EXECUTE WINNT32.EXE.

Table 8.4	*Documentation to check compatibility*
Folder	**Notes**
1386	Includes WINNT.EXE and WINN32T.EXE and other files needed for the Windows 2000 installation
BOOTDISK	Contains image files to create the 4-disk boot disks for Windows 2000, plus the MAKEBOOT.EXE and MAKEBT32.EXE command line programs that are used to create the boot disks
SETUPTXT	Contains release notes and setup documentation within two separate Windows 9X Notepad compatible files
SUPPORT	Holds the TOOLS folder; this has a subset of the full resource kit, a version of the HCL and the APCOMPAT.EXE utility – the Windows 2000 version of the DOS SETVER command

◆ For an upgradable system, placing the CD-ROM in the drive should automatically load and run the setup program.

There are then three basic stages of installation:

◆ During **setup loading**, the installation files and SETUPLDR are copied from the CD to the hard drive. This either creates or modifies the BOOT.INI file. SETUPLDR loads NTDETECT.COM and NTBOOTDD.SYS and does some initial checking of hardware, loads the device driver for the hard disk controller and passes control to the kernel. Depending on how this stage started, the end-user licence agreement (EULA) and the product ID dialogue are displayed at this point (see Figure 8.7). See page 251 for details of BOOT.INI.

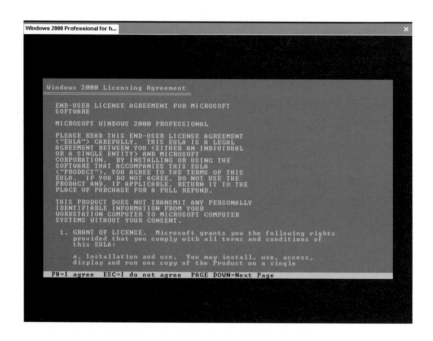

Figure 8.7
Setup loading

◆ During **text-mode setup**, the screen goes blue. The operating system makes an inventory of the systems hardware (motherboard, CPU and hard drives), creates the registry, detects PnP devices partitions and formats the hard disk and then creates the files systems (or converts any existing system NTFS file system).

◆ In the **GUI-mode setup**, the Setup wizard appears on the screen. This detects and configures devices found on the PC and creates Setup log files in the installation directory on the hard drive.

What does it mean?

GUI (graphical user interface): a category of user interface in which the style of communication uses icons to replace some or all of the text.

Notice that lots of log files (Table 8.5) are created during the installation of Windows 2000.

Filename	Notes
SETUPACT.LOG	Files copied during setup
SETUPERR.LOG	Errors that occurred during setup
SETUPAPI.LOG	Device drivers copied to the PC during setup
SETUPLOG.TXT	Extra information on device driver files

Table 8.5 *Log files*

These text files can be opened using Windows *Notepad* (or any other text editor) and can be useful for troubleshooting problems that might arise.

When asked if you want to run a System Compatibility report, answer yes. This will reveal any incompatibility problems with hardware and/or device drivers. If any device drivers are missing, you will need to load them.

What can go wrong? If your BIOS is not compatible with Windows 2000, the advanced power management and device configuration features of Windows 2000 may not work.

The final stage is to create a **start-up disk**. See page 306 to find out how to set up a start-up disk.

Go and try out 8.5

1 Go through the Windows 2000 installation.
2 Compare it with that of Windows 9X, and make notes on how they differ.

Upgrading an operating system

You need to know how to – and have experience in – upgrading an operating system:

◆ From Windows 95 to Windows 98

◆ From Windows NT Workstation 4.0 to Windows 2000

◆ Replacing Windows 9X with Windows 2000

If you are upgrading from one operating system to another, you don't need so much free hard disk space, because many of your OS files will be overwritten during the upgrade process.

Go and try out 8.6

1 Working with two friends, tackle each of the three types of upgrade:
  ◆ From Windows 95 to Windows 98
  ◆ From Windows NT Workstation 4.0 to Windows 2000
  ◆ Replacing Windows 9X with Windows 2000
2 Plan what you are going to do beforehand. Read all available documentation. Make notes at each stage, and check that you understand every step along the way.
3 When you have completed all three upgrades, compare your notes to see what is the same and what is different about the processes.

You also need to know how to dual boot Windows 9X/Windows NT 4.0/2000.

Dual booting

Dual booting means installing more than one operating system on a single PC, each on a separate partition. You must be sure that you have enough disk space in total to support both operating systems and, if you plan to dual boot with MS-DOS, your version of DOS must be able to able to support disk partition greater than 32 MB.

Not all operating systems support dual booting:

◆ Windows 9X and Windows ME do not support it.

◆ Windows NT, Windows 2000 and Windows XP do support dual booting.

To overcome this, third-party software is available, but you can manage to dual boot one of each without third-party software. If you install the non-supporting one first so that it is in the primary partition, the operating system that does support dual booting will recognise that another operating system is in place, and co-operate.

CASE STUDY   Installing Windows 98 and Windows 2000 on the same PC

Suppose you want to install Windows 98 and Windows 2000 on the same PC. The process is straightforward:

◆ Install two hard disks in the PC or partition a single hard disk so you have multiple drive letters, e.g. C: and F:. (D: and E: are usually assigned to CD drives.)

◆ Install the non-supporting operating software, Windows 98, on the primary partition, i.e. on the C: drive.

◆ Boot from the Windows 2000 CD-ROM. The Setup program will notice that Windows 98 is already installed and ask whether you want to upgrade or install a new copy. Opt for 'New copy' and use the drive letter for the second partition, F:.

◆ Complete the installation for Windows 2000 as normal.

A hidden file called BOOT.INI will be created in the root directory of the primary partition, and this contains a menu so that, when you turn on the computer, you are offered a choice of both operating systems. You can choose which operating system to work with or, if you fail to respond quickly enough, the system will assume you want the default operating system in the primary partition:

1 Follow the steps given above to install Windows 98 on the primary partition.

2 Then install Windows 2000 by booting from the Windows 2000 CD-ROM.

3 Restart the PC to see the menu offered at start up.

3   Booting up

During an **MS-DOS boot up**, these steps are followed:

1 The BIOS performs the POST.

2 The BIOS searches the drives for an MBR.

POST = power-on self-test.

The MBR (master boot record) contains data about partitions, including which partition is active.

3   The MBR takes control and loads IO.SYS.

4   IO.SYS takes control, identifying all installed hardware. It looks for CONFIG.SYS and – if it finds it – executes the instructions in CONFIG.SYS.

5   MSDOS.SYS takes control and loads the operating system kernel into memory. It looks for AUTOEXEC.BAT and – if it finds it – executes the instructions in AUTOEXEC.BAT.

6   COMMAND.COM displays the prompt, showing that the system is now booted up and ready to take input from the user.

During the boot, there are therefore three files that are needed: IO.SYS, MSDOS.SYS and COMMAND.COM. CONFIG.SYS and AUTOEXEC.BAT are optional.

Having booted up MS-DOS, the user is then in MS-DOS mode and can enter commands. See page 306 for more information about MS-DOS mode.

Booting up in Windows 9X is a more complex process. The OS has two parts:

◆ The **DPMI (DOS-protected mode interface)** is like the MS-DOS command prompt interface, except that it is protected mode rather than real mode. (See page 268 for an explanation of protected mode and real mode.)

◆ The **GUI (graphical user interface)** presents the WIMP environment that epitomises the Windows OS family: windows, icons, menus, pointers.

During a **Windows 9X boot up**, these steps are followed:

1   As with an MS-DOS boot up, the BIOS performs a POST and searches the drives for the MBR. The MBR takes control and loads the IO.SYS.

2   Unlike MS-DOS, the IO.SYS incorporates the role of MSDOS.SYS and IO.SYS. The MSDOS.SYS is no longer in charge of anything but supplies a list of settings that the IO.SYS needs. So the IO.SYS retains control, following the instructions in MSDOS.SYS and then looks for and checks the registry files: SYSTEM.DAT and USER.DAT. IO.SYS then loads SYSTEM.DAT.

3   IO.SYS then looks for CONFIG.SYS and AUTOEXEC.BAT and – if it finds them – executes them. They are not necessary files, but might exist for backward compatibility reasons. (See page 248 for explanation of backward compatibility.)

4   IO.SYS loads HIMEM.SYS if it has not already been loaded through CONFIG.SYS.

5   IO.SYS then loads WIN.COM and hands control to it.

6   WIN.COM is the main Windows program. It loads VMM386.VXD, the virtual memory manager.

7   VMM386.VXD then loads the 32-bit device drivers into memory.

8 WIN.COM reads SYSTEM.INI – the Windows 3.1 equivalent of SYSTEM.DAT – if it is present, and executes its instructions.

9 WIN.COM loads three files for the GUI: KRNL32.DLL, GDI.EXE and USER.EXE.

10 WIN.COM reads WIN.INI – the Windows 3.1 equivalent of USER.DAT – if it is present, and executes its instructions.

11 WIN.COM refers to the Start Up folder on the Start menus and executes any programs that you have specified there.

The **Windows 2000 boot process** is different again because, instead of having the DPMI+GUI setup, Windows 2000 is based on Windows NT. It therefore uses completely different systems files:

1 As with an MS-DOS boot up or the Windows 9X boot up, the BIOS performs a POST and searches the drives for the MBR. However, when the MBR takes control it loads NTLDR – the NT equivalent of the IO.SYS.

2 The NTLDR switches the CPU into 32-bit protected mode.

What does it mean?

NTLDR = NT loader.

3 NTLDR then finds BOOT.INI and displays any dual-booting menus for 30 seconds. If the user opts for a particular OS, then the chosen OS takes control. Otherwise, Windows 2000 continues with the boot process.

4 NTLDR runs NTDETECT.COM to detect installed hardware and feeds this information into the Registry.

5 NTLDR reads into memory the program NTOSKRNL.EXE – the equivalent of the DOS kernel loaded into memory by MSDOS.SYS in MS-DOS.

6 NTLDR locates device drivers as per the hardware that the Registry reports as installed.

7 NTLDR hands control to NTOSKRNL.EXE which then loads the device drivers and the GUI.

Go and try out 8.7

1 In Activities 4.8 and 4.9 on pages 207 and 208, you studied the boot process. Refer to your notes to refresh your memory.
2 Interrupt the boot process – and look again at what happens. Amend your notes as necessary so that you have full details of what happens and are familiar with the process.

Discuss with friends any messages that you still are not sure about on the BIOS start-up screen.

Creating an emergency repair disk (ERD)

What does it mean? *An ERD (emergency repair diskette) is created during or after installation using RDISK.EXE.*

An ERD is also called a **rescue disk**, or **start-up disk**. Ideally, you should create one or more of these disks before anything goes wrong with the PC.

A start-up disk is a bootable disk that includes the internal DOS commands (Table 8.6) and other useful command line utilities (Table 8.7) that will help you to troubleshoot when confronted with a PC that will not boot Windows.

A start-up disk can only be made for the 9X versions. This is because later versions of Windows (2000, XP) are based on Windows NT rather than a command line OS like DOS. For Windows 2000 and Windows XP, instead, a Recovery Console (page 305) is provided with the OS.

Table 8.6 *Internal DOS commands*

Command	Stands for	Notes
CD	Change directory	In MS-DOS, what are now called folders were referred to as directories, so the letter D appears in several DOS commands. CD changes the active directory to one that you specify. The prompt will then appear with a changed drive letter.
COPY	Copy	The COPY command allows you to copy one or more files from one directory to another.
DEL	Delete	DEL deletes one or more files. The syntax allows **wild card** characters, so you can delete many files with the same extension with a single command.
DIR	Directory	
MD	Make directory	MD creates a new directory, i.e. a new folder.
RD	Remove directory	RD deletes a directory. The directory has to be empty before this command can be executed.
REN	Rename	REN renames a file.

Table 8.7 *Windows-based utilities*

Utility	Notes	See these pages
ATTRIB.EXE	Displays and can be used to set and change file attributes	File attributes (pages 278–9)
EDIT.COM	A text editor that is not Windows-based	Command and prompt procedures, page 273
EXTRACT.EXE	Extracts files from compressed archives as on the start-up disk	Start-up disk, page 306
FDISK.EXE	The Fixed Disk Management partitioning utility used to create and delete disk partitions	Partitioning, page 33
FORMAT	Formats both floppy and hard disks so that they can be written to	Formatting a disk, page 34
ScanDisk/ Check disk	Checks the integrity of data on the disk and physically checks the surface of the disk	

How to make a start-up disk for Windows 9X

1 Place a blank floppy disk in your floppy drive.

2 Click on Start and go to the Control Panel.

3 Select Add/Remove programs and click on the Startup Disk tab.

4 Click on Create Disk and follow the prompts from there (Figure 8.8).

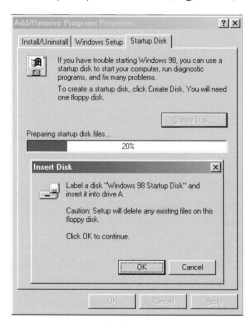

Figure 8.8
The Create Disk sequence

5 Label the disk 'Startup Disk' and write the Windows version, today's date and store this floppy disk somewhere safe.

The Startup Disk holds more files than could normally be held on a 1.44 Mb floppy disk, so the files are compressed into an **archive file**. When you use the disk to boot up, in Windows 98, you are given the option to start with or without CD-ROM support. If you opt for no CD support – or if you are in Windows 95 and are not given the option – it will then create a **RAM disk** as drive D:, and extract the boot files from the archive on to that drive. This results in a renaming of the logical drives beyond D. You then need manually to correct the CONFIG.SYS and AUTOEXECT.BAT files.

Since a Windows 98 Startup Disk will work on a Windows 95 PC, it makes sense to use this and take advantage of the CD-ROM support option.

When the system boots up, you are presented with the Command prompt, so you can start to troubleshoot straightaway.

How to use the Recovery Console for Windows 2000/ME

1 The Recovery Console exists on the Windows CD-ROM, so boot from that CD. It will start the Windows Setup program.

2 Key R (for recovery) at the Welcome to Setup screen.

3 Key 1 to select the first Windows installation of your PC.

4 Enter a password if asked.

You could decide to install the Recovery Console on your hard disk, so that it is more convenient to use.

How to install the Recovery Console

1 While you are running Windows, insert the Windows 2000 CD in the CD drive. If it starts automatically, close it.

2 Click on Start and select Run.

3 Key in D:i386\winnt32/cmdcons and click OK. (This assumes your CD is in drive D:. Amend the drive letter if necessary.)

4 Confirm by clicking on Yes.

5 After the installation is confirmed, click OK

Having the Recovery Console on the hard disk makes the PC act in dual-booting mode. Each time you boot, you will see a menu and one of the options is Recovery Console.

Once you are in the Recovery Console, you will see a prompt. Keying in HELP (and pressing Return) will give you a list of available commands. These are the same ones as for Windows 9X (Tables 8.6 and 8.7) plus some more as listed in Table 8.8.

Go and try out 8.8

1 Create an emergency repair disk for a PC running under Windows 9X.
2 On a Windows 2000 PC, install the Recovery Console. Check that the menu appears when you start up.
3 Experiment with Windows Recovery Console commands.

Table 8.8 *Windows Recovery Console commands*

Utility	Notes	See these pages
BATCH	Executes batch commands in a given text file	
DISABLE	Disables a given Windows 2000 service or driver; see ENABLE below	
DISKPART	Similar to FDISK, manages hard disk partitions	FDISK, Table 7.11, page 282
ENABLE	Enables a given Windows 2000 service or driver; see DISABLE above	
FIXBOOT	Writes a boot sector on the disk	Boot sector (page 35)
FIXMBR	Repairs the master boot record	MBR (page 301)
LISTSYC	Lists all drivers, service and start-up types that are available	

CHAT

Share your experiences of creating the Startup Disk – and using the Recovery Console commands – with friends.

Safe mode

In safe mode, the PC boots up as normal, except it does not load drivers for non-essential devices. It also uses a **generic VGA display**, rather than using the driver that you will have installed for your video card.

Booting up in safe mode (see Figure 8.9) dodges any start-up problems that may be due to device conflicts. So, if you installed a device and it prevented Windows from starting, safe mode would allow you to uninstall the software and undo the damage done. You then have a working PC again, although you have not managed to install the new device.

You should restart the PC normally before using any applications. It is unlikely that applications will enjoy much functionality in safe mode, and you will want the display to return to the normal standard. Also, it is likely that you need to study the documentation for the new hardware more carefully, visit the vendor's website and, maybe, download a fix, before you attempt the installation again.

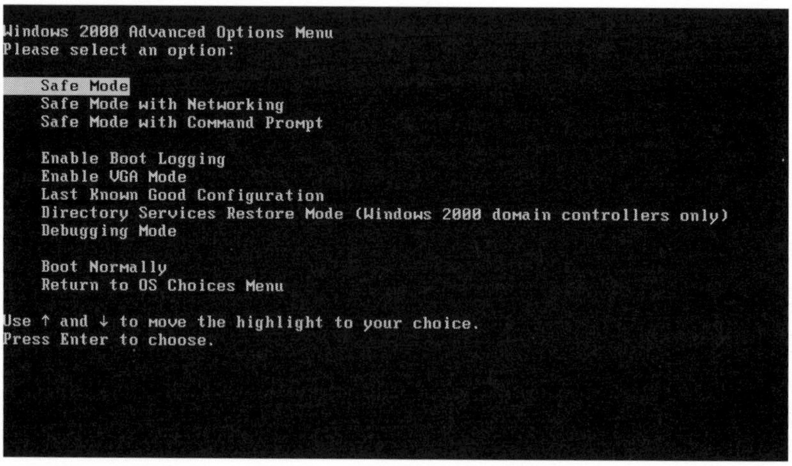

```
Windows 2000 Advanced Options Menu
Please select an option:

   Safe Mode
   Safe Mode with Networking
   Safe Mode with Command Prompt

   Enable Boot Logging
   Enable VGA Mode
   Last Known Good Configuration
   Directory Services Restore Mode (Windows 2000 domain controllers only)
   Debugging Mode

   Boot Normally
   Return to OS Choices Menu

Use ↑ and ↓ to move the highlight to your choice.
Press Enter to choose.
```

Figure 8.9   **Safe mode**

MS-DOS mode

This mode of boot up is only available in Windows 9X. It is useful if you need to use some DOS commands or a utility that might be incompatible with Windows. You can also use it to run a DOS application.

To go into DOS, from any other operating system, is achievable, though. You can boot straight to the **Command prompt** using **Restart in MS-DOS mode**, or it is available through the Accessories Folder. Chapter 7, section 6 explains the syntax of DOS commands.

How to create a DOS boot disk

You need an operational PC running under Windows 98 or an earlier system, and a blank floppy disk.

1   Make sure the PC is booted up and at the DOS prompt: C:\>

2   Key in the DOS command: FORMAT A:/

Be sure not to format the hard disk!

3 Check the contents of the disk using the DIR command. You should see five files: AUTOEXEC.BAT, COMMAND.COM, CONFIG.SYS, IO.SYS and MSDOS.SYS. Three of these are needed for the disk to be bootable: IO.SYS, MSDOS.SYS and COMMAND.COM. The other two files (AUTOEXEC.BAT and CONFIG.SYS) specify your hardware configuration and system settings.

4 Check that the disk does boot up. Leave the floppy disk in the drive and reboot.

Check Your Understanding 8.2

1 In what order are the five files on the boot disk used during the boot process?
2 If you boot using a DOS boot disk in drive A:, what prompt are you given at the end of the boot process?
3 What would happen if you had a floppy disk in the drive when powering up – on any operating system – that was not a bootable disk?

NTLDR (NT LOADER) is a leading player in the boot process of Windows 2000 systems. See page 302 to see NTLDR's involvement.

BOOT.INI is an essential Windows 2000 file. It is a hidden file, located in the root directory of the Primary partition. It contains the menu that appears each time the PC is started. If the user does not react within 30 seconds the PC automatically boots to the default OS.

Go and try out 8.9

1 Find out how to start in safe mode. Make notes.
2 Create a DOS boot disk.

CHAT *Discuss any problems you had in starting in safe mode and/or creating a DOS boot disk.*

4 Application device drivers

A **device resource** is something that enables a device to communicate with the CPU and the operating system. You have already met the four main types of device resource:

◆ IRQ (see page 75).
◆ I/O addresses (see page 78).
◆ Memory addresses (see pages 269 and 300).
◆ DMA channels (see page 77).

Ports are assigned device resources when you boot up. Expansion slots on a motherboard have to wait until you connect a device and the OS spots this. At this point, a **device driver** is needed:

◆ If the device is Plug and Play, and your OS supports Plug and Play, the device will automatically be recognised and the device driver installed for you.

What does it mean?

The device driver for a particular peripheral provides data – such as which codes mean which keys on the keyboard, how to achieve particular characters on a printer, what capabilities a monitor has – so that the operating system can manage the interface with that particular peripheral.

◆ Otherwise, you have to install the driver for yourself. You may also have to set jumpers on the expansion board to set the IRQ and I/O address.

See Chapter 1, page 53, for more information on jumpers.

CHAT

Discuss which devices on your PC are Plug and Play.
Does your operating system recognise these devices as Plug and Play?

Application device drivers

Some applications rely on a particular item of hardware and so the device driver is built into the application software.

CHAT

Think of some hardware which is sold with its own special software – or software that is only needed to use a particular piece of hardware.

TWAIN (technology without an interesting name) (Figure 8.10) is an example of an application device driver, used for image acquisition devices such as scanners and digital cameras.

Figure 8.10
A TWAIN option

Alternate CDFS.VXD

CDFS.VXD is an alternative Windows 9X CD-ROM driver that offers access to audio CD tracks as WAV files. Once installed, an array of folders is listed for the audio CD in the CD-ROM's drive. All the tracks are listed as WAV files in each of the folders made for each combination of formats (Mono/Stereo, 8 bit/16 bit, 11025 Hz/22050 Hz/44100 Hz). When you access the files, e.g. from Windows *Explorer*, CDFS.VXD automatically converts your CD's audio data to WAV file data in the correct format.

What does it mean?

VXD: a virtual device driver.

Installation, configuration and upgrading

1 Search the Internet for information about this VXD and others. Compare notes with others in your group.
2 Identify software applications that utilise TWAIN, and experiment with its use. Make notes.

Go and try out 8.10

5 Printing within Windows

Figure 8.11
The printer icon

Printing within Windows can be activated by clicking the printer icon in the menu bar at the top of the screen (Figure 8.11).

An alternative is to select Print from the File drop-down menu. Using the icon is slightly quicker, but it makes assumptions:

◆ The printout is to go to the default printer.

◆ Only one copy is required.

The File/Print route provides for a change of printer, more than one copy and many more options (Figure 8.12).

It is possible to set up several printers, i.e. to install their device drivers, so that any one of them could be used to create hard copy output. One of the printers is then identified as the **default printer**:

◆ Clicking on the Print icon sends data to the default printer.

◆ Going via File/Print will offer the default printer as the default, but it can be changed (Figure 8.13).

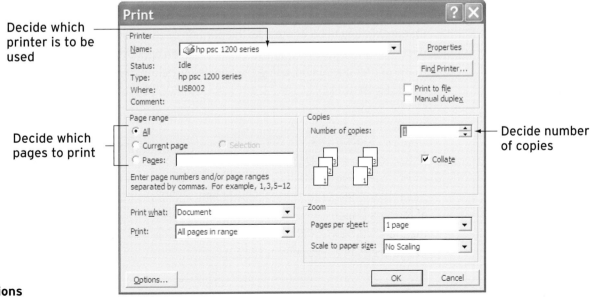

Decide which printer is to be used

Decide which pages to print

Decide number of copies

Figure 8.12
File/Print options

309

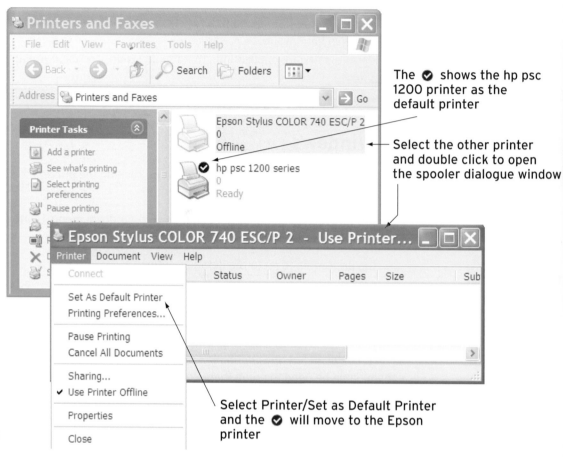

The ✓ shows the hp psc 1200 printer as the default printer

Select the other printer and double click to open the spooler dialogue window

Select Printer/Set as Default Printer and the ✓ will move to the Epson printer

Figure 8.13
Setting the default printer

Installing/spool setting

A **spooler** is a program installed as part of the device driver that forms a queue of documents that are waiting to be printed. As the printing of each document is completed, all other documents move further up the queue. From an application, it is possible to send documents to the printer queue and, using the Spooler, to delete them from the queue if you change your mind (Figure 8.14).

Select a document entry

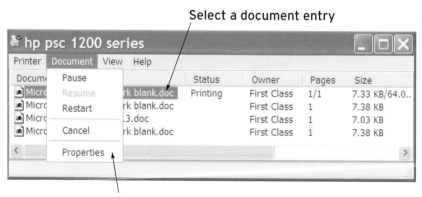

Figure 8.14
Printer queue options

Then click on Document to see the options available. Or, right click on the entry

Network printing (with the help of LAN admin)

Figure 5.9 (page 226) shows how a printer might be attached to a network and Figure 6.13 (page 240) shows how a printer can be assigned as a network printer.

1 A user complains that he or she cannot print a document on a networked printer. List what steps you might take to resolve this problem.
2 Experiment with a spooler: add documents to the queue to be printed and remove documents from the queue.

In a small group, share your ideas for troubleshooting printer problems on a network.

6 Installing and launching typical Windows and non-Windows applications

There are two types of Windows programs:

◆ Some programs are supplied with the Windows operating system and are called **Windows components**. You need not install all of these when you first install Windows. Not installing Windows components – especially those that you know you do not plan to use – will prevent unnecessary wastage of memory space on your hard drive.

◆ Any other programs – applications software – are installed separately from the Windows operating system. You can install just the ones you plan to use, as and when you buy them.

Then, there are the non-Windows applications. For example, on some hardware such as PDAs, the manufacturer may include software that is not Windows-compatible. Special installation arrangements will be needed for any non-Windows software to be installed on a PC, and these will be supplied with the CD.

Look at the applications installed on your PC and identify any non-Windows applications.

Installing Windows components

When you install Windows and choose the 'default install' option, some of the programs that appear in the Accessories folder (see Figure 8.15) are installed automatically – such as *Calculator* and *Notepad*.

If you don't want these installed, or want others to be installed, you can use Add/Remove Programs to select exactly what mix of accessories you want to have installed on your PC.

With a friend, compare notes as to what Windows components you have installed on your PC – and which you actually use.

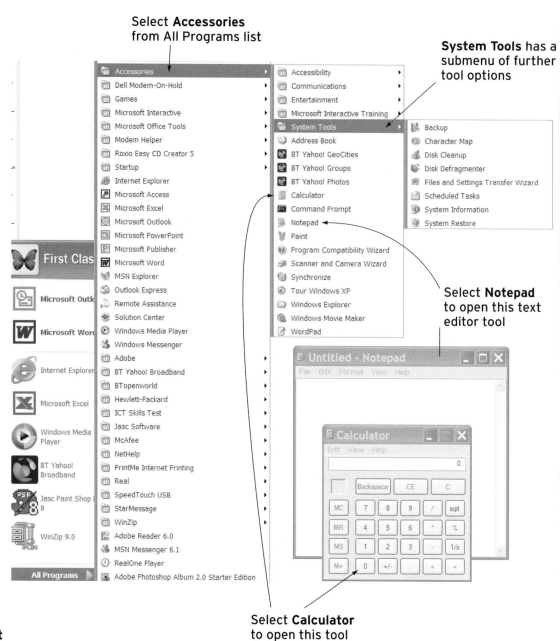

Select **Accessories** from All Programs list

System Tools has a submenu of further tool options

Select **Notepad** to open this text editor tool

Select **Calculator** to open this tool

Figure 8.15
The Accessories list

Installing applications that run under Windows

There four ways of installing and running applications software that runs under Windows:

◆ You may receive the application on CD and, when you place the CD in the drive, it automatically installs itself.

◆ Installing the software using the Control Panel/Add Software wizard (Figure 8.16), and then double-clicking on the application icon.

◆ The application may have a self-extracting or self-installing file such as SETUP.EXE or INSTALL.EXE.

If you want to free up space, consider removing programs that are large and that you use rarely

This shows how much you use the program

This gives the date you last used the program

You can also add/remove Windows Components

Figure 8.16   The Control Panel/Add Software wizard

◆ If the application does not install itself, you can use Start/Run to run SETUP.EXE or INSTALL.EXE (Figure 8.17).

Once an application is installed, it will appear on the list of programs.

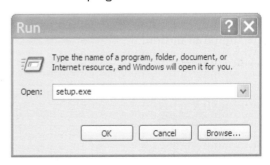

Figure 8.17
Start/Run to run SETUP.EXE

If you want to delete unwanted applications from a PC, it is not sufficient to delete all the files that appear to have been installed. The installation may have resulted in changes to other files such as the CONFIG.SYS or AUTOEXEC.BAT file and these files also need to be amended. Most software application vendors supply an uninstall program so that you can remove all traces of an application (see Figure 8.18).

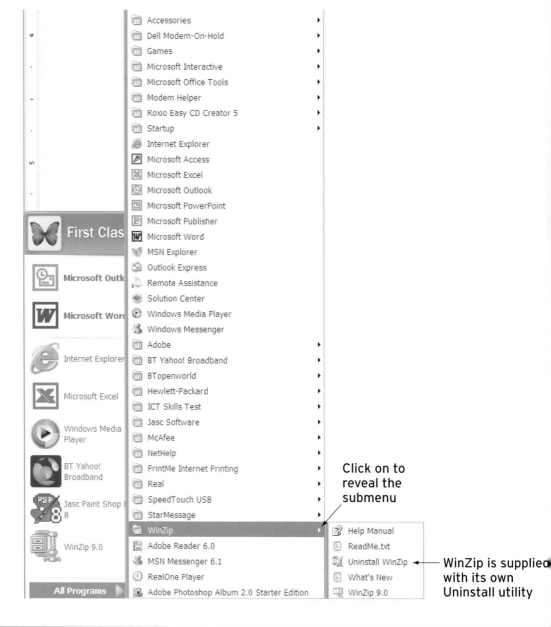

Figure 8.18
The Uninstall option

1 Experiment with installing applications software from a CD. Do all operating systems automatically install the software?
2 Use the Start/Run option to install an application.
3 Having installed an application, find out how to uninstall the application.

Discuss why it is important to use a utility to uninstall software that you no longer need on your PC.

Windows 9X/2000 procedures

With Windows 9X, there are many programs available as Windows components, so you can customise accessories for a particular end user. Windows 2000 is more prescriptive; you may not be able to remove many accessories. Windows XP returns to a more flexible arrangement.

Go and try out 8.13

1 Check out which Windows components are installed automatically during a 'default install' for at least two different versions of Windows.

2 Identify how to Add/Remove Windows components in Windows 9X, and then in Windows 2000. Figure 8.19 shows how to do this for Windows XP. Note the main differences in these three procedures.

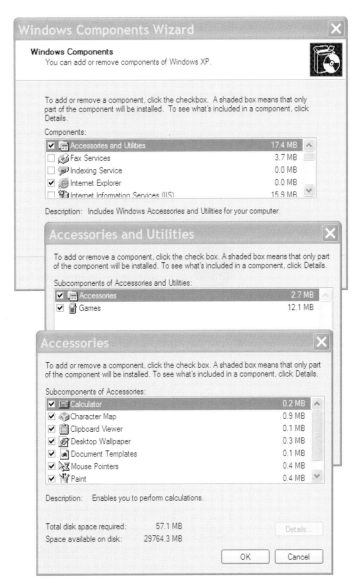

Figure 8.19
Windows XP Add/Remove

Programs options

Within applications software, such as Microsoft *Office*, there are also components that you may or may not want installed. These can be added/removed using Add/Remove programs from the Windows Control Panel.

If while using an application you choose a menu option for which the software has not yet been installed, you will be asked to add this software. This may happen when trying to insert clipart into a *Word* document, or using some special tool/feature.

Start-up configuration

You may decide to switch on your PC in a number of different ways:

◆ **Safe mode** starts using only the most basic files and drivers.

◆ **Safe mode with Command Prompt** starts as with safe mode, except that after logging on, the Command Prompt is displayed instead of the Windows graphical interface.

◆ **Enable boot logging mode** keeps track of all the drivers and services that were loaded (or not loaded) by the system to a file called ntbtlog.txt located in the %windir% directory. Safe mode starts this boot log so this can prove useful in determining the exact cause of system start-up problems.

◆ **Enable VGA mode** starts using only the basic VGA driver, which can be useful when you have installed a new driver for your video card and it seems to be causing Windows problems in starting properly.

◆ The **LKG (last known good) configuration** starts using information from the Registry and drivers that Windows saved at the last shutdown. So any changes that you made since the last successful start-up will be lost, and you may solve problems that were caused by your own erroneous changes to the configuration settings.

Discuss with friends how to start your PC in different ways.
Find out how to start with the LKG configuration.

When you switch on your PC, after the boot-up process has almost been completed, you may also be offered a choice of operating system. This occurs if you have installed more than one operating system. (See page 300 for details of how to dual boot).

Once the PC is on, and the operating system installed, you may also arrange for some programs to start up automatically. These programs are listed in the Startup folder (Figure 8.20).

Desktop access

The desktop is the on-screen work area on which windows, icons, menus and dialogue boxes appear. For your desktop, you have the option to make lots of decisions:

◆ You decide which windows to have open, which to minimise and which window is to be the active window. You can also move windows around the screen (by dragging the window to a new position) and resize them (by dragging the corners of the window until it is the size and shape you want).

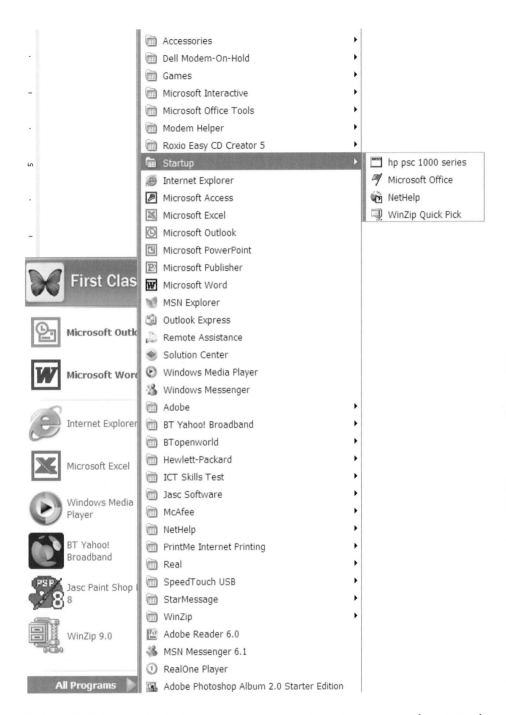

Figure 8.20
The Startup folder

◆ You decide which icons to include, and can set up new icons for shortcuts (see below).

◆ You decide which menus to display, i.e. which toolbars to include, and where these should appear on the screen (e.g. at the top/bottom of the window or down one side).

CHAT *Compare your desktop options with friends. Check that you know how to change the desktop options.*

You can also choose the theme for your desktop so that it suits your personal preferences for colour, etc. (see Figure 8.21).

Icons provide shortcuts to your programs

You can choose a background for your desktop

Figure 8.21 **A desktop**

It is also possible, over a network, to access your desktop on one computer remotely from another. The **remote desktop** option allows you to lock one PC so that no one can access the programs and files on it, but you can access them remotely, e.g. from home.

 Discuss situations where the remote desktop option might prove useful.

Shortcuts

A shortcut provides a route to a feature that avoids going through the normal menu route. There are lots of situations where you might choose to set up a shortcut, and the Windows Help Centre provides an online tutorial to take you through all the options.

1 Experiment with your desktop, changing the settings for colour theme, screen saver and so on. Compare what you have done with others in your group.
2 Use the Microsoft Help Centre to look at how to set up shortcuts or, if you feel confident about shortcuts, explore some other feature of Windows through the tutorial system.

 Discuss the benefits of online tutorials with others in your group.

Revision 8

Remember these facts:

1 Operating system: uses BIOS at start-up; manages primary and secondary storage; interface between hardware and applications software; housekeeping and diagnosing faults.

2 An operating system has requirements: processor, memory and hard drive space. An operating system can be installed with minimum requirements but will perform better with recommended requirements.

3 Windows 98 needs 486DX/66 process (min) or Pentium (rec) with 16 MB (min) or 24 MB (rec) of RAM and 180 MB (min) or 295 MB (rec) hard drive space.

4 Windows 2000 needs 133 MHz or higher Pentium-compatible CPU with 64 MB (min) of RAM and 2 GB hard drive with free space of 650 MB.

5 Hardware essentials for Windows operating system: mouse, VGA video card. CD-ROM drive also necessary when software is supplied on CD-ROM.

6 HCL (hardware compatibility list) shows which peripherals can be supported on a particular Windows operating system.

7 Stages of installation of an operating system: partition, format drive, run appropriate setup utility, load drivers, start up.

8 Files are created during installation according to the operating system, e.g. FAT32 for Windows 9X, NTFS for Windows 2000.

9 Partitioning is done using the FDISK command on Windows 9X. Windows 2000 and XP provide a Disk Management utility.

10 Formatting is done using the FORMAT command or using formatting tools available within Windows.

11 For Windows 9X, a start-up disk is a bootable disk that includes the internal DOS commands and other useful command line utilities that will help you to troubleshoot when confronted with a PC that will not boot Windows.

12 For Windows 2000 and Windows XP, a Recovery Console is used instead of the start-up disk, and this can be installed on the hard disk.

13 TWAIN (technology without an interesting name) is an example of an application device driver, used for image acquisition devices such as scanners and digital cameras.

14 A spooler is a program installed as part of the device driver that forms a queue of documents that are waiting to be printed.

15 An uninstaller program removes all traces of an application – not just the program files.

16 The LKG (last known good) configuration starts up a PC using information from the Registry and drivers that Windows saved at the last shutdown.

17 The desktop is the on-screen work area on which windows, icons, menus and dialogue boxes appear.

18 A shortcut provides a route to a feature that avoids going through the normal menu route.

Chapter 9 **Diagnosing and troubleshooting**

The Windows Help feature (Figure 9.1) can prove useful if you forget where to find an option within the menu system. It may also help you if you need specific information on a topic.

CHAT

Discuss with friends the times you have used the Windows Help feature. How helpful was it?

Access from Windows Explorer by selecting the Help menu

Put a keyword here

The Overviews, Articles and Tutorials are useful when you are new to a topic, or as a refresher

The Microsoft Knowledge Base is the place to find information about particular error codes

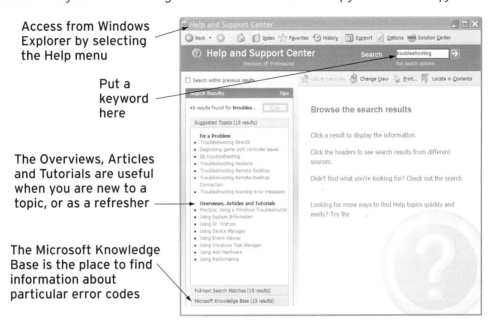

Figure 9.1
The Windows Help feature

1 Common error codes and start-up messages from the boot sequence: how to correct the problems

Chapter 8, page 300, explains the boot process in details. See also pages 17–24.

Until the video is checked, you will only hear beeps if there is a problem during start-up. The number of beeps tells you what might be wrong; Table 9.1 lists some examples of what the beeps might mean. You will need to check your operating system documentation to interpret the beeps on your own PC.

Table 9.1 *Beep codes during the boot process*

Number of beeps	Meaning
1 beep, and then 3, 4 or 5 beeps	Problem with motherboard, e.g. CMOS setup chip, DMA, system bus or timer
2 beeps, and then 3, 4 or 5 beeps	Errors in first 64 K of RAM
3 beeps, and then 3, 4 or 5 beeps	Failure of keyboard controller or video controller
4 beeps, and then 2, 3 or 4 beeps	Fault within serial/parallel ports, system timer or time of day
Continuous beeping	PSU problem

Table 9.2	POST codes
POST code	**Location of error**
1 – –	Motherboard
2 – –	Main memory/RAM
3 – –	Keyboard
5 – –	Video controller/monitor
6 – –	Floppy disk controller
7 – –	Coprocessor
9 – –	Parallel port
11 – –/12 – –	Async (comms adaptor)
13 – –	Game controller/joystick
14 – –	Printer
17 – –	Hard disk controller
60 – –	SCSI device/network card
73 – –	Floppy drive
86 – –	Mouse

Once the video is checked, any error messages will appear on the screen.

Table 9.2 lists some sample POST codes which identify the location of a problem found during the boot process. You need to check the documentation of your own PC, or visit the manufacturer's website, to interpret the POST codes correctly for your own PC. The dashes in Table 9.2 appear on screen as actual numbers, e.g. 201, and this gives more details as to what the problem is (see Figure 9.2).

If there are no POST codes, you might assume all is well, but you might then be presented with an error message at start-up (Figure 9.3). Table 9.3 lists common messages that may arise during the boot sequence or, later, while you are using the PC. You need to know how to correct these problems.

CHAT *Discuss with others any other error messages that you have seen while working on your PC. How did you resolve the problem?*

Turning the PC off and starting in **safe mode** might eliminate an error message, and this will help you to locate the source of the fault. Chapter 8 (page 306) explains more about starting in safe mode.

POST code 201

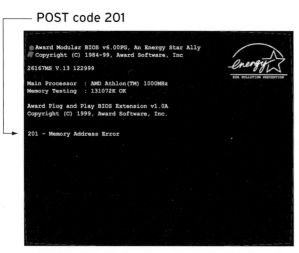

Figure 9.2   POST code error 201-Memory Address Error

Common start up message, caused by keyboard not being connected correctly

Figure 9.3   Example start-up error message

Check Your Understanding 9.1

1 You turn on your PC and you hear continuous beeping.
   What might be the problem?
2 Find out what POST code would be displayed if your keyboard was not connected properly.
3 What files must be present to make a disk bootable?
4 What will happen if you leave a floppy disk in drive A: when you boot up?
5 What might happen if you try to run many applications at the same time on your PC?

Table 9.3 Common error messages

Message	What can you do to overcome the problem?
Bad or missing COMMAND.COM	You may have a non-booting disk in drive A:. If so, remove it and press any key to continue. If not, there is a problem with COMMAND.COM on drive C:. Check the path and reinstall if necessary.
Bad command or file not found	There is a problem with the OS command that your PC has just tried to execute. This may be due to a syntax error in the command, or an invalid path to a program. Check the syntax, the path to the file and the filename. Check that the file has not been moved, deleted or renamed. Reinstall the program if necessary.
Bad sector	If this error message appears while you are reading from/writing to a disk, then sector markings on the disk may be fading. You could use ScanDisk to check it, but will probably need to reformat the disk. Try to retrieve data from the disk before you reformat; otherwise it will be lost.
CMOS error	The configuration that your CMOS seems to think you have does not match the hardware. The battery may be at fault; if so, replace it. If you have changed the configuration of hardware without changing the setup, check the setup settings.
Error in CONFIG.SYS line xx	Check line xx to make sure there is no syntax error. Or your PC is having a problem loading a device driver so check that the path to the driver is correct. Try reinstalling the driver, in case it has been corrupted.
Hard drive not found Fixed disk error	Your OS cannot find the hard drive (!) so your controller card is probably at fault. Or there may be a problem with internal connections. Check cables, connections to the motherboard, PSU connections and setup data.
HIMEM.SYS not loaded Missing or corrupt HIMEM.SYS	Your HIMEM.SYS file may be corrupted, in the wrong directory or not match the OS. You may need to replace it.
Insufficient memory	Your PC cannot cope with the number of applications that you are running simultaneously. Close some applications.
No operating system found	May be caused by a new hard disk not having been partitioned or formatted.
No boot device available	Your hard drive may not have been formatted – or the formatting may have been corrupted, and the OS cannot find a disk in drive A:. Boot up from a floppy start-up disk and check your hard drive for flaws.
Non-system disk	The disk in drive A: is not bootable and/or lacks the required files. Remove the floppy and boot up from the hard drive. Use SYS command to restore the systems files on the floppy.
Not ready reading drive A: Abort, Retry, Fail?	You may have forgotten to push the floppy into place, or to close the floppy drive door. The disk may be faulty, either because the data has been corrupted or because it has not yet been formatted.
Write-protect error writing drive A:	The floppy disk may be physically set to prevent writing. Check the write-protect tab.

1 Check your user documentation to find out what these errors messages mean, and how you might solve the problem:
   a Swap file
   b Registry is not to be found
   c Failure to start GUI
   d Event log is full
2 Working in pairs, sharing one (working!) PC, one of you should disconnect a peripheral. The other should turn on the PC and, using POST codes, identify what the problem might be. Take it in turns to present the other with a problem to solve.

2 Printing problems in Windows: how to correct them

Chapter 5 (page 214) focuses on printers and the problems that arise in their use. Here, we consider how to correct these problems.

The problems with printers tend to fall into two groups:

- Installing the printer and its drivers and managing to start printing successfully
- Problems that happen once the printer is up and running

As with any problem on your PC, you can always look at the Windows Help and Support Centre. Figure 5.7 (page 223) lists the problems you might have experienced with a printer.

Discuss other problems that you have experienced while trying to print in Windows.

Chapter 5 (page 224) focuses on how printers ought to be connected and how they should work. Maintenance of a printer is essential; otherwise, it will soon fail. It will run out of ink and you may experience paper jams, if only due to a build-up of dust.

Common problems, together with what you should check, are listed in Table 5.3 (page 224) but this section considers three particular problems that were not covered in Chapter 5:

- Print spool is stalled.
- Incorrect/incompatible driver for print.
- Incorrect parameter.

Print spool is stalled

A spool is a bobbin, cylinder or reel on to which yarn can be wound. On a PC, a print spool runs together, one after another, the documents that are in the queue to be printed.

The print spool has a list of documents that are due to be printed (Figure 9.4).

If the print spool stalls, none of these documents will be printed, and so you need to make a note of them. Then, when the problem is fixed, you can arrange for them to be sent to the printer again.

Figure 9.4
A spooler

Select Printers and Faxes from the Start menu, or Control Panel

Double click on the active printer to see this dialogue box

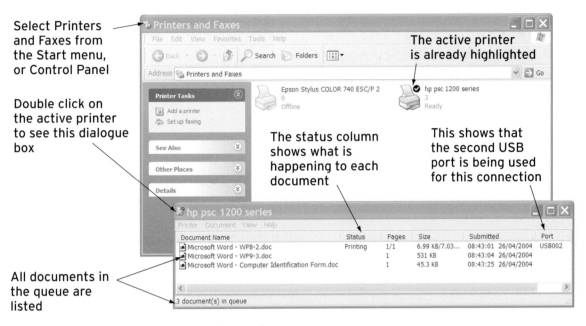

The active printer is already highlighted

The status column shows what is happening to each document

This shows that the second USB port is being used for this connection

All documents in the queue are listed

You can try to close down the spooler program:

◆ Click on the cross icon at the top right-hand corner.

◆ Go through the Task Manager, by pressing Ctrl – Alt – Del.

It is quite likely that neither of these will work or, if they do, the spooler will not function properly when you try to send documents to the printer. The cleanest option is to close down your PC and restart. Save the latest versions of any files you are working on, before you restart. If the spooler seems to be playing up, make sure that you save documents regularly – just in case you experience a complete crash.

Incorrect/incompatible driver for print

What does it mean?

A printer driver specifies information that the operating system needs to know before it can send data to the printer. Each different make and model of printer has its own special printer driver.

It is essential that your printer driver matches the make and model of printer that is installed on your PC.

How to install a printer driver

1 If your PC recognises Plug and Play devices, and your new printer is a Plug and Play printer, then – while the PC is turned off – connect the printer. Then when you turn on the PC, it will be recognised and the correct printer driver installed automatically.

2 If you do not have the Plug and Play option, Windows provides a wizard to install a new printer, and with it the appropriate printer driver. From the Start menu, select Printers and Faxes and choose Add a printer (Figure 9.5).

Figure 9.5
Add a printer

Select Add a printer

Follow the Wizard to install a new printer

3 The available printers that are supported by your PC are listed by manufacturer and model of printer (Figure 9.6). Select the one that matches your printer, and follow the on-screen instructions to complete the printer driver installation.

Work through the Add Printer Wizard screens

Select the manufacturer of the new printer

Choose the model from the list offered for the chosen manufacturer

Figure 9.6   Printer driver options

4 Some printers may be supplied with the printer driver on a CD. If so, follow the instructions supplied. You will normally be asked to connect the printer while the PC is turned off, and to insert a CD in the CD-ROM drive as soon as boot up has been completed. The CD should self-start and take you through a wizard.

Incorrect parameter

A parameter is a value (number or text) that is needed by a program to allow it to do something general in a specific way. For example, a program – more likely a macro or procedure – may draw a square; to draw any size of square one variable may be set up as a parameter to allow the length of the side of the square to be input to the procedure.

In sending a document to the printer, parameters are used to specify relevant details:

◆ The logical or physical drive on which the file you want to print is located, if different from the current drive

◆ The path – i.e. where, on the drive, the file you want to print is located, if this is different from the current directory

◆ The filename of the file you want to print

◆ The printer on which you want to print the job

You can specify a local printer by specifying the port on your computer to which the printer is connected. Valid values for parallel ports are LPT1 (the default printer, if you do not specify one), LPT2 and LPT3. Valid values for serial ports are COM1, COM2, COM3 and COM4. You can also specify a network printer by its queue name: \ServerName\ShareName.

If any of these parameters are incorrect, the error message 'incorrect parameter' may appear. Careful checking of the file and its whereabouts – in case it has been moved or deleted or renamed – is needed. You may also need to check that the setup for the printer is correct.

Check Your Understanding 9.2

1 List four errors that might arise while using a printer.
2 What is a spooler? How does it work?
3 What is the purpose of a printer driver?
4 What is a parameter? Give two examples of parameters.

Go and try out 9.2

1 Working with a friend, install a new printer on a PC.
2 Experiment with deleting, adding or replacing printer drivers on your PC. What happens if you delete the driver from your printer and then try to print a document?

CHAT · *Discuss with others in your group your experiences with printers and how you solved problems that arose.*

3 Common problems: how to resolve them

While working on a PC, a user might meet any of a number of problems:

◆ If a **system error** occurs, the computer may display a blue screen containing error codes, and all computer operations stop; this is a system crash.

◆ When an error occurs in a program (such as Microsoft *Word*) that causes a **program error**, and the program just stops working.

When an error occurs, a dialogue box may ask whether you want to report the problem. If you choose to report the problem, technical information about the problem is collected from your PC and can be sent to Microsoft over the Internet.

It is advisable to report system and program errors to Microsoft so that Microsoft can track and address these errors. You have the option to configure error reporting to send only specified information, e.g. only to report system errors. The same is true for Windows components, such as Windows *Explorer*, and for programs installed on your computer, such as Microsoft *Word*.

Then, if a similar problem has been reported by other people, and more information is available, a link to that information will be provided.

A **general protection fault** may be the result of using poor-quality chips or a clash of personalities between your operating system and one of your software applications. Some are recognised by Windows as being their fault and fixes are issued. It is therefore important to keep up to date and to check regularly for Windows Updates (see Figure 9.7).

CASE STUDY   Nigel the novice PC user

Nigel is trying to remove a modem from his Windows 95 PC, using the Modem tool in the Control Panel, and he receives this error message:

Rundll32.exe Has Performed an Illegal Operation

He goes to the Help and Support Centre and discovers that this fault is known to Microsoft, and that an article (Q135224) had been published about it. However, he does not read the article because the Help screen tells Nigel that the error happens because he has the Device Manager open while trying to remove the modem. He follows the instructions given on-screen and the problem is solved.

1 Working in small groups, use the Help and Support Centre – and other sources – to find out about other types of errors:

a Invalid working directory
b System lock-up
c Option (sound cards, modem, input device) will not function
d Applications that won't install
e Applications that will not start or load
f Network connection failure
g User cannot log on to network (option NIC not functioning)

2 Explore the tutorial options available on your PC, and watch/listen to one or two of them, e.g. the Accessibility wizard.

Figure 9.7
Windows Update

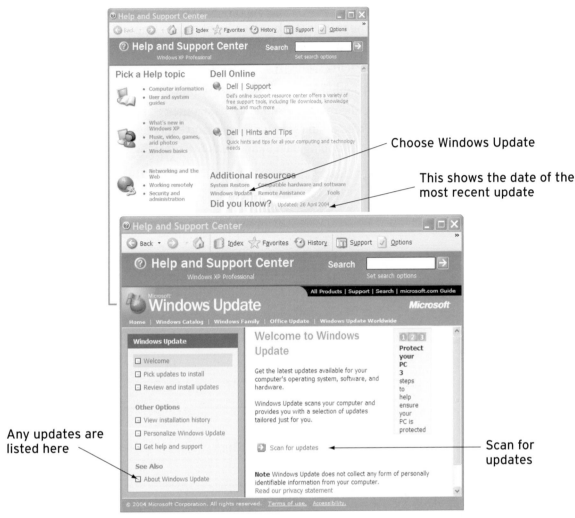

Choose Windows Update

This shows the date of the most recent update

Any updates are listed here

Scan for updates

To find out if a fix exists for a particular error, such as an **illegal error**, use the Help and Support Centre to locate any relevant information.

TSR programs and viruses (see page 331) are another potential source of problems for a user.

What does it mean?

TSR = terminate stay resident.

The fact that Windows supports TSR programs is useful in that you can access, very quickly, more than one program at a time. So you could be working on a *Word* document and have the Calculator or some other TSR utility open, even though you are not using it right now.

TSRs that are essential can be included in the AUTOEXEC.BAT file. They will be loaded during the boot process and be ready for your use as soon as booting up is complete. This applies to essential utilities such as anti-virus software.

When an application program is loaded into memory, it is given some memory space (within the transient program area shown in Figure 9.8). This memory is not released for other programs to use until that program is exited. However, once you close the application, the memory is freed up.

With TSRs, the memory is allocated within the user area, is not released when you exit it and won't be released until you restart your PC. So, if you have too many TSRs running, you could begin to run out of space and experience a slowing down of your system, while it is busy swapping data in and out of virtual memory.

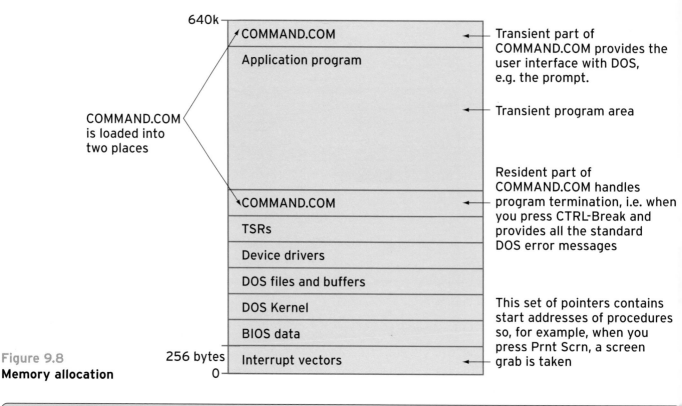

Figure 9.8
Memory allocation

Check Your Understanding 9.3

1 What is the difference between a system error and a program error?
2 What is a fix?
3 What is a general protection fault?
4 What is a TSR? Give two examples of TSRs.

Go and try out 9.3

1 On a PC, systematically open as many software applications as you can and, within these applications, open as many different files as you can. At what point does the PC complain of lack of memory?
2 On your PC, check which TSRs are installed during the boot process.

CHAT *Discuss with friends which applications seem to need the most space on your PC.*

4   Viruses

This section considers how to protect against viruses, and how to identify and remove them.

What does it mean?

A virus is a program written so that it will spread itself from one PC to another, infecting each machine as it spreads, and either damaging the PC by corrupting data or just causing a nuisance to the user.

The **Computer Misuse Act (1990)** defines **electronic vandalism** and makes it a criminal activity to write viruses that can cause damage to software and data and disrupt the operation of a computer system. The Act also covers **hacking** through a **firewall** and theft of data.

Types of virus

The least offensive form of a virus is the **impostor virus**. An email will warn you of a virus and suggest that you check whether you have a particular file somewhere on your hard disk. When you check, you find that indeed you do have this file, and set about deleting the offending file as per instructions given in the email, only to find that it was a hoax. Apart from the waste of time, and the stress involved in thinking you have a virus, you may delete an important file and reduce the functionality of your PC software.

Watch out

If you hear of a virus, check on the Internet for details of the virus, before you do anything else.

Other forms of virus are less acceptable and can do positive damage to your PC data:

◆ A **boot sector virus** plants itself in the boot sector of every bootable floppy disk or hard disk. This guarantees that it will run each time you boot up. These viruses spread from disk to disk and, hence, from PC to PC if you take a floppy disk from one PC to another.

◆ **File viruses** are infected program files with extensions of .exe or .com; when the program is run it does whatever damage it is designed to do.

◆ **Macro viruses** hide within the macro of applications such as *Word* and *Excel*. Such viruses spread from one open document or spreadsheet to another.

◆ **BIOS viruses** are the most harmful; they attack the flash BIOS, overwriting the system BIOS and making the PC unbootable.

◆ A **Trojan horse** is special kind of virus. It infiltrates a PC by pretending to be a file or program that would normally be found on a PC. However, it can still cause grief and can be difficult to track down. It takes it name from the Greek myth in which a gift of a wooden horse was a ruse to smuggle soldiers, hidden inside the horse, inside the city walls. When executed, the Trojan horse program tends to create yet more Trojan horses.

◆ A **worm** – or **email virus** such as the famous Melissa virus – can send on emails – the virus – to all your contacts using data from your address book. It tends to create a spoof message which might fool someone who receives the email into thinking it is genuinely from the sender.

Some viruses hide by using a double file extension. A file may be called harmlessfun.jpg.vbs. The 'vbs' part shows that it is a Visual Basic program – and a potential virus – but, if you have opted to hide file extensions, it will show in a folder listing as harmlessfun.jpg and look just like an image file to you.

Discuss your experiences of viruses. What damage have they done?

How viruses infect a PC

Viruses/Trojan horses/worms can be introduced to a PC by one of two sources:

◆ If you save data on to a floppy disk from one PC that is infected with a virus then, when you read that floppy into a second PC, the virus can infect the second PC. This can happen when a file is opened from the floppy, or when you boot from the floppy disk.

◆ Files can arrive at a PC as attachments to emails. If the file was saved from a PC that was infected, the receiving PC can become infected as soon as the attached file is opened.

Because viruses are programs, they can only infect programs. However, having done so, they can wipe files from your hard disk and/or make your PC crash and/or become inoperable.

If you accidentally leave a floppy disk in the drive and boot up, you will get an error message at start-up. Do not remove the disk and press any key as suggested. If the floppy disk had a virus, it has already infected your PC and has transferred itself to the memory. Instead, remove the floppy disk and press Reset – this dumps the memory (losing the virus infection) and starts to reboot again.

How to display file extensions

1 From My Computer or *Explorer*, select the folder containing the files for which you want to check the file extensions.

2 On the menu bar, select Tools and then, from the drop-down menu, select Folder Options.

3 Click on the View tab and make sure that the item that reads 'Hide extensions for known file types' is not checked (see Figure 9.9).

How to determine the presence of a virus

Viruses show themselves in various ways:

◆ Spontaneous rebooting of an infected PC

◆ Crashes: system, application

Figure 9.9
How to display file extensions

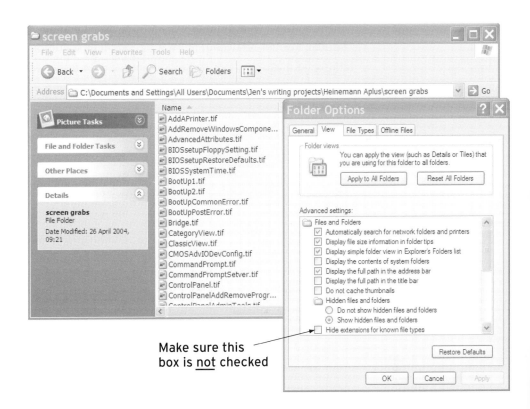

Make sure this box is <u>not</u> checked

- Sound card problems
- Speaker problems
- Screen display anomalies: distortion, misshapen images, missing video
- Missing files or corrupted files
- Disk partitions that disappear
- Boot disks that become unbootable

How to combat viruses

Almost at the same rate as virus writers invent new viruses, so do anti-virus software vendors produce updated versions of their software.

Anti-virus software attempts to trace viruses by looking for the **virus signature**. This sequence of characters can be recognised by the anti-software vendors, having analysed the virus code. Meanwhile, virus writers adopt **cloaking techniques**:

- **Polymorphing**: just as cells in a diseased body mutate, this type of virus is designed to change its appearance, size and signature each time it infects another PC, making it harder for anti-virus software to recognise it.
- A **stealth virus** hides its damage so that, for all intents and purposes, it looks like nothing is wrong.
- A **directory virus** corrupts a directory entry so that it points to itself instead of to the file the virus is actually replacing.

The only defence against viruses is to subscribe to a reliable anti-virus software vendor's virus protection service (Figure 9.10). Regular scanning of the PC is recommended, as is immediate update of virus software as soon as one is released.

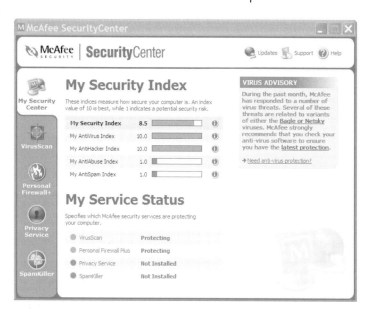

Figure 9.10   McAfee's security centre

There are a variety of products available:

◆ **Virus scanner software** is the most common form of anti-virus software. The scan is initiated by the user.

◆ **Start-up virus scanner software** runs each time the PC is booted up. It checks only for boot sector viruses.

◆ **Memory-resident virus scanner software** stays in memory and checks incoming emails and browser documents, and so automatically checks the environment in which your PC operates.

◆ A **behaviour-based detector** is a form of memory-resident virus scanner software that watches for behaviour that would indicate the presence of a virus.

The anti-virus software vendors maintain a database of information about viruses: a DAT file of their profiles and signatures. Users who subscribe to an online anti-virus protection service may have this database downloaded to their PC automatically each time an update is released. Other users may receive an email telling them that an update is available.

Having the most up-to-date DAT file, scanning regularly and avoiding opening emails that look like they may contain viruses are all that PC users can do to protect themselves. If the software detects a virus, a pop-up screen informs the user and may offer options: to quarantine the file (i.e. move it somewhere it can do no harm), to repair the file (i.e. delete the virus but retain the file) or to delete the file.

Anti-virus software vendors may include the option to create a rescue disk. This is a bootable disk that also contains anti-virus software. If your system fails due to a virus and will not boot, this rescue disk should solve the problem. Write-protecting the disk will prevent it becoming infected with a virus.

Check Your Understanding 9.4

1 Explain the difference between a Trojan and a worm.
2 Explain how viruses, Trojans and worms can infect a PC.
3 Explain these terms: 'polymorphing', 'stealth virus' and 'directory virus'.
4 Distinguish between start-up scanner software and memory-resident scanner software.
5 What is a DAT file?
6 What is a rescue disk?

5   Diagnosing system faults

Chapter 2 (page 128) looked in detail at how you should diagnose problems and troubleshoot.

Check Your Understanding 9.5

1   Outline your problem-solving strategy.
2   Why is it helpful to know when the problem started?
3   Why is it helpful if the user can recreate the problem?
4   What tools might prove useful when troubleshooting?

In this section, the focus is on system faults, i.e. those faults that lie within the software rather than the hardware. Once you work out what the problem is, you may have two scenarios to consider:

◆ You may need to change the settings on the software, e.g. to recognise a peripheral or load a different device driver.

◆ What the user wants to do, perhaps, cannot be done using the software currently installed on the PC. You may need to arrange for the purchase of new software, and upgrade the PC in some way to support this software.

In any event, you cannot decide on a course of action until you have fully understood the user's problem.

Eliciting problem system status from customers

Chapter 2, page 160, stressed the importance of finding out as much as possible from the user:

◆ When did the problem start?
◆ What actually happened?
◆ Had any equipment been installed, or removed, prior to the problem arising?

Go and try out 9.4

Working in groups of four, split into two teams of two.

1   In your team, plan a fault – hardware or software – that you will present to the other pair, e.g. disconnected cabling, unseated expansion board, the wrong setting for a monitor. Agree between you what symptoms your PC would show if this fault were to happen.
2   Taking turns, act as user pair and technician pair. The technician pair ask questions to try to find out what the problem is. The user pair answer these questions (honestly!).
3   Write down what you, as the technician pair, think may be the source of the problem. Is it hardware? Or, is it software?
4   Write down what you would do to isolate the fault and, hopefully, fix it.
5   With permission of your tutor, as the user pair, and out of sight of the technician pair, set up a PC with the fault as planned.
6   As the technician pair, follow your plan to isolate the fault and then fix it.
7   Discuss what you found difficult about this process, and what you found easy.
8   Repeat the activity, taking turns and choosing different faults.

Reproducing errors as part of the diagnostic process

If you can reproduce an error, working backwards, you might be able to determine what caused the fault.

Share experiences of times when you have managed successfully to reproduce a fault.

Identifying recent changes to the computer environment from the user

If a PC was working fine last Tuesday, but now is not working, then what happened between last Tuesday and now must provide some explanation as to where the fault lies – and once you know that, you are halfway to solving the problem.

There are situations where wear and tear can cause a PC to fail:

◆ Build-up of dust

◆ Corrosion

◆ Wearing out of moving parts

Most of the time, though, problems arise because a change to the computer settings is completed unsatisfactorily.

Check Your Understanding 9.6

1 Suggest three questions you might ask a user who reports a fault.
2 How does the reproduction of an error help you to troubleshoot?
3 Give three examples of wear and tear on a PC.

Revision 9

Remember these facts:

1 Until the video is checked, you will only hear beeps if there is a problem during start-up.

2 The number of beeps in the beep code tells you what might be wrong.

3 During the boot-up process, once the video is checked, any error messages will appear on the screen.

4 Trying to boot from a non-bootable disk, or just leaving a data disk in the floppy drive, will cause problems when you turn on the PC.

5 OS commands need to obey syntax rules, and refer to valid path names; otherwise, you will see a bad command error message.

6 A low battery can cause a CMOS error.

7 Problems with connections within the PC casing (e.g. to/from the motherboard or to/from the PSU) can result in error messages such as 'hard drive not found'.

8   Running too many application programs at the same time, or having too many TSRs, can result in an 'insufficient memory' error.

9   Failure to partition a hard disk and/or failure to format any type of disk will prevent you from writing to that disk.

10 The write-protect tab prevents you from writing to a floppy disk.

11 A print spool runs together, one after another, the documents that are in the queue to be printed.

12 A printer driver specifies information that the operating system needs to know before it can send data to the printer. Each different make and model of printer has its own special printer driver.

13 A parameter is a value (number or text) that is needed by a program to allow it to do something general in a specific way.

14 If a system error occurs, the computer may display a blue screen containing error codes, and all computer operations stop; this is a system crash.

15 When an error occurs in a program (such as Microsoft *Word*) that causes a program error, the program just stops working.

16 A general protection fault may be the result of using poor-quality chips, or a clash of personalities between your operating system and one of your software applications.

17 TSR stands for terminate stay resident. It refers to programs that are loaded into a special area in memory, and this space is not made available to other programs even when you exit from the program.

18 The Computer Misuse Act (1990) defines electronic vandalism and makes it a criminal activity to write viruses that can cause damage to software and data and disrupt the operation of a computer system. The Act also covers hacking through a firewall and theft of data.

19 A boot sector virus plants itself in the boot sector of every bootable floppy disk or hard disk.

20 File viruses are infected program files with extensions of .exe or .com; when the program is run, it does whatever damage it is designed to do.

21 Macro viruses hide within the macro of applications such as *Word* and *Excel*. Such viruses spread from one open document or spreadsheet to another.

22 BIOS viruses are the most harmful; they attack the flash BIOS, overwriting the system BIOS and making the PC unbootable.

23 A Trojan horse is special kind of virus which infiltrates a PC by pretending to be a file or program that would normally be found on a PC.

24 A worm can send on emails – and the virus – to all your contacts using data from your address book by creating a spoof message which might fool someone who receives the email into thinking it is genuinely from the sender.

25 Anti-virus software attempts to trace viruses by looking for the virus signature.

26 Virus writers adopt cloaking techniques, such as polymorphing, to avoid detection.

27 A stealth virus hides its damage so that, for all intents and purposes, it looks like nothing is wrong.

28 A directory virus corrupts a directory entry so that it points to itself instead of to the file the virus is actually replacing.

29 Virus scanner software is the most common form of anti-virus software. The scan is initiated by the user. Start-up virus scanner software runs each time the PC is booted up. It checks only for boot sector viruses.

30 Memory-resident virus scanner software stays in memory and checks incoming emails and browser documents, and so automatically checks the environment in which your PC operates.

31 A behaviour-based detector is a form of memory-resident virus scanner software that watches for behaviour that would indicate the presence of a virus.

32 A rescue disk is a bootable disk that also contains anti-virus software. If your system fails due to a virus and will not boot, this rescue disk should solve the problem.

33 Troubleshooting relies on eliciting as much information from the user as possible: When did the problem start? What actually happened? Had any equipment been installed, or removed, prior to the problem arising?

34 If you can reproduce an error, working backwards, you might be able to determine what caused the fault.

35 PCs suffer from wear and tear: build-up of dust; corrosion; and wearing out of moving parts.

Chapter 10 **Networks**

Chapter 6 (page 227) the concept of networks. This chapter gives more background information and looks in more detail at networks, concentrating on the software aspects of networking.

Check Your Understanding 10.1

1 Distinguish between two types of network: LAN and WAN.
2 Explain these terms: 'client/server' and 'peer-to-peer'.
3 Explain the topologies: bus, ring and star.
4 List the types of cabling that might be used in a network.
5 Explain what these network components do: hub, switch, gateway, repeater, bridge, router.
6 What is bandwidth?

CHAT *In a small group, discuss what you remember about networks from Chapter 6. Are you familiar with all the terminology and concepts?*

Network operating systems operate in two modes:

◆ **User mode** is a non-privileged mode. Programs only have limited access to system information and cannot directly access hardware.

◆ **Kernel mode** is a privileged mode. Programs have full access to system information and can directly access the hardware.

Each PC on a network is given a name – a **network name** – that is used to identify it on the network as the sender or receiver of data to other users on the same network. For example, the **NetBIOS** name is a unique 15-character name that is displayed in the Windows Network Neighborhood. The **WINS** then translates this network name into an IP address for that particular PC.

What does it mean?

WINS = Windows Internet naming service.

Having identified a PC on a network, addressing – and therefore accessing drives and folders located on that PC – is achievable.

Resources are made available to everyone in the domain through the use of **share names** as assigned by the network administrator – or as set up by you during installation (Figure 10.1). For users to access a resource, they need to have **permission** to do so, and to know the share name of the resource.

Figure 10.1
Share names

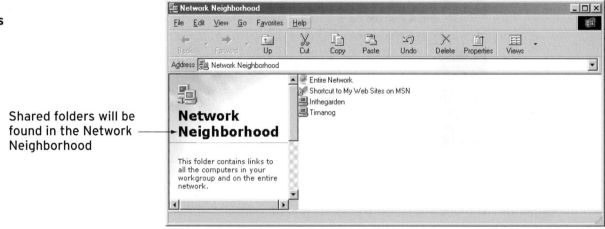

Shared folders will be found in the Network Neighborhood

IP addresses

An IP address uniquely identifies each node in a network (Figure 10.2). The IP address for a networked PC is a 32-bit address expressed as four 8-bit octets which combine information about the network and the node within it.

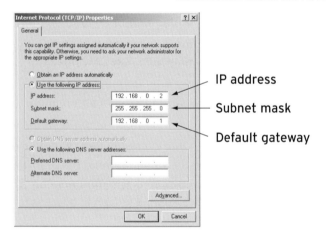

IP address
Subnet mask
Default gateway

Figure 10.2   IP address for a networked PC

The **DHCP protocol** is used automatically to configure a node with its IP address. Then, each time a user logs on to the network, the DHCP server software, which is on the network server or router, renews the IP address.

When you set up an Internet connection, you could enter a **fixed IP address** for it, as assigned by your ISP. However, there are only so many IP addresses, and not every ISP customer is online at the same time. So, instead, a **dynamic IP address** is assigned, just for as long as you are connected. The same number can then be released for someone else to use.

You can use IPCONFIG.EXE or WINIPCFG.EXE (depending on the version of Windows) to view the IP address of your PC. These programs can also be used to renew or release an IP address.

What does it mean?

DHCP = **dynamic host configuration protocol.**

ISP = **Internet service provider.**

Go and try out 10.1

1   Identify which of the executable files is available on your operating system: IPCONFIG.EXE or WINIPCFG.EXE.

2   Run the file to discover the IP address of your PC. Use the RUN command, or the Command Prompt as shown in Figure 10.3.

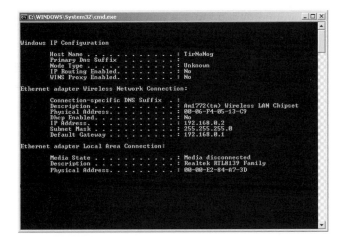

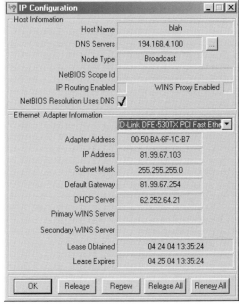

Figure 10.3　**IPCONFIG displays the IP address**

Domains

The term 'domain' is defined in a dictionary as 'what one is master of or has dominion over'. In the world of networks, it describes a group of computers that work together.

The term domain is used in three particular contexts:

◆ An Internet domain

◆ A NetWare domain

◆ A Windows NT/2000 domain

On the Internet, the highest level of domain is given by the tail end of the Internet address:

◆ .com

◆ .org

◆ .gov

This describes the type of organisation (commercial, charitable or non-profit making, government). Domains can also indicate the location, e.g. the country, as in .co.uk.

In a group, brainstorm other domains given by the Internet address.
List domains for countries apart from the UK.

The DNS server is used to translate the Internet address that you key, e.g. heinemann.co.uk, into the relevant IP address. DNS servers exist all over the world and share information with each other. Your browser will use the DNS lookup service to convert what you key as the URL into an IP address. If you get **DNS Lookup Error** in a web browser, this will be because there is no information available or the DNS server is not working for some reason (Figure 10.4).

Figure 10.4
A 'page not found' error

DNS = domain name system.

A NetWare domain is a memory segment within NetWare that is used to separate NLMs from the operating system.

In a **Windows NT/2000 domain**, groups of NT, 2000 or XP machines share a centralised security database or **SAM**.

NLM = NetWare-loadable modules.

SAM = security access manager.

One PC – or workstation – has to be assigned as the **PDC (primary domain controller)** where the SAM is stored.

The PDC is a PC which runs an NT or 2000 server, and manages all security aspects of the network: user logons and permissions. In a large network, you would also assign a **BDC (backup domain controller)**, in which case the BDC would hold and maintain the **user account database** for the network.

All the domain user accounts are created on the PDC. When a domain user logs on from his or her workstation, the PDC controls what happens:

◆ The user presses Ctrl + Alt + Del, enters his or her username, password and selects the domain.

◆ The workstation checks the user's credentials with the PDC.

◆ If the user has entered valid domain user details then the PDC returns details about that user to the workstation which builds a security access token for that user.

Check Your Understanding 10.2

1 What is the difference between user mode and kernel mode?
2 Explain these terms: 'WINS', 'DNS', 'IP address', 'SAM' and 'PDC'.
3 What is a share name?
4 What does the DHCP protocol do?
5 Distinguish between a fixed IP address and a dynamic IP address.
6 Give four examples of domains for countries, excluding the UK.

1 Networking capabilities of Windows

One of the main benefits of a network is the facility to share with other users: files and printers. However, when a network is set up, the default option is not to share anything with anyone. So, control lies with the user as to how much to share with others.

Discuss the disadvantages of working on a network.

Sharing files

To share anything at all – a file, a folder or the entire contents of the hard disk – a **service** has to be installed: File and Printer Sharing for Microsoft Networks (Figure 10.5):

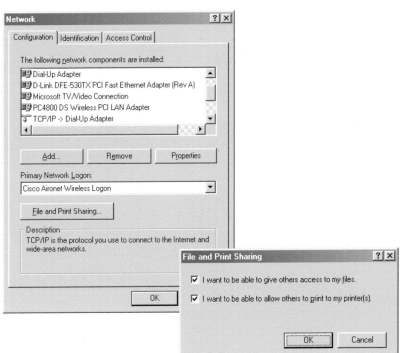

Figure 10.5   **Shared files**

◆ In Windows 9X, go to Control Panel/Network/File and Print Sharing. Confirm that you want to share by checking the relevant box(es).

◆ In Windows 2000/XP, in Control Panel/Network/Dial-up Connections, select the particular connection. Then, right-click to select Properties. If the File and Printer Sharing for Microsoft Networks has not already been installed, click Install. Then click Service and Add. Select File and Printer Sharing for Microsoft Networks and click OK. You are then ready to share a specific resource.

How to share a folder

The instructions in this 'How to' show you how to share a folder (Figure 10.6):

◆ To arrange to **share a drive**, at step 2, you need to right-click on a drive.

◆ To arrange to **share a single file**, save the file, by itself in a folder, and arrange to share that folder.

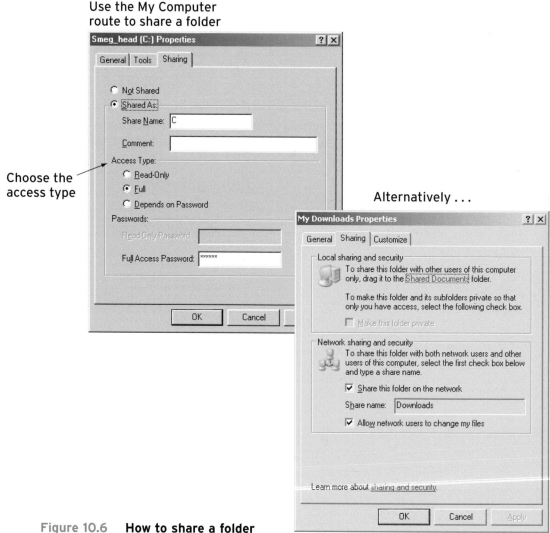

Figure 10.6   **How to share a folder**

1 Make sure that File and Printer Sharing service is installed.

2 Browse through My Computer until the folder that you want to share is listed.

3 Right-click on the folder, and select Sharing (Windows 9X, 2000) or Sharing and Security (Windows XP).

4 For Windows 9X: click on Shared As. For Windows 2000/XP: click on Share This Folder.

5 Enter a name that you want to use to refer to this shared folder. This can be the same name as the folder or you might decide to use an alternative name.

6 Decide what level of access/permissions you want – Read-only, Full or Depends on Password – and enter any passwords.

7 Click OK to accept the new sharing arrangements that you have set up.

Once folders have been set up for sharing, users (at least those with the password to access password-protected folders) can access the file through My Computer. Shared files can be found in the Network Neighborhood – also known as **My Network Places**.

Go and try out 10.2

1 Working with a friend, agree to share a folder that is on your PC with your partner and vice versa, and agree the names by which these two folders will be known.

2 Each of you should ensure that your networked PC will allow sharing.

3 Each of you should set up the agreed folder so that it can be shared, using the agreed name.

4 Access the shared folder that your partner has set up for you.

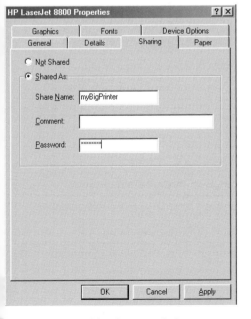

Sharing printers

You may also arrange to share print services.

How to share a printer

1 Access the Printers dialogue box via the Start button. For XP, look for Printers and Faxes. For other versions of Windows, you need to select Settings/Printers (Figure 10.7).

2 Right-click on the printer that you want to share. Indicate that you do want to share the printer and then enter a name that you want the shared printer to be known as.

3 Consider whether you want to set a password, and enter the password as prompted.

4 Click OK to confirm your settings.

Figure 10.7 **Sharing a printer**

Go and try out 10.3

With the permission of your tutor, arrange to share a printer on your network.

Network type and network card

The network type and card must be compatible. Chapter 6 lists the different network types (page 227) and explains NICs (page 238).

The NIC type has to match the expansion bus for the slot but it must also match the network type and, in particular, the speed of the network.

Check Your Understanding 10.3

1 Explain these terms: 'Ethernet', 'token ring' and 'FDDI'.
2 What is a MAC address?
3 What different speeds of data transfer are supported in Ethernet networks?
4 Explain these terms: 'header', 'trailer' and 'packet'.

Protocols

CHAT

Brainstorm to produce a list of protocols.

You have met several protocols so far. Table 10.1 lists them all – and some others that you need to be aware of.

Table 10.1 *Protocols used in networking*	
Protocol	**Function**
FTP (file transfer protocol)	Allows a user to send/receive a message using a copy of a file to be transferred between two computers, i.e. uploading and downloading; file is sent in blocks
HTTP (hypertext transfer protocol)	Used for WWW pages, this lets your browser view pages encoded in HTML
IPX/SPX (Internetwork packet exchange/sequenced packet exchange)	Used on Novell network operating systems
NetBEUI (NetBIOS extended user interface)	Used on Microsoft Windows systems for LANs with no external connections, i.e. no Internet access and no routing to other networks via a router
NFS (network file services)	Allows access to network drives as if they were local drives, folders and files
PPP (point-to-point protocol)	Used to make the connection and manage network communications with a modem
SMTP (simple mail transfer protocol)	Used for email across a network
TCP/IP (transmission control protocol/Internet protocol)	Not a single protocol, but a collection of working practices that allow all Internet users to communicate, regardless of what equipment they are using Determines how individual signal are sent over the Internet
Telnet	Allows a user to connect and log in to a remote host computer

What does it mean? *HTML (Hypertext Markup Language) is used to create multimedia pages to go on a website on the WWW.*

Check Your Understanding 10.4

1 What do these stand for: FTP, HTTP, PPP, SMTP, HTML?
2 What is TCP/IP?

Configuring the OS for network connection

Having installed NICs in the PCs and connected them to a hub, the next step is to configure the software:

◆ If you are using Windows XP, everything is done automatically for you.
◆ If you are using earlier versions of Windows you need to do some or all of the configuring manually.

For Windows to manage the communication of the network, three pieces of software are needed:

◆ The NIC is a Plug and Play device so the **NIC driver** should be installed automatically as soon as Windows realises you have installed the NIC. If not, as with any driver for any piece of equipment, go through Control Panel/Add New Hardware.
◆ A **client driver** is needed to manage the interface. The default client program is called Client for Microsoft Networks – easy to remember!
◆ There must be at least one **protocol** installed that is acceptable to all the PCs on the network. This could be TCP/IP for a Windows network, or some other protocol for another type of network.

Before trying to install software, it makes sense to check what may have already been installed automatically:

Discuss how you might find out what is already installed on a PC. (Hint: Think Control Panel – what icon might lead you to information about the network?)

◆ In Windows 9X, the Control Panel/Network/Configuration tab lists network components that have been installed.
◆ With Windows 2000, you can set up different connections for each NIC, each with different protocols; this allows more flexibility. Access details of a particular connection through Control Panel/Network/Dial-up Connections/Properties.
◆ For Window XP, Control Panel/Network Connections lists all the connections that have been set up. Most of these will have been set up automatically for the user (Figure 10.8).

If you do have to install the client driver and/or a protocol, there may be a wizard to help you:

◆ In Windows 2000, head for Control Panel/Network/Dial-up Connections/New Connection.

Figure 10.8
Network connections

◆ In Windows XP, the wizard is available in the Accessories program folder.

In earlier versions of Windows, there is no wizard, so you need to go to Control Panel/Network and select Add. Choose between Client or Protocol and click on Add. From the list of manufacturers offered, select the one that you want to install, and click OK.

Watch out

Remember to reboot your PC. Settings will not work until you have restarted the PC.

Go and try out 10.4

1 On two separate networks, identify what network protocols have been installed.
2 On an early version of Windows, use Add to install a protocol.

Installing and configuring browsers

A **browser** is a program which lets you view web pages on the Internet (Figure 10.9). If you know the **URL** of the site, you can go straight to the site.

Figure 10.9   **A browser**

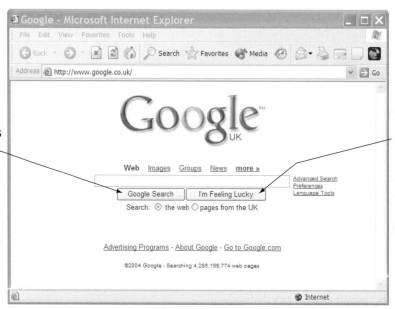

A search produces a hot list of sites that may - or may not - suit your needs

If your search key is precise enough, clicking on I'm Feeling Lucky could take you direct to the website you want

URL = uniform resource locator.

If you don't know the name, a **search engine** will allow you to find websites that match criteria set by you. You need to enter a word phrase that can be used as a **search key**. The browser then presents you with a **hot list**, which includes brief details of relevant sites and hotlinks to these sites.

CHAT

With a friend, discuss search engines that you have used.
Which ones give the best results?

Most popular browsers – Internet *Explorer*, Netscape *Navigator* and *Opera* – are self-configuring. Some of the settings can affect how the PC works and you need to know about these:

◆ To reduce the time it takes to display a page that has been downloaded from the Internet, the browser stores the page in a **disk cache** on the hard disk. If you navigate backwards and forwards, then instead of downloading again, the pages are displayed straight from the cache. These temporary Internet files can take up a lot of space, so part of the maintenance of your PC should include cleaning the disk of such temporary files.

Chapter 1 (page 28) explains how caching works, and Table 3.1 (page 167) includes disk cleaning as part of a regular maintenance programme.

◆ The browser keeps a record of all sites that you have visited in the History folder. If you visit a lot of sites every day, you might consider reducing the number of days records that you want to retain. This will reduce the amount of space used by the History folder (Figure 10.10).

◆ Several **players** and **handlers** are included in the most popular browsers (Table 10.2).

Table 10.2 *Players and handlers*

Player/handler	Function
Adobe Acrobat	To read PDF files
Flash	To play Macromedia Flash animations
Windows Media Player Apple Quick Time Real Player	To play back streaming audio, video and multimedia

PDF = portable data format.

Check Your Understanding 10.5

1 What three pieces of software are needed for Windows to manage communication on a network?
2 What is a protocol? Give two examples.
3 What is a URL?
4 What is a hot list?
5 Give two examples of players or handlers.

Figure 10.10
History folder

Select Tools for Internet Options

Displays the History panel

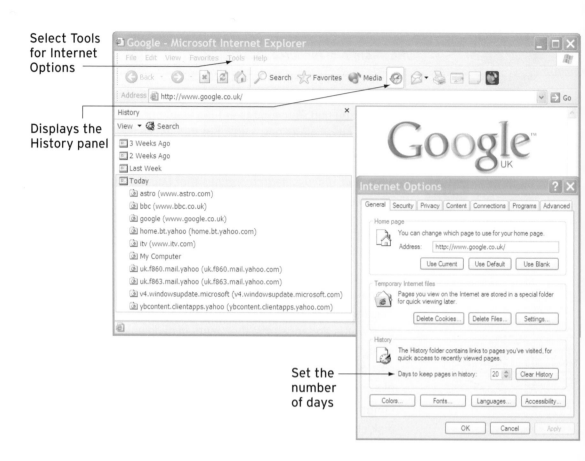

Set the number of days

Go and try out 10.5

1 Use Accessories/Systems Tools/Disk Clean to identify files which could be deleted from your PC. How much space would you save by deleting web pages?
2 Visit a few sites and check how much extra memory these pages are taking up in your temporary files.
3 Amend the number of days records that are retained in your History folder. See what effect this has on the amount of temporary space being used.

2 Internet concepts and capabilities: setting up a system for Internet access

The Internet is one huge network, providing access to information and a wide variety of services for those who are connected. As with any other client–server network, you can identify two categories of computer on the Internet:

- The **Internet clients** – the end users – enjoy access to the Internet to send and receive emails, and surf the web.
- The **Internet server** provides its clients with an access point, from where they can tap into the Internet. Some **ISPs** also retain email messages for the clients, rather than the client downloading them using communications software like Microsoft Outlook.

What does it mean?

ISP = Internet service provider.

The Internet client computer can be connected to the ISP computer using a telephone line in a number of ways:

- A **cable link** may be available, e.g. through a television cable service. This is only available as a residential service, but does provide good transfer speeds: 512 Kbps to 2 Mbps.

- A **modem** may be used, linked to a telephone line, and a **dial-up connection** made each time the client wants to access the net. This system is available wherever there are phone links, but it does tie up the phone line and is slow: 56 Kbps.

- The client may have a **Broadband connection** which allows data transfer at the same time as voice conversations – or a connection may be via a mobile phone, using **Bluetooth technology**.

- With **ISDN** phone lines, the data transfer speed is much faster: 64 to 200 Kbps.

What does it mean?

ISDN = integrated digital subscriber network.

Communication may be by satellite:

- In a **one-way satellite system**, the satellite is used for downloading only, and the satellite dish can be used to receive TV signals. A modem is needed and DUN achieves 56 Kbps for uploading and 512 Kbps for downloading.

- A **two-way satellite service** requires a special two-way satellite dish, but this does improve the speeds of transfer: 512 Kbps to 1.5 Mbps.

There are also options to have special T1 or T3 lines connected from the phone company to an organisation, and these provide very fast speeds: 1.5 to 44 Mbps. These are expensive and would suit larger organisations that have many employees all requiring Internet access. Such large organisations are most likely to set aside at least one computer to act as a **web server** for the other client computers on the organisation's network.

For the very largest organisations, **fibre-optic technology** offers an expensive but very fast Internet connection: 155 Mbps.

Check Your Understanding 10.6

1 What does ISP stand for?
2 Distinguish between one-way and two-way satellite systems.
3 What is the benefit of fibre-optic technology for Internet connections?

Email protocols

One of the most popular uses for the Internet is to send and receive email (Figure 10.11).

As with just about everything else on the Internet, email has its own protocols:

351

Figure 10.11
Email communications software: Outlook Express

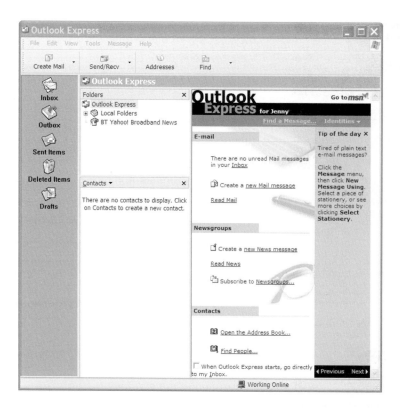

- If you use an email program like Outlook or Eudora, then **POP (post office protocol)** or **IMAP (Internet message access protocol)** may be used to pick up emails. **SMTP (simple mail transfer protocol)** will then be used to send emails.
- Some email accounts are entirely web-based and so they follow the **HTTP protocol** (hypertext transfer protocol).

Discuss with a friend the availability of free email accounts. Who provides these?

Setting up a system for Internet access

For Windows systems, there are two main types of communications link:

- those that require dial-up networking (DUN)
- those that do not require DUN.

Those that do not require DUN tend to be supplied with their own setup software. So the cable, DSL or satellite service provider will supply a CD-ROM and/or specific instructions for setting up the service. You may be supplied with a 'box' which acts like a modem and is to be connected to a USB port. You will have to consult the provider's instructions and follow them carefully.

Dial-up networking (DUN)

To access the Internet using DUN, you would probably use a modem and a telephone line (Figure 10.12): Chapter 1, page 79, explains how modems work.

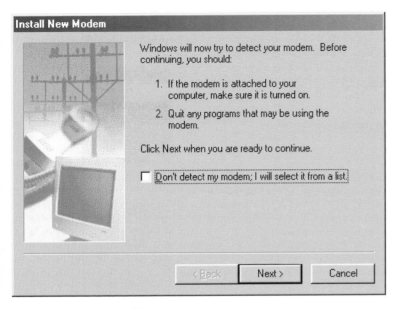

Windows will now try to detect your modem. Before continuing, you should:

1. If the modem is attached to your computer, make sure it is turned on.

2. Quit any programs that may be using the modem.

Click Next when you are ready to continue.

☐ Don't detect my modem; I will select it from a list.

< Back   Next >   Cancel

Figure 10.12   Installing a new modem

◆ **Standard modems** are operating systems neutral and need a generic device driver.

◆ The **Windows modem** is an internal Plug and Play device that needs a special device driver as supplied with the Windows operating system.

An ISP provides a host computer to which users can connect by dialling in. This host computer manages all communications, storing emails, web pages and files for its subscribers. The host computer is connected to the Internet and this allows the subscribers to communicate with other computers and hence other users who subscribe to other ISPs.

Windows NT and Windows 2000 Server both support RAS, the service used to manage and control incoming dial-up connections.

What does it mean?

RAS = remote access services.

Note that not all outgoing connections are made to the Internet. It is possible, instead, to connect to a corporate server. For example, you may be working from a laptop and need to access data on the company network. Having dialled up, you can then log on to the corporate LAN and gain access to the WAN.

How to set up an Internet connection

You need lots of parameters before working your way through the Windows wizard to set up an Internet connection:

◆ Your **username** is the name that you will use to establish your dial-up link. This could be the same as your email username.

◆ You can set a **password** so that no one else can connect to the Internet using your PC.

◆ You need a phone number that has to be dialled to make the connection. For Broadband connections, this is the number of the phone you are ringing from. For other dial-up connections, it may be a free-phone number.

◆ Your ISP will provide you with the names of the incoming and outgoing **mail servers**, the **server type** (e.g. POP) and your email username and password.

If you are using Windows 9X, you may need manually to install DUN and TCP/IP (although both may be installed as defaults for Windows 98):

1   Go to Add/Remove Programs to install DUN and check that the icon for DUN appears in My Computer. Then go to Network Properties to install TCP/IP (Figure 10.13).

Figure 10.13
Setting up a DUN communications link

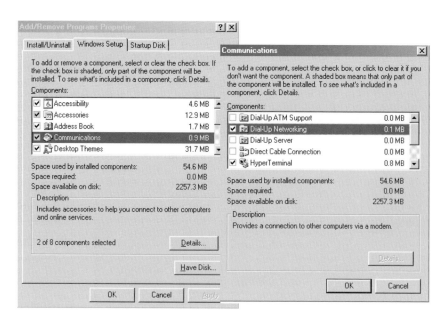

Figure 10.14   The Internet connection wizard

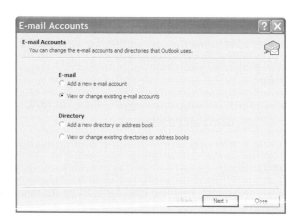

Figure 10.15   Setting up new email accounts

2 Alternatively, open Internet Explorer or Microsoft Outlook, or Outlook Express. If no Internet connection has been set up, each of these programs will lead you to the Internet Connection Wizard (Figure 10.14).

3 When setting up an Internet connection, you can set up the email account at the same time, or leave this until later. If you leave it until later, you will need to do it via your email program (Figure 10.15).

If you are using Windows 2000, the process is automated for you. Simply go to the Internet Connection wizard via Start/Programs/Accessories/ Communications and choose 'I want to set up my Internet connection manually' and follow the on-screen instructions.

Having set up a connection you may decide to place a shortcut for the connection on your desktop. See page 318 for details of shortcuts.

Troubleshooting

If your connection is not working, the fault could lie with the phone line, the hardware or the software:

◆ Check that your phone line is working okay. If you can get a dial tone to make an outgoing call, the PC should be able to dial out too. If you set the properties to allow you to hear the dialling tone – and the other noises the modem makes – you will be able to tell that your phone line is operational without attaching an ordinary phone to the socket (Figure 10.16).

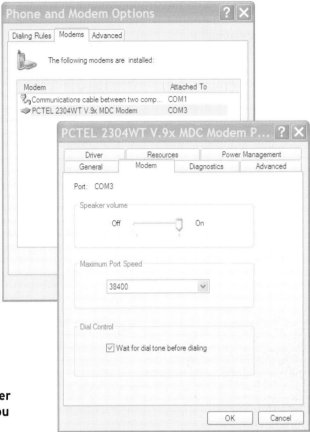

Figure 10.16 **Setting the speaker volume on the modem so that you can hear when it is dialling out**

◆ Check that the hardware is properly connected. If the phone jack is not connected, you will not be able to dial out!

◆ Check that the correct modem is shown in the properties for the DUN connection.

◆ If you still cannot make a connection or if the connection breaks down soon after you have made a connection, it is more likely to be a fault with the ISP's equipment. Be patient. Most ISP's have a help line so that you can check the status of the service.

◆ If you can connect to the Internet, but you cannot retrieve your mail, check your email settings. Your ISP will have a help desk to assist you, if you still have problems. It may be that the problem lies with the ISP, and will be fixed soon.

◆ If you have problems sending or receiving emails through communications software like Microsoft Outlook – e.g. it takes ages to download – access your email by going to the ISP's website. You can then view your emails, without necessarily downloading them to your PC. It may be that you don't want to receive the emails that are taking so long to download, and can delete them from the website.

Check Your Understanding 10.7

1 What do these stand for: POP, IMAP, SMTP, HTTP, DUN?
2 What is a username?
3 Why should you password-protect your Internet connection?

Go and try out 10.6

Set up an Internet connection, with an email address. Send test emails to each other.

Revision 10

Remember these facts:

1 User mode is a non-privileged mode that allows only limited access to system information; such users cannot directly access hardware.

2 Kernel mode is a privileged mode that allows full access to system information so such users can directly access the hardware.

3 A network name is used to identify a PC on the network as the sender or receiver of data to other users on the same network.

4 An IP address uniquely identifies each node in a network.

5 The DHCP (dynamic host configuration protocol) is used to configure a node with its IP address automatically.

6 The WINS (Windows Internet naming service) translates the network name into an IP address for a particular PC.

7 Resources (drives, folders, printers) are made available to everyone in the domain through the use of share names. Shared files can be found in the Network Neighborhood – also known as My Network Places.

8 On the Internet, the highest level of domain is given by the tail end of the Internet address, and this describes the type of organisation (commercial, charitable or non-profit making, government).

9 The DNS (domain name system) server is used to translate the Internet address that you key, e.g. heinemann.co.uk, into the relevant IP address.

10 The network type and card must be compatible. The NIC type has to match the expansion bus for the slot but it must also match the network type and in particular the speed of the network.

11 Protocols are used in networking to define how communication takes place.

12 FTP (file transfer protocol) allows a user to send/receive a message using a copy of a file to be transferred between two computers, i.e. uploading and downloading.

13 HTTP (hypertext transfer protocol) lets a browser view pages encoded in HTML.

14 NFS (network file services) allows access to network drives as if they were local drives, folders and files.

15 PPP (point-to-point protocol) is used to make the connection and manage network communications with a modem.

16 SMTP (simple mail transfer protocol) is used for email across a network.

17 TCP/IP (transmission control protocol/Internet protocol) determines how individual signals are sent over the Internet. It is not a single protocol, but a collection of working practices that allows all Internet users to communicate, regardless of what equipment they are using.

18 For Windows to manage the communication of the network, it needs an NIC driver, a client driver and a protocol.

19 A browser is a program which lets you view web pages on the Internet.

20 If you enter a search key into a browser, its search engine will search the Internet and present you with a hot list of sites, the contents of which match your search key.

21 The browser keeps a record of all sites that you have visited in the History folder.

22 The Internet server provides its clients with an access point, from where they can tap into the Internet. Some ISPs also retain the email messages for the clients, rather than the client downloading them using communications software like Microsoft Outlook.

23 Fibre-optic technology offers an expensive but very fast Internet connection for the very largest organisations.

24 Your username is the name that you will use to establish your dial-up link.

Chapter 11 Electricity, electronics and ESD

Electricity is an energy force with properties that can be measured. It is invisible, but you may be able to visualise the flow of electricity if you think of it like water passing through a hose pipe (see Figure 11.1 and Table 11.1).

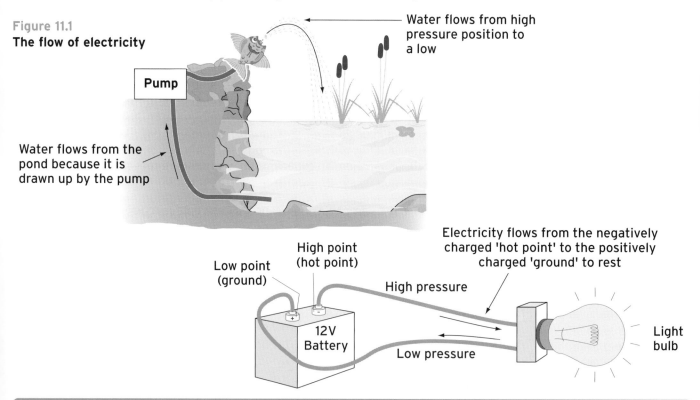

Figure 11.1
The flow of electricity

Water flows from high pressure position to a low

Pump

Water flows from the pond because it is drawn up by the pump

Low point (ground)

High point (hot point)

Electricity flows from the negatively charged 'hot point' to the positively charged 'ground' to rest

High pressure

Low pressure

12V Battery

Light bulb

Water	Electricity	Example
Water flows through a hose pipe.	Electricity flows through cables. It is called a **current**, and flows in a circuit.	
How much water is flowing through the hose?	The volume of the flow of electricity is measured in **amperes** (**amps** for short). This is the strength of the current.	A hard drive may need 2 amps to start up, and 0.35 amps while running.
What is the pressure of the water as it comes out of the hose?	Pressure is measured as a **voltage**. Pressure exists even when no electricity is flowing.	There are several levels of voltage within a PC: +3.3 V, ±5 V and ±12 V.
Is there any friction on the inside of the hose?	Resistance of the cable/wire is measured in **ohms**.	There are many circuits in a PC. The higher the resistance the less current will flow.
What is the total supply of water?	Power supply is measured as a wattage and is calculated as volts × amps.	For a PC, the power supply could be in the range 200–600 watts.

Table 11.1 *The analogy between water and electricity*

Figure 11.4 then illustrates the three measures (voltage, current and resistance) and defines the volt. V stands for volts and actually measures the pressure difference – called the **potential difference** – between two points. Voltage is measured when the power is turned on. **Ohm's law** links the volts, amps and ohms in a circuit: I = V/R, where I = current (in amps); V = volts; R = resistance (in ohms). So, if you know two of these values for a circuit, you could calculate the third one.

Electricity only travels in a circuit. If you act as a bridge and connect two parts of an open circuit, making a closed circuit, the electricity will pass through you – and you will experience an **electrical shock**. If there are enough volts, this can kill you.

There are two types of current: **AC** (**alternating current**) and **DC** (**direct current**):

- DC is used inside computers. The 230 V AC mains provides the primary power and this is converted to low-voltage DC power inside the computer. The flow of electricity is in only one direction. Negatively charged particles flow towards positively charged particles (just as water flows down, not up, an incline) and this creates a current in that direction. The DC current is constant, and always from a negative charge to a positive charge.

- AC is used for most electrical appliances in the home: the washing machine, fridge and TV. In alternating current, the current changes directions – it alternates, moving first one way and then the other way. This alternation happens very frequently, about 50 or 60 times per second depending on the standard for any particular country. The change in direction is created by switching the charge from negative to positive and back again repeatedly. AC power is used for generating and transmitting electricity because it can be easily transformed to different voltages and gives more efficient transmission of power through the national grid network.

Another form of electricity is **static electricity**. This can be created simply be walking across a carpet. It is not a problem until you touch something and discharge that power. With the delicate components inside a computer this can cause severe damage. Static electricity is an electrical charge at rest which can build up on non-conductive surfaces such as clothing or plastic and on the surface of an ungrounded conductor.

ESD (electrostatic discharge) is a real source of danger – to computers – and can cause catastrophic damage, if some simple precautions are not heeded:

- ESD of just 30 V can destroy a computer circuit.
- ESD which you can feel, e.g. when you touch something metal, may be around 3,000 V, but low energy and not enough to kill you. It can be painful all the same.
- ESD that you can see may be 20,000 V.

ESD can damage a circuit without you realising it. The circuit just stops working. To prevent ESD, you need to make sure that the charge between you and the PC is equalised. One way – the best way – to do this is to wear an antistatic wrist strap (see page 179).

Now – some electronics!

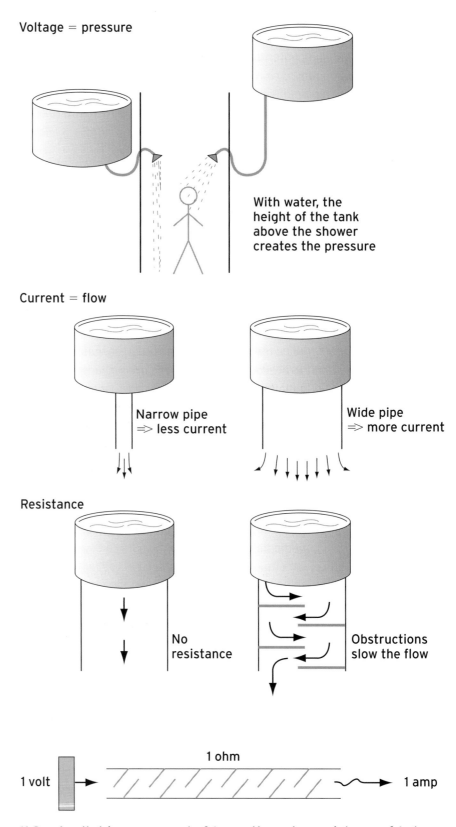

Voltage = pressure

With water, the
height of the tank
above the shower
creates the pressure

Current = flow

Narrow pipe
⇒ less current

Wide pipe
⇒ more current

Resistance

No
resistance

Obstructions
slow the flow

1 ohm

1 volt

1 amp

Figure 11.2   **1 volt drives a current of 1 amp through a resistance of 1 ohm**

- For electrical current to flow, it needs a **conductor** – such as copper or gold – that allows current to flow through it.
- An **insulator** – such as rubber, glass or ceramic – prevents the current flowing.

These two facts explain why copper wire is placed within a rubber outer sheath. Current will flow along the wire without harming anyone who handles the rubber sheath.

Circuit boards are full of semiconductors. So are these halfway between a conductor and an insulator? Not quite! A **semiconductor** is neither a conductor nor an insulator. However, when supplied with a jolt of electricity, it can toggle between the two states: allowing current, or preventing it. These two extreme states can be thought of as 0 and 1 – the two values in a binary system.

A circuit can be built from a variety of components:

- A **transistor** is a semiconductor that stores just one value: 0 or 1. According to the charge (positive or negative) applied to one layer of the transistor, its circuit is either completed (on) or not (off). Setting the transistor on/off requires very little power, and it needs even less to maintain this state. It can act as a 'gate' or switch for an electrical signal and because it takes so little charge to create a charge, it can be used to amplify the flow of electricity through a system. The transistor is the basic building block of the integrated circuit (IC) which is then used to create a microchip.
- A **diode** acts as a one-way valve. It lets current (data) pass one way, but not the other way, within the circuit. (Note that a transistor contains two diodes.) Groups of 1–4 diodes can be used to convert AC power to DC; this is then called a **rectifier**.
- A **resistor** acts like a sticky patch in the circuit. It slows down the current, by limiting the amount of current that can flow through it.
- A **capacitor** is like a bucket; it can store electricity. It holds the charge and so can be lethal if you touch it.

These four components, and ground, have special symbols when drawn on a circuit diagram (Figure 11.3).

There are other electrical components that you might meet in a PC:

- A **varistor** is used within a surge suppressor (see MOV, page 174). Its resistance varies with its temperature. For example, when cold it will have a high resistance. As the current passes through it, it heats up and the resistance reduces. These characteristics can be used to prevent surges of power when appliances are first switched on.
- A coil is like a resistor to AC power only. It can have very little resistance to DC power when measuring ohms, but a high resistance to AC power which is measured as **inductance**. (It also has more complex characteristics that can cause phase shift between current and voltage.)

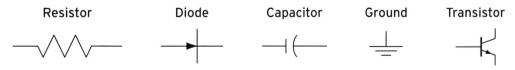

| Resistor | Diode | Capacitor | Ground | Transistor |

Figure 11.3 **The symbols for components found in a PC**

The design of a circuit board includes an arrangement of **logic gates**. These logic gates – AND, OR, NOT – rely on Boolean algebra to determine the output signal according to the input signals. A current (data) flows in and through these gates and, in this way, data is processed.

Nanoseconds and megahertz

The hertz (Hz) is a measure of frequency: in cycles per second. A megahertz (MHz) is a million cycles per second. So an 83 MHz RAM performs 83 million cycles per second.

The RAM clock speed may be given in **nanoseconds**: 1 billion nanoseconds = 1 second.

The speed of SDRAM is rated in MHz rather than nanoseconds because this makes it easier to compare the bus speed with the RAM chip speed.

What does it mean?

SDRAM (synchronous dynamic RAM) is a form of RAM tied to the system clock that reads/writes memory in burst mode.

How to convert between the RAM clock speed in nanoseconds to the frequency in megahertz

83 megahertz means 83 million cycles per second. The clock speed is how long 1 cycle takes.

If there are	83,000,000 cycles in 1 second
then	1 cycle takes 1/83,000,000 seconds
but	1 second = 1 billion nanoseconds = 1000,000,000 ns
so	1 cycle takes 1000,000,000/83,000,000 ns = 12 ns (approximately)

So, a frequency of 83 MHz is equivalent to a clock speed of 12 ns.

Check Your Understanding 11.2

1 What is used to measure potential difference?
2 State Ohm's law.
3 Distinguish between AC and DC.
4 Give two examples of how static electricity is created.
5 Explain these terms: 'conductor' and 'insulator'.
6 What is a transistor?
7 What is a capacitor?
8 Within what IT equipment is a varistor used?
9 What is measured in megahertz?

Tools for the job

Your **ESD wrist strap** includes a 1-megaohm resistor without which it is useless. So don't remove this resistor and, if it is damaged, dispose of the wrist strap completely, and buy a new one.

Apart from your ESD wrist strap, you should have a few well chosen tools to take with you to the poorly PC:

◆ You will need a variety of **screwdrivers**: Phillips, slotted, hex head or Torx (Figure 11.4).

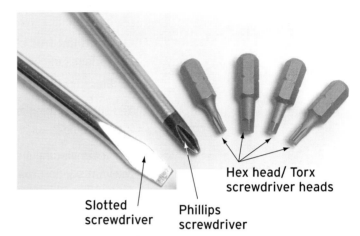

Hex head/ Torx
screwdriver heads

Slotted
screwdriver

Phillips
screwdriver

Figure 11.4
**Different types of screw-
driver and a parts
retriever**

**Watch
out**

Avoid magnetic screwdrivers. Its electromagnetic field can damage components within the PC. Instead, use a parts retriever to retrieve things that fall inside the PC case.

◆ **Needle-nose pliers** can be used to hold screws and/or connectors, and would be handy for handling wire. They might also have a wire cutter.

**Watch
out**

Rubber-handled pliers are easy to grip but are unlikely to protect you from electrical shock.

◆ A **dike** (diagonal cutter) will be needed to cut through cable ties.
◆ A **torch** or flashlight will help you to spot things in dark corners of your PC. It may also help you to read the small print on some components.
◆ A **multimeter** will let you test and measure the electrical properties of your PC and its components. See page 366 for instructions on how to use a multimeter.
◆ A **loop-back plug** can be used to isolate a problem with a port. This plug is constructed so that data that is sent out is immediately sensed on the receiving pins of the port. For more details, visit www.eurosoft-use.com, www.symnantec.com or www.touchstonesoftware.com
◆ **Angled mirrors** (Figure 11.5), like the kind used by a dentist, can help you to see around corners within your PC. You might also use some **cleaning materials** while you have the PC open. See page 169 for details of cleaning materials.

In particular, these might come in handy:

◆ **Compressed air** comes in an aerosol can and may be used to clean fans and grills, or keyboards. To direct the air more precisely, use the long thin plastic tube, taking care to blow the air in a direction which will take the dust away from the PC.

◆ A **soft lint-free cloth** will prove invaluable for cleaning glass and the plastic surfaces of components.

◆ **Electrical tape** can be used to wrap wire ends and insulating components.

You should also collect an assortment of spare parts: screws, expansion card inserts, etc.

If you are visiting a site to try to fix a PC, you will need to have with you all relevant support materials, including reference disks.

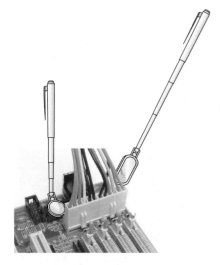

Figure 11.5
Angled mirrors

A notepad and pen will prove useful, to write down details of components such as the model number and serial number, or to note settings when installing or configuring a system. Sometimes, a diagram is more useful than long-hand notes. Just to be safe, you should boot the system and write down the system setup configuration data. Then if disaster strikes you have the relevant details to set the system up again. (See page 204 to find out how to access the configuration data held within CMOS.)

A simple thing like a paper clip can prove very useful when trying to make a connection to a pin on a female connector. Straighten it out and you can poke it into the hole, leaving yourself with a convenient length of wire to which you can attach a probe.

Some tools are best left in the workshop. If you are going to need these, you probably need to bring the PC back to the workshop to be mended:

◆ A **wire stripper/cutter** can be used to prepare wires, cutting them to length and stripping back the insulating sheath.

◆ **Chip tools** are used either to insert DIP chips – or to take them out.

◆ A **soldering iron** might be needed to repair a cable.

Watch out

Keep your soldering iron well away from circuit boards.

All about multimeters

You need to know when a multimeter (Figure 11.6) would be useful, what it measures (Table 11.2) and how to use it, i.e. what setting to use (Table 11.3).

A multimeter can be three machines in one: a voltmeter, an ammeter and an ohmmeter.

CHAT *Discuss with friends: do you understand what is measured in volts, amps and ohms?*

Figure 11.6   **A multimeter**

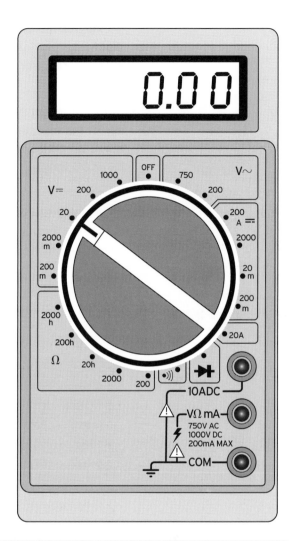

Table 11.2   *What does a multimeter measure?*

Meter type	What it measures	Units
Voltmeter	**Potential difference** between two points	volts
Ammeter	**Current**	amps
Ohmmeter	Resistance between two points, i.e. **continuity**	ohms

Note: Volts and ohms are measured between two points in a circuit. The **capacitance** of an electrical device (in farads) can also be measured using a multimeter.

Table 11.3   *What settings to use?*

What type of current?	AC or DC (or VDC, voltage direct current)
Measurement?	Voltage (volts) OR current (amps) OR resistance (ohms)
Range?	Power supply: 3–12 V AC wall plug output: 105–125 V (USA) or 230 (UK)

On a **digital multimeter**, the LCD displays the measurement as digits. On an **analogue multimeter**, values are shown by a needle on a numbered dial. Digital multimeters can use **switched range** or **autoranging**.

What does it mean?

Switched range: select AC or DC and the maximum voltage expected. Autoranging: select the measure (volts or amps) and the multimeter automatically sets the range according to the source of electricity. It also identifies the current as being AC or DC for you.

Table 11.4 gives examples of when to use a multimeter. There are two **probes**. To test a device, put the red (positive) probe on the 'hot point', i.e. high point of the circuit. Put the black (negative) probe on the 'ground', i.e. low point of the circuit; see Figure 11.1 on page 358.

Watch out

Do not connect a multimeter to the main supply line, which carries 20 kW or more. It will damage the multimeter – and you!

Table 11.4 *When to use a multimeter?*

What might be wrong?	Symptoms	What to measure
A defective power supply	A beep code indicating a CPU fault (see page 321)	Voltage
A defective cable	A device such as the printer stops working (see Chapter 2, page 130)	Voltage and resistance
A defective cable connector		Voltage and resistance
Broken/defective shielding of a cable		Resistance

Watch out

When using an ammeter, the current will flow through the ammeter, so check the rating of the ammeter to make sure it can cope with the flow. More flow than the ammeter is designed to handle may blow a fuse in the meter.

How to measure volts (general principles)

Follow these steps carefully . . . keeping your fingers clear of any contacts.

1 Set dial to DC.
2 Select voltage rating (see Table 11.3).
3 Hold the black/negative probe to a grounding point.
4 Touch the red/positive probe to a hot point (Figure 11.7).

Figure 11.7
Using a multimeter to measure volts

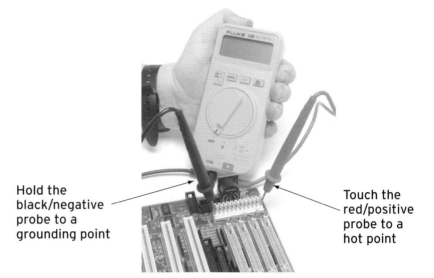

Hold the black/negative probe to a grounding point

Touch the red/positive probe to a hot point

5 Note the reading (in volts).

How to measure volts on a power supply connector

> **Watch out**
>
> Before you start, check: are you wearing your ESD wrist strap? Is it connected to a static ground mat – or to the PC case?

1 Switch off the PC, leaving it connected at the wall socket.

2 Prepare the multimeter: DC, 20 V.

3 Open the computer case and remove the cover.

4 Identify one unused power supply connecter. (You could remove one, e.g. from a CD-ROM drive or the hard/floppy disk drive.)

5 Turn on the PC.

6 Using the black probe touch any of the black wires in the unused power supply connector (Figure 11.8). At the same time, use the read probe to touch the connector's yellow wire.

7 Check that the multimeter shows a reading of +12 V. Anything in the range +11.5 V to +12.6 V is okay. What if your reading is very different (e.g. 5 V)? Check that you are using the correct probes with the correct coloured wires.

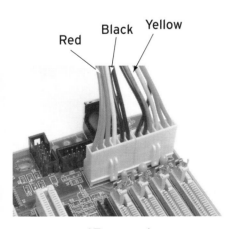

Red   Black   Yellow

AT connector

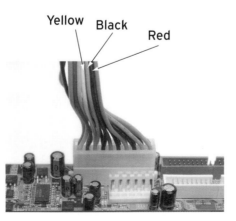

Yellow   Black   Red

ATX connector

Figure 11.8
The wires on a power supply connector: (a) AT commector and (b) ATX connector

8 Keeping the black probe in place, now move the red probe to touch the connector's red wire.

9 Check that the multimeter shows a reading of $+5$ V. Anything in the range $+4.8$ V to $+5.2$ V is okay.

CHAT *What if these readings do not show? What might this indicate? (Hint: See page 153.)*

Watch out — Using a multimeter to test a circuit which has power running through it can damage the multimeter.

How to measure resistance (general principles)

1 Make sure that the circuit has no power running through it. For example, to test circuits inside the PC, turn off the PC.

2 Prepare the multimeter to test ohms with an appropriate range.

CHAT *Discuss how you would know the appropriate range.*

3 Using both probes, touch two different metal points in the circuit, but very close to each other. Make sure that the multimeter reading shows zero – and adjust it if necessary so that it does show zero.

4 Move the two probes so that they are either side of any suspected source of resistance. Check the multimeter reading. If it still shows zero, there is no resistance. If it shows a value, that is the resistance between the two points.

How to measure resistance in a cable

You can use this test for a cable from any external serial device, and for a null modem cable.

1 Disconnect the cable at both ends.

2 Prepare the multimeter to test ohms with an appropriate range.

3 Identify Pin 2 of the cable's connectors at each end (see Figure 11.9).

4 Touch one Pin 2 with the black probe, and the other Pin 2 with the red probe.

If you cannot make a good connection at the female end, poke a wire segment (e.g. a paperclip) into the pin hole.

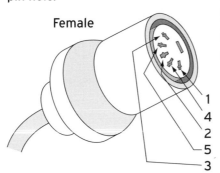
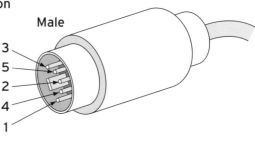

Figure 11.9
Identifying Pin 2

5   Check that the multimeter indicates continuity (by its reading, a beep or a buzzing noise, according to the model of multimeter). What if the multimedia does not indicate continuity? Check your connections! If you are making good connections and there is no reading, then the cable is defective.

Check Your Understanding 11.3

1   When should you use an ESD wrist strap? When should you not use an ESD wrist strap?
2   Explain the difference between a Phillips screwdriver and a Torx screwdriver.
3   What might needle-nose pliers be used for?
4   What might a dike be used for?
5   What is a loop-back plug?
6   What is compressed air useful for?

Revision 11

1   Electricity is an energy force with properties that can be measured in amps, ohms and volts.

2   There are two types of current: AC (alternating current) and DC (direct current).

3   The volume of the flow of electricity – the strength of the current – is measured in amperes (amps for short).

4   Resistance of a cable/wire is measured in ohms.

5   V stands for volts and measures the pressure difference – the potential difference – between two points.

6   Power supply is measured as a wattage and is calculated as volts × amps.

7   Static electricity is an electrical charge at rest which can build up on non-conductive surfaces such as clothing or plastic and on the surface of an ungrounded conductor.

8   ESD is a real source of danger – to computers – and can cause catastrophic damage.

9   For electrical current to flow, it needs a conductor – such as copper or gold – that allows current to flow through it.

10   An insulator – such as rubber, glass or ceramic – prevents the current flowing.

11   A semiconductor is neither a conductor nor an insulator. However, when supplied with jolt of electricity, it can toggle between the two states: allowing current or preventing it. These two extreme states can be thought of as 0 and 1 – the two values in a binary system.

12   A transistor is a semiconductor that stores just one value: 0 or 1.

13   A loop-back plug is constructed so that data that is sent out is immediately sensed on the receiving pins of the port; it can therefore be used to isolate a problem with a port.

Index